728.37

600 Most Popular
HOME PLANS

TABLE OF CONTENTS

Library of Congress
Catalogue Card No.: 98-85181
IBSN: 1-58011-023-1

CREATIVE HOMEOWNER®
A Division of
Federal Marketing Corp.
24 Park Way,
Upper Saddle River, NJ 07458

Manufactured in the
United States of America

Current Printing (last digit)
10 9 8 7 6 5 4 3 2

Cover Photography
Supplied by Design Basics

Builder
Tweedt Construction

CREATIVE
HOMEOWNER®

Country Styled Home

■ Total living area 1,833 sq. ft. ■ Price Code C ■

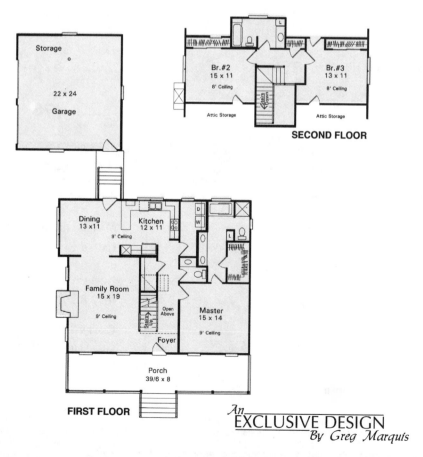

Storage

22 x 24

Garage

SECOND FLOOR

Br.#2
15 x 11
8' Ceiling

Br.#3
13 x 11
8' Ceiling

Attic Storage

Attic Storage

Stairs Down

Dining
13 x11
9' Ceiling

Kitchen
12 x 11

D

W

L

Family Room
15 x 19
9' Ceiling

Open Above

Master
15 x 14
9' Ceiling

Foyer

Porch
39/6 x 8

FIRST FLOOR

An
EXCLUSIVE DESIGN
By Greg Marquis

No. 93432

■ This plan features:

— Three bedrooms

— Two full and one half baths

■ A country styled front Porch provides a warm welcome

■ The Family Room is highlighted by a fireplace and front windows

■ The Dining Room is separated from the U-shaped Kitchen by only an extended counter

■ The first floor Master Suite pampers the owners with a walk-in closet and a five-piece bath

■ There are two additional bedrooms with a convenient bath in the hall

First floor — 1,288 sq. ft.
Second floor — 545 sq. ft.
Garage — 540 sq. ft.
Width — 50'-8"
Depth — 74'-0"

■ *Total living area 2,194 sq. ft.* ■ *Price Code C* ■

No. 10507

■ This plan features:

— Three bedrooms

— One full and one three quarter baths

■ A central courtyard complete with a pool

■ A secluded Master Bedroom accented by a skylight, a spacious walk-in closet, and a private bath

■ A convenient Kitchen easily serving the patio for comfortable outdoor entertaining

■ A detached two-car garage

Main floor — 2,194 sq. ft.
Garage — 576 sq. ft.

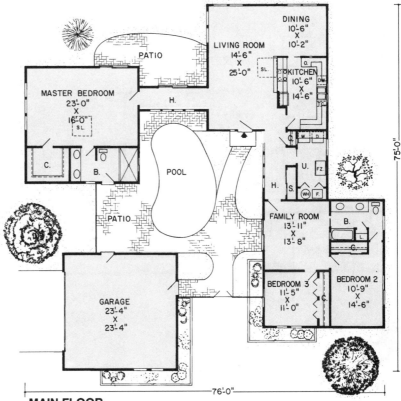

MAIN FLOOR

Perfect for Family Gatherings

© 1994 Donald A. Gardner Architects, Inc.

■ *Total living area 1,346 sq. ft.* ■ *Price Code B* ■

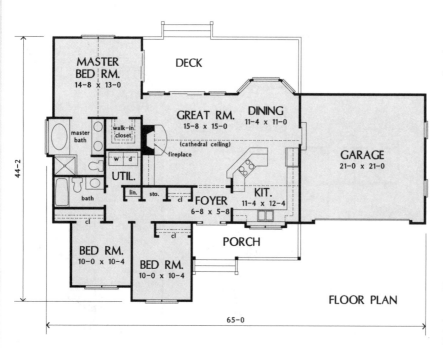

FLOOR PLAN

No. 99826 ✖

■ **This plan features:**

— Three bedrooms

— Two full baths

■ An open layout between the Great Room, Kitchen, and Breakfast Bay sharing a cathedral ceiling and a fireplace

■ Master Bedroom with a soaring cathedral ceiling, direct access to the deck and a well appointed bath with a large walk-in closet

■ Additional bedrooms sharing a full bath in the hall

■ Centrally located utility and storage spaces

Main floor — 1,346 sq. ft.
Garage & storage — 462 sq. ft.

■ *Total living area 2,608 sq. ft.* ■ *Price Code E* ■

No. 92156 ⚒

■ This plan features:

— Four bedrooms

— Two full and one three-quarter baths

■ Creates an indoor/outdoor relationship with terrific Decks and large glass expanses

■ Family Room and Living Room enjoy highly glassed walls taking in the vistas

■ Living Room enhanced by a cathedral ceiling and a warm fireplace

■ Dining Room and Kitchen are in an open layout and a center cooktop island/snack bar highlight the Kitchen

■ Master Bedroom enhanced by floor-to-ceiling windowed area allowing natural light to filter in

■ Two additional bedrooms, a three-quarter bath and a Family Room complete the lower level

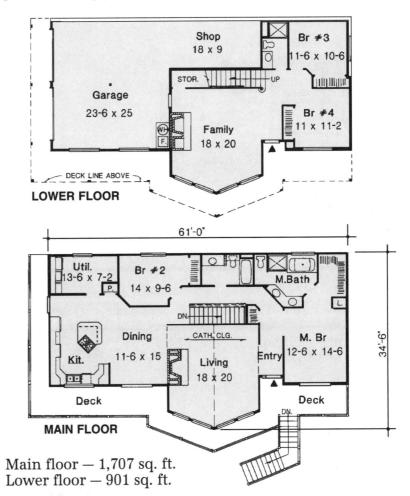

Main floor — 1,707 sq. ft.
Lower floor — 901 sq. ft.

French Country Styling

■ *Total living area 2,567 sq. ft.* ■ *Price Code D* ■

Main Floor

First floor — 1,765 sq. ft.
Second floor — 802 sq. ft.
Bonus room — 275 sq. ft.
Garage — 462 sq. ft.

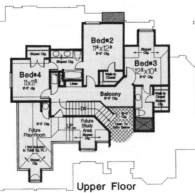

Upper Floor

No. 98533

■ **This plan features:**

— Four bedrooms

— Two full, one half and one three-quarter baths

■ A bay window with a copper roof, a large eyebrow dormer and an arched covered entry

■ The Great Room includes a brick fireplace and a built-in entertainment center

■ An elegant formal Dining Room and angled Study are located to each side of the entry

■ Convenient Kitchen with an informal Dining Area

■ The Master Suite is located on the first floor and has a large bath

■ An optional basement or slab foundation — please specify when ordering

■ No materials list is available for this plan

Stately Exterior with an Open Interior

■ *Total living area 2,655 sq. ft.* ■ *Price Code E* ■

No. 99424

■ **This plan features:**

— Four bedrooms

— Two full and one half baths

■ Open Entry accented by a lovely landing staircase and access to Study and formal Dining Room

■ Central Family Room with an inviting fireplace and a cathedral ceiling extending into Kitchen

■ Spacious Kitchen offers a work island/snackbar, built-in pantry, glass Breakfast Area and nearby Porch, Utilities and Garage entry

■ Secluded Master Bedroom enhanced by a large walk-in closet and lavish bath

■ No materials list is available for this plan

First floor — 1,906 sq. ft.
Second floor — 749 sq. ft.
Basement — 1,906 sq. ft.
Garage — 682 sq. ft.

© Carmichael & Dame

FIRST FLOOR

SECOND FLOOR

For First Time Buyers

■ *Total living area 1,310 sq. ft.* ■ *Price Code A* ■

WIDTH 49-10

BRKFST RM
9-4 X 11-0
42" LEDGE
10 FT CLG
SLOPE
10 FT CLG

KITCHEN
9-6 X 11-0

STORAGE

ARCH

FP

SLOPE

MASTER BEDRM
14-8 X 12-6
10 FT CLG

LIVING RM
14-6 X 17-8
10 FT CLG

DEPTH 40-6

MASTER BATH

SHLV

GARAGE

FOYER

BATH 2

PORCH

BEDRM 2
10-0 X 11-0

LIN

BEDRM 3
11-0 X 10-0

© Larry E. Belk

OPTIONAL BAY
WINDOW

MAIN FLOOR

No. 93048

■ **This plan features:**

— Three bedrooms

— Two full baths

■ An efficiently designed Kitchen with a corner sink, ample counter space and a peninsula counter

■ A sunny Breakfast Room with a convenient hide-away laundry center

■ An expansive Family Room that includes a corner fireplace and direct access to the Patio

■ A private Master Suite with a walk-in closet and a double vanity bath

■ Two additional bedrooms, both with walk-in closets, that share a full hall bath

■ No materials list is available for this plan

Main floor — 1,310 sq. ft.
Garage — 449 sq. ft.

Open Plan Accented By Loft and Decks

■ *Total living area 2,015 sq. ft.* ■ *Price Code C* ■

No. 10515 ✕✎

■ This plan features:

— Three bedrooms

— Two full and one half baths

■ A fireplaced Family Room and Dining Room

■ A large Kitchen sharing a preparation/eating bar with Dining Room

■ A first floor Master Bedroom featuring two closets and a five-piece bath

■ An ample Utility Room designed with a Pantry and room for a freezer, a washer and dryer, plus a furnace and a hot water heater

Main floor — 1,280 sq. ft.
Upper floor — 735 sq. ft.
Greenhouse — 80 sq. ft.

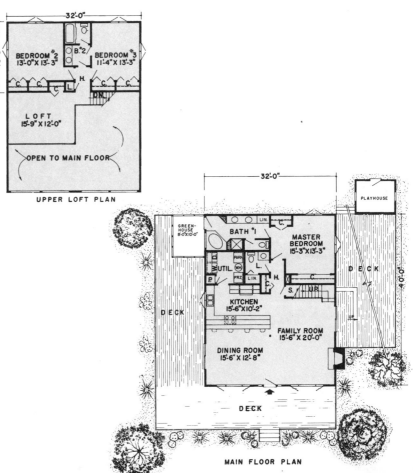

Covered Porch on Farm Style Traditional

■ *Total living area 1,763 sq. ft.* ■ *Price Code B* ■

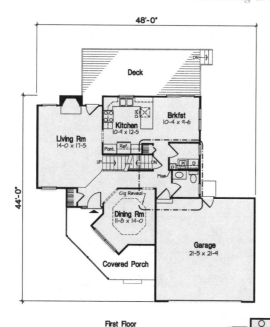

First Floor

Deck

Living Rm
14-0 x 17-5

Kitchen
10-9 x 12-5

Brkfst
10-4 x 9-6

Dining Rm
11-8 x 14-0

Clg Reveal

Garage
21-5 x 21-4

Covered Porch

48'-0"

44'-0"

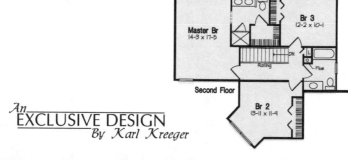

Second Floor

Line of Floor Below

Master Br
14-3 x 17-5

Br 3
12-2 x 10-1

Railing

Br 2
13-11 x 11-9

No. 34901

■ This plan features:

— Three bedrooms

— Two full and one half baths

■ A Dining Room with bay window and elevated ceiling

■ A Living Room complete with gas-light fireplace

■ A two-car Garage

■ Ample storage space throughout the home

First floor — 909 sq. ft.
Second floor — 854 sq. ft.
Basement — 899 sq. ft.
Garage — 491 sq. ft.

An
EXCLUSIVE DESIGN
By Karl Kreeger

■ *Total living area 2,223 sq. ft.* ■ *Price Code D* ■

No. 91126

■ **This plan features:**

— Four bedrooms

— Two full baths

■ This home is characterized by volume ceilings and open rooms

■ A cozy see-through fireplace is set between the Family Room and the Living Room

■ The Kitchen has an open bar area and an abundance of cabinet and workspace

■ The Master Suite is set away from the other bedrooms and enjoys a walk-in closet and a plush bath

■ A third bedroom, optional Study, with French doors at the entrance

■ Generously sized secondary bedrooms share the full hall bath

■ No materials list is available for this plan

Main floor — 2,223 sq. ft.
Garage & storage — 445 sq. ft.

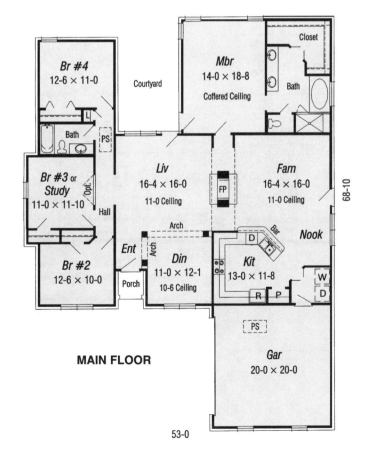

MAIN FLOOR

Striking Facade of Stone and Wood

■ *Total living area 2,450 sq. ft.* ■ *Price Code D* ■

MAIN FLOOR

Main Floor — 2,450 sq. ft.
Basement — 2,450 sq. ft.
Garage — 739 sq. ft.

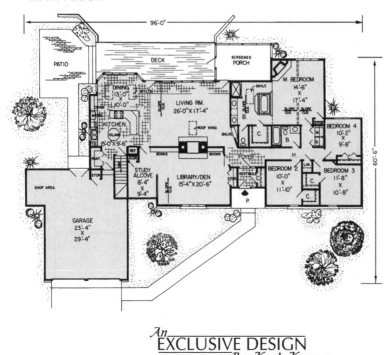

An
EXCLUSIVE DESIGN
By Karl Kreeger

No. 10570

■ **This plan features:**

— Four bedrooms

— Two full baths

■ Recessed entrance leads into the tiled Foyer and bright, expansive Living Room with a skylight and a double fireplace below a sloped ceiling

■ The Library/Den features a Study Alcove, a storage space, a decorative window and a fireplace between built-in bookshelves

■ Ideal Kitchen with a work island, a cooktop snackbar, a walk-in pantry and a tiled Dining area with a built-in china cabinet, skylights and wall of windows overlooking the Deck

■ Master Suite with a corner fireplace, a walk-in closet and a plush bath with two vanities and a raised, tiled tub below a skylight

Inviting Porch Has Dual Function

■ *Total living area 1,295 sq. ft.* ■ *Price Code A* ■

No. 91021

■ **This plan features:**

— Three bedrooms

— One full and one three quarter baths

■ An inviting, wrap-around porch Entry with sliding glass doors leading right into a bayed Dining Room

■ A Living Room with a cozy feeling, enhanced by the fireplace

■ An efficient Kitchen opening to both Dining and Living rooms

■ A Master Suite with a walk-in closet and private master bath

■ An optional basement, slab or crawl space foundation — please specify when ordering

Main floor — 1,295 sq. ft.
Garage — 400 sq. ft.

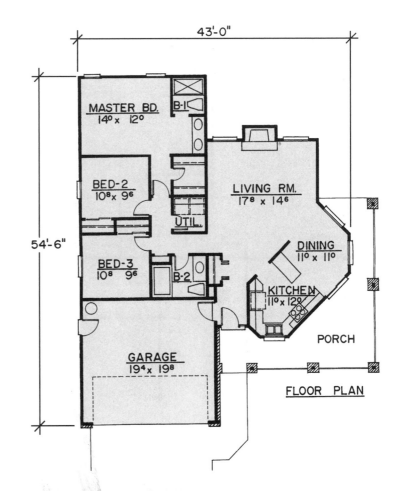

FLOOR PLAN

Style and Convenience

■ *Total living area 1,373 sq. ft.* ■ *Price Code A* ■

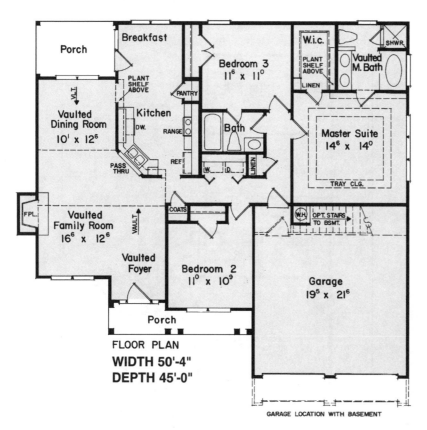

FLOOR PLAN
WIDTH 50'-4"
DEPTH 45'-0"

GARAGE LOCATION WITH BASEMENT

No. 98411

This plan features:

— Three bedrooms

— Two full baths

■ Large front windows, dormers and an old-fashioned porch

■ A vaulted ceiling in the Foyer

■ A Formal Dining Room crowned in an elegant vaulted ceiling

■ An efficient Kitchen enhanced by a pantry, and a pass through to the Family Room

■ A decorative tray ceiling, a five piece private bath and a walk-in closet in the Master Suite

■ An optional basement or crawl space foundation available — please specify when ordering

Main floor — 1,373 sq. ft.
Basement — 1,386 sq. ft.

Two-Story Farmhouse

Total living area 2,263 sq. ft. ■ Price Code D

No. 90458

This plan features:

— Three bedrooms

— Two full and one half baths

- The wrap-around Porch gives a nostalgic appeal to this home

- The Great Room with fireplace is accessed directly from the Foyer

- The formal Dining Room has direct access to the efficient Kitchen

- An island, double sink, plenty of counter/cabinet space and a built-in pantry complete the Kitchen

- The second floor Master Suite has a five-piece, private bath and a walk-in closet

- Two other bedrooms have walk-in closets and share a full bath

- An optional basement or crawl space foundation — please specify when ordering

First floor — 1,125 sq. ft.
Second floor — 1,138 sq. ft.
Basement — 1,125 sq. ft.

SECOND FLOOR PLAN

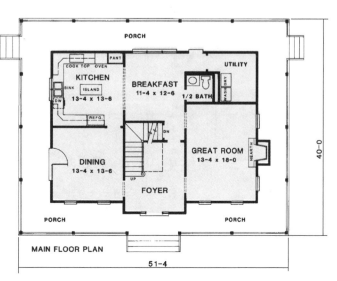

MAIN FLOOR PLAN

Eye Catching Tower

■ *Total living area 3,323 sq. ft.* ■ *Price Code E* ■

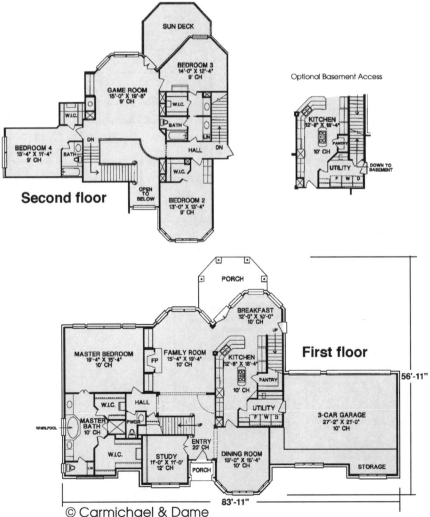

Second floor

Optional Basement Access

First floor

© Carmichael & Dame

No. 99438

■ **This plan features:**

— Four bedrooms

— Four full and one half baths

■ Dining Room with bay is perfect for special dinner parties

■ Study with high ceiling and windows

■ Family Room with fireplace is open to the Breakfast Bay and gourmet Kitchen

■ First floor Master Bedroom spans the width of the home and contains every luxury imaginable

■ Located upstairs are three bedrooms, a Game Room, a Sun Deck and two full baths

■ This plan has a three-car garage with storage space

First floor — 2,117 sq. ft.
Second floor — 1,206 sq. ft.
Garage — 685 sq. ft.

High Ceilings and Arched Windows

■ *Total living area 1,502 sq. ft.* ■ *Price Code B* ■

No. 98441

■ **This plan features:**

— Three bedrooms

— Two full baths

■ Natural illumination streaming into the Dining Room and Sitting Area of the Master Suite

■ Kitchen with convenient pass-through to the Great Room and a serving bar for the Breakfast Room

■ Great Room topped by a vaulted ceiling accented by a fireplace and a French door

■ Decorative columns accent the entrance of the Dining Room

■ Tray ceiling over the Master Suite and a vaulted ceiling over the sitting room and the master bath

■ An optional basement or crawl space foundation — please specify when ordering

■ No materials list is available for this plan

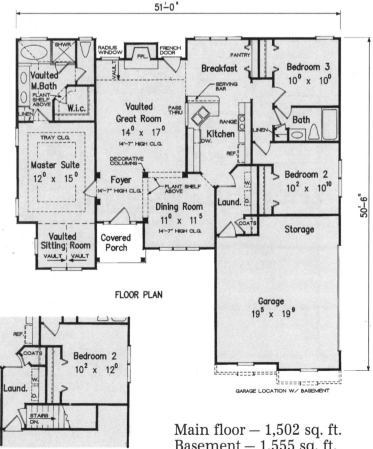

Main floor — 1,502 sq. ft.
Basement — 1,555 sq. ft.
Garage — 448 sq. ft.

Keystone Arches and Decorative Windows

■ Total living area 1,666 sq. ft. ■ Price Code B ■

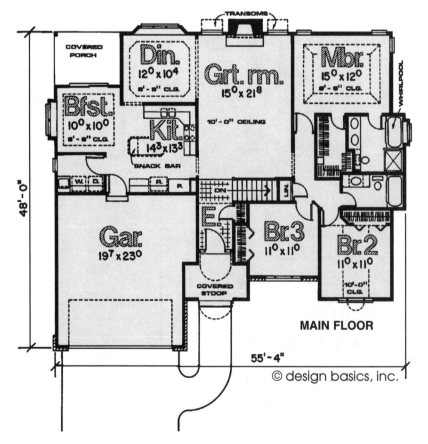

MAIN FLOOR

© design basics, inc.

No. 94923 ✕

■ **This plan features:**

— Three bedrooms

—Two full baths

■ Brick and stucco enhance the dramatic front elevation and volume entrance

■ Inviting Entry leads into expansive Great Room with hearth fireplace framed by transom window

■ Dining Room topped by decorative ceiling is convenient to the Great Room and the Kitchen/ Breakfast area

■ Corner Master Suite enjoys a tray ceiling, roomy walk-in closet and a plush bath with a double vanity and whirlpool window tub

Main floor — 1,666 sq. ft.
Basement — 1,666 sq. ft.
Garage — 496 sq. ft.

■ *Total living area 2,466 sq. ft.* ■ *Price Code D* ■

No. 9850

■ This plan features:

— Three bedrooms

— Two full and one half baths

■ A Master Bedroom Suite with a private Study

■ Fireplaces enhancing the formal Living Room and spacious Family Room

■ A lovely, screened porch/patio skirting the Family Room and the Kitchen

■ A Utility Room with access into the storage and garage areas

Main area — 2,466 sq. ft.
Basement — 1,447 sq. ft.
Garage — 664 sq. ft.

19

■ *Total living area 1,498 sq. ft.* ■ *Price Code B* ■

No. 99860

■ This plan features:

— Three bedrooms

— Two full baths

■ Down-sized country plan for home builder on a budget

■ Columns punctuate open, one-level floor plan and connect Foyer with clerestory window dormers

■ Front Porch and large, rear Deck extend living space outdoors

■ Tray ceilings decorate Master Bedroom, Dining Room and Bedroom/Study

■ Private Master Bath features garden tub, double vanity, separate shower and skylights

Main floor — 1,498 sq. ft.
Garage & storage — 427 sq. ft.

■ *Total living area 2,965 sq. ft.* ■ *Price Code F* ■

No. 92535 ✗

■ This plan features:

— Four bedrooms

— Three full and one half baths

■ An open Foyer flanked by formal areas, left to the Dining Room, right to the Living Room

■ An expansive Den with a large fireplace with a flat tiled hearth fireplace warming the room

■ Built-in cabinets and shelves providing an added convenience in the Den

■ A well-appointed Kitchen serving the formal Dining Room and the informal Kitchen with equal ease and providing a snack bar for meals on the run

■ A Master Bedroom with a lavish bath and a walk-in closet

■ An optional crawl space or slab foundation — please specify when ordering

First floor — 2,019 sq. ft.
Second floor — 946 sq. ft.
Garage — 577 sq. ft.

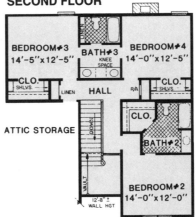

SECOND FLOOR

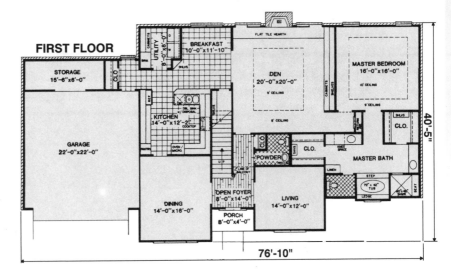

FIRST FLOOR

Split Bedroom Plan

■ *Total living area 1,429 sq. ft.* ■ *Price Code A* ■

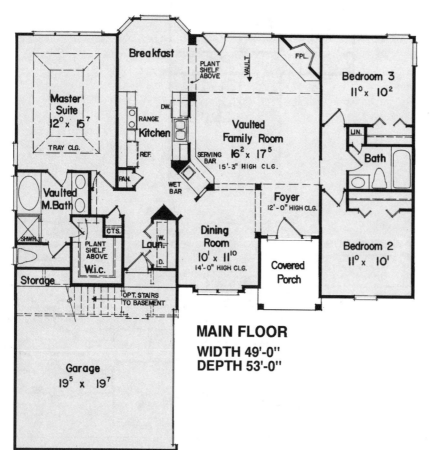

MAIN FLOOR

WIDTH 49'-0"
DEPTH 53'-0"

No. 98415 ☒

■ **This plan features:**

— Three bedrooms

— Two full baths

■ A tray ceiling adds a decorative touch the Master Bedroom

■ A full bath is located between the secondary bedrooms

■ A corner fireplace and a vaulted ceiling highlight the Family Room

■ A wetbar/serving bar in the Family Room and a built-in pantry add to the convenience of the Kitchen

■ The Dining Room is crowned by an elegant high ceiling

■ An optional basement, crawl space or slab foundation — please specify when ordering

Main floor — 1,429 sq. ft.
Basement — 1,472 sq. ft.
Garage — 438 sq. ft.

Family Room at Heart of the Home

■ *Total living area 2,558 sq. ft.* ■ *Price Code D* ■

No. 94640

■ **This plan features:**

— Four bedrooms

— Three full baths

■ The Living Room and Dining Room are to the left and right of the Foyer

■ The Dining Room with French doors opens to the Kitchen

■ An extended counter maximizes the workspace in the Kitchen

■ The Breakfast Room includes access to the Utility Room and to the secondary bedroom wing

■ The Master Bedroom is equipped with a double vanity bath, two walk-in closets and a linear closet

■ A cozy fireplace and a decorative ceiling highlight the Family Room

■ Secondary bedrooms have easy access to two full baths

■ No materials list is available for this plan

Main floor — 2,558 sq. ft.
Garage — 549 sq. ft.

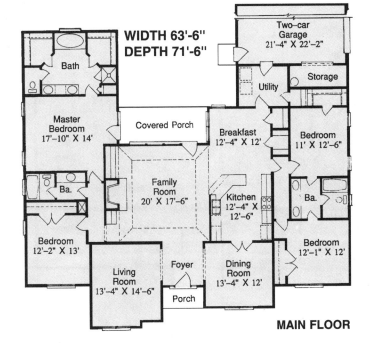

WIDTH 63'-6"
DEPTH 71'-6"

Two-car Garage
21'-4" X 22'-2"

Utility

Storage

Bath

Master Bedroom
17'-10" X 14'

Covered Porch

Breakfast
12'-4" X 12'

Bedroom
11' X 12'-6"

Ba.

Family Room
20' X 17'-6"

Kitchen
12'-4" X 12'-6"

Ba.

Bedroom
12'-2" X 13'

Living Room
13'-4" X 14'-6"

Foyer

Porch

Dining Room
13'-4" X 12'

Bedroom
12'-1" X 12'

MAIN FLOOR

Three Bedroom Ranch

■ Total living area 1,575 sq. ft. ■ Price Code B ■

No. 98414

■ This plan features:

— Three bedrooms

— Two full baths

■ Formal Dining Room enhanced by a plant shelf and a side window

■ Wetbar located between the Kitchen and the Dining Room

■ Built-in pantry, a double sink and a snack bar highlight the Kitchen

■ Breakfast Room containing a radius window and a French door to the rear yard

■ Large cozy fireplace framed by windows in the Great Room

■ Master Suite with a vaulted ceiling over the sitting area, a master bath and a walk-in closet

■ An optional basement or crawl space foundation available — please specify when ordering

Main floor — 1,575 sq. ft.
Garage — 459 sq. ft.
Basement — 1,658 sq. ft.

Floor Plan Labels

50'-0"

52'-6"

RADIUS WDW.

OPT. FRENCH DR.

Vaulted Sitting Room

Master Suite
13⁰ x 15⁰

TRAY CLG.

Vaulted M. Bath

SHWR.

W.i.c.

PLANT SHELF ABOVE

LIN.

Bath

Foyer

LIN.

COATS

Bedroom 3
11⁰ x 11⁰

Bedroom 2
11² x 11⁰

MAIN FLOOR

FPL.

Great Room
17⁰ x 15¹⁰
16'-0" HIGH CLG.

SERVING BAR

PLANT SHELF ABOVE

WET BAR

RADIUS WDW.

Vaulted Breakfast

FRENCH DOOR

PLANT SHELF ABOVE

REF.

RANGE

Kitchen

D.W.

PAN.

Laun.

D. W.

Dining Room
11³ x 10⁷

Storage

Garage
19⁵ x 19⁸

GARAGE LOCATION W/ BASEMENT

■ *Total living area 2,747 sq. ft.* ■ *Price Code E* ■

No. 91109

■ **This plan features:**

— Five bedrooms

— Three full baths

■ A beautiful brick exterior is accentuated by double transoms over double windows

■ Big bedrooms and an oversized Great Room, desirable for a large family

■ Volume ceilings in the Master Suite, Great Room, Dining Room, Kitchen, Breakfast Nook and bedroom four

■ Three bathrooms, including a plush master bath, with a double vanity and knee space

■ Plenty of room to spread out in the Sun Room adjacent to the Great Room, and a Game Room above the Garage

■ No materials list is available for this plan

First floor — 2,307 sq. ft.
Second floor — 440 sq. ft.
Garage & Storage — 517 sq. ft.

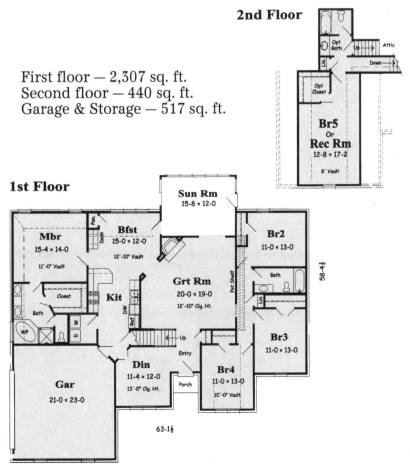

2nd Floor

Opt Bath

Attic

Up

Down

Lin

Opt Closet

Br5 Or **Rec Rm**
12-8 x 17-2

8' Vault

1st Floor

Sun Rm
15-8 x 12-0

Mbr
15-4 x 14-0
11'-0" Vault

Pan.
Desk

Bfst
15-0 x 12-0
12'-10" Vault

Br2
11-0 x 13-0

Bath

Closet

Kit

Grt Rm
20-0 x 19-0
12'-10" Clg. Ht.

Pot Shelf

Bath

Lin

Bath

WP

DW

Ref

D W

Up

Entry

Br3
11-0 x 13-0

Gar
21-0 x 23-0

Din
11-4 x 12-0
13'-0" Clg. Ht.

Porch

Br4
11-0 x 13-0
10'-0" Vault

63-1½

58-4½

25

Old-Fashioned Country Porch

■ *Total living area 1,668 sq. ft.* ■ *Price Code B* ■

An
EXCLUSIVE DESIGN
By Jannis Vann & Associates, Inc.

No. 93219

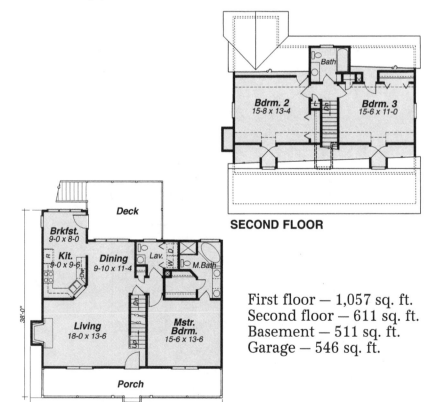

SECOND FLOOR

FIRST FLOOR

First floor — 1,057 sq. ft.
Second floor — 611 sq. ft.
Basement — 511 sq. ft.
Garage — 546 sq. ft.

■ **This plan features:**

— Three bedrooms

— Two full and one half baths

■ A Traditional front Porch, with matching dormers above and a garage hidden below, leading into an open, contemporary layout

■ A Living Area with a cozy fireplace visible from the Dining Room for warm entertaining

■ An efficient U-shaped Kitchen featuring a corner, double sink and pass-thru to the Dining Room

■ A convenient half bath with a laundry center on the first floor

■ A spacious, first floor Master Suite with a lavish bath including a double vanity, walk-in closet and an oval, corner window tub

■ Two large bedrooms with dormer windows sharing a full hall bath

Grand Four Bedroom Farmhouse

© 1992 Donald A. Gardner Architects, Inc.

■ *Total living area 2,561 sq. ft.* ■ *Price Code E* ■

No. 99891

■ This plan features:

— Four bedrooms

— Two full and one half baths

■ Double gables, wrap-around Porch and custom window details add appeal to farmhouse

■ Formal Living and Dining rooms connected by Foyer in front, while casual living areas expand rear

■ Efficient Kitchen with island cooktop and easy access to all eating areas

■ Fireplace, wetbar and rear Porch/Deck provide great entertainment space

■ Spacious Master Bedroom features walk-in closet and pampering bath

First floor — 1,357 sq. ft.
Second floor — 1,204 sq. ft.
Garage & storage — 546 sq. ft.

SECOND FLOOR PLAN

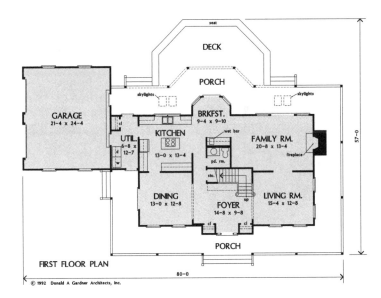

FIRST FLOOR PLAN

© 1992 Donald A Gardner Architects, Inc.

Tandem Garage

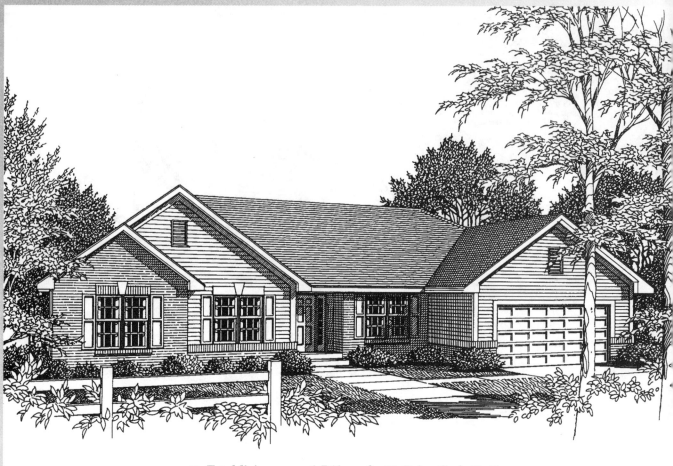

■ *Total living area 1,761 sq. ft.* ■ *Price Code B* ■

No. 93133

■ This plan features:

— Three bedrooms

— Two full baths

■ Open Foyer leads into spacious Living highlighted by a wall of windows

■ Country-size Kitchen with efficient, U-shaped counter, work island, eating Nook with back yard access, and nearby laundry/Garage entry

■ French doors open to pampering Master Bedroom with window alcove, walk-in closet and double vanity bath

■ Two additional bedrooms with large closets, share a full bath

■ No materials list is available for this plan

Main floor — 1,761 sq. ft.
Garage — 658 sq. ft.
Basement — 1,761 sq. ft.

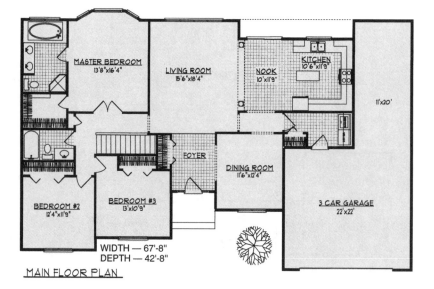

MASTER BEDROOM
13'8"x16'4"

LIVING ROOM
15'6"x18'4"

NOOK
10'x11'9"

KITCHEN
10'6"x11'9"

11'x20'

FOYER

DINING ROOM
11'6"x12'4"

3 CAR GARAGE
22'x22'

BEDROOM #2
12'4"x11'9"

BEDROOM #3
13'x10'9"

WIDTH — 67'-8"
DEPTH — 42'-8"

MAIN FLOOR PLAN

Whimsical Two-story Farmhouse

© 1993 Donald A. Gardner Architects, Inc.

B. NATHAN

■ *Total living area 2,182 sq. ft.* ■ *Price Code D* ■

No. 96442

■ This plan features:

— Four bedrooms

— Three full and one half baths

■ Double gable with palladian, clerestory window and wrap-around Porch provide country appeal

■ First floor enjoys nine foot ceilings throughout

■ Palladian windows flood two-story Foyer and Great Room with natural light

■ Both Master Bedroom and Great Room access covered, rear Porch

■ One upstairs bedroom offers a private bath and walk-in closet

First floor — 1,346 sq. ft.
Second floor — 836 sq. ft.

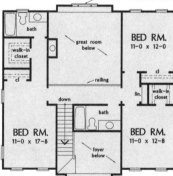

clerestory with palladian window

bath

walk-in closet

cl

BED RM.
11-0 x 17-8

great room below

railing

down

bath

foyer below

BED RM.
11-0 x 12-0

cl

lin.

walk-in closet

BED RM.
11-0 x 12-8

clerestory with palladian window

SECOND FLOOR PLAN

PORCH

GREAT RM.
15-4 x 14-8

BRKFST.
11-0 x 9-0

w   d

UTIL.
6-2 x
cl 5-10

MASTER BED RM.
12-0 x 15-0

fireplace

balcony above

KIT.
11-0 x 12-0

45-4

cl

walk-in closet

cl

pd. rm.

master bath

FOYER
9-10 x 8-6

up

DINING
13-4 x 12-8

PORCH

49-5

FIRST FLOOR PLAN

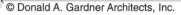

© Donald A. Gardner Architects, Inc.

Quaint and Cozy

© 1993 Donald A. Gardner Architects, Inc.

B. NATHAN

■ *Total living area 1,864 sq. ft.* ■ *Price Code C* ■

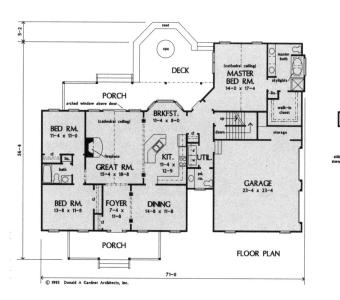

FLOOR PLAN

© 1993 Donald A Gardner Architects, Inc.

No. 99878

■ This plan features:

— Three bedrooms

— Two full and one half baths

■ Spacious floor plan with large Great Room crowned by cathedral ceiling

■ Central Kitchen with angled counter opens to the Breakfast Area and Great Room

■ Privately located Master Bedroom has a cathedral ceiling

■ Operable skylights over the tub accent the luxurious master bath

■ Bonus Room over the Garage makes expanding easy

■ An optional crawl space or basement foundation — please specify when ordering

Main floor — 1,864 sq. ft.
Garage — 614 sq. ft.
Bonus — 420 sq. ft.

Total living area 2,690 sq. ft. ■ *Price Code E* ■

No. 94810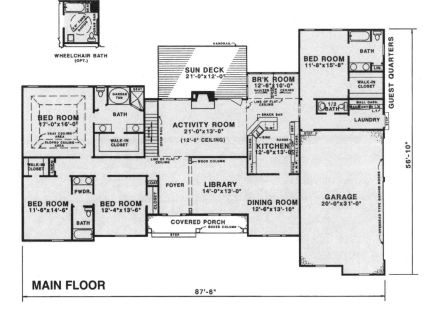

■ This plan features:

— Four bedrooms

— Three full and one half baths

■ Attractive styling using a combination of stone and siding and a covered porch add to the curb appeal

■ Former foyer giving access to the bedroom wing, library or activity room

■ Activity room showcasing a focal point fireplace and including direct access to the rear Deck and the Breakfast Room

■ Breakfast Room is topped by a vaulted ceiling and flows into the kitchen

■ A secluded Guest Suite is located off the kitchen area

■ Master Suite topped by a tray ceiling and pampered by five-piece bath

Main floor — 2,690 sq. ft.
Basement — 2,690 sq. ft.
Garage — 660 sq. ft.

Elegance And A Relaxed Lifestyle

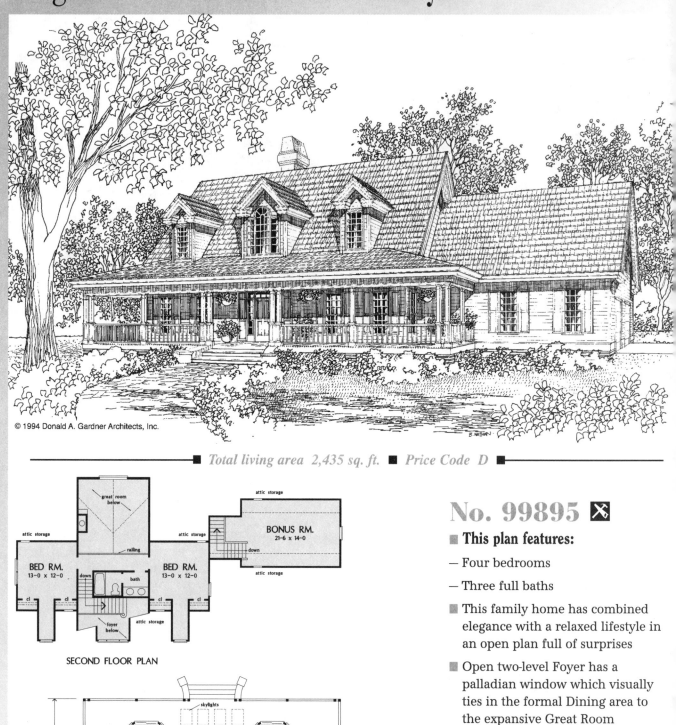

© 1994 Donald A. Gardner Architects, Inc.

B. NATHAN

■ *Total living area 2,435 sq. ft.* ■ *Price Code D* ■

SECOND FLOOR PLAN

FIRST FLOOR PLAN

No. 99895 ⚒

■ **This plan features:**

— Four bedrooms

— Three full baths

■ This family home has combined elegance with a relaxed lifestyle in an open plan full of surprises

■ Open two-level Foyer has a palladian window which visually ties in the formal Dining area to the expansive Great Room

■ Windows all around, including bays in Master Bedroom and Breakfast area provide natural light, while nine foot ceilings create volume

■ Master Bedroom features a whirlpool tub, separate shower and his-n-her vanities

First floor — 1,841 sq. ft.
Second floor — 594 sq. ft.
Bonus room — 411 sq. ft.
Garage & storage — 596 sq. ft.

Double Decks Adorn Luxurious Master Suite

■ Total living area 2,700 sq. ft. ■ Price Code E ■

No. 91022

■ This plan features:

— Three bedrooms

— Two full and one half baths

■ Abundant windows, indoor planters and three decks uniting every room with the outdoors

■ An efficient Kitchen with direct access to the Nook and the formal Dining Room

■ A wood stove warming the spacious Family Room

■ A secluded Master Suite with private Deck, Den and master bath

■ An optional basement, slab or crawl space foundation — please specify when ordering

Main floor — 1,985 sq. ft.
Upper floor — 715 sq. ft.
Basement — 1,985 sq. ft.
Garage — 608 sq. ft.

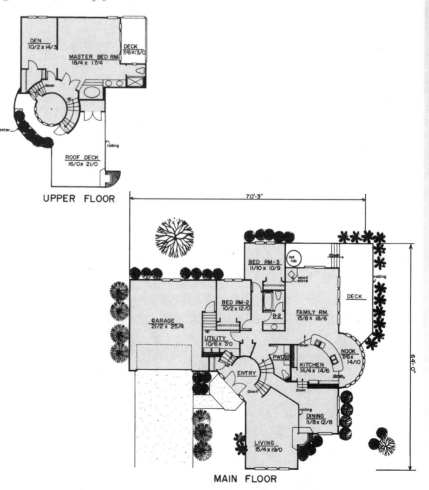

Gingerbread Charm

■ *Total living area 2,281 sq. ft.* ■ *Price Code D* ■

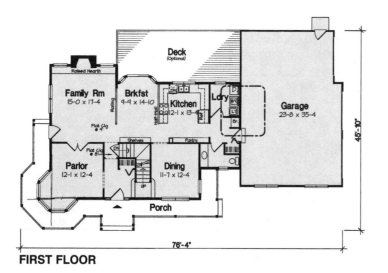

FIRST FLOOR

76'-4"

45'-10"

Alternate Crawl/Slab Plan

SECOND FLOOR

No. 10690

■ This plan features:

— Three bedrooms

— Two full and one half baths

■ A wrap-around Porch and rear Deck adding lots of outdoor living space

■ A formal Parlor and Dining Room just off the central entry

■ A Family Room with a fireplace

■ A Master Suite complete with a five-sided Sitting Nook, walk-in closets and a sunken tub

First floor — 1,260 sq. ft.
Second floor — 1,021 sq. ft.
Basement — 1,186 sq. ft.
Garage — 851 sq. ft.

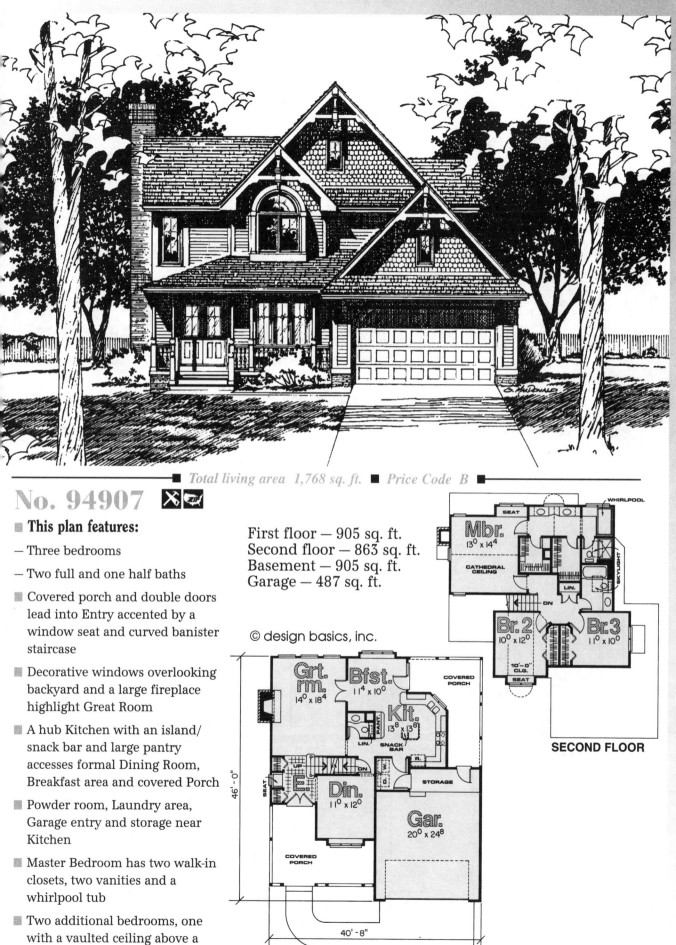

Total living area 1,768 sq. ft. ■ Price Code B ■

No. 94907

■ This plan features:

— Three bedrooms

— Two full and one half baths

■ Covered porch and double doors lead into Entry accented by a window seat and curved banister staircase

■ Decorative windows overlooking backyard and a large fireplace highlight Great Room

■ A hub Kitchen with an island/snack bar and large pantry accesses formal Dining Room, Breakfast area and covered Porch

■ Powder room, Laundry area, Garage entry and storage near Kitchen

■ Master Bedroom has two walk-in closets, two vanities and a whirlpool tub

■ Two additional bedrooms, one with a vaulted ceiling above a window seat, share a full bath

First floor — 905 sq. ft.
Second floor — 863 sq. ft.
Basement — 905 sq. ft.
Garage — 487 sq. ft.

© design basics, inc.

SECOND FLOOR

FIRST FLOOR

Small, Yet Lavishly Appointed

■ *Total living area 1,845 sq. ft.* ■ *Price Code C* ■

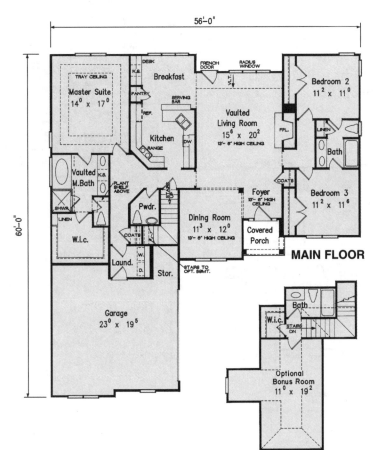

MAIN FLOOR

OPT. BONUS FLOOR PLAN

No. 98425

■ This plan features:

— Three bedrooms

— Two full and one half baths

■ The Dining Room, Living Room, Foyer and master bath all topped by high ceilings

■ Master Bedroom includes a decorative tray ceiling and a walk-in closet

■ Kitchen open to the Breakfast Room and enhanced by a serving bar and a pantry

■ Living Room with a large fireplace and a French door to the rear yard

■ An optional basement or crawl space foundation — please when ordering

Main floor — 1,845 sq. ft.
Bonus — 409 sq. ft.
Basement — 1,845 sq. ft.
Garage — 529 sq. ft.

Dignified Family Home

■ *Total living area 2,578 sq. ft.* ■ *Price Code D* ■

No. 24653

An
EXCLUSIVE DESIGN
By Plan One Homes, Inc.

■ **This plan features:**

— Three bedrooms

— Two full and one half baths

■ A formal Living Room that adjoins the formal Dining Room with columns

■ U-shaped Kitchen equipped with a built-in Pantry, a built-in planning desk and an island

■ Family Room with a focal point fireplace and a bright bay window

■ A second floor Master Suite topped by a decorative ceiling

■ A convenient second floor Laundry

■ A Bonus Room for future needs

■ No materials list is available for this plan

First floor — 1,245 sq. ft.
Second floor — 1,333 sq. ft.
Bonus room — 192 sq. ft.
Basement — 1,245 sq. ft.
Garage — 614 sq. ft.

Second Floor

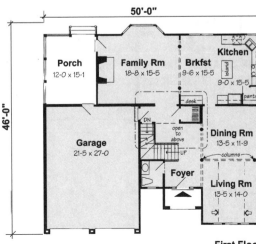

First Floor

**Crawl Space/
Slab Option**

Charming Brick Ranch

■ *Total living area 1,782 sq. ft.* ■ *Price Code B* ■

No. 92630

■ **This plan features:**

— Three bedrooms

— Two full baths

■ Sheltered entrance leads into open Foyer and Dining Room defined by columns

■ Vaulted ceiling spans Foyer, Dining Room and Great Room with corner fireplace and atrium door to rear yard

■ Central Kitchen with separate Laundry and Pantry easily serves Dining Room, Breakfast Area and Screened Porch

■ Luxurious Master Bedroom offers tray ceiling and French doors to double vanity, walk-in closet and whirlpool tub

■ Two additional bedrooms, one which easily converts to a Study, share a full bath

■ No materials list is available for this plan

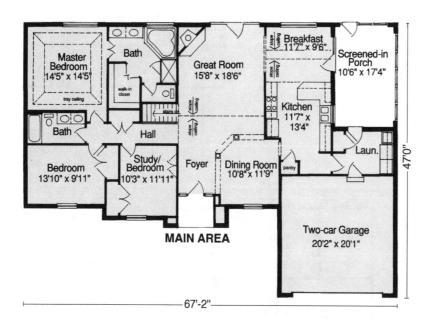

Main area — 1,782 sq. ft.
Garage — 407 sq. ft.
Basement — 1,735 sq. ft.

Comfortable Design Encourages Relaxation

© 1997 Donald A. Gardner Architects, Inc.

B. NATHAN

■ *Total living area 2,349 sq. ft.* ■ *Price Code D* ■

No. 96413

■ **This plan features:**

— Four bedrooms

— Three full baths

■ A wide front Porch providing a warm welcome

■ Center dormer lights Foyer, as columns punctuate the entry to the Dining Room and Great Room

■ Spacious Kitchen with angled countertop opens to the Breakfast Bay

■ Tray ceilings add elegance to the Dining Room and the Master Suite

■ Master Suite, privately located, features an arrangement for the physically challenged

Main floor — 2,349 sq. ft.
Bonus — 435 sq. ft.
Garage — 615 sq. ft.

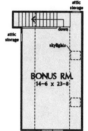

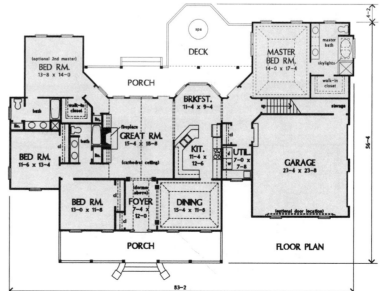

Balcony Offers Sweeping Views

■ *Total living area 3,746 sq. ft.* ■ *Price Code F* ■

No. 10778

■ **This plan features:**

— Three bedrooms

— Three full and one half baths

■ A Living Room and a formal Dining Room located off the Foyer

■ A convenient island Kitchen steps away from both the Dining Room and the Three Season Porch

■ A cozy Master Suite including a fireplace and large bath area

First floor — 1,978 sq. ft
Second floor — 1,768 sq. ft.
Basement — 1,978 sq. ft.

■ *Total living area 1,715 sq. ft.* ■ *Price Code B* ■

No. 98456 ⚔

■ This plan features:

— Three bedrooms

— Two full baths

■ A covered entry gives way to a 14-foot high ceiling in the Foyer

■ An arched opening greets you in the Great Room that also has a vaulted ceiling and a fireplace

■ The Dining Room is brightened by triple windows with transoms above

■ The Kitchen is a gourmet's delight and is open to the Breakfast Nook

■ The Master Suite is sweet with a tray ceiling, vaulted Sitting Area and private bath

■ Two bedrooms on the opposite side of the home share a bath in the hall

■ An optional basement, slab or crawl space foundation — please specify when ordering

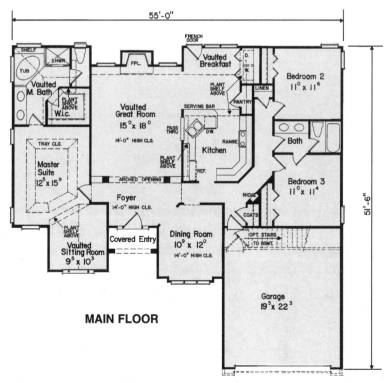

MAIN FLOOR

Main floor — 1,715 sq. ft.
Basement — 1,715 sq. ft.
Garage — 450 sq. ft.

Fan-lights Highlight Facade

■ *Total living area 1,312 sq. ft.* ■ *Price Code A* ■

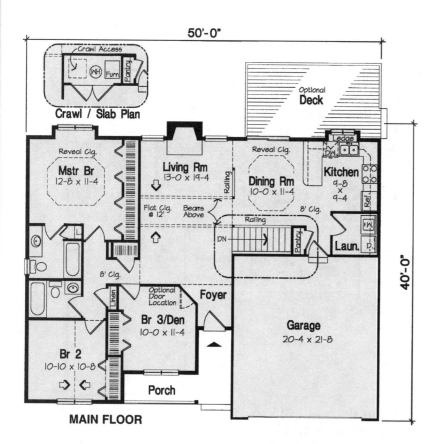

Crawl / Slab Plan

Crawl Access
WH Furn.
Pantry

50'-0"

Optional
Deck

Reveal Clg.

Mstr Br
12-8 x 11-4

Living Rm
13-0 x 19-4

Reveal Clg.

Dining Rm
10-0 x 11-4

Railing

Kitchen
9-8 x 9-4

DW

Ledge

Ref.

Flat Clg. Beams
@ 12'   Above

8' Clg.

Railing

8' Clg.

DN

Pantry

Laun.   D.

Linen

Optional
Door
Location

Foyer

Br 3/Den
10-0 x 11-4

Garage
20-4 x 21-8

40'-0"

Br 2
10-10 x 10-8

Porch

MAIN FLOOR

No. 24700

■ **This plan features:**

— Three bedrooms

— Two full baths

■ Front Porch entry leads into an open Living Room, accented by a hearth fireplace below a sloped ceiling

■ Efficient Kitchen with a peninsula counter convenient to the Laundry, Garage, Dining area and Deck

■ Master Bedroom accented by a decorative ceiling, a double closet and a private bath

■ Two additional bedrooms with decorative windows and ample closets share a full bath

Main floor — 1,312 sq. ft.
Basement — 1,293 sq. ft.
Garage — 459 sq. ft.

Bricks and Arches Detail this Ranch

■ *Total living area 2,512 sq. ft.* ■ *Price Code D* ■

No. 94973 ✕

■ **This plan features:**

— Two bedrooms

— Two full and one half baths

■ A Master Bedroom with a vaulted ceiling and luxurious bath further complimented by a skylit walk-in closet

■ A second bedroom that shares a full bath with the Den/optional bedroom which has built-in curio cabinets

■ Columns and arched windows defining the elegant Dining Room

■ A Great Room sharing a see-through fireplace with the Hearth Room, which also has a built-in entertainment center

■ A gazebo-shaped Nook opening into the Kitchen with center island, snack bar and desk

Main floor — 2,512 sq. ft.
Garage — 783 sq. ft.

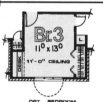
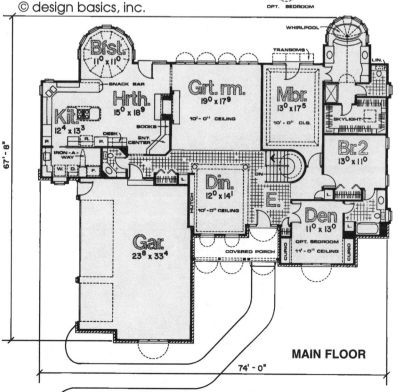

© design basics, inc.

MAIN FLOOR

43

Soft Arches Enhance Style

■ *Total living area 3,393 sq. ft.* ■ *Price Code F* ■

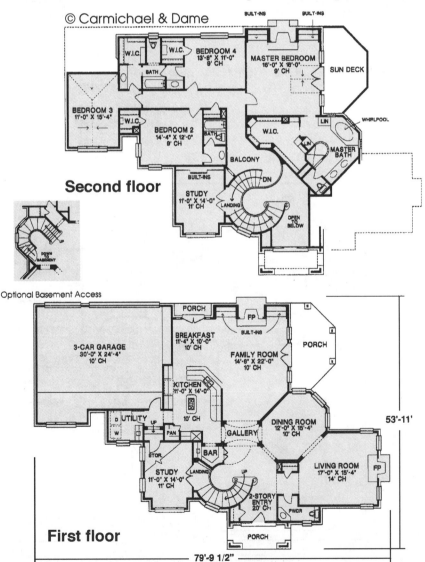

© Carmichael & Dame

Second floor

Optional Basement Access

First floor

No. 99442

■ **This plan features:**

— Four bedrooms

— Three full and one half baths

■ Open layout of rooms separated by arched openings

■ Living Room is graced by a fireplace and adjoins the Dining Room

■ Family Room has a second fireplace and is open to the Breakfast Nook and Kitchen

■ A mid-level Study is brightened by a large front window

■ This plan has four huge bedrooms and three full baths upstairs

■ No materials list is available for this plan

First floor — 1,786 sq. ft.
Second floor — 1,607 sq. ft
Garage — 682 sq. ft.

■ Total living area 3,169 sq. ft. ■ Price Code E ■

No. 20071 ✕

■ This plan features:

— Four bedrooms

— Three full and one half baths

■ A heat storing floor in the Sun Room adjoining the Living Room and Breakfast Room

■ A Living Room with French doors and a massive fireplace

■ A balcony overlooking the soaring two-story Foyer and Living Room

■ An island Kitchen centrally-located between the formal and informal Dining rooms

First floor — 2,186 sq. ft.
Second floor — 983 sq. ft.
Basement — 2,186 sq. ft.
Garage — 704 sq. ft.

An EXCLUSIVE DESIGN
By Karl Kreeger

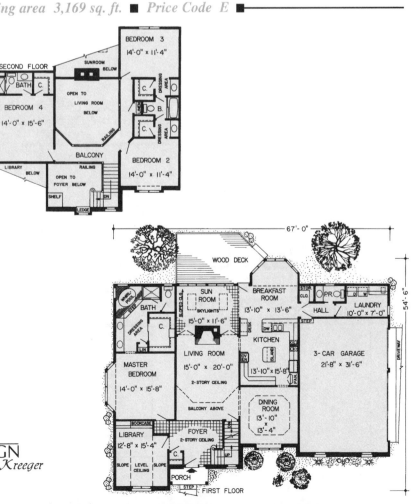

■ *Total living area 2,165 sq. ft.* ■ *Price Code D* ■

No. 94811

■ This plan features:

—Three bedrooms

—Two full and one half baths

■ Privately located Master Suite is complimented by a luxurious bath with two walk-in closets

■ Two additional bedrooms have ample closet space and share a full bath

■ The Activity Room has a sloped ceiling, large fireplace and is accented with columns

■ Access to Sun Deck from the Dining Room

■ The island Kitchen and Breakfast Brea have access to Garage for ease when bringing in groceries

Main floor — 2,165 sq. ft.
Garage — 484 sq. ft.
Basement — 2,165 sq. ft.

MAIN FLOOR

■ *Total living area 3,870 sq. ft.* ■ *Price Code F* ■

No. 92274

■ This plan features:

— Four bedrooms

— Three full and one half baths

■ Two-story glass Entry enhanced by a curved staircase

■ Open Living/Dining Room with decorative windows makes entertaining easy

■ Large, efficient Kitchen with cooktop/work island, huge walk-in pantry, Breakfast Area, butler's Pantry and Utility/Garage entry

■ Comfortable Family Room with hearth fireplace, built-ins and access to covered Patio

■ Cathedral ceiling tops luxurious Master Bedroom offering a private Lanai, skylit bath, double walk-in closet and adjoining Study

■ No materials list is available for this plan

Main floor — 2,807 sq. ft.
Upper floor — 1,063 sq. ft.
Garage — 633 sq. ft.

Upper Floor

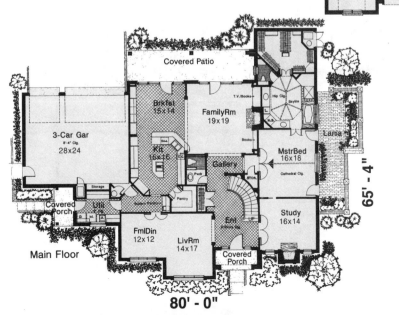

Main Floor

80' - 0"

65' - 4"

Distinctive Ranch

Total living area 1,802 sq. ft. ■ *Price Code C* ■

No. 93143

■ **This plan features:**

— Three bedrooms

— Two full baths

■ This hipped roofed ranch has an exterior that mixes brick and siding

■ The cozy front Porch leads into a recessed Entry with sidelights and transoms

■ The Great Room has a cathedral ceiling, and a rear wall fireplace

■ The Kitchen has a center island and opens into the Nook

■ The Dining Room features a high ceiling and a bright front window

■ The bedroom wing has three large bedrooms and two full baths

■ The two-car garage could easily be expanded to three with a door placed in the rear storage area

■ No materials list is available for this plan

Main floor — 1,802 sq. ft.
Basement — 1,802 sq. ft.

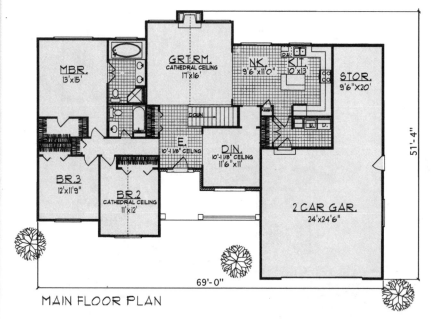

MAIN FLOOR PLAN

Wrapping Front Porch and Gabled Dormers

©1997 Donald A. Gardner Architects, Inc.

■ *Total living area 2,596 sq. ft.* ■ *Price Code E* ■

No. 96411

■ This plan features:

— Four bedrooms

— Three full baths

■ Generous Great Room with a fireplace, cathedral ceiling and a balcony above

■ Flexible bedroom/Study having a walk-in closet and an adjacent full bath

■ Master Suite with a sunny bay window and a private bath topped by a cathedral ceiling and highlighted by his-n-her vanities, and a separate tub and shower

■ Two additional bedrooms, each with dormer windows, sharing a full bath with a cathedral ceiling, palladian window and double vanity

■ Bonus Room over the garage for future expansion

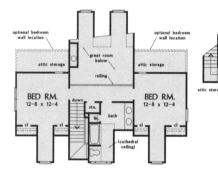

SECOND FLOOR PLAN

First floor — 1,939 sq. ft.
Second floor — 657 sq. ft.
Garage & Storage — 526 sq. ft.
Bonus room — 386 sq. ft.

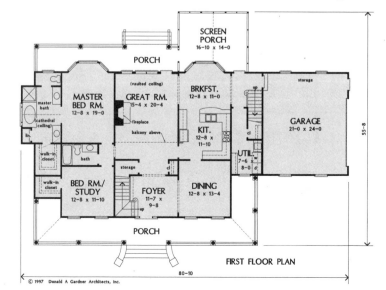

FIRST FLOOR PLAN

© 1997 Donald A Gardner Architects, Inc.

49

Compact Plan

© 1996 Donald A. Gardner Architects, Inc.

■ *Total living area 1,372 sq. ft.* ■ *Price Code B* ■

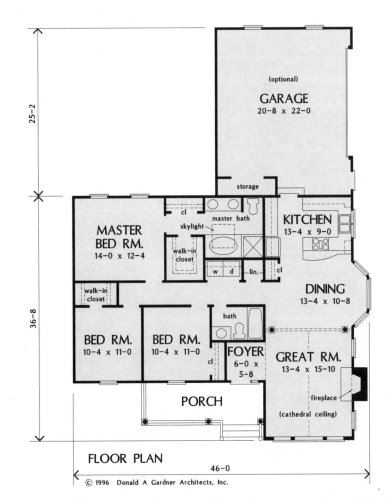

FLOOR PLAN

© 1996 Donald A Gardner Architects, Inc.

No. 99830

■ **This plan features:**

— Three bedrooms

— Two full baths

■ A Great Room topped by a cathedral ceiling, combining with the openness of the adjoining Dining Room and Kitchen, to create a spacious living area

■ A bay window enlarging the Dining Room and a palladian window allowing ample light into the Great Room

■ An efficient U-shaped Kitchen leading directly to the garage, convenient for unloading groceries

■ A Master Suite highlighted by ample closet space and a private skylit bath enhanced by a dual vanity and a separate tub and shower

Main floor — 1,372 sq. ft.
Garage & Storage — 537 sq. ft.

Welcoming Wrap-Around Country Porch

■ *Total living area 2,083 sq. ft.* ■ *Price Code C* ■

No. 24245

■ This plan features:

— Three bedrooms

— Two full and one half baths

■ Formal areas flanking the entry hall

■ A Living Room that includes a wonderful fireplace

■ A U-shaped Kitchen including a breakfast bar, double sink, built-in pantry and planning desk

■ A Mudroom entry that will help keep the tracked-in dirt under control

■ An expansive Family Room with direct access to the rear Deck

■ A Master Suite highlighted by a walk-in closet and a private master bath

First floor — 1,113 sq. ft.
Second floor — 970 sq. ft.
Garage — 480 sq. ft.
Basement — 1,113 sq. ft.

Crawl Space/Slab Option

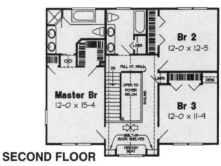

SECOND FLOOR

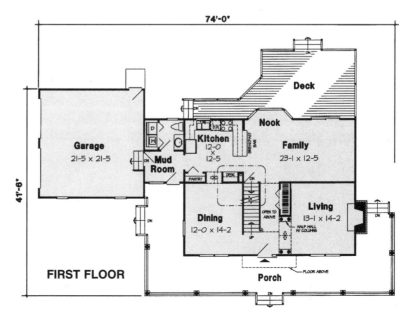

FIRST FLOOR

Charm and Personality

© 1996 Donald A. Gardner Architects, Inc.

■ *Total living area 1,655 sq. ft.* ■ *Price Code C* ■

Main floor — 1,655 sq. ft.
Garage — 434 sq. ft.

FLOOR PLAN

© 1996 Donald A Gardner Architects, Inc.

No. 99871

■ **This plan features:**

— Three bedrooms

— Two full baths

■ Charm and personality radiate through this country home

■ Interior columns dramatically open the Foyer and Kitchen to the spacious Great Room

■ Drama is heightened by the Great Room cathedral ceiling and fireplace

■ Master Suite with a tray ceiling combines privacy with access to the rear Deck with spa, while the skylit bath has all the amenities expected in a quality home

■ Tray ceilings with arched picture windows bring a special elegance to the Dining Room and the front Swing Room

■ An optional basement or crawl space foundation — please specify when ordering

■ *Total living area 2,425 sq. ft.* ■ *Price Code E* ■

No. 98419

■ This plan features:

— Three bedrooms

— Two full and one half baths

■ Vaulted Great Room is highlighted by a fireplace

■ Decorative columns define the Dining Room

■ A built-in pantry and a radius window in the Kitchen

■ The Breakfast Bay is crowned by a vaulted ceiling

■ A tray ceiling over the Master Bedroom and Sitting Area

■ Two additional bedrooms, each with a walk-in closet, share the full, double vanity bath in the hall

■ An optional basement, crawl space or slab foundation — please specify when ordering

■ No material list is available for this plan

First floor — 1,796 sq. ft.
Second floor — 629 sq. ft.
Bonus room — 208 sq. ft.
Basement — 1,796 sq. ft.
Garage — 588 sq. ft.

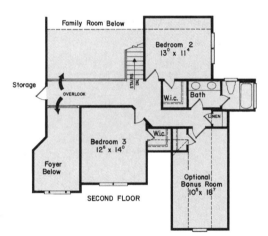

Family Room Below

Bedroom 2
13⁰ x 11⁴

Storage

OVERLOOK

W.i.c. Bath

LINEN

W.i.c.

Foyer
Below

Bedroom 3
12⁶ x 14⁰

Optional
Bonus Room
10⁵ x 18⁷

SECOND FLOOR

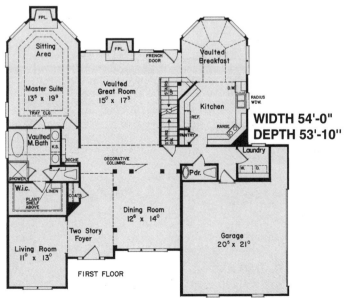

FPL.

Sitting
Area

FPL.

FRENCH
DOOR

Vaulted
Breakfast

Master Suite
13⁵ x 19⁹

Vaulted
Great Room
15⁰ x 17³

Kitchen

STAIRS UP

D.W.

RADIUS
WDW.

TRAY CLG.

REF.

Vaulted
M. Bath

K.S.

NICHE

RANGE

PANTRY

STAIRS DN

WIDTH 54'-0"
DEPTH 53'-10"

SHOWER

W.i.c.

DECORATIVE
COLUMNS

Laundry

W. D.

PLANT
SHELF
ABOVE

LINEN

COATS

Pdr.

Dining Room
12⁶ x 14⁰

Garage
20⁵ x 21⁰

Two Story
Foyer

Living Room
11⁰ x 13⁰

FIRST FLOOR

Appealing Farmhouse Design

© 1995 Donald A. Gardner Architects, Inc.

■ *Total living area 1,792 sq. ft.* ■ *Price Code C* ■

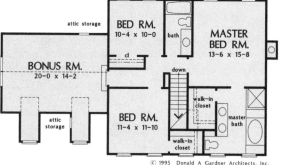

© 1995   Donald A Gardner Architects, Inc.

SECOND FLOOR PLAN

First floor — 959 sq. ft.
Second floor — 833 sq. ft.
Bonus room — 344 sq. ft.
Garage & storage — 500 sq. ft.

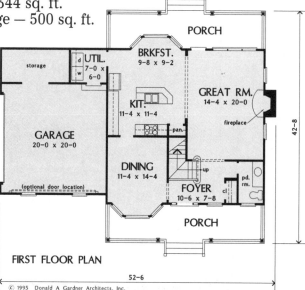

FIRST FLOOR PLAN

© 1995   Donald A Gardner Architects, Inc.

No. 99836 ✕

■ **This plan features:**

— Three bedrooms

— Two full and one half baths

■ Comfortable farmhouse features an easy to build floor plan with all the extras

■ Active families will enjoy the Great Room which is open to the Kitchen and Breakfast bay, as well as expanded living space provided by the full back Porch

■ For narrower lot restrictions, the Garage can be modified to open in front

■ Second floor Master Bedroom contains a walk-in closet and a private bath with a garden tub and separate shower

■ Two more bedrooms on the second floor, one with a walk-in closet, share a full bath

Executive Home

© 1994 Donald A. Gardner Architects, Inc.

■ *Total living area 2,211 sq. ft.* ■ *Price Code D* ■

No. 96449

■ This home features:

— Three bedrooms

— Two full baths

■ Exciting roof lines and brick detailing fit in the finest neighborhood

■ Open Kitchen assures great cooks lots of company

■ Large Deck easily accessible from Breakfast area, Great Room and Master Bedroom

■ Great Room also offers cathedral ceiling above arched windows and fireplace nestled between built-ins

■ Private Master Suite features walk-in closet and plush bath with twin vanities, shower and corner window tub

Main floor — 2,211 sq. ft.
Bonus room — 408 sq. ft.
Garage & storage — 700 sq. ft.

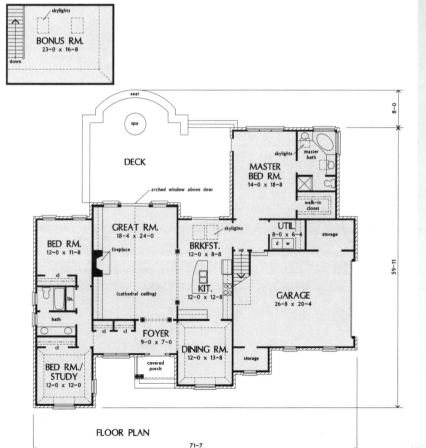

FLOOR PLAN

© Donald A. Gardner Architects, Inc.

Distinctive Design

■ *Total living area 1,998 sq. ft.* ■ *Price Code C* ■

© design basics, inc.

FIRST FLOOR

Sto. 10⁰ x 8⁴
Gar. 20⁸ x 21⁰
D. W.
SHELVES
HUTCH
Kit. 10⁷ x 14⁰
Bfst. 10⁰ x 11⁸
Fam. rm. 13⁰ x 17⁰
P.
CURIO
DESK
Din. 11⁰ x 13⁰
LIN.
UP
Liv. rm. 13⁰ x 11⁸
DN

37' - 8"
55' - 4"

COVERED PORCH

SECOND FLOOR

WHIRLPOOL
Br. 3 10⁰ x 11⁰
10'-0" CLG.
DN
LIN.
Br. 2 11⁰ x 13⁶
Mbr. 13⁰ x 15⁰
OPEN TO BELOW
10'-0" CEILING
PLANT SHELF

No. 94904

■ **This plan features:**

— Three bedrooms

— Two full and one half baths

■ Living Room is distinguished by warmth of bayed window and French doors leading to Family Room

■ Built-in curio cabinet adds interest to formal Dining Room

■ Well-appointed Kitchen with island cooktop and Breakfast area designed to save you steps

■ Family Room with focal point fireplace for informal gatherings

■ Spacious Master Suite with vaulted ceiling over decorative window and plush dressing area

■ Secondary bedrooms share a double vanity bath

First floor — 1,093 sq. ft.
Second floor — 905 sq. ft.
Basement — 1,093 sq. ft.
Garage — 527 sq. ft.

■ *Total living area 2,464 sq. ft.* ■ *Price Code D* ■

No. 93209 ✕⬛

■ **This plan features:**

— Four bedrooms

— Two full and one half baths

▨ A wrap-around Porch adding a cozy touch to this classic style

▨ A two-story Foyer area that is open to the formal Dining and Living rooms

▨ A large Family Room accentuated by columns and a fireplace

▨ A sunny Breakfast area with direct access to the Sun Deck, Screen Porch and Kitchen

▨ A convenient Kitchen situated between the formal Dining Room and informal Breakfast Area has a Laundry Center and a Pantry

▨ A private Deck highlights the Master Suite which includes a luxurious bath and a walk-in closet

An
EXCLUSIVE DESIGN
By Jannis Vann & Associates, Inc.

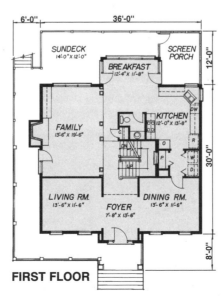

First floor — 1,250 sq. ft.
Second floor — 1,166 sq. ft.
Finished stairs — 48 sq. ft.
Basement — 448 sq. ft.
Garage — 706 sq. ft.

57

Stately Stone and Stucco

■ *Total living area 3,027 sq. ft.* ■ *Price Code F* ■

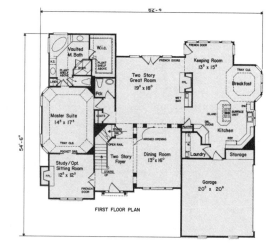

FIRST FLOOR PLAN

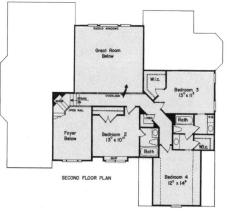

SECOND FLOOR PLAN

No. 98402

■ This plan features:

— Four bedrooms

— Three full and one half baths

■ Two-story Foyer with angled staircase welcomes all

■ Large Great Room has a fireplace, wetbar and French doors

■ Kitchen with a cooktop island, pantry and Breakfast alcove

■ Open Keeping Room accented by a wall of windows

■ Master Suite wing offers a tray ceiling, a plush bath and roomy walk-in closet

■ An optional basement, slab or crawl space foudation — please specify when ordering

First floor — 2,130 sq. ft.
Second floor — 897 sq. ft.
Garage — 494 sq. ft.
Basement — 2,130 sq. ft.

Four Bedroom 1-1/2 Story Design

■ *Total living area 1,531 sq. ft.* ■ *Price Code B* ■

No. 90358 ✂

■ This plan features:

— Three bedrooms

— Two full baths

■ A vaulted ceiling in the Great Room and a fireplace

■ An efficient Kitchen with a peninsula counter and double sink

■ A Family Room with easy access to the wood Deck

■ A Master Bedroom with private bath entrance

■ Convenient laundry facilities outside the Master Bedroom

■ Two additional bedrooms upstairs with walk-in closets and the use of the full hall bath

Main floor — 1,062 sq. ft.
Upper floor — 469 sq. ft.

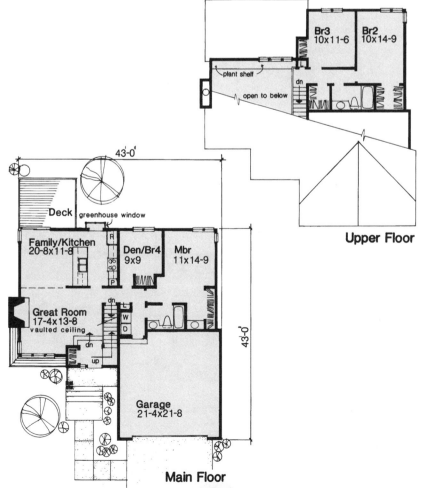

Br3 10x11-6

Br2 10x14-9

plant shelf

open to below

dn

Upper Floor

43'-0"

Deck greenhouse window

Family/Kitchen 20-8x11-8

Den/Br4 9x9

Mbr 11x14-9

Great Room 17-4x13-8 vaulted ceiling

L W D

dn

up

43'-0"

Garage 21-4x21-8

Main Floor

Fashionable Country Style

■ Total living area 2,695 sq. ft. ■ Price Code E ■

No. 99450

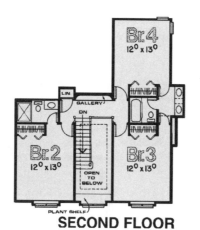

SECOND FLOOR

© design basics, inc.

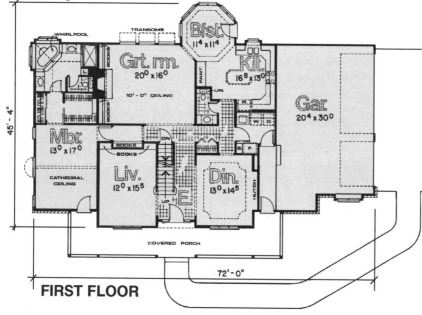

FIRST FLOOR

■ This plan features:

— Four bedrooms

— Two full, one three quarter, and one half baths

■ The large covered front Porch adds old fashioned appeal to this modern floor plan

■ The Dining Room features a decorative ceiling and a built in hutch

■ The Kitchen has a center island and is adjacent to the gazebo-shaped Nook

■ The Great Room is accented by transom windows and a fireplace with bookcases on either side

■ The Master Bedroom has a cathedral ceiling, a door to the front porch, and a large bath with a whirlpool tub

■ Upstairs are three additional bedrooms and two full baths

■ An optional basement or slab foundation — please specify when ordering

First floor — 1,881 sq. ft.
Second floor — 814 sq. ft.
Basement — 1,020 sq. ft.
Garage — 534 sq. ft.

■ *Total living area 3,034 sq. ft.* ■ *Price Code E* ■

No. 91111

■ This plan features:

— Four bedrooms

— Two full and one half baths

■ Dramatic roof lines and a seven foot tall arched transom above front door

■ Columns, arches, angled stairs, a high ceiling and a large plant ledge in the Foyer

■ High vaulted ceilings and an abundance of windows in the Sun Room, Breakfast Nook and Living Room

■ The Master Bedroom has a lavish whirlpool bath and a large walk-in closet

■ No materials list is available for this plan

First floor — 2,123 sq. ft.
Second floor — 911 sq. ft.
Garage & storage — 565 sq. ft.

FIRST FLOOR

Nook 13-0 × 12-6 Vaulted
Grt Rm 24-0 × 15-8 15'-4" Vault
Sun 11-2 × 12-2 Vaulted
Kit 10'-0" Clg. Ht
Up
Entertainment
Mbr 19-2 × 15-8 10'-0" Ceiling Ht
Entry
Bath
Din 12-4 × 15-0 Vaulted
Arch
Coat
Utility
Bath
Closet
WP
Lin
W D
Porch
Gar 25-6 × 20-10
Storage
50-3¼
66-11½

SECOND FLOOR

Plant Ledge
Open to Below
Down
Closet
Br #4 17-6 × 12-0
PS
Bath
Br #2 12-4 × 12-4
Br #3 16-2 × 12-8
Closet
Closet

Easy One Floor Living

■ *Total living area 1,671 sq. ft.* ■ *Price Code B* ■

WIDTH 50'-0"
DEPTH 51'-0"

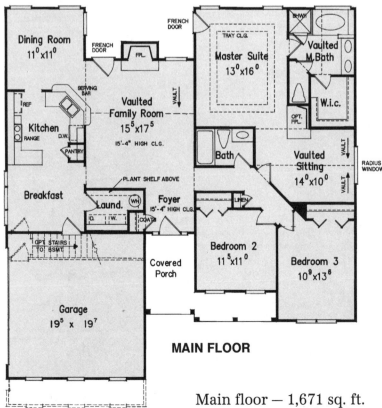

MAIN FLOOR

Main floor — 1,671 sq. ft.
Basement — 1,685 sq. ft.
Garage — 400 sq. ft.

No. 98423

■ **This plan features:**

— Three bedrooms

— Two full baths

■ A spacious Family Room topped by a vaulted ceiling and highlighted by a large fireplace and a French door to the rear yard

■ A serving bar open to the Family Room and the Dining Room, a pantry and a peninsula counter adds more efficiency to the Kitchen

■ A crowning tray ceiling over the Master Bedroom and a vaulted ceiling over the master bath

■ A vaulted ceiling over the cozy Sitting Room in the Master Suite

■ Two additional bedrooms, roomy in size, share the full bath in the hall

■ An optional basement, crawl space or slab foundation — please specify when ordering

Delightful Doll House

■ *Total living area 1,307 sq. ft.* ■ *Price Code A* ■

No. 20161

■ This plan features:

— Three bedrooms

— Two full baths

■ A sloped ceiling in the Living Room which also has a focal point fireplace

■ An efficient Kitchen with a peninsula counter and a built-in pantry

■ A decorative ceiling and sliding glass doors to the Deck from the Dining Room

■ A Master Suite with a decorative ceiling, ample closet space and a private full bath

■ Two additional bedrooms that share a full hall bath

Main floor — 1,307 sq. ft.
Basement — 1,298 sq. ft.
Garage — 462 sq. ft.

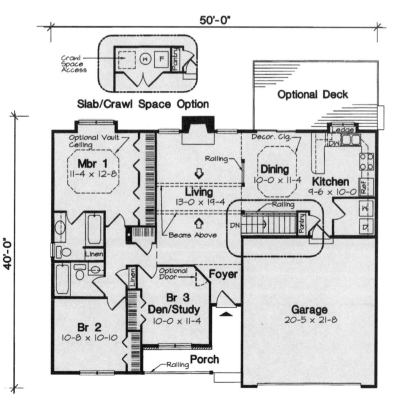

50'-0"

40'-0"

Crawl Space Access

Slab/Crawl Space Option

Optional Deck

Optional Vault Ceiling

Mbr 1
11-4 x 12-8

Railing

Decor. Clg.

Dining
10-0 x 11-4

Kitchen
9-6 x 10-0

Living
13-0 x 19-4

Railing

Beams Above

DN

Linen

Linen

Optional Door

Foyer

Br 3
Den/Study
10-0 x 11-4

Br 2
10-8 x 10-10

Garage
20-5 x 21-8

Railing

Porch

MAIN AREA

An
EXCLUSIVE DESIGN
By Karl Kreeger

Ideal Plan for a Sloping Lot

■ *Total living area 2,534 sq. ft.* ■ *Price Code D* ■

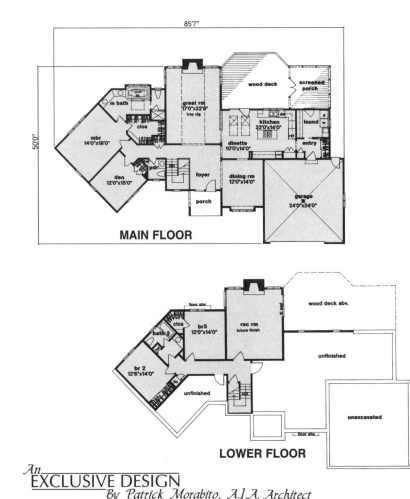

MAIN FLOOR

85'7"

500"

m bath
mbr 14'0"x18'0"
clos
great rm 17'0"x22'0" tray clg
wood deck
screened porch
kitchen 22'0"x14'0"
laund
dinette 10'0"x14'0"
entry
den 12'0"x15'0"
pdr
foyer
dining rm 12'0"x14'0"
porch
garage 24'0"x24'0"

LOWER FLOOR

floor abv.
clos
bath 2
br3 12'0"x14'0"
rec rm future finish
wood deck abv.
br 2 12'6"x14'0"
unfinished
unfinished
up
unexcavated
floor abv.

No. 93312

■ **This plan features:**

—Three bedrooms

—Two full and one half baths

■ The Great Room adds interest to the home with a tray ceiling and focal point fireplace

■ Sunlight streams into the Dinette area through skylights above

■ The cooktop island, double sinks and ample cabinet and counter space make the Kitchen great

■ The Master Suite is spacious and has a private bath with a double vanity, a separate tub and shower

■ The lower level has two additional bedrooms and a second full bath

■ No materials list is available for this plan

Main floor — 1,947 sq. ft.
Lower floor — 587 sq. ft.
Basement — 1,360 sq. ft.
Garage — 576 sq. ft.

An
EXCLUSIVE DESIGN
By Patrick Morabito, A.I.A. Architect

Updated Victorian

■ *Total living area 2,099 sq. ft.* ■ *Price Code C* ■

No. 91053 ⚒

■ **This plan features:**

— Three bedrooms

— Two full and one half baths

■ A classic Victorian exterior design accented by a wonderful turret room and second floor covered Porch above a sweeping veranda

■ A spacious formal Living Room

■ An efficient, U-shaped Kitchen with a peninsula snackbar, opens to an eating Nook and Family Room for informal gatherings

■ An elegant Master Suite with a unique, octagon Sitting area, a private Porch, an oversized, walk-in closet and private Bath with a double vanity and a window tub

■ Two bedrooms with ample closets sharing a full hall bath

First floor — 1,150 sq. ft.
Second floor — 949 sq. ft.
Garage — 484 sq. ft.

SECOND FLOOR

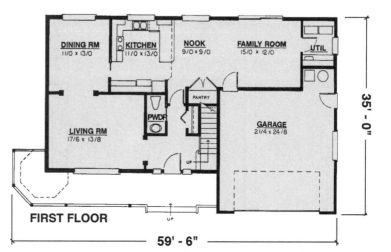

FIRST FLOOR

Fieldstone Facade and Arched Windows

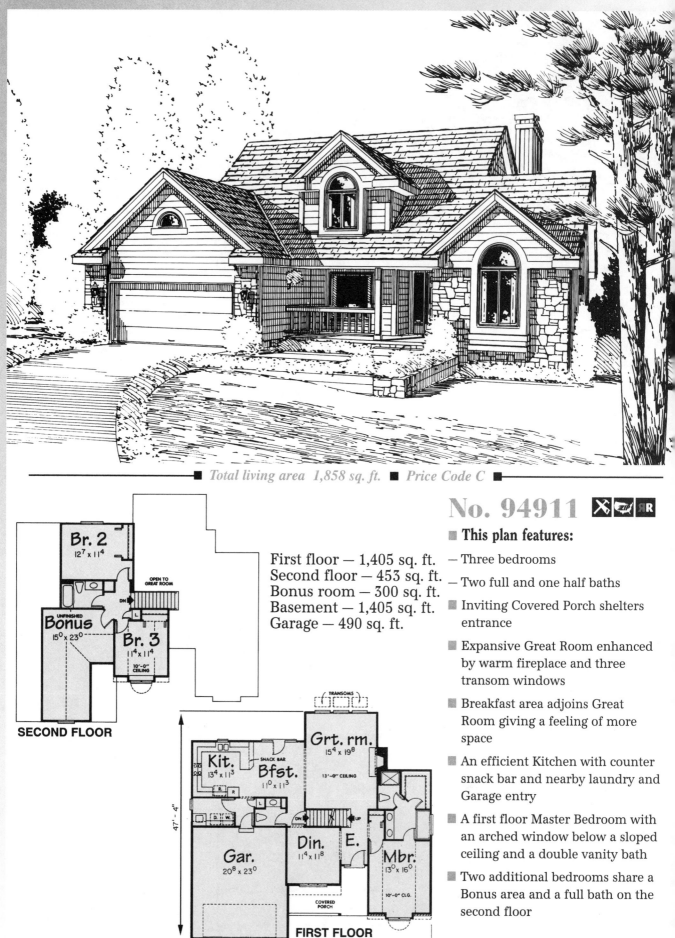

■ *Total living area 1,858 sq. ft.* ■ *Price Code C* ■

No. 94911

■ This plan features:

First floor — 1,405 sq. ft.
Second floor — 453 sq. ft.
Bonus room — 300 sq. ft.
Basement — 1,405 sq. ft.
Garage — 490 sq. ft.

- Three bedrooms
- Two full and one half baths
- Inviting Covered Porch shelters entrance
- Expansive Great Room enhanced by warm fireplace and three transom windows
- Breakfast area adjoins Great Room giving a feeling of more space
- An efficient Kitchen with counter snack bar and nearby laundry and Garage entry
- A first floor Master Bedroom with an arched window below a sloped ceiling and a double vanity bath
- Two additional bedrooms share a Bonus area and a full bath on the second floor

SECOND FLOOR

Br. 2
12⁷ x 11⁴

OPEN TO GREAT ROOM

Bonus
UNFINISHED
15⁰ x 23⁰

Br. 3
11⁴ x 11⁴
10'-0" CEILING

FIRST FLOOR
52' - 0"

47' - 4"

Grt. rm.
15⁴ x 19⁸
13'-0" CEILING

TRANSOMS

Kit.
13⁴ x 11³

SNACK BAR

Bfst.
11⁰ x 11³

Gar.
20⁸ x 23⁰

Din.
11⁴ x 11⁸

E.

Mbr.
13⁰ x 16⁰
10'-0" CLG.

COVERED PORCH

© design basics, inc.

■ *Total living area 1,528 sq. ft.* ■ *Price Code B* ■

No. 98522

■ **This plan features:**

— Three bedrooms

— Two full baths

■ The covered front Porch opens into the entry that has a 10-foot ceiling and a coat closet

■ The large Living Room is distinguished by a fireplace and a front window wall

■ The Dining Room features a 10-foot ceiling and access to the rear covered Patio

■ The Kitchen is angled and has a pantry, and a cooktop island

■ The Master Bedroom is located in the rear for privacy and boasts a triangular walk-in closet, plus a private bath

■ No materials list is available for this plan

Main floor — 1,528 sq. ft.
Garage — 440 sq. ft.

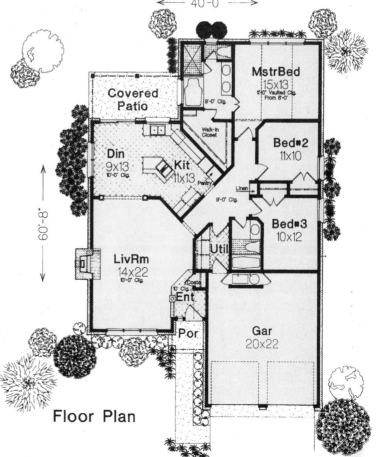

Floor Plan

A Statuesque Look

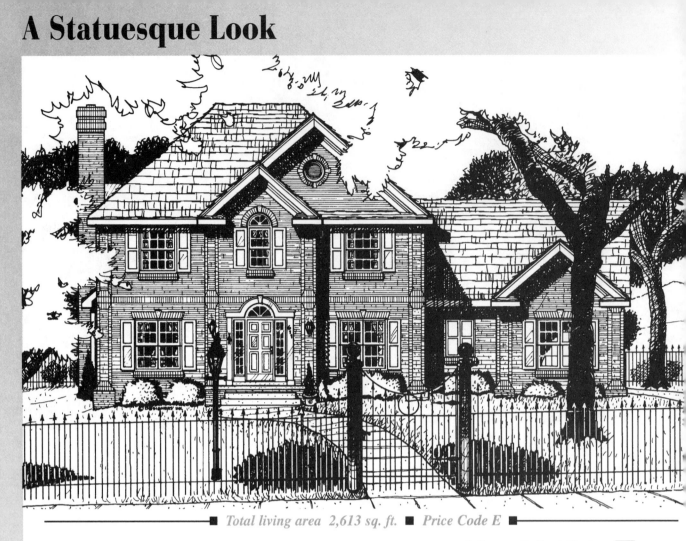

■ *Total living area 2,613 sq. ft.* ■ *Price Code E* ■

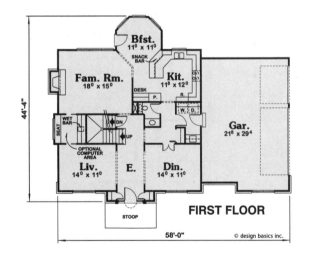

FIRST FLOOR

- Bfst. 11⁰ x 11⁰
- SNACK BAR
- Fam. Rm. 18⁰ x 15⁰
- Kit. 11⁸ x 12⁰
- DESK
- P.
- R.
- Gar. 21⁸ x 29⁴
- WET BAR
- SEAT
- DN
- UP
- W. D.
- OPTIONAL COMPUTER AREA
- Liv. 14⁰ x 11⁰
- E.
- Din. 14⁰ x 11⁰
- STOOP
- 44'-4"
- 58'-0"
- © design basics inc.

SECOND FLOOR

- WHIRLPOOL TUB
- CATHEDRAL CEILING
- Mbr. 15⁰ x 15⁰
- 9'-0" CEILING
- Br. 2 12⁰ x 12⁰
- DN
- Unfinished Bonus 21⁸ x 14⁰
- Br. 3 13⁰ x 11⁰
- Br. 4 13⁰ x 11⁰
- CATHEDRAL CEILING

No. 99494

■ **This plan features:**

— Four bedrooms

— Two full, one three quarter, and one half baths

■ The formal rooms flank the Entry

■ An angled snack bar in the Kitchen serves the Breakfast Area

■ Bedroom two is the perfect Guest Suite with a private bath

■ His-n-her walk-in closets and an extravagant whirlpool tub set the tone in the Master Suite

■ A large Bonus Room with many potential uses

■ An optional basement or slab foundation — please specify when ordering

First floor — 1,333 sq. ft.
Second floor — 1,280 sq. ft.
Bonus room — 323 sq. ft.
Garage — 687 sq. ft.

■ *Total living area 3,063 sq. ft.* ■ *Price Code E* ■

No. 98211

■ This plan features:

— Four bedrooms

— Three full and one half baths

■ High volume ceilings

■ An extended staircase highlights the Foyer as columns define the Dining Room and the Grand Room

■ A massive glass exterior rear wall and high ceiling in the Master Suite

■ His-n-her walk-in closets and a five-piece lavish bath highlight the master bath

■ The island Kitchen, Keeping Room and Breakfast Room create an open living space

■ A fireplace accents both the Keeping Room and the two-story Grand Room

■ An optional basement, slab or crawl space foundation — please specify when ordering

■ No materials list is available for this plan

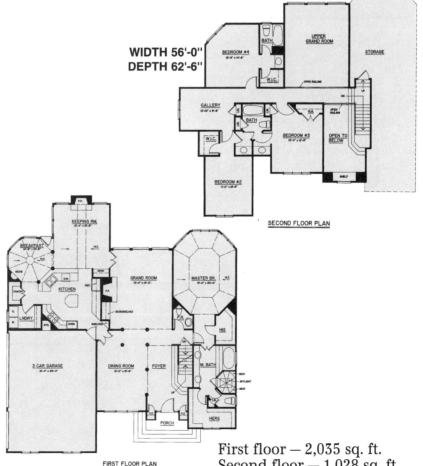

WIDTH 56'-0"
DEPTH 62'-6"

SECOND FLOOR PLAN

FIRST FLOOR PLAN

First floor — 2,035 sq. ft.
Second floor — 1,028 sq. ft.
Basement — 2,035 sq. ft.
Garage — 530 sq. ft.

Split Bedroom Plan

■ *Total living area 2,051 sq. ft.* ■ *Price Code C* ■

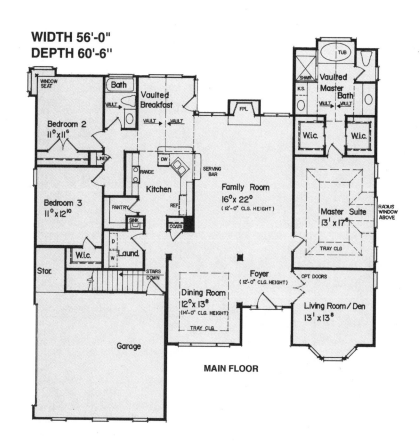

WIDTH 56'-0"
DEPTH 60'-6"

MAIN FLOOR

No. 98427

■ **This plan features:**

— Three bedrooms

— Two full baths

■ Dining Room is crowned by a tray ceiling

■ Living Room/Den privatized by double doors at its entrance, and is enhanced by a bay window

■ The Kitchen includes a walk-in pantry and a corner double sink

■ The vaulted Breakfast Room flows naturally from the Kitchen

■ The Master Suite is topped by a tray ceiling, and contains a compartmental bath plus two walk-in closets

■ An optional basement, slab or crawl space foundation — please specify when ordering

Main floor — 2,051 sq. ft.
Basement — 2,051 sq. ft.
Garage — 441 sq. ft.

Country Style Home With Corner Porch

© 1997 Donald A Gardner Architects, Inc.

■ *Total living area 1,815 sq. ft.* ■ *Price Code C* ■

No. 99804

■ This plan features:

— Three bedrooms

— Two full baths

■ Dining Room has four floor-to-ceiling windows that overlook front Porch

■ Great Room topped by a cathedral ceiling, enhanced by a fireplace, and sliding doors to the back Porch

■ Utility Room located near Kitchen and Breakfast Nook

■ Master Bedroom has a walk in closet and private bath

■ Two additional bedrooms with ample closet space share a full bath

■ A skylight Bonus Room over the two-car Garage

Main floor — 1,815 sq. ft.
Garage — 522 sq. ft.
Bonus — 336 sq. ft.

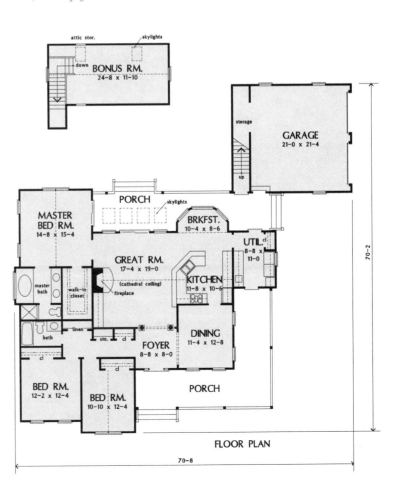

FLOOR PLAN

Sophisticated Southern Styling

■ *Total living area 2,858 sq. ft.* ■ *Price Code E* ■

First floor — 2,256 sq. ft.
Second floor — 602 sq. ft.
Bonus — 264 sq. ft.
Garage — 484 sq. ft.

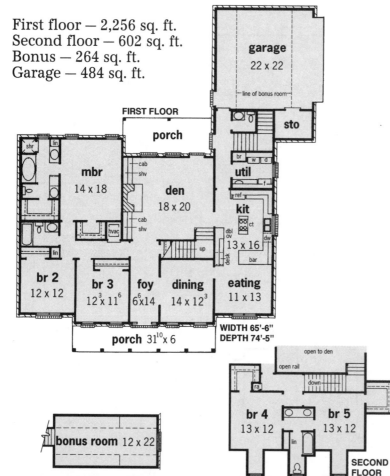

No. 92576

■ **This plan features:**

— Five bedrooms

— Three full and one half baths

■ Covered front and rear Porches expanding the living space to the outdoors

■ A Den with a large fireplace and built-in cabinets and shelves

■ A cooktop island, built-in desk, and eating bar complete the Kitchen

■ The Master Suite has two walk-in closets and a luxurious bath

■ Four additional bedrooms, two on the main level and two on the upper level, all have easy access to a full bath

■ An optional slab or crawl space foundation — please specify when ordering

■ *Total living area 1,500 sq. ft.* ■ *Price Code A* ■

No. 20062

■ **This plan features:**

— Three bedrooms

— Two full baths

■ A large picture window brightening the Breakfast Area

■ A well planned Kitchen

■ A Living Room which is accented by an open beam across the sloping ceiling and wood burning fireplace

■ A Master Bedroom with an extremely large bath area

Main floor — 1,500 sq. ft.
Basement — 1,500 sq. ft.
Garage — 482 sq. ft.

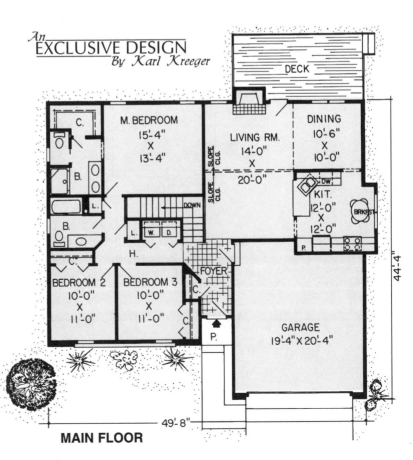

An
EXCLUSIVE DESIGN
By Karl Kreeger

DECK

M. BEDROOM
15'-4"
X
13'-4"

LIVING RM.
14'-0"
X
20'-0"

DINING
10'-6"
X
10'-0"

KIT.
12'-0"
X
12'-0"

BRKFST.

DOWN

BEDROOM 2
10'-0"
X
11'-0"

BEDROOM 3
10'-0"
X
11'-0"

FOYER

GARAGE
19'-4" X 20'-4"

44'-4"

49'-8"

MAIN FLOOR

A Magnificent Manor

■ *Total living area 2,389 sq. ft.* ■ *Price Code D* ■

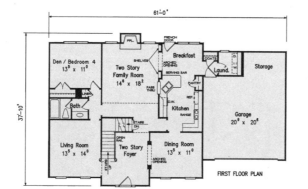

FIRST FLOOR PLAN

SECOND FLOOR PLAN

First floor — 1,428 sq. ft.
Second floor — 961 sq. ft.
Basement — 1,428 sq. ft.
Garage — 507 sq. ft.
Bonus — 472 sq. ft.

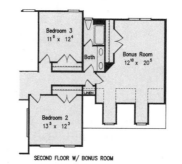

SECOND FLOOR W/ BONUS ROOM

No. 98410

■ This plan features:

— Three bedrooms

— Three full baths

■ The two-story Foyer is dominated by a lovely staircase

■ The Living Room is located directly off the Foyer

■ An efficient Kitchen accesses the formal Dining Room with ease

■ The Breakfast area is separated from the Kitchen by an extended counter/serving bar

■ The two-story Family Room is highlighted by a fireplace

■ Decorative ceilings crown Master Bedroom and bath

■ An optional basement or crawl space foundation available — please specify when ordering

© 1991 Donald A. Gardner Architects, Inc.

■ *Total living area 1,898 sq. ft.* ■ *Price Code C* ■

No. 99852

■ This plan features:

— Three bedrooms

— Two full and one half baths

■ Ready, set, grow with this lovely country home enhanced by wrap-around Porch and rear Deck

■ Palladian window in clerestory dormer bathes two-story Foyer in natural light

■ Private Master Bedroom offers everything: walk-in closet, whirlpool tub, shower and double vanity

■ Two upstairs bedrooms with dormers and storage access share a full bath

■ An optional basement or crawl space foundation — please specify when ordering

First floor — 1,356 sq. ft.
Second floor — 542 sq. ft.
Bonus room — 393 sq. ft.
Garage & storage — 543 sq. ft.

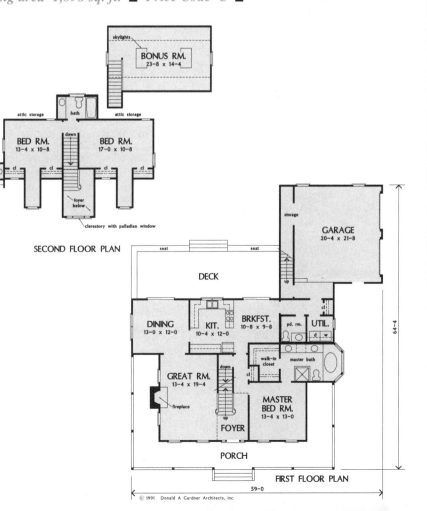

Luxury on One Level

■ *Total living area 2,196 sq. ft.* ■ *Price Code C* ■

No. 93190

■ This plan features:

— Three bedrooms

— Two full and one half baths

■ Covered front Porch leads into Entry and Great Room with vaulted ceilings

■ Huge Great Room perfect for entertaining or family gatherings with cozy fireplace

■ Arched soffits and columns surround the formal Dining Room

■ Country-size Kitchen with a pantry, work island, bright eating Nook with Screen Porch beyond, and nearby Laundry/Garage entry

■ No materials list is available for this plan

Main floor — 2,196 sq. ft.
Basement — 2,196 sq. ft.

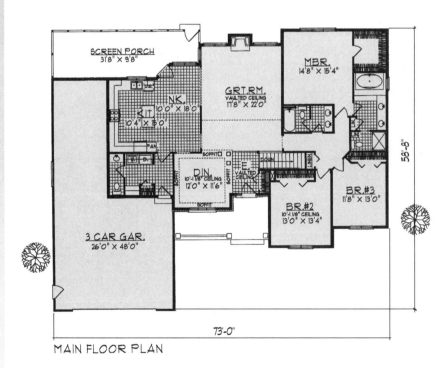

MAIN FLOOR PLAN

■ *Total living area 2,685 sq. ft.* ■ *Price Code E* ■

An
EXCLUSIVE DESIGN
By Westhome Planners, Ltd.

No. 90838 ⊠

■ This plan features:

— Three bedrooms

— Three full baths

■ A corner gas fireplace in the spacious Living Room

■ A Master Suite including a private bath with a whirlpool tub, separate shower and a double vanity

■ An island Kitchen that is well-equipped to efficiently serve both formal Dining Room and informal Nook

■ Two additional bedrooms share a full bath on the second floor

First floor — 1,837 sq. ft.
Second floor — 848 sq. ft.
Basement — 1,803 sq. ft.
Bonus room — 288 sq. ft.

SECOND FLOOR

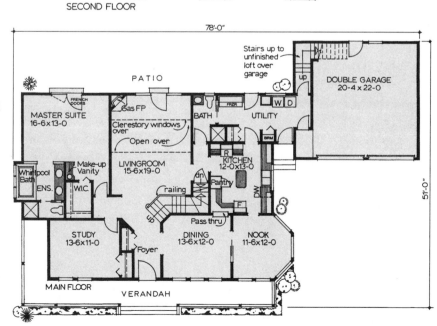

Traditional Home

© design basics inc.

■ *Total living area 2,979 sq. ft.* ■ *Price Code E* ■

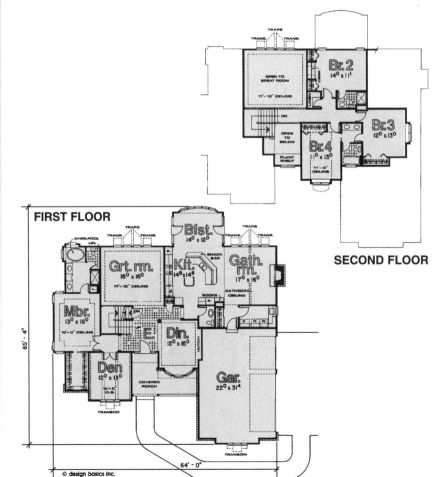

SECOND FLOOR

FIRST FLOOR

No. 99452

■ This plan features:

— Four bedrooms

— Two full and one half baths

■ Dining Room has a built-in hutch and a bay window

■ Cozy Den and Great Room have high ceilings and transom windows

■ Conveniently arranged Kitchen adjoins the Breakfast Nook

■ The warm Gathering Room features a fireplace and a cathedral ceiling

■ The secluded Master Bedroom is a world away from the busy areas of the home

■ Upstairs are three bedrooms and two full baths

First floor — 2,158 sq. ft.
Second floor — 821 sq. ft.
Basement — 2,158 sq. ft.
Garage — 692 sq. ft.

© 1995 Donald A Gardner Architects, Inc.

■ *Total living area 1,246 sq. ft.* ■ *Price Code B* ■

No. 99806

■ **This plan features:**

— Three bedrooms

— Two full baths

■ Great Room topped by a cathedral ceiling and enhanced by a fireplace

■ Great Room, Dining Room and Kitchen open to each other for a feeling of spaciousness

■ Pantry, skylight and peninsula counter add to the comfort and efficiency of the Kitchen

■ Cathedral ceiling crowns the Master Suite and has these amenities; walk-in and linen closet, a luxurious private bath

■ Swing Room, bedroom or Study, topped by a cathedral ceiling

■ Skylight over full hall bath naturally illuminates the room

Main floor — 1,246 sq. ft.
Garage — 420 sq. ft.

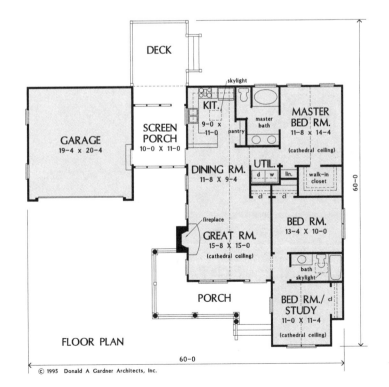

FLOOR PLAN

© 1995 Donald A Gardner Architects, Inc.

Glorious Gables

■ *Total living area 3,306 sq. ft.* ■ *Price Code F* ■

No. 94933

■ **This plan features:**

— Four bedrooms

— Two full, one three-quarter and one half baths

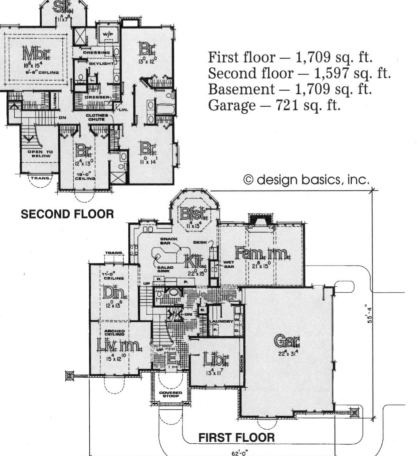

SECOND FLOOR

© design basics, inc.

FIRST FLOOR

First floor — 1,709 sq. ft.
Second floor — 1,597 sq. ft.
Basement — 1,709 sq. ft.
Garage — 721 sq. ft.

■ Arched windows and entry graciously greet one and all

■ Arched ceiling topping decorative windows highlights Living and Dining rooms

■ Double door leads into quiet Library with book shelves

■ Hub Kitchen with angled, work island/snackbar, built-in pantry and desk

■ Comfortable Family Room with hearth fireplace framed by decorative windows

■ Private Master Suite offers a Sitting area, two walk-in closets and luxurious bath

■ Three additional bedrooms with ample closets and private access to a full bath

■ *Total living area 1,808 sq. ft.* ■ *Price Code C* ■

No. 93413

■ **This plan features:**

— Three bedrooms

— Two full and one half baths

■ The Foyer is naturally lit by a dormer window above

■ Family Room is highlighted by two front windows and a fireplace

■ Kitchen includes an angled extended counter/snack bar and an abundance of counter/cabinet space

■ Dining Area opens to the Kitchen, for a more spacious feeling

■ The roomy Master Suite is located on the first floor and has a private five-piece bath plus a walk-in closet

■ Laundry Room doubles as a mud room from the side entrance

■ No materials list is available for this plan

An
EXCLUSIVE DESIGN
By Greg Marquis

SECOND FLOOR

First floor — 1,271 sq. ft.
Second floor — 537 sq. ft.
Basement — 1,271 sq. ft.
Garage — 555 sq. ft.

Rambling Ranch

■ *Total living area 1,689 sq. ft.* ■ *Price Code B* ■

No. 97251

■ This plan features:

— Three bedrooms

— Two full baths

■ Decorative columns define the Foyer area

■ The Family Room is topped by a vaulted ceiling

■ A serving bar in the Kitchen doubles as a snackbar

■ The Breakfast Area flows from the Kitchen and directly accesses the rear yard

■ Secondary bedrooms are to the left of the Breakfast Room

■ A tray ceiling tops the Master Suite

■ An optional basement or crawl space foundation — please specify when ordering

■ No materials list is available for this plan

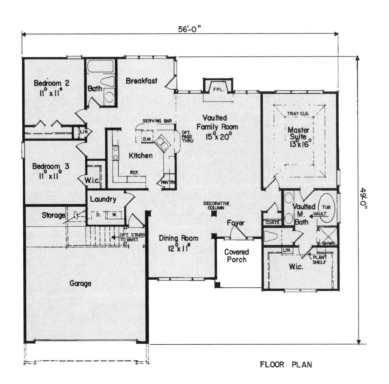

FLOOR PLAN

Main floor — 1,689 sq. ft.
Basement — 1,689 sq. ft.
Garage — 478 sq. ft.

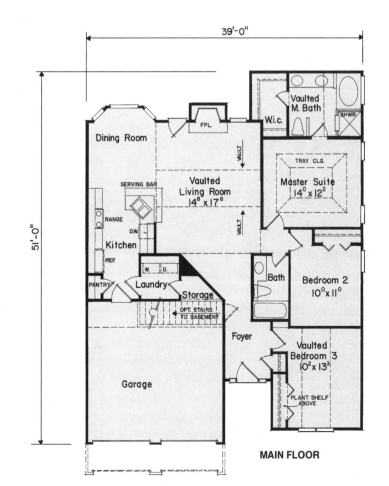

■ *Total living area 1,346 sq. ft.* ■ *Price Code A* ■

No. 98434

■ This plan features:

— Three bedrooms

— Two full baths

■ Vaulted ceiling crowns spacious Living Room highlighted by a fireplace

■ Built-in pantry and direct access from the garage adding to the conveniences of the Kitchen

■ Walk-in closet and a private five piece bath topped by a vaulted ceiling in the Master Bedroom suite

■ Proximity to the full bath in the hall from the secondary bedrooms

■ An optional basement, slab or crawl space foundation available — please specify when ordering

Main floor — 1,346 sq. ft.
Basement — 1,358 sq. ft.
Garage — 395 sq. ft.

MAIN FLOOR

Designed for Today's Family

■ *Total living area 2,192 sq. ft.* ■ *Price Code D* ■

No. 99838

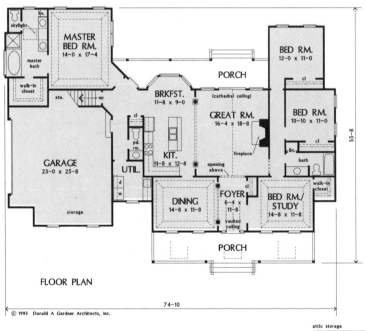

FLOOR PLAN

■ **This plan features:**

— Three bedrooms

— Two full and one half baths

■ Volume and 9' ceilings add elegance to a comfortable, open floor plan

■ Secluded bedrooms designed for pleasant retreats at the end of the day

■ Airy Foyer topped by a vaulted dormer sends natural light streaming in

■ Formal Dining Room delineated from the Foyer by columns and topped with a tray ceiling

■ Extra flexibility in the front bedroom which could double as a study

■ Tray ceiling, skylights and a garden tub, in the bath highlight the Master Suite

Main floor — 2,192 sq. ft.
Garage & Storage — 582 sq. ft.
Bonus — 390 sq. ft.

■ *Total living area 1,619 sq. ft.* ■ *Price Code B* ■

No. 98416

■ This plan features:

— Three bedrooms

— Two full and one half baths

■ A high arched window illuminates the Foyer and adds style to the exterior of the home

■ Vaulted ceilings in the formal Dining Room, Breakfast Room and Great Room create volume

■ The Master Suite is crowned with a decorative tray ceiling

■ The master bath has a double vanity, oval tub, separate shower and a walk-in closet

■ The Loft, with the option of becoming a fourth bedroom, highlights the second floor

■ An optional basement or crawl space foundation — please specify when ordering

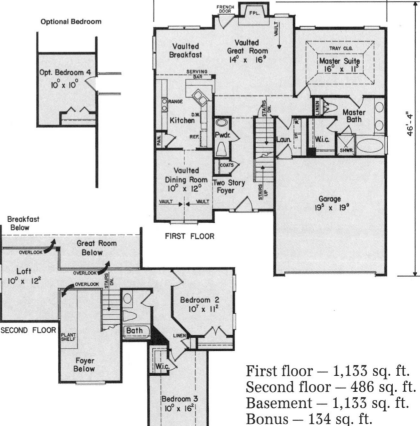

First floor — 1,133 sq. ft.
Second floor — 486 sq. ft.
Basement — 1,133 sq. ft.
Bonus — 134 sq. ft.
Garage — 406 sq. ft.

Home Sweet Home

■ *Total living area 2,588 sq. ft.* ■ *Price Code D* ■

FIRST FLOOR

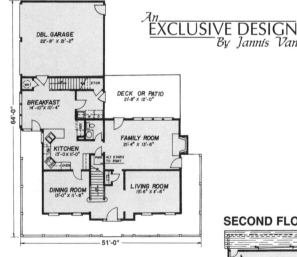

An
EXCLUSIVE DESIGN
By Jannis Vann & Associates, Inc.

DBL. GARAGE
22'-8" X 21'-2"

BREAKFAST
14'-10"X 10'-4"

DECK OR PATIO
21'-8" X 12'-0"

KITCHEN
13'-0 X 11'-0"

FAMILY ROOM
21'-4" X 13'-6"

DINING ROOM
13'-0"X 11'-6"

LIVING ROOM
15'-6" X 8'-6"

64'-0"

51'-0"

First floor — 1,320 sq. ft.
Second floor — 1,268 sq. ft.
Bonus room — 389 sq. ft.
Basement — 1,320 sq. ft.
Garage — 482 sq. ft.

SECOND FLOOR

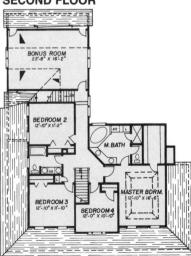

BONUS ROOM
22'-8" X 16'-2"

BEDROOM 2
12'-10"X 11'-2"

M. BATH

BEDROOM 3
12'-10"X 11'-10"

BEDROOM 4
12'-0" X 10'-0"

MASTER BDRM.
12'-10" X 16'-6"

No. 93205

■ This plan features:

— Four bedrooms

— Two full and one half baths

■ Foyer with formal Living Room to the right

■ Dining Room convenient to the Kitchen

■ A U-shaped Kitchen equipped with a peninsula counter

■ A spacious Breakfast Room with direct access to the Garage

■ Family Room with a large fireplace and direct access to the rear Deck and Porch

■ Second floor Master Suite crowned by a decorative ceiling treatment

■ A Bonus Room for future expansion

■ An optional basement, crawl space or slab foundation — please specify when ordering

Rocking Chair Living

■ *Total living area 1,670 sq. ft.* ■ *Price Code B* ■

No. 90409 ⚒

■ This plan features:

— Three bedrooms

— Two full baths

■ A massive fireplace separating Living and Dining Rooms

■ An isolated Master Suite with a walk-in closet and handy compartmentalized bath

■ A galley-type Kitchen between the Breakfast Room and Dining Room

■ An optional basement, slab or crawl space foundation — please specify when ordering

Main area — 1,670 sq. ft.

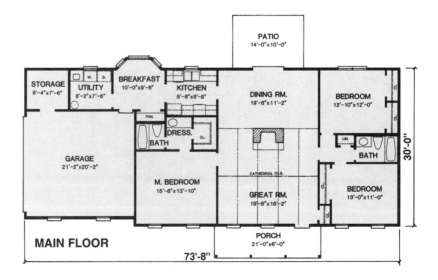

PATIO 14'-0"x10'-0"

STORAGE 8'-4"x7'-6"

UTILITY 8'-2"x7'-6"

W. D.

BREAKFAST 10'-0"x9'-6"

KITCHEN 9'-8"x8'-8"

DINING RM. 19'-8"x11'-2"

BEDROOM 12'-10"x12'-0"

PAN.

BATH

DRESS.

CL.

GARAGE 21'-2"x20'-2"

LIN.

BATH

M. BEDROOM 15'-8"x13'-10"

CATHEDRAL CLG.

GREAT RM. 19'-8"x18'-2"

BEDROOM 13'-0"x11'-0"

MAIN FLOOR

PORCH 21'-0"x6'-0"

73'-8"

30'-0"

Traditional Splendor

■ *Total living area 3,688 sq. ft.* ■ *Price Code F* ■

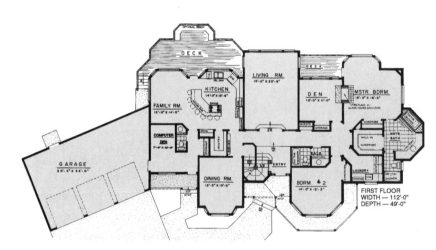

FIRST FLOOR
WIDTH — 112'-0"
DEPTH — 49'-0"

SECOND FLOOR

No. 91339

■ This plan features:

— Six bedrooms

— Four full and one half baths

■ This home easily accommodates large or extended families with style and grace

■ Two-story Entry illuminated by palladian window opens to gracious Living Room

■ Bright and efficient Kitchen with angled counter/eating bar and walk-in Pantry opens to Family Room and Deck

■ Luxurious Master Suite shares two-way fireplace with Den

■ Four second floor bedrooms share two full baths

■ No materials list is available for this plan

First floor — 2,498 sq. ft.
Second floor — 1,190 sq. ft.

Perfect Compact Ranch

■ *Total living area 1,738 sq. ft.* ■ *Price Code B* ■

No. 10839

■ **This plan features:**

— Two bedrooms

— Two full baths

■ A large, sunken Great Room, centralized with a cozy fireplace

■ A Master Bedroom with an unforgettable bathroom including a skylight

■ A huge three-car Garage, including a work area for the family carpenter

■ A Kitchen, including a Breakfast Nook for family gatherings

Main floor — 1,738 sq. ft.
Basement — 1,083 sq. ft.
Garage — 796 sq. ft.

Crawl / Slab Option

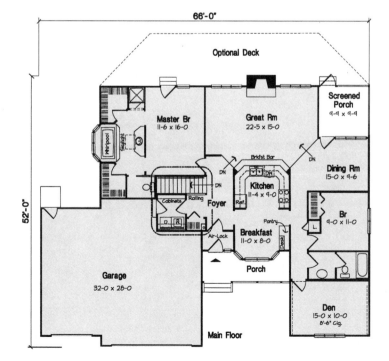

66'-0"

Optional Deck

52'-0"

Master Br
11-6 x 16-0

Great Rm
22-5 x 15-0

Screened Porch
9-9 x 9-9

Whirlpool

Skylight

Brkfst Bar

DN

Dining Rm
15-0 x 9-6

DN

DN

Kitchen
11-4 x 9-0

Cabinets

Railing

Ref.

Foyer

Br
9-0 x 11-0

Pantry

Air-Lock

Breakfast
11-0 x 8-0

Garage
32-0 x 28-0

Porch

Den
15-0 x 10-0
8'-6" Clg.

Main Floor

89

Captivating Colonial

© design basics inc.

■ *Total living area 2,585 sq. ft.* ■ *Price Code D* ■

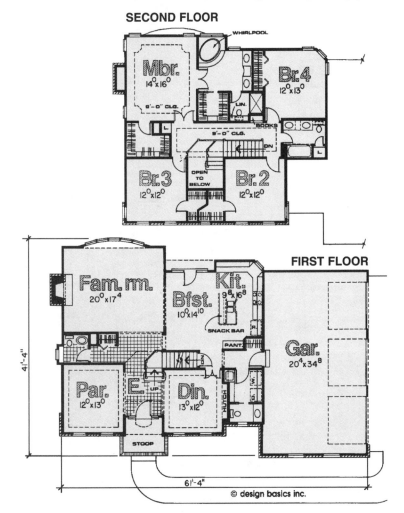

SECOND FLOOR

WHIRLPOOL

Mbr.
14⁰x16⁰

Br. 4
12⁰x13⁰

8'-0" CLG.

LIN.

BOOKS

8'-0" CLG.

DN

Br. 3
12⁰x12⁰

OPEN TO BELOW

Br. 2
12⁰x12⁰

FIRST FLOOR

Fam. rm.
20⁰x17⁴

Kit.
9⁸x16⁸

Bfst.
10⁰x14¹⁰

SNACK BAR

PANT.

Gar.
20⁴x34⁸

Par.
12⁰x13⁰

E.

UP

Din.
13⁰x12⁰

HUTCH

W

D

STOOP

41'-4"

61'-4"

© design basics inc.

No. 99454 ✕

■ This plan features:

— Four bedrooms

— Two full and one half baths

■ Decorative windows and brick detailing

■ Dining room highlighted by decorative ceiling, French doors and hutch space

■ The Family Room has a fireplace and a bow window

■ The Breakfast Nook and Kitchen are perfectly set up for meals on the run

■ Upstairs find the Master Bedroom and bath fully complemented

■ Three more bedrooms and a bath completed the second floor plan

■ This plan is available with a basement or slab foundation — please specify when ordering

First floor — 1,362 sq. ft.
Second floor — 1,223 sq. ft.
Basement — 1,362 sq. ft.
Garage — 734 sq. ft.

■ Total living area 1,675 sq. ft. ■ Price Code B ■

No. 98431 ✕

■ This plan features:

— Three bedrooms

— Two full and one half baths

■ An impressive two-story Foyer

■ The Kitchen is equipped with ample cabinet and counter space

■ Spacious Family Room flows from the Breakfast Bay and is highlighted by a fireplace and a French door to the rear yard

■ The Master Suite is topped by a tray ceiling and is enhanced by a vaulted, five-piece master bath

■ An optional basement, slab or crawl space foundation — please specify when ordering

First floor — 882 sq. ft.
Second floor — 793 sq. ft.
Bonus room — 416 sq. ft.
Basement — 882 sq. ft.
Garage — 510 sq. ft.

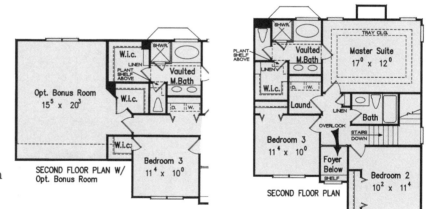

SECOND FLOOR PLAN W/ Opt. Bonus Room

Opt. Bonus Room 15⁵ x 20³

W.I.C.

W.I.C.

LINEN

PLANT SHELF ABOVE

SHWR.

Vaulted M.Bath

W.I.C.

Bedroom 3 11⁴ x 10⁰

SECOND FLOOR PLAN

PLANT SHELF ABOVE

SHWR.

Vaulted M.Bath

LINEN

W.I.C.

Laund.

Master Suite 17⁰ x 12⁰

TRAY CLG.

Bath

OVERLOOK

STAIRS DOWN

Bedroom 3 11⁴ x 10⁰

Foyer Below

SHELF

LINEN

Bedroom 2 10² x 11⁴

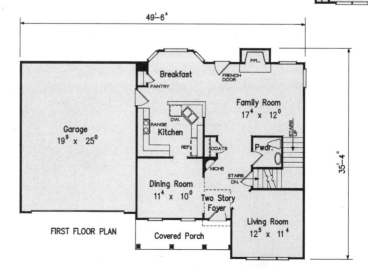

FIRST FLOOR PLAN

49'-6"

35'-4"

Garage 19⁹ x 25⁰

Breakfast

PANTRY

RANGE

Kitchen

DW.

REF.

COATS

NICHE

FPL.

FRENCH DOOR

Family Room 17⁴ x 12⁰

STAIRS UP

Pwdr.

Dining Room 11⁴ x 10⁰

STAIRS DN.

Two Story Foyer

Living Room 12⁵ x 11⁴

Covered Porch

Mixture of Traditional and Country Charm

© 1994 Donald A. Gardner Architects, Inc.

■ *Total living area 1,954 sq. ft.* ■ *Price Code C* ■

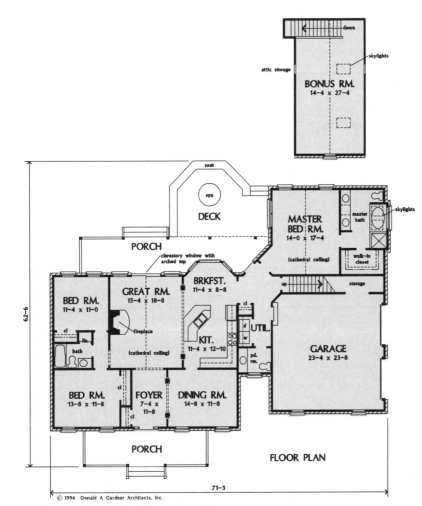

No. 99845

■ This plan features:

— Three bedrooms

— Two full and one half baths

■ Stairs to the skylit bonus room located near the Kitchen and Master Suite

■ Master Suite crowned in cathedral ceilings has a skylit bath that contains a whirlpool tub and dual vanity

■ Great Room, topped by a cathedral ceiling and highlighted by a fireplace, is adjacent to the country Kitchen

■ Two additional bedrooms share a hall bath

Main floor — 1,954 sq. ft.
Bonus area — 436 sq. ft.
Garage — 649 sq. ft.

© 1994 Donald A Gardner Architects, Inc.

Total living area 1,782 sq. ft. ■ *Price Code B* ■

No. 94917 ✖

■ This plan features:

— Three bedrooms

— Two full baths

■ Entry opens to formal Dining Room with arched window

■ Angles and transom windows add interest to the Great Room

■ Bright Hearth area expands Breakfast/Kitchen area and shares three-sided fireplace

■ Efficient Kitchen offers an angled snack bar, a large pantry and nearby laundry/Garage entry

■ Secluded Master Suite crowned by decorative ceiling, a large walk-in closet and a plush bath with a whirlpool tub

■ Two secondary bedrooms in separate wing from Master Suite for added privacy

Main floor — 1,782 sq. ft.
Basement — 1,782 sq. ft.
Garage — 466 sq. ft.

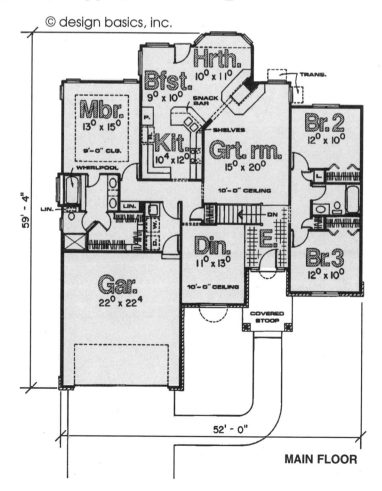

© design basics, inc.

MAIN FLOOR

Traditional Two-Story Home

© 1997 Donald A. Gardner Architects, Inc.

■ *Total living area 2,250 sq. ft.* ■ *Price Code D* ■

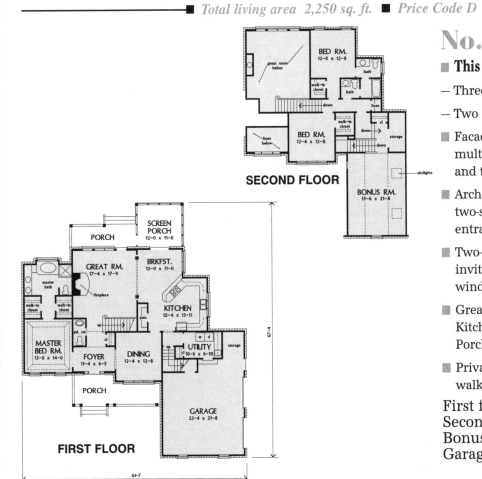

SECOND FLOOR

FIRST FLOOR

© 1997 Donald A. Gardner Architects, Inc.

No. 96491 ✕

■ **This plan features:**

— Three bedrooms

— Two full and two half baths

■ Facade handsomely accented by multiple gables, keystone arches and transom windows

■ Arched clerestory window lights two-story Foyer for a dramatic entrance

■ Two-story Great Room with inviting fireplace, wall of windows and back Porch access

■ Great cooks will enjoy open Kitchen with easy access to Screen Porch and Dining Room

■ Private Master Bedroom has two walk-in closets and deluxe bath

First floor — 1,644 sq. ft.
Second floor — 606 sq. ft.
Bonus room — 548 sq. ft.
Garage & storage — 657 sq. ft.

Hip Roof Ranch

■ *Total living area 1,540 sq. ft.* ■ *Price Code B* ■

No. 93161

■ This plan features:

— Three bedrooms

— Two full baths

■ Cozy front Porch leads into Entry with vaulted ceiling and sidelights

■ Open Living Room enhanced by a cathedral ceiling, a wall of windows and corner fireplace

■ Large and efficient Kitchen with an extended counter and a bright Dining area with access to Screen Porch

■ Convenient Utility area with access to Garage and Storage area

■ Spacious Master Bedroom with a walk-in closet and private bath

■ Two additional bedrooms with ample closets share a full bath

■ No materials list is available for this plan

Main floor — 1,540 sq. ft.
Basement — 1,540 sq. ft.

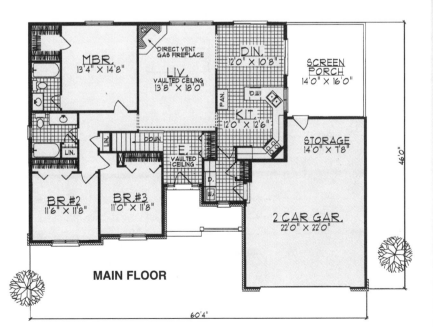

MAIN FLOOR

Windows Distinguish Design

■ Total living area 3,525 sq. ft. ■ Price Code F ■

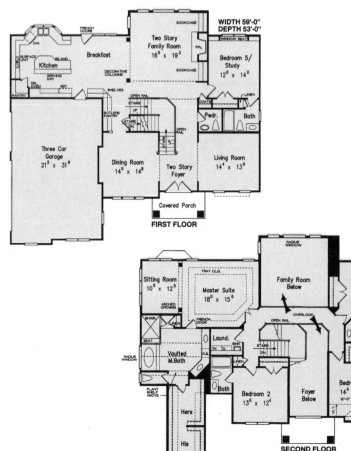

WIDTH 59'-0"
DEPTH 53'-0"

FIRST FLOOR

SECOND FLOOR

No. 98438

■ This plan features:

— Five bedrooms

— Four full and one half baths

■ Light shines into the Dining Room and the Living Room through their respective elegant windows

■ A hall through the Butler's Pantry leads the way into the Breakfast Nook

■ The two-story Family Room has a fireplace with built-in bookcases on either side

■ The upstairs Master Suite has a sitting room and a French door that leads into the vaulted master bath

■ An optional basement or crawl space foundation — please specify when ordering

First floor — 1,786 sq. ft.
Second floor — 1,739 sq. ft.
Basement — 1,786 sq. ft.
Garage — 704 sq. ft.

Updated Tudor

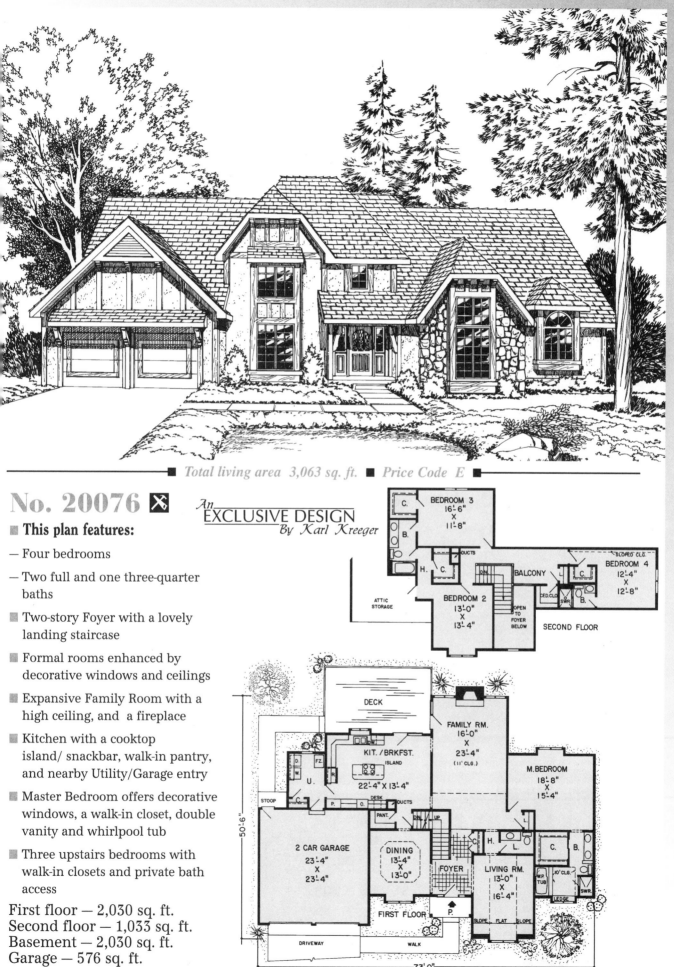

■ Total living area 3,063 sq. ft. ■ Price Code E ■

No. 20076 ✖

An EXCLUSIVE DESIGN
By Karl Kreeger

■ This plan features:

— Four bedrooms

— Two full and one three-quarter baths

■ Two-story Foyer with a lovely landing staircase

■ Formal rooms enhanced by decorative windows and ceilings

■ Expansive Family Room with a high ceiling, and a fireplace

■ Kitchen with a cooktop island/ snackbar, walk-in pantry, and nearby Utility/Garage entry

■ Master Bedroom offers decorative windows, a walk-in closet, double vanity and whirlpool tub

■ Three upstairs bedrooms with walk-in closets and private bath access

First floor — 2,030 sq. ft.
Second floor — 1,033 sq. ft.
Basement — 2,030 sq. ft.
Garage — 576 sq. ft.

Feels Like Home

Total living area 2,038 sq. ft. ■ Price Code C ■

No. 91121 ℞

This plan features:

— Three bedrooms

— Three full baths

■ An eleven foot ceiling in the Foyer

■ The Kitchen, Dining and Great Room flow together to create a perfect layout for entertaining

■ The fireplace helps to divide space and create a cozy atmosphere

■ The first floor Master Suite is topped by a tray ceiling and is completed by a five-piece bath

■ Bedroom two is equipped with private access to a full bath and a walk-in closet

■ Bedroom three has a walk-in closet and direct access to a full bath

■ The Loft area could easily become a study or home office

■ No materials list is available for this plan

First floor — 1,553 sq. ft.
Second floor — 485 sq. ft.
Garage & storage — 477 sq. ft.

FIRST FLOOR

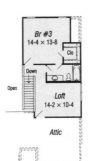

SECOND FLOOR

Perfect Home for Narrow Lot

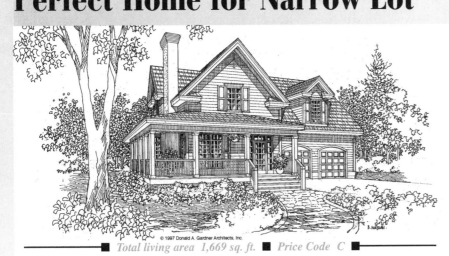

© 1997 Donald A. Gardner Architects, Inc.

Total living area 1,669 sq. ft. ■ Price Code C ■

No. 96487 ⚒

This plan features:

— Three bedrooms

— Two and one half baths

■ Narrow lot floor plan featuring wrap-around Porch and two-car Garage

■ Alcove of windows and columns add distinction to Dining Room

■ Cathedral ceiling above inviting fireplace accent spacious Great Room

■ Efficient Kitchen with peninsula counter accesses side Porch and Deck

■ Master Suite on first floor and two additional bedrooms and Bonus Room on second floor

First floor — 1,219 sq. ft.
Second floor — 450 sq. ft.
Bonus Room — 406 sq. ft.
Garage — 473 sq. ft.

FIRST FLOOR

SECOND FLOOR

Spectacular Sophistication

■ *Total living area 1,933 sq. ft.* ■ *Price Code C* ■

No. 94944

■ **This plan features:**

— Four bedrooms

— Two full and one half baths

■ Open Foyer with circular window and a plant shelf leads into the Dining Room

■ Great Room with an inviting fireplace and windows, front and back

■ Open Kitchen has a work island and accesses the Breakfast Area

■ Master Suite features a nine-foot boxed ceiling, a walk-in closet and whirlpool bath

■ Three additional bedrooms share a full bath with a double vanity

First floor — 941 sq. ft.
Second floor — 992 sq. ft.
Basement — 941 sq. ft.
Garage — 480 sq. ft.

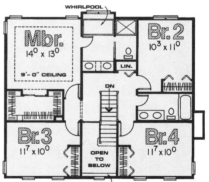

SECOND FLOOR

© design basics, inc.

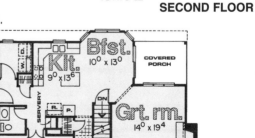

FIRST FLOOR

Cozy Cottage

■ *Total living area 1,249 sq. ft.* ■ *Price Code A* ■

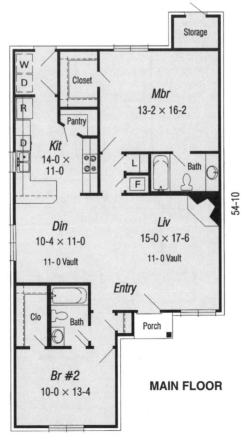

MAIN FLOOR

No. 91120

■ **This plan features:**

— Two bedrooms

— Two full baths

■ Living and Dining rooms with vaulted ceilings flowing into each other

■ Corner fireplace adding to the cozy cottage atmosphere

■ Kitchen efficiency is enhanced by a large Pantry, lots of corner space and a window over the sink for natural lighting

■ Two large bedrooms placed at opposite ends of the home for privacy each with a walk-in closet and a full bath

■ Master Bedroom has a vaulted ceiling and a view of the backyard

■ No materials list is available for this plan

Main floor — 1,249 sq. ft.

Design Features Six Sides

No. 1074

This plan features:

— Three bedrooms

— One full and one three-quarter baths

■ Active living areas centrally located between two quiet bedroom and bath areas

■ A Living Room that can be closed off from bedroom wings giving privacy to both areas

■ Kitchen features breakfast bar for quick meals

■ A bath located behind a third bedroom

Main floor — 1,040 sq. ft.
Storage — 44 sq. ft.
Deck — 258 sq. ft.
Carport — 230 sq. ft.

■ Total living area 1,040 sq. ft. ■ Price Code A ■

MAIN FLOOR

Cozy Three-Bedroom

No. 94800

This plan features:

— Three bedrooms

— Two full baths

■ Covered entry leads into Activity Room highlighted by a double window and a vaulted ceiling

■ Efficient Kitchen with work island, nearby laundry and Garage entry, opens to Dining area with access to Sun Deck

■ Plush Master Bedroom offers a decorative ceiling, walk-in closet and whirlpool tub

■ Two additional bedrooms, one with a vaulted ceiling, share a full bath

■ Garage with entry into Laundry Room serving as a Mud Room

■ An optional basement, slab or crawl space foundation — please specify when ordering

Main floor — 1,199 sq. ft.
Basement — 1,199 sq. ft.
Garage — 287 sq. ft.

■ Total living area 1,199 sq. ft. ■ Price Code B ■

ALT. PART FLOOR PLAN
(OMITTING BASEMENT STAIR)

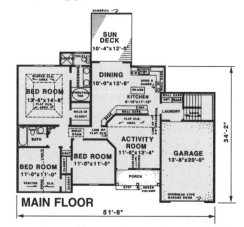

MAIN FLOOR

Cathedral Window Graced by Massive Arch

■ Total living area 1,850 sq. ft. ■ Price Code C ■

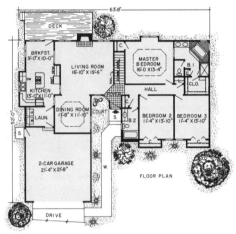

FLOOR PLAN

No. 20066

■ **This plan features:**

— Three bedrooms

— Two full baths

■ A tiled threshold providing a distinctive entrance

■ A comfortable Living Room with a wood-burning fireplace and tiled hearth

■ A Dining Room with vaulted ceiling

■ A Kitchen with central work island, Pantry, planning desk, and Breakfast area

■ A Master Suite with decorative ceilings, master bath and bow window

Main area — 1,850 sq. ft.
Basement — 1,850 sq. ft.
Garage — 503 sq. ft.

An
EXCLUSIVE DESIGN
By Karl Kreeger

Living Room Features Exposed Beams

■ Total living area 1,876 sq. ft. ■ Price Code C ■

Floor Plan

No. 98503

■ **This plan features:**

— Three bedrooms

— Two full baths

■ A covered Porch shelters the entry to this home

■ The large Living Room with exposed beams includes a fireplace and built-ins

■ The bright Dining Room is located next to the Kitchen which features a center island

■ The bedroom wing features three spacious bedrooms and two full baths

■ The two-car Garage has a handy workshop area

■ An optional crawl space or slab foundation — please specify when ordering

■ No materials list is available for this plan

Main floor — 1,876 sq. ft.
Garage — 619 sq. ft.

Lavish Accommodations

■ *Total living area 2,733 sq. ft.* ■ *Price Code F* ■

No. 92538 ✕

■ **This plan features:**

— Four bedrooms

— Three full baths

■ A central Den with a large fireplace, built-in shelves and cabinets and a decorative ceiling

■ Columns defining the entrance to the formal Dining Room, adding a touch of elegance

■ An island Kitchen that has been well thought out and includes a walk-in pantry

■ An informal Breakfast Room

■ A Master Bedroom with a decorative ceiling, a walk-in closet, and a luxurious Master Bath

■ Four additional bedrooms, each with private access to a full bath, two of which have walk-in closets

■ An optional crawl space or slab foundation available — please specify when ordering

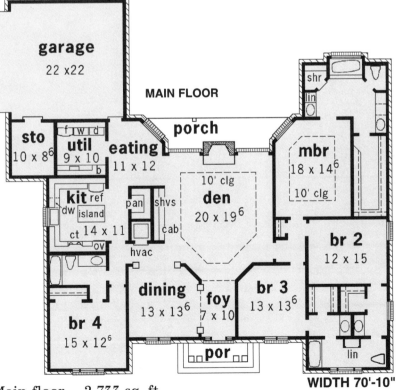

MAIN FLOOR

garage
22 x22

sto
10 x 8⁶

util
9 x 10

eating
11 x 12

porch

mbr
18 x 14⁶

10' clg

kit
14 x 11

den
20 x 19⁶

10' clg

br 2
12 x 15

dining
13 x 13⁶

foy
7 x 10

br 3
13 x 13⁶

br 4
15 x 12⁶

por

WIDTH 70'-10"
DEPTH 67'-4"

Main floor — 2,733 sq. ft.
Garage and storage — 569 sq. ft.

103

Your Classic Hideaway

■ *Total living area 1,773 sq. ft.* ■ *Price Code B* ■

No. 90423

■ **This plan features:**

— Three bedrooms

— Two full baths

■ A lovely fireplace in the Living Room which is both cozy and a source of heat for the core area

■ An efficient country Kitchen, connecting the large Dining and Living Rooms

■ A lavish Master Suite enhanced by a step-up sunken tub, more than ample closet space, and separate shower

■ A screened porch and patio area for outdoor living

■ An optional basement, slab or crawl space foundation — please specify when ordering

Main area — 1,773 sq. ft.
Screened porch — 240 sq. ft.

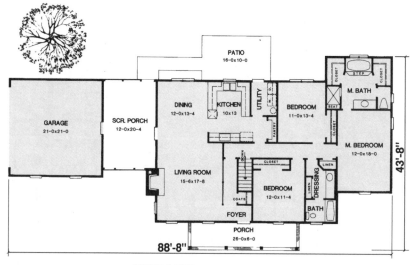

MAIN AREA

Designed For Easy Building And Easy Living

No. 99814

This plan features:

— Three bedrooms

— Two full baths

■ Refined, traditional exterior created by brick, double dormers and a hip roof

■ Foyer opens to a generous Great Room with cathedral ceiling and fireplace

■ Columns define entrance to Kitchen with a center island

■ Master Bedroom, Dining Room, and front Bedroom/Study receive distinction from tray ceilings

Main floor — 1,800 sq. ft.
Garage — 477 sq. ft.

© 1996 Donald A Gardner Architects, Inc.

■ *Total living area 1,800 sq. ft.* ■ *Price Code C* ■

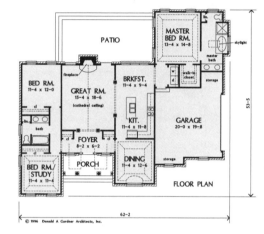

FLOOR PLAN

© 1996 Donald A Gardner Architects, Inc.

Relax on the Veranda

No. 91749

This plan features:

— Four bedrooms

— Three full and one half baths

■ A wrap-around veranda

■ A skylit Master Suite with elevated custom spa, twin basins, a walk-in closet, and an additional vanity outside the bathroom

■ A vaulted ceiling in the Den

■ A fireplace in both the Family Room and the formal Living Room

■ An efficient Kitchen with a peninsula counter and a double sink

■ Two additional bedrooms with walk-in closets, served by a compartmentalized bath

■ A Guest Suite with a private bath

Main floor — 3,051 sq. ft.
Garage — 646 sq. ft.

■ *Total living area 3,051 sq. ft.* ■ *Price Code E* ■

MAIN FLOOR

Comfortable Vacation Living

■ *Total living area 2,017 sq. ft.* ■ *Price Code C* ■

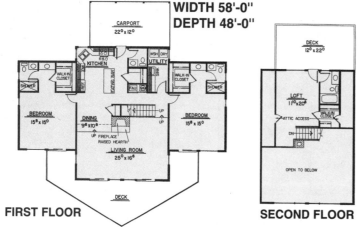

WIDTH 58'-0"
DEPTH 48'-0"

CARPORT
22⁰ x 12⁰

R.O KITCHEN
EATING BAR
WSH DRY
UTILITY

WALK-IN CLOSET
SHOWER

WALK-IN CLOSET
SHOWER

BEDROOM
15⁸ x 15⁰

BEDROOM
15⁸ x 15⁰

DINING
9⁶ x10⁸

UP   UP

UP FIREPLACE
RAISED HEARTH

LIVING ROOM
25⁰ x 16⁸

DECK

FIRST FLOOR

DECK
12⁰ x 22⁰

LOFT
11¹⁰ x 20⁰

WALK-IN CLOSET

ATTIC ACCESS

DN

OPEN TO BELOW

SECOND FLOOR

No. 98714

■ **This plan features:**

— Three bedrooms

— One full, two three-quarter and one half baths

■ A wrap-around Deck offering views and access into the Living Room

■ A sunken Living Room with a vaulted ceiling, and a raised-hearth fireplace adjoining the Dining area

■ An open Kitchen with a corner sink and windows, an eating bar and a walk-in storage/pantry

■ Two private bedroom suites with sliding glass doors leading to a Deck, walk-in closets and plush baths

■ A Loft area with a walk-in closet, attic access, a private bath and a Deck

First floor — 1,704 sq. ft.
Second floor — 313 sq. ft.

For Four or More

■ *Total living area 1,713 sq. ft.* ■ *Price Code C* ■

© 1993 Donald A. Gardner Architects, Inc.

PORCH
33-10 x 6-4

DINING
12-0 x 12-2

KIT.
9-4 x 12-2

BED RM.
11-8 x 12-8

balcony above

bath

GREAT RM.
17-4 x 16-6

fireplace

up

PORCH
21-6 x 6-4

BED RM./
STUDY
11-8 x 14-0

43-8

FIRST FLOOR PLAN

36-5

LOFT/
STUDY
10-4 x 14-0

master
bath

walk-in
closet

railing

down

(cathedral ceiling)
great room below

MASTER
BED RM.
11-8 x 15-8

attic storage

clerestory windows

SECOND FLOOR PLAN

No. 96440

■ **This plan features:**

— Three bedrooms

— Two full baths

■ Covered porches, front and back, with an open interior capped by a cathedral ceiling

■ Cathedral ceiling timing the Great Room, Kitchen/Dining and loft/study into an impressive living space

■ Kitchen equipped with an island cooktop and counter opening to both the Great Room and the Dining Room

■ A cathedral ceiling topping the front bedroom/study

■ A large bay cozies up the rear bedroom

■ Luxurious Master Suite located upstairs for extra privacy

First floor — 1,146 sq. ft.
Second floor — 567 sq. ft.

Distinctive Brick with Room to Expand

■ Total living area 2,645 sq. ft. ■ Price Code E ■

No. 93206

■ This plan features:

— Four bedrooms

— Two full and one half baths

■ Arched entrance with decorative glass leads into two-story Foyer

■ Formal Dining Room with tray ceiling above decorative window

■ Efficient Kitchen with island cooktop, built-in desk and pantry

■ Master Bedroom topped by tray ceiling with French door to Patio, huge private bath with garden tub and two walk-in closets

■ Three additional bedrooms with ample closets share laundry and full bath

■ Optional space for Storage and Future Bedroom with full bath

■ An optional basement, crawl space or slab foundation — please specify when ordering

First Floor — 2,577 sq. ft.
Future Second Floor — 619 sq. ft.
Bridge — 68 sq. ft.
Basement — 2,561 sq. ft.
Garage — 560 sq. ft.

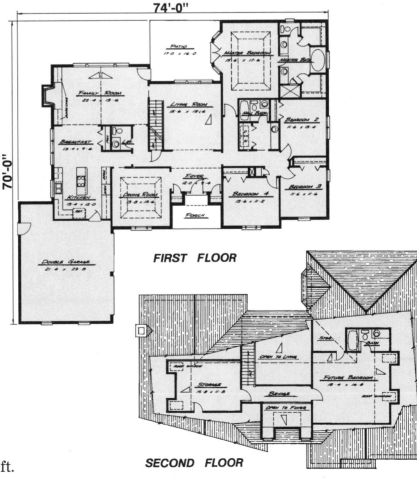

FIRST FLOOR

SECOND FLOOR

An
EXCLUSIVE DESIGN
By Jannis Vann & Associates, Inc.

Four Bedroom Charmer

■ *Total living area 2,185 sq. ft.* ■ *Price Code C* ■

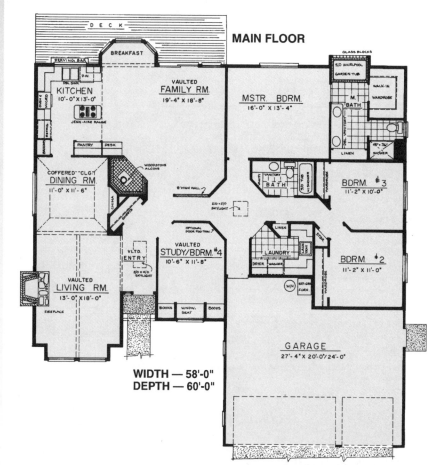

MAIN FLOOR

WIDTH — 58'-0"
DEPTH — 60'-0"

No. 91346

■ **This plan features:**

— Four bedrooms

— Two full baths

■ A Living Room with a masonry fireplace, large windowed bay and vaulted ceiling

■ A coffered ceiling and built-in china cabinet in the Dining Room

■ A large Family Room with a wood stove alcove

■ An island cook top, built-in pantry and a telephone desk in the efficient Kitchen

■ A luxurious Master Bedroom with whirlpool garden tub, walk-in closet and double sink vanity

■ Two bedrooms share a full bath

■ A Study with a window seat and built-in bookshelves

Main floor — 2,185 sq. ft.

Plan for the Future

No. 93265

This plan features:

— Three bedrooms

— Two full baths

- Entry leads up to Living area accented by a vaulted ceiling and arched window

- Compact, efficient Kitchen with serving counter/snack bar serves Dining area and Deck

- Comfortable Master Bedroom with a walk-in closet and double vanity bath with a window tub

- Two additional bedrooms with large closets share a full bath

- Entry leads down to laundry, Garage and future Playroom

- No materials list is available for this plan

Main floor — 1,269 sq. ft.
Lower floor — 56 sq. ft.
Basement — 382 sq. ft.
Garage — 598 sq. ft.

■ Total living area 1,325 sq. ft. ■ Price Code A ■

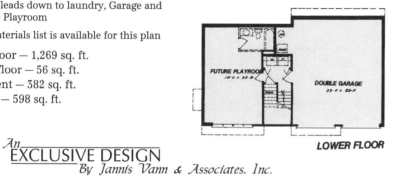

LOWER FLOOR

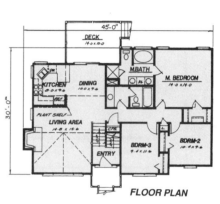

FLOOR PLAN

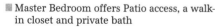

An
EXCLUSIVE DESIGN
By Jannis Vann & Associates, Inc.

Clerestory Windows Add Light

No. 90926

This plan features:

— Three bedrooms

— One full and one three-quarter baths

- Striking contemporary exterior compliments an exceptional design

- Open Foyer leads to sunken Living Room with a vaulted ceiling, a hearth fireplace with wood box and sliding glass doors to Patio

- Hub Kitchen easily serves Dining Room, Family Room and Covered Patio

- Comfortable Family Room with Patio and Utility/Garage access

- Master Bedroom offers Patio access, a walk-in closet and private bath

- Two additional bedrooms with ample closets, share a full bath

Main floor — 1,589 sq. ft.
Garage — 474 sq. ft.

■ Total living area 1,589 sq. ft. ■ Price Code B ■

WIDTH 60'-0"
DEPTH 56'-0"

MAIN AREA

PLANS
INCLUDE
ALTERNATE
OPT. WASHRM
LAYOUT OFF
UTILITY

An
EXCLUSIVE DESIGN
By Westhome Planners, Ltd.

Three Bedroom Traditional Country Cape

Total living area 1,494 sq. ft. ■ *Price Code A* ■

No. 99022

■ **This plan features:**

— Three bedrooms

— Two full and one half baths

■ Entry area with a coat closet

■ An ample Living Room with a fireplace

■ A Dining Room with a view of the rear yard and located conveniently close to the Kitchen and Living Room

■ A U-shaped Kitchen with a double sink, ample cabinet and counter space and a side door to the outside

■ A first floor Master Suite with a private master bath

■ Two additional, second floor bedrooms that share a full, double vanity bath with a separate shower

First floor — 913 sq. ft.
Second floor — 581 sq. ft.

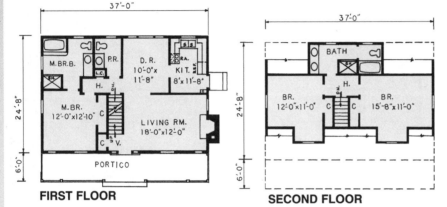

FIRST FLOOR

SECOND FLOOR

Deck Doubles Outdoor Living Space

Total living area 2,352 sq. ft. ■ *Price Code D* ■

No. 10619 ✕

■ **This plan features:**

— Three bedrooms

— Two full and one half baths

■ A design made for the sun lover with a front Deck and Patio

■ A sunken Living Room with three window walls and a massive fireplace

■ A hot tub with skylight, a vaulted Master Suite and a Utility Area

First floor — 2,352 sq. ft.
Basement — 2,352 sq. ft.
Garage — 696 sq. ft.

An
EXCLUSIVE DESIGN
By Karl Kreeger

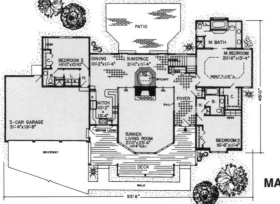

MAIN FLOOR

An Open Concept Home

■ *Total living area 1,282 sq. ft.* ■ *Price Code A* ■

No. 93021

■ **This plan features:**

— Three bedrooms

— Two full baths

■ An angled Entry creating the illusion of space

■ Two square columns that flank the bar and separate the Kitchen from the Living Room

■ A Dining Room that may service both formal and informal occasions

■ A Master Bedroom with a large walk-in closet

■ A large Master Bath with double vanity, linen closet and whirlpool tub/shower combination

■ Two additional bedrooms that share a full bath

■ No materials list is available for this plan

Main floor — 1,282 sq. ft.
Garage — 501 sq. ft.

WIDTH 48–10

DEPTH 52–6

OPTIONAL BAY WINDOW

LIN

MASTER BATH

SLOPE

MASTER BEDRM
11-0 X 14-0
10 FT CLG

STORAGE

GARAGE

DINING
9-8 X 9-6
10 FT CLG

FP

SLOPE

10 FT CLG
KITCHEN
13-4 X 9-6

ARCH

FOYER

ARCH

PORCH

LIVING ROOM
16-0 X 17-6
10 FT CLG

BEDRM 3
10-0 X 10-0

ARCH

BATH 2

LIN

BEDRM 2
10-0 X 12-0

MAIN FLOOR

© Larry E. Belk

Classic Exterior with Modern Interior

■ *Total living area 1,876 sq. ft.* ■ *Price Code C* ■

WIDTH 56'-2"
DEPTH 48'-0"

Screened-in Porch

Master Bedroom 14'1" x 15'1"

Great Room 16'8" x 15'4"

Dining Area 10'1" x 14'1"

Bath

Laun.

slope ceiling

slope ceiling

Dressing

Foyer

walk-in closet

Kitchen 13'2" x 11'8"

pantry

Porch

Two-car Garage 20' x 27'5"

FIRST FLOOR

Bedroom 10'5" x 12'

Foyer Below

Bedroom 11'6" x 11'5"

Hall

Bath

wood rail

stairs dn

computer desk

SECOND FLOOR

Bonus Bedroom 10' x 18'2"

No. 92674

■ **This plan features:**

– Three or four bedrooms

– Two full and one half baths

■ Front Porch leads into an open Foyer and Great Room beyond accented by a sloped ceiling, corner fireplace and multiple windows

■ An efficient Kitchen with a cooktop island, walk-in pantry, a bright Dining Area and nearby Screened Porch, Laundry and Garage entry

■ Deluxe Master Bedroom wing with a decorative ceiling, large walk-in closet and plush bath

■ No materials list is available for this plan

First floor — 1,348 sq. ft.
Second floor — 528 sq. ft.
Bonus — 195 sq. ft.
Basement — 1,300 sq. ft.

Compact Comfort

No. 10787

This plan features:

— Three bedrooms

— Two full and one half baths

■ Soaring ceilings and a wall of stacked windows

■ A formal Dining Room perfect for entertaining

■ A Kitchen/Family Room combination with a cozy fireplace

■ An efficient Kitchen layout

■ Three bedrooms upstairs and two full baths, including the luxury bath in the Master Bedroom

First floor — 1,088 sq. ft.
Second floor — 750 sq. ft.
Basement — 750 sq. ft.
Garage — 548 sq. ft.

■ *Total living area 1,838 sq. ft.* ■ *Price Code C* ■

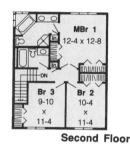

Second Floor

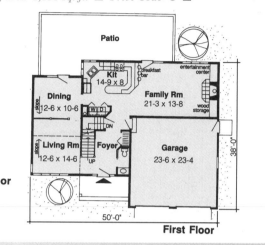

First Floor

Perfect for a Woodland Setting

No. 35007 X

This plan features:

— Two bedrooms

— One full bath

■ A Living Room and Dining Room/Kitchen located to the front of the house

■ A sloped ceiling adding to the cozy feeling of the home

■ A built-in entertainment center in the Living Room adding convenience

■ An L-shaped Kitchen that includes a double sink and Dining area

■ A full hall bath easily accessible from either bedroom

■ A Loft and Balcony that overlooks the Living Room and the Dining area

■ Storage on either side of the Loft

First floor — 763 sq. ft.
Second floor — 264 sq. ft.

■ *Total living area 1,027 sq. ft.* ■ *Price Code A* ■

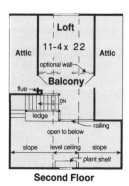

Second Floor

Slab/ Crawl Space Option

First Floor

Victorian Details Add Visual Delight

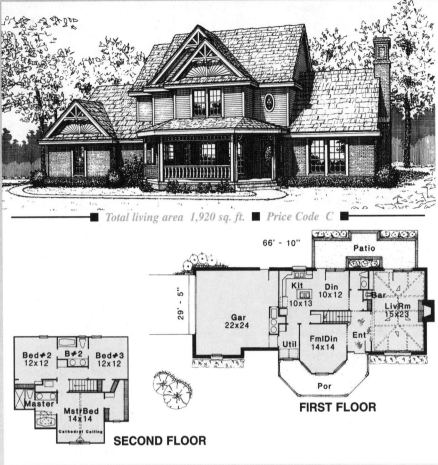

Total living area 1,920 sq. ft. ■ **Price Code C**

FIRST FLOOR

SECOND FLOOR

No. 92218

■ **This plan features:**

— Three bedrooms

— Two full and one half baths

■ Quaint country Porch provides a warm welcome

■ Expansive Living Room with a cozy fireplace and beamed ceiling

■ Formal Dining Room highlighted by an alcove of windows

■ An open Kitchen with cooktop work island, Dining area with Patio access and nearby Utility room with Garage entry

■ Comfortable Master Suite offers a cathedral ceiling, huge walk-in closet and a pampering bath

■ Two secondary bedrooms with ample closets and private access to a full bath

■ No materials list is available for this plan

First floor — 1,082 sq. ft.
Second floor — 838 sq. ft.
Basement — 1,082 sq. ft.
Garage — 500 sq. ft.

Yesteryear Flavor

Total living area 2,356 sq. ft. ■ **Price Code D**

No. 24404

■ **This plan features:**

— Three or four bedrooms

— Three full baths

■ Wrap-around Porch invites visiting and access into gracious Foyer with landing staircase

■ Formal Living Room doubles as a Guest Room

■ Huge Family Room highlighted by a decorative ceiling, cozy fireplace, book shelves and Porch access

■ Country-size Kitchen with island snackbar, built-in desk and nearby Dining Room, laundry/Workshop and Garage access

■ Corner Master Bedroom enhanced by a large walk-in closet and plush bath with a whirlpool tub

■ Two additional bedrooms with walk-in closets share a full bath and Sitting area

First floor — 1,236 sq. ft.
Second floor — 1,120 sq. ft.

An EXCLUSIVE DESIGN *By Upright Design*

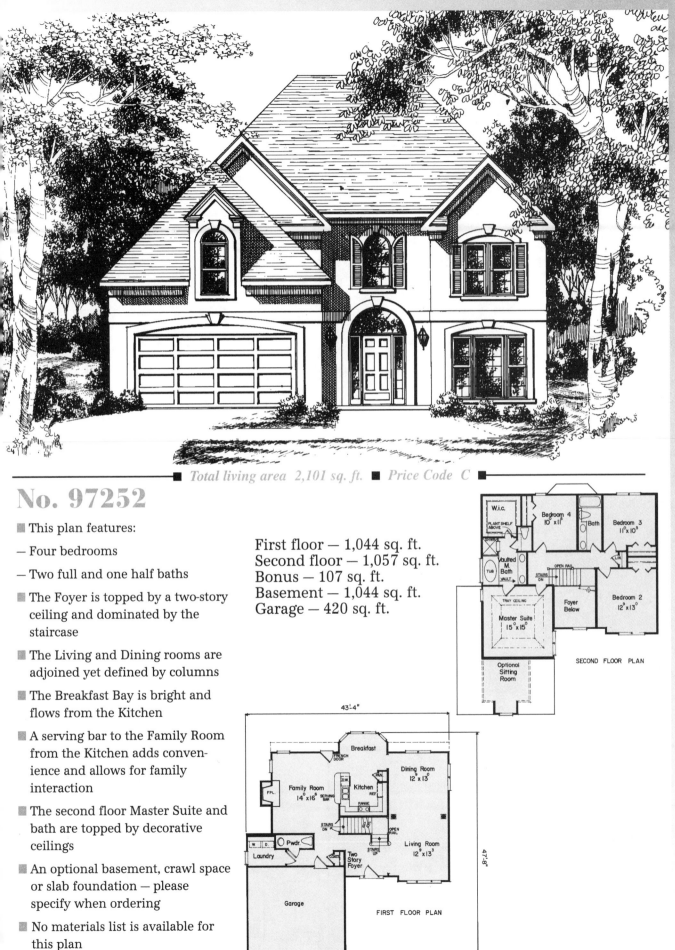

■ *Total living area 2,101 sq. ft.* ■ *Price Code C* ■

No. 97252

■ This plan features:

— Four bedrooms

— Two full and one half baths

■ The Foyer is topped by a two-story ceiling and dominated by the staircase

■ The Living and Dining rooms are adjoined yet defined by columns

■ The Breakfast Bay is bright and flows from the Kitchen

■ A serving bar to the Family Room from the Kitchen adds convenience and allows for family interaction

■ The second floor Master Suite and bath are topped by decorative ceilings

■ An optional basement, crawl space or slab foundation — please specify when ordering

■ No materials list is available for this plan

First floor — 1,044 sq. ft.
Second floor — 1,057 sq. ft.
Bonus — 107 sq. ft.
Basement — 1,044 sq. ft.
Garage — 420 sq. ft.

SECOND FLOOR PLAN

FIRST FLOOR PLAN

Elegant Presence

■ *Total living area 2,980 sq. ft.* ■ *Price Code E* ■

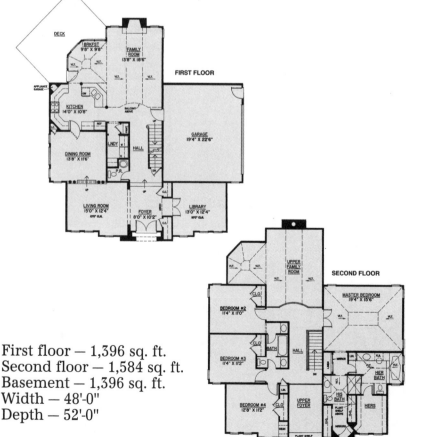

First floor — 1,396 sq. ft.
Second floor — 1,584 sq. ft.
Basement — 1,396 sq. ft.
Width — 48'-0"
Depth — 52'-0"

No. 98231

■ **This plan features:**

— Four bedrooms

— Two full, one three-quarter and one half baths

■ A double door entrance into the grand Foyer, and an attached double door entry accesses the Library

■ The Living Room is to the left of the Foyer and steps up into the Dining Room

■ A vaulted ceiling crowns the Family Room and the Breakfast Room

■ The Master Suite is topped by a vaulted ceiling and includes a his-n-her bath

■ An optional basement or slab foundation — please specify when ordering

■ No material list is available for this plan

Turret Dining Views

No. 93061

■ This plan features:

— Three bedrooms

— Two full baths

■ Front Porch and Entry lead into the Dining and Great rooms

■ Expansive Great Room with a focal point fireplace and access to the rear yard

■ Unique Dining Room with an alcove of windows adjoins the Kitchen

■ Angled counter with an eating bar and a built-in pantry in the Kitchen easily serves the Breakfast area and Great Room

■ Comfortable Master Bedroom and bath with a corner whirlpool tub, a double vanity and a huge walk-in closet

■ Two additional bedrooms with oversized closets share a full bath

■ An optional slab or crawl space foundation — please specify when ordering

■ No materials list is available for this plan

Main floor — 1,742 sq. ft.
Garage — 566 sq. ft.

■ *Total living area 1,742 sq. ft.* ■ *Price Code B* ■

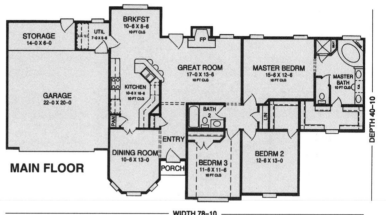

MAIN FLOOR

© Larry E. Belk

Roomy, Yet Practical Home

No. 96406

■ This plan features:

— Three bedrooms

— Two full and one half baths

■ A smart exterior conceals an economical use of interior space

■ The two-story Foyer leads to the Great Room with a fireplace, a wall of windows and access to the back Porch

■ Columns divide the Great Room from the Breakfast Room which is open to an angled Kitchen with Pantry

■ A handy Utility Room leads to a two-car Garage with ample storage space

■ A split bedroom plan places the Master Suite with two walk-in closets on the second floor

First floor — 1,489 sq. ft.
Second floor — 534 sq. ft.
Garage & Storage — 568 sq. ft.
Bonus — 393 sq. ft.

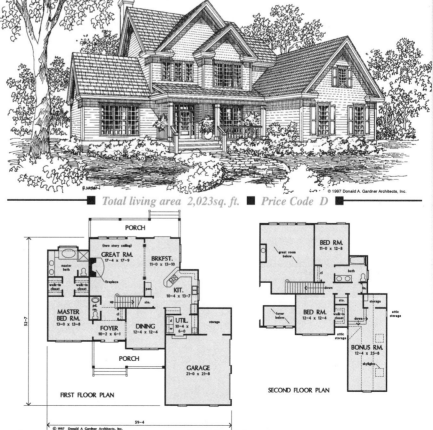

■ *Total living area 2,023 sq. ft.* ■ *Price Code D* ■

FIRST FLOOR PLAN

SECOND FLOOR PLAN

© 1997 Donald A Gardner Architects, Inc.

Country Charmer

■ *Total living area 1,438 sq. ft.* ■ *Price Code A* ■

MAIN FLOOR

No. 96509

■ This plan features:

— Three bedrooms

— Two full baths

■ Quaint front Porch is perfect for sitting and relaxing

■ Great Room opening into Dining Area and Kitchen

■ Corner Deck in rear of home accessed from Kitchen and Master Suite

■ Master Suite with a private bath, walk-in closet and built-in shelves

■ Two large secondary bedrooms in the front of the home share a hall bath

■ Two-car Garage located in the rear of the home

Main floor — 1,438 sq. ft.
Garage — 489 sq. ft.

Victorian Accents the Exterior

© 1991 Donald A. Gardner Architects, Inc.

■ *Total living area 1,865 sq. ft.* ■ *Price Code C* ■

MAIN FLOOR

© 1991 Donald A. Gardner Architects, Inc.

No. 99857

■ This plan features:

— Three bedrooms

— Two full baths

■ The covered wrap-around Porch connects to the rear Deck

■ The Foyer opens into the octagonal Great Room that is warmed by a fireplace

■ The Dining Room has a tray ceiling and convenient access to the Kitchen

■ The galley Kitchen opens into the Breakfast bay

■ The Master Bedroom has a bay area in the rear, a walk-in closet, and a fully appointed bath

■ Two more bedrooms and another full bath complete this plan

Main floor — 1,865 sq. ft.
Garage — 505 sq. ft.

© design basics inc.

■ *Total living area 3,057 sq. ft.* ■ *Price Code E* ■

No. 99456 ⊠

■ This plan features:

- Four bedrooms

- Two full, one three-quarter and one half baths

■ Stucco accents and graceful window treatments enhance the front of this home

■ French doors open to a large screened-in verandah ideal for outdoor entertaining

■ The open Living Room and handsome curved staircase add drama to the entry area

■ The gourmet Kitchen, dinette bay and Family Room flow together for easy living

■ Elegant Master Bedroom has a ten foot vaulted ceiling and two walk-in closets, his-n-her vanities and a whirlpool tub highlight the master bath

■ An optional basement or slab foundation — please specify when ordering

First floor — 1,631 sq. ft.
Second floor — 1,426 sq. ft.
Basement — 1,631 sq. ft.
Garage — 681 sq. ft.

FIRST FLOOR

SECOND FLOOR

One Floor Convenience

■ Total living area 1,359 sq. ft. ■ Price Code A ■

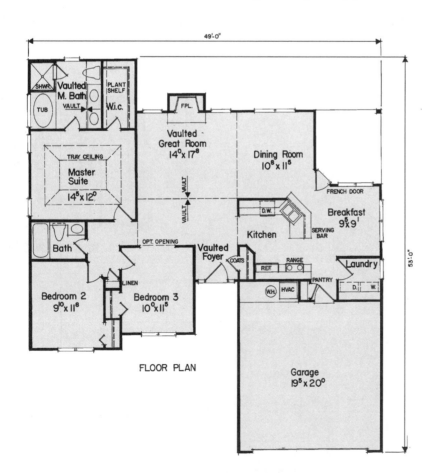

FLOOR PLAN

No. 98443

■ This plan features:

— Three bedrooms

— Two full baths

■ Vaulted Foyer blends with the vaulted Great Room giving a larger feeling to the home

■ Formal Dining Room opens into the Great Room

■ Kitchen includes a serving bar, flows into the Breakfast Room

■ Master Suite topped by a decorative tray ceiling and a vaulted ceiling in the Master Bath

■ Two additional bedrooms share the full bath in the hall

■ An optional crawl space or slab foundation available — please specify when ordering

■ No materials list is available for this plan

Main floor — 1,359 sq. ft.
Garage — 439 sq. ft.

Traditional Transom Windows Add Appeal

No. 90396

This plan features:

— Three bedrooms

— Two full and one half baths

▪ A vaulted ceiling in both the Living and adjoining Dining rooms, accentuated by a fireplace

▪ A well-appointed, skylit Kitchen which easily serves the Dining Room

▪ A first floor Master Suite with a dramatic vaulted ceiling and private patio access

▪ A private master bath with double vanity and walk-in closet

Main floor — 1,099 sq. ft.
Upper floor — 452 sq. ft.
Basement — 1,099 sq. ft.
Garage — 412 sq. ft.

Total living area 1,551 sq. ft. ▪ Price Code B

Arched Windows Add Natural Light

No. 94609

This plan features:

— Four bedrooms

— Three full baths

▪ Welcoming porch shelters entry into Foyer

▪ Dining Room highlighted by alcove of windows

▪ Spacious Living Room enhanced by a hearth fireplace, built-in shelves and glass access to Covered Porch

▪ Efficient, U-shaped Kitchen with a peninsula serving bar, nearby laundry and bright Breakfast area with access to Porch

▪ Pampering bedroom one offers a large walk-in closet and double vanity bath

▪ Three additional bedrooms with walk-in closets have access to full baths

▪ No materials list is available for this plan

▪ An optional crawl space or slab foundation— please specify when ordering

First floor — 1,505 sq. ft.
Second floor — 555 sq. ft.
Garage — 400 sq. ft.

Total living area 2,060 sq. ft. ▪ Price Code C

121

Comfortable Contemporary

Total living area 1,591 sq. ft. ■ Price Code B

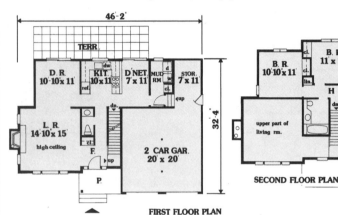

FIRST FLOOR PLAN

SECOND FLOOR PLAN

No. 99652

■ **This plan features:**

— Three bedrooms

— Two full and one half baths

■ Covered Porch entrance into convenient Foyer with closet and powder room

■ High ceiling accenting arched window in Living Room opens to Dining Room with sliding glass door to Patio

■ Efficient U-shaped Kitchen with serving counter, Dinette Area and indispensable Mud Room

■ Private, corner Master Bedroom with two closets and plush bath with whirlpool tub

■ Two additional bedrooms with ample closets share a full bath

First floor — 810 sq. ft.
Second floor — 781 sq. ft.
Basement — 746 sq. ft.
Garage/Storage — 513 sq. ft.

Impressive Brick and Wood Facade

Total living area 1,651 sq. ft. ■ Price Code B

© design basics, inc.

MAIN FLOOR

No. 94921

■ **This plan features:**

— Two or three bedrooms

— Two full baths

■ Covered front and rear Porches expand living space outside

■ Handy serving area located between formal Dining Room and expansive Great Room

■ Transom windows frame hearth fireplace in Great Room and highlight Breakfast Room

■ Hub Kitchen with built-in pantry, snack bar and adjoining laundry/Garage entry

■ French doors lead into Den with wetbar that can easily convert to third bedroom

■ Exclusive Master Suite includes decorative ceiling, walk-in closet, dual vanity and a corner whirlpool tub

Main floor — 1,651 sq. ft.
Basement — 1,651 sq. ft.
Garage — 480 sq. ft.

Brick Detail with Arches

■ *Total living area 1,987 sq. ft.* ■ *Price Code D* ■

No. 92544 ⚒

■ **This plan features:**

— Four bedrooms

— Two full and one half baths

■ Front and back porches expand the living space and provide inviting access to the open layout

■ Spacious Den with a fireplace flanked by built-in shelves and double access to the rear Porch

■ Formal Dining Room with an arched window

■ Efficient, U-shaped Kitchen with a snackbar counter, a bright Breakfast area and an adjoining laundry and Garage

■ Secluded Master Bedroom suite

■ Three additional bedrooms with walk-in closets, share one and half baths

■ An optional slab or crawl space foundation available — please specify when ordering

Main floor — 1,987 sq. ft.
Garage/Storage — 515 sq. ft.

Spacious Family Living

■ Total living area 2,303 sq. ft. ■ Price Code D ■

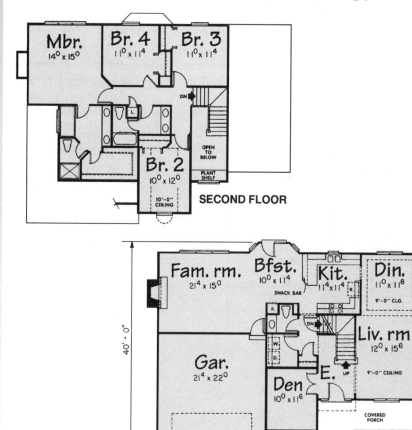

Mbr. 14⁰ x 15⁰

Br. 4 11⁰ x 11⁴

Br. 3 11⁰ x 11⁴

DN

Br. 2 10⁰ x 12⁰

OPEN TO BELOW

PLANT SHELF

10'-0" CEILING

SECOND FLOOR

Fam. rm. 21⁴ x 15⁰

Bfst. 10⁰ x 11⁴

SNACK BAR

Kit. 11⁴ x 11⁴

Din. 11⁰ x 11⁸

9'-0" CLG.

Gar. 21⁴ x 22⁰

W. D.

DN

Liv. rm. 12⁰ x 15⁶

Den 10⁰ x 11⁶

E.

UP

9'-0" CEILING

COVERED PORCH

FIRST FLOOR

© design basics inc.

40' - 0"

52' - 0"

No. 94956

■ This plan features:

— Four bedrooms

— Two full and one half baths

■ Front Porch welcomes friends and family

■ Entry opens to spacious Living Room with a tiered ceiling and Dining Room beyond

■ Hub Kitchen easily serves the Dining Room, the Breakfast bay and the Family Room

■ Corner Master Bedroom has access to a private bath

■ Three additional bedrooms share a double vanity bath

First floor — 1,269 sq. ft.
Second floor — 1,034 sq. ft.
Basement — 1,269 sq. ft.
Garage — 485 sq. ft.

Dignified French Country Style

No. 92517

This plan features:

- Three bedrooms

- Two full baths

- Sheltered Porch leads into an open Foyer and Great Room enhanced by raised hearth fireplace between book shelves, access to Patio and a vaulted ceiling

- Hub Kitchen with a peninsula counter and Utility Garage entry easily serves Breakfast area and formal Dining Room

- Spacious Master Bedroom offers a Sitting area and a plush Master Bath

- Two additional roomy bedrooms with over-sized closets share a double vanity bath

- An optional crawl space or slab foundation — please specify when ordering

Main floor — 1,805 sq. ft.
Garage & Storage — 524 sq. ft.

Total living area 1,805 sq. ft. ■ Price Code D

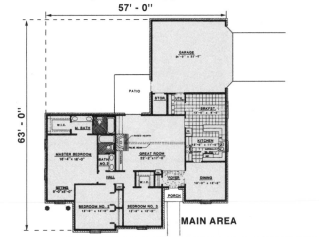

MAIN AREA

Affordable Energy-Saver

No. 90680

This plan features:

- Three bedrooms

- Two full baths

- A covered Porch leading into an open Foyer and Living/Dining Room with skylights and front to back exposure

- An efficient Kitchen with a bay window and a walk-in Pantry is adjacent to the Mud Room, Garage area

- A private Master Bedroom with a luxurious master bath leading to a private Deck complete with a hot tub

- Two additional bedrooms with access to a full hall bath

Main floor — 1,393 sq. ft.
Basement — 1,393 sq. ft.

Total living area 1,393 sq. ft. ■ Price Code A

MAIN FLOOR

Highly Unpretentious

Total living area 2,060 sq. ft. ■ *Price Code C* ■

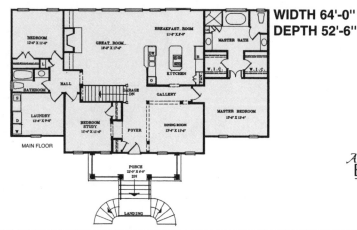

WIDTH 64'-0"
DEPTH 52'-6"

MAIN FLOOR

No. 93608

■ **This plan features:**

— Three bedrooms

— Two full baths

■ A graceful front portico leads past the Foyer to the open Grand Room

■ Ten-foot ceilings and three large, full radius windows draw in the sunlight

■ A large Kitchen with an island opens to the Breakfast Room and an optional Porch in the rear

■ The split-bedroom design affords the utmost in privacy for all

■ An oversized Laundry/Sewing Room that is rarely seen in a home of this size

■ A drive under Garage has plenty of room for three vehicles, or two vehicles and a boat

■ No materials list is available for this plan

Main floor — 2,060 sq. ft.
Garage — 1,000 sq. ft.

An
EXCLUSIVE DESIGN
By Garrell Associates Inc.

Details, Details, Details

Total living area 2,155 sq. ft. ■ *Price Code C* ■

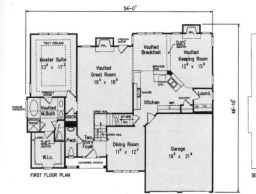

FIRST FLOOR PLAN

SECOND FLOOR PLAN

No. 98447

■ **This plan features:**

— Three bedrooms

— Two full and one half baths

■ This elevation is highlighted by stucco, stone and detailing around the arched windows

■ The two-story Foyer allows access to the Dining Room and Great Room

■ A vaulted ceiling and a fireplace can be found in the Great Room

■ The Breakfast Room has a vaulted ceiling and flows into the Kitchen and the Keeping Room

■ Two secondary bedrooms, each with a walk-in closet, share a full hall bath

■ The Master Suite has a tray ceiling a huge walk-in closet and a compartmental bath

■ An optional basement or crawl space foundation — please specify when ordering

First floor — 1,682 sq. ft.
Second floor — 527 sq. ft.
Bonus room — 207 sq. ft.
Basement — 1,628 sq. ft.
Garage — 440 sq. ft.

■ *Total living area 3,192 sq. ft.* ■ *Price Code E* ■

No. 91319 ⚒

■ This plan features:

— Three bedrooms

— One full, one three quarter baths

■ A wall of windows taking full advantage of the front view

■ A large, two-way staircase

■ A Master Bedroom with a private master bath and a walk-in wardrobe

■ An efficient Kitchen including a breakfast bar that opens into the Dining Area

■ A formal Living Room with a vaulted ceiling and a stone fireplace

First floor — 1,306 sq. ft.
Second floor — 598 sq. ft.
Lower level — 1,288 sq. ft.

WIDTH 46'-0"
DEPTH 30'-0"

SECOND FLOOR

FIRST FLOOR

Luxuriant Living

■ *Total living area 2,869 sq. ft.* ■ *Price Code E* ■

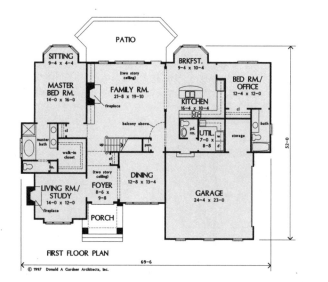

PATIO

SITTING
9-4 x 4-4

MASTER
BED RM.
14-0 x 16-0

FAMILY RM.
21-8 x 19-10
(two story ceiling)
fireplace

BRKFST.
9-4 x 10-4

KITCHEN
16-4 x 10-4

BED RM./
OFFICE
12-4 x 12-0

master bath

walk-in closet

lin.

balcony above

UTIL.
7-0 x
8-8

storage

bath

pd. rm.

LIVING RM./
STUDY
14-0 x 12-0
fireplace

FOYER
8-6 x
9-8

DINING
12-8 x 13-4
(two story ceiling)

GARAGE
24-4 x 23-0

PORCH

52-0

FIRST FLOOR PLAN

© 1997 Donald A Gardner Architects, Inc.

69-6

First floor — 2,249 sq. ft.
Second floor — 620 sq. ft.
Bonus — 308 sq. ft.
Garage — 642 sq. ft.

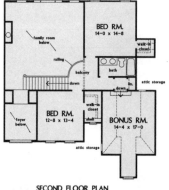

family room below

railing

balcony

BED RM.
14-0 x 14-8

walk-in closet

bath

attic storage

foyer below

down

down

BED RM.
12-8 x 13-4

walk-in closet
shelf

BONUS RM.
14-4 x 17-0

attic storage

SECOND FLOOR PLAN

No. 99825 ⚒

■ **This plan features:**

— Four bedrooms

— Three full and one half baths

■ French doors, windows and a high gabled Entry make a dramatic entrance

■ Living Room features a box bay window and a fireplace

■ Dining Room is illuminated by a bank of windows

■ Family Room has a two-story ceiling, a fireplace and access to the rear Patio

■ Kitchen and Nook adjoin handy home Office

■ The Master Suite features a private bath and a Sitting Area

■ Upstairs find two bedrooms, each with a walk-in closet, a full bath and a Bonus Room

Great As A Mountain Retreat

No. 99815

This plan features:

— Three bedrooms

— Two full baths

■ Board and batten siding, stone and stucco combine to give this popular plan a casual feel

■ User friendly Kitchen with huge Pantry for ample storage, and island counter

■ Casual family meals in sunny Breakfast Bay; formal gatherings in the columned Dining Area

■ Master Suite is topped by a deep tray ceiling, has a large walk-in closet, an extravagant private bath and direct access to back porch

Main floor — 1,912 sq. ft.
Bonus — 398 sq. ft.
Garage — 580 sq. ft.

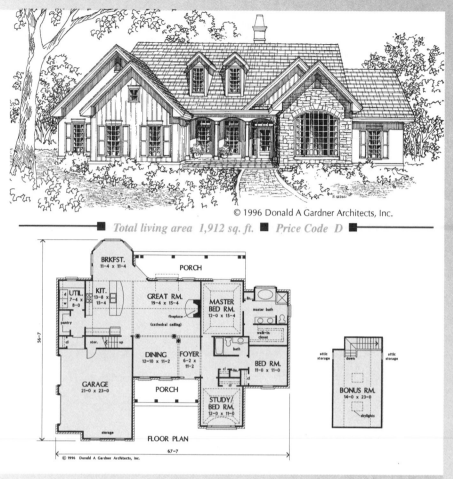

© 1996 Donald A Gardner Architects, Inc.

■ *Total living area 1,912 sq. ft.* ■ *Price Code D* ■

FLOOR PLAN

© 1996 Donald A Gardner Architects, Inc.

Two-story Bay Window Adds Appeal

No. 91543

This plan features:

— Three bedrooms

— Two full and one half baths

■ Portico entrance leads into central Foyer with banister staircase

■ Ease in entertaining with combination Living/Dining Room brightened by lovely bay window

■ Open Family Room with cozy fireplace and corner windows opens to Nook/Kitchen area

■ Compact Kitchen with peninsula serving/eating counter and built-in Pantry adjoins Nook and Dining Area

■ French doors into Master Suite with vaulted ceiling over another lovely bay window and double vanity bath

■ Two additional bedrooms share a full bath and laundry closet

■ Second floor Bonus Room offers many options

First floor — 972 sq. ft.
Second floor — 843 sq. ft.
Bonus Room — 180 sq. ft.
Garage — 437 sq. ft.

■ *Total living area 1,815 sq. ft.* ■ *Price Code C* ■

FIRST FLOOR

SECOND FLOOR

Distinguished Look

Total living area 1,906 sq. ft. ■ *Price Code C* ■

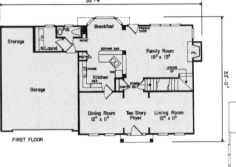

FIRST FLOOR

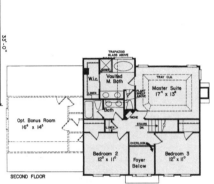

SECOND FLOOR

No. 98429

■ This plan features:

— Three bedrooms

— Two full and one half baths

■ The Family Room, Breakfast Room and the Kitchen are presented in an open layout

■ A fireplace in the Family Room provides a warm atmosphere

■ The plush Master Suite pampers the owner and features a trapezoid glass above the tub

■ Two additional bedrooms share the use of the double vanity bath in the hall

■ An optional basement, crawl space or slab foundation — please specify when ordering

First floor — 1,028 sq. ft.
Second floor — 878 sq. ft.
Bonus room — 315 sq. ft.
Basement — 1,028 sq. ft.
Garage — 497 sq. ft.

Turret Adds Appeal

Total living area 2,214 sq. ft. ■ *Price Code D* ■

MAIN FLOOR

No. 94206

■ This plan features:

— Three bedrooms

— Two full baths

■ A garden Entry with double door leading into an open Foyer and Great Room

■ Vaulted ceilings above a decorative window in the Dining area and sliding glass doors to the Veranda in the Great Room

■ A private Study with double door and turret windows

■ A large, efficient Kitchen featuring a walk-in pantry and glassed Nook with skylights, near the laundry area and Garage

■ A Master Suite with a vaulted ceiling, two huge, walk-in closets, a luxurious bath and sliding glass doors to the Veranda

■ Two additional bedrooms with over-sized closets sharing a full bath

■ No materials list is available for this plan

Main floor — 2,214 sq. ft.
Garage — 652 sq. ft.

■ Total living area 2,707 sq. ft. ■ Price Code E ■

No. 91509 ✕ ℞

■ This plan features:

— Three bedrooms

— Two full and one half baths

■ A unique Living Room with a vaulted ceiling, and columns separating it from the formal Dining Room

■ A wide-open arrangement between the Family Room, Nook and island Kitchen

■ A fireplace in both the Family Room and the Living Room

■ A skylight and double vanity in the full hall bath

■ A Master Suite with a walk-in closet, garden spa tub and bay window

First floor — 1,675 sq. ft.
Second floor — 1,032 sq. ft.
Bonus room — 450 sq. ft.
Basement — 642 sq. ft.
Garage — 725 sq. ft.

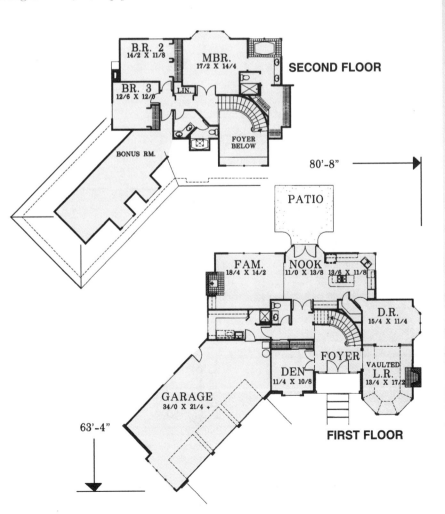

SECOND FLOOR

B.R. 2
14/2 X 11/8

MBR.
17/2 X 14/4

BR. 3
12/6 X 12/8

LIN.

FOYER
BELOW

BONUS RM.

80'-8"

PATIO

FAM.
18/4 X 14/2

NOOK
11/0 X 13/8

13/6 X 11/8

D.R.
15/4 X 11/4

FOYER

DEN
11/4 X 10/8

VAULTED
L.R.
13/4 X 17/2

GARAGE
34/0 X 21/4 +

63'-4"

FIRST FLOOR

Champagne Style on a Soda-Pop Budget

■ *Total living area 988 sq. ft.* ■ *Price Code A* ►

No. 24302

■ **This plan features:**

— Three bedrooms

— One full and one three quarter baths

■ Multiple gables, circle-top windows, and a unique exterior set this delightful Ranch apart in any neighborhood

■ Living and Dining Rooms flow together to create a very roomy feeling

■ Sliding doors lead from the Dining Room to a covered Patio

■ A Master Bedroom with a private Bath

Main floor — 988 sq. ft.
Basement — 988 sq. ft.
Garage — 280 sq. ft
Optional 2-car garage — 384 sq. ft.

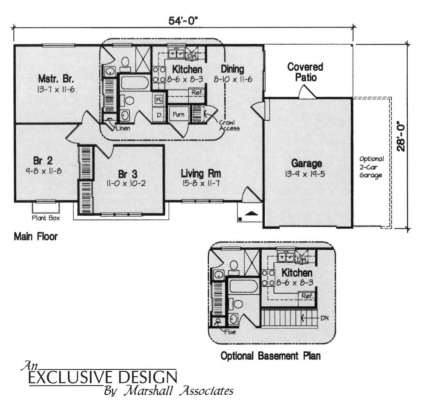

Main Floor

Optional Basement Plan

An EXCLUSIVE DESIGN
By Marshall Associates

Appealing Master Suite

No. 92239

■ **This plan features:**

— Three bedrooms

— Two full baths

■ Sheltered Entry into spacious Living Room with a corner fireplace and Patio access

■ Efficient Kitchen with a serving counter for Dining Area and nearby Utility/Garage entry

■ Private Master Bedroom offers a vaulted ceiling and pampering bath with two vanities and walk-in closets, and a garden window tub

■ Two additional bedrooms with ample closets share a full bath

■ No materials list is available for this plan

Main floor — 1,198 sq. ft.

■ *Total living area 1,198 sq. ft.* ■ *Price Code A* ■

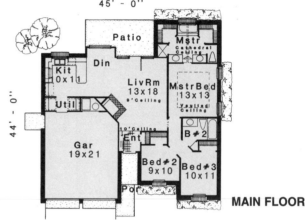

MAIN FLOOR

Master Suite Crowns Plan

No. 10394

■ **This plan features:**

— Three bedrooms

— Two full baths

■ A Master Bedroom which occupies the entire second level

■ A passive solar design

■ An exciting Living Room which rises two stories in the front

■ Skylights in the sloping ceilings of the Kitchen and master bath

First floor — 1,306 sq. ft.
Second floor — 472 sq. ft.
Garage — 576 sq. ft.

■ *Total living area 1,778 sq. ft.* ■ *Price Code B* ■

Nostalgia Returns

■ *Total living area 1,368 sq. ft.* ■ *Price Code A* ■

Floor Plan

- Mas. Suite 14x12-6 vaulted
- Br 2 12x10
- Patio
- Den/ Br 3 11x9
- Kit/Brkfst 19x10-8 vaulted
- Dining
- Garage 21-4x19-4
- Great Room 19x18 vaulted

48'-4"
48'-4"

No. 99321

■ This plan features:

— Three bedrooms

— Two full baths

■ A half-round transom window with quarter-round detail and a vaulted ceiling in the Great Room

■ A cozy corner fireplace brings warmth to the Great Room

■ A vaulted ceiling in the Kitchen/Breakfast Area

■ A Master Suite with a walk-in closet and a private master bath

■ Two additional bedrooms which share a full hall bath

Main area — 1,368 sq. ft.
Garage — 412 sq. ft.

One-Level Beauty

■ *Total living area 2,355 sq. ft.* ■ *Price Code D* ■

MAIN FLOOR

- Brkst.
- Kit.
- Hrth. 14x12
- Grt. rm. 16x20
- Br 2 11x13
- Din.
- Br3 12x11
- Gar.
- Mbr 14x15

No. 94967

■ This plan features:

— Three bedrooms

— Two full and one half baths

■ From the tiled entry one can view the terrific Great Room

■ A built-in wetbar and a three-sided fireplace, shared with the hearth room highlight the Great Room

■ A built-in entertainment center in the Hearth Room, which is open to the Kitchen and Breakfast Room

■ A sloped gazebo ceiling and a built-in hutch highlighting the Breakfast Room

■ Master Bedroom with an impressive and luxurious bath and a walk-in closet

■ Secondary bedrooms having private access to a full bath

Main floor — 2,355 sq. ft.
Garage — 673 sq. ft.

An Old-Fashioned Country Feel

■ *Total living area 2,091 sq. ft.* ■ *Price Code C* ■

No. 93212

■ This plan features:

— Three bedrooms

— Two full and one half baths

■ Living Room with a cozy fireplace

■ A formal Dining Room with a bay window and direct access to the Sun Deck

■ U-shaped Kitchen efficiently arranged with ample work space

■ Master Suite with an elegant private bath complete with jacuzzi and a step-in shower

■ A future Bonus Room to finish, tailored to your needs

■ An optional basement, crawl space or slab foundation — please specify when ordering

■ No materials list is available for this plan

First floor — 1,362 sq. ft.
Second floor — 729 sq. ft.
Bonus room — 384 sq. ft.
Basement — 988 sq. ft.
Garage — 559 sq. ft

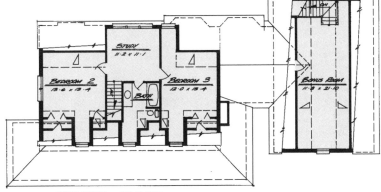

SECOND   FLOOR

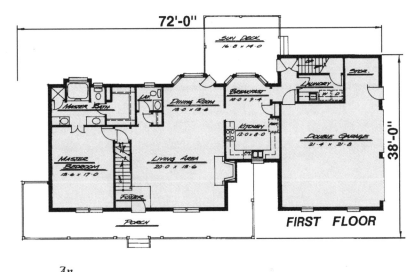

FIRST   FLOOR

An
EXCLUSIVE DESIGN
By Jannis Vann & Associates, Inc.

Family-Sized Accommodations

■ *Total living area 1,874 sq. ft.* ■ *Price Code C* ■

SECOND FLOOR

FIRST FLOOR

No. 98454 ✖

■ This plan features:

— Four bedrooms

— Two full and one half baths

■ A spacious feeling provided by a vaulted ceiling in Foyer

■ A fireplace is nestled by an alcove of windows in the Family Room

■ An angled Kitchen with a work island and a pantry easily serves the Breakfast area and the Dining Room

■ The Master Bedroom is accented by a tray ceiling, a lavish bath and a walk-in closet

■ An optional basement or crawl space foundation — please specify when ordering

First floor — 1,320 sq. ft.
Second floor — 554 sq. ft.
Bonus room — 155 sq. ft.
Basement — 1,320 sq. ft.
Garage — 406 sq. ft.

Relaxed Style

No. 94985

This plan features:

- Three bedrooms

- Two full and one half baths

- Lovely covered Porch fostering the desire to relax and enjoy a cool breeze on the end of the day

- One bedroom for an empty-nest lifestyle, with an option for two additional bedrooms in the basement

- Kitchen, Breakfast Area, and Great Room flowing into each other for ease in every-day living

- Cathedral ceiling topping the Great Room while a fireplace enhances the atmosphere

Main floor — 1,279 sq. ft.
Bonus lower floor — 984 sq. ft.
Garage — 509 sq. ft.

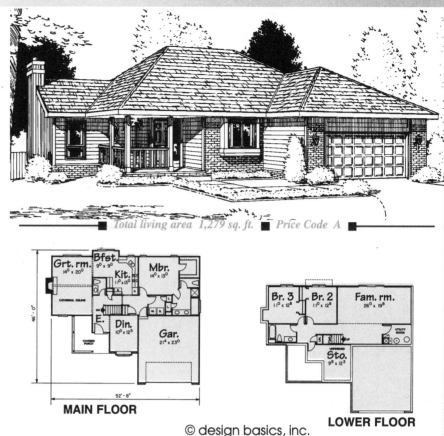

Total living area 1,279 sq. ft. ■ Price Code A

MAIN FLOOR

LOWER FLOOR

© design basics, inc.

Foyer Isolates Bedroom Wing

No. 20087

This plan features:

- Three bedrooms

- Two full baths

- A Living Room complete with a window wall flanking a massive fireplace

- A Dining Room with recessed ceilings and a pass-through for convenience

- A Master Suite tucked behind the two-car garage for maximum noise protection

- A spacious Kitchen with built-ins and access to the two-car garage

Main floor —1,568 sq. ft.
Basement — 1,568 sq. ft.
Garage — 484 sq. ft.

Total living area 1,568 sq. ft. ■ Price Code B

MAIN FLOOR

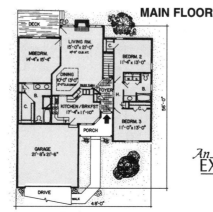

An
EXCLUSIVE DESIGN
By Karl Kreeger

Lap of Luxury

■ Total living area 2,445 sq. ft. ■ Price Code D ■

FLOOR PLAN

No. 98511

■ **This plan features:**

— Four bedrooms

— Three full and one half baths

■ Entertaining in grand style in the formal Living Room, the Dining Room, or under the covered Patio in the backyard

■ A Family Room crowned in a cathedral ceiling, enhanced by a center fireplace, and built-in book shelves

■ An efficient Kitchen highlighted by a wall oven, plentiful counter space and a Pantry

■ A Master Bedroom with a sitting area, huge walk-in closet, private bath and access to a covered lanai

■ A secondary bedroom wing containing three additional bedrooms with ample closet space and two full baths

■ No materials list is available for this plan

Main floor — 2,445 sq. ft.
Garage — 630 sq. ft.

Tower Stimulates Interest

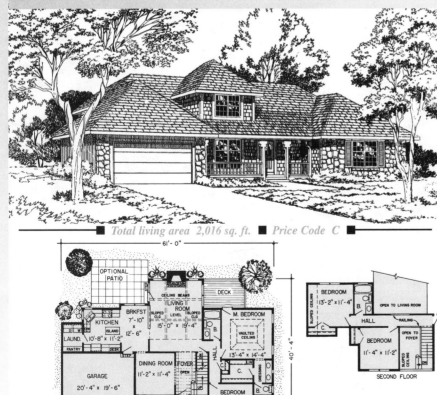

■ Total living area 2,016 sq. ft. ■ Price Code C ■

No. 34049

■ **This plan features:**

— Four bedrooms

— Three full baths

■ Sloping ceilings and lofty open spaces

■ A rustic, fireplaced Living Room with sloped ceilings to enhance the atmosphere

■ A Master Suite with vaulted ceilings, walk-in closet, dressing area and master bath

■ Two upstairs bedrooms share a full bath

First floor — 1,496 sq. ft.
Second floor — 520 sq. ft.
Basement — 1,487 sq. ft.
Garage — 424 sq. ft.

An
EXCLUSIVE DESIGN
By Karl Kreeger

■ *Total living area 2,387 sq. ft.* ■ *Price Code E* ■

No. 92546 ⚒

■ This plan features:

— Four bedrooms

— Two full and one half baths

■ Dining Room accented by an arched window and pillars

■ Decorative ceiling crowns the Den which contains a hearth fireplace, built-in shelves and large double window

■ Kitchen with a peninsula serving counter and Breakfast area, adjoining the Utility Room and Garage

■ Master Bedroom Suite with a decorative ceiling, two vanities and a large walk-in closet

■ Three additional bedrooms with double closets share a full bath

■ An optional slab or crawl space foundation — please specify when ordering

Main floor — 2,387 sq. ft.
Garage — 505 sq. ft.

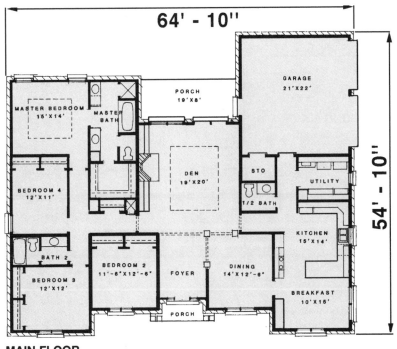

MAIN FLOOR

A Livable Home

■ Total living area 2,715 sq. ft. ■ Price Code E ■

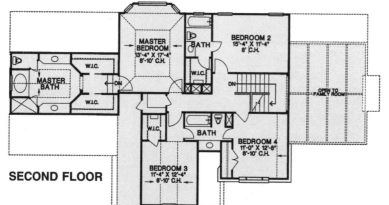

SECOND FLOOR

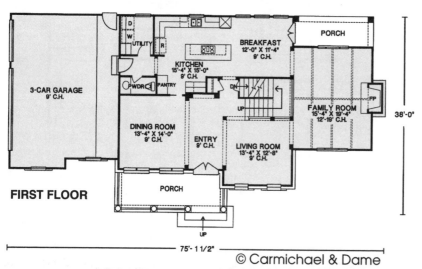

FIRST FLOOR

75'- 1 1/2"

© Carmichael & Dame

No. 94965

■ This plan features:

— Four bedrooms

— Two full, one three quarter and one half baths

■ The Master Bedroom is complete with a tray ceiling, two walk in closets and a large bath

■ Three additional Bedrooms upstairs, all have ample closet space and share two full baths

■ The Dining and Living rooms both have decorative windows that let in plenty of light

■ The Family Room has a beamed ceiling and a fireplace

■ A three-car Garage with plenty of storage space

■ No materials list is available for this plan

First floor — 1,400 sq. ft.
Second floor — 1,315 sq. ft.
Basement — 1,400 sq. ft.
Garage — 631 sq. ft.

Imposing and Practical Design

No. 93213

■ This plan features:

— Three bedrooms

— Two full and one half baths

■ Two-story keystone entrance with sidelights leads into Foyer with balcony above

■ Bay windows illuminate formal Dining and Living rooms elegantly

■ Expansive Family Room with cozy fireplace and a wall of windows with access to Patio

■ Efficient, U-shaped Kitchen convenient to both formal and informal dining areas

■ Private Master Bedroom crowned by decorative ceiling, features a walk-in closet, two vanities and garden tub bath

■ Two additional bedrooms, full bath and convenient laundry closet complete second floor

■ An optional basement or slab foundation — please specify when ordering

■ No materials list is available for this plan

First floor — 1,126 sq. ft.
Second floor — 959 sq. ft.
Basement — 458 sq. ft.
Garage — 627 sq. ft.

An
EXCLUSIVE DESIGN
By Jannis Vann & Associates, Inc.

■ *Total living area 2,085 sq. ft.* ■ *Price Code C* ■

SECOND FLOOR

FIRST FLOOR

Arches Add Ambiance

No. 92539 ✖

■ This plan features:

— Four bedrooms

— Two full and one half baths

■ Arched two-story entrance highlighted by a lovely arched window

■ Expansive Den offers hearth fireplace between book shelves, raised ceiling and access to rear yard

■ Efficient Kitchen with peninsula counter, built-in pantry, Breakfast bay, Garage entry, laundry and adjoining Dining Room

■ Private Master Bedroom enhanced by a large walk-in closet and plush bath

■ Three second floor bedrooms with walk-in closets share a double vanity bath

■ An optional slab or crawl space foundation — please specify when ordering

First floor — 1,250 sq. ft.
Second floor — 783 sq. ft.
Garage and Storage — 555 sq. ft.

■ *Total living area 2,033 sq. ft.* ■ *Price Code D* ■

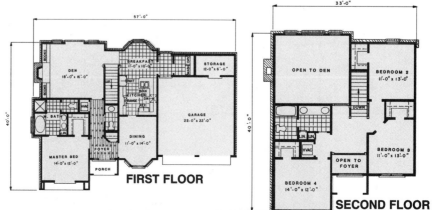

FIRST FLOOR

SECOND FLOOR

Sprawling Wrap-Around Porch

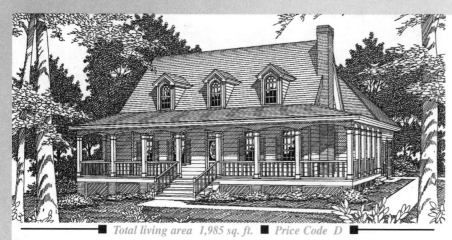

Total living area 1,985 sq. ft. ■ **Price Code D** ■

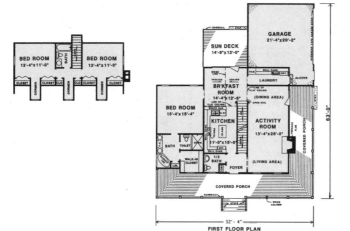

No. 94812 ⚒

■ This plan features:

— Three bedrooms

— Two full and one half baths

■ Old-fashioned quality with dormers and a covered Porch leading into a modern floor plan

■ Activity Room has a fireplace for warmth and comfort

■ Efficient, U-shaped Kitchen has a work island, a snack bar and a vaulted Breakfast Room with Sun Deck access

■ First floor Master Bedroom enjoys a plush bath and a walk-in closet

■ Two additional bedrooms on the second floor each have dormer windows and access to a full bath

First floor — 1,426 sq. ft.
Second floor — 559 sq. ft.
Basement — 1,426 sq. ft.
Garage — 500 sq. ft.

Executive Two-Story

Total living area 2,116 sq. ft. ■ **Price Code C** ■

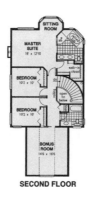

No. 98800 ⚒

■ This plan features:

— Three bedrooms

— Two full and one half baths

■ Gracefully curving staircase dominating the Foyer and leading to the bedrooms

■ Kitchen and Breakfast Nook separated from the Family Room by only a railing and a step down

■ Built-in entertainment center and a warming fireplace highlighting the sunken Family Room

■ Formal Living Room and Dining Room adjoin and include a fireplace in the Living Room and a built-in china cabinet in the Dining Room

■ Lavish Master Suite boasts a Sitting Room and a deluxe five-piece bath

■ Bonus Room to be finished for future needs

First floor — 1,258 sq. ft.
Second floor — 858 sq. ft.
Bonus — 263 sq. ft.
Basement — 1,251 sq. ft.
Garage — 441 sq. ft.

■ *Total living area 1,345 sq. ft.* ■ *Price Code A* ■

No. 91342

■ This plan features:

— Three bedrooms

— Two full baths

■ A handicaped Master Bath plan is available

■ Vaulted Great Room, Dining Room and Kitchen areas

■ A Kitchen accented with angles and an abundance of cabinets for storage

■ A Master Bedroom with an ample sized wardrobe, large covered private deck, and private bath

Main area — 1,345 sq. ft.

MAIN AREA

ALTERNATE BATH

143

Amenities Normally Found In Larger Homes

© 1995 Donald A Gardner Architects, Inc.

■ Total living area 1,253 sq. ft. ■ Price Code B ■

No. 99858

■ **This plan features:**

—Three bedrooms

—Two full baths

■ A continuous cathedral ceiling in the Great Room, Kitchen, and Dining Room giving a spacious feel to this efficient plan

■ Skylighted Kitchen with a seven foot high wall by the Great Room and a popular plant shelf

■ Master Bedroom suite opens up with a cathedral ceiling and contains walk-in and linen closets and a private bath with garden tub and dual vanity

■ Cathedral ceiling as the crowning touch to the front bedroom/study

Main floor — 1,253 sq. ft.
Garage & Storage — 420 sq. ft.

FLOOR PLAN

© 1995 Donald A Gardner Architects, Inc.

Brick Details Add Class

No. 93165

This plan features:

— Three bedrooms

— Two full baths

- Keystone entrance leads into easy care, tile Entry with plant ledge and convenient closet

- Expansive Great Room with cathedral ceiling over triple window and a corner gas fireplace

- Hub Kitchen accented by arches and columns serving Great Room and Dining area, near laundry area and Garage

- Adjoining Dining area with large windows, access to rear yard and Screen Porch

- Private Master Bedroom Suite with a walk-in closet and plush bath with corner whirlpool tub

- Two additional bedrooms share a full bath

- No materials list is available for this plan

- This plan is not to be built within a 20 mile radius of Iowa City, IA

Main floor — 1,472 sq. ft.
Basement — 1,472 sq. ft.
Garage — 424 sq. ft.

■ *Total living area 1,472 sq. ft.* ■ *Price Code A* ■

MAIN FLOOR PLAN

Abundance of Closet Space

No. 20204

This plan features:

— Three bedrooms

— Two full baths

- Roomy walk-in closets in all the bedrooms

- A Master Bedroom with decorative ceiling and a private full bath

- A fireplaced Living Room with sloped ceilings and sliders to the Deck

- An efficient Kitchen, with plenty of cupboard space and a pantry

Main area —1,532 sq. ft.
Garage — 484 sq. ft.

■ *Total living area 1,532 sq. ft.* ■ *Price Code B* ■

An

EXCLUSIVE DESIGN
By Karl Kreeger

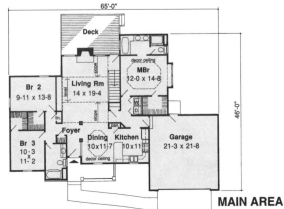

MAIN AREA

145

Detailed Brick and Fieldstone Facade

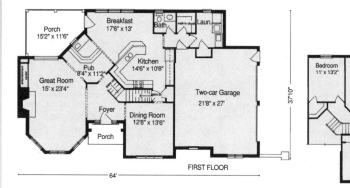

Total living area 2,205 sq. ft. ■ *Price Code D* ■

FIRST FLOOR

SECOND FLOOR

No. 92675

■ **This plan features**

— Three bedrooms

— Two full and one half baths

■ Open Foyer enhanced by a graceful, banister staircase

■ Great Room highlighted by a twelve foot ceiling topping an alcove of windows, fireplace, built-in entertainment center and Porch access

■ Spacious Kitchen and Breakfast Area with extended counter/snackbar and nearby Pub, walk-in closet, Laundry and Garage

■ Comfortable Master Bedroom with a large walk-in closet and double vanity bath

■ Two additional bedrooms share a double vanity bath

■ No materials list is available for this plan

First floor — 1,192 sq. ft.
Second floor — 1,013 sq. ft.
Basement — 1,157 sq. ft.

Rich Classic Lines

Total living area 2,212 sq. ft. ■ *Price Code D* ■

FIRST FLOOR

SECOND FLOOR

No. 91901

■ **This plan features:**

— Four bedrooms

— Three full and one half baths

■ A two-story Foyer flooded by light through an arched transom

■ A vaulted ceiling in the Great Room that continues into the Master Suite

■ A corner fireplace in the Great Room with French doors to the Breakfast/Kitchen area

■ A center island in the Kitchen with an angled sink and a built-in desk and Pantry

■ A tray ceiling and recessed hutch area in the formal Dining Room

■ A Master Suite with a walk-in closet, a whirlpool tub and two vanities

■ No materials list is available for this plan

First floor — 1,496 sq. ft.
Second floor — 716 sq. ft.
Basement — 1,420 sq. ft.
Garage — 460 sq. ft.

Spacious Elegance

■ *Total living area 2,349 sq. ft.* ■ *Price Code D* ■

No. 98455

■ This plan features:

— Four bedrooms

— Three full baths

■ The two-story Foyer with palladian window illuminates a lovely staircase and the Dining Room entry way

■ The Family Room has a vaulted ceiling and an inviting fireplace

■ Vaulted ceiling and a radius window highlight the Breakfast area and the efficient Kitchen

■ The Master Suite boasts a tray ceiling, luxurious bath and a walk-in closet

■ An optional basement or crawl space foundation — please specify when ordering

First floor — 1,761 sq. ft.
Second floor — 588 sq. ft.
Bonus Room — 267 sq. ft
Basement — 1,761 sq. ft.
Garage — 435 sq. ft.

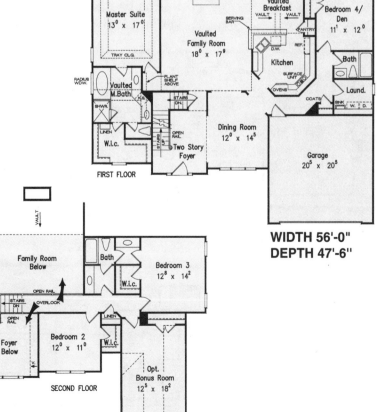

WIDTH 56'-0"
DEPTH 47'-6"

Flexibility to Expand

■ *Total living area 1,831 sq. ft.* ■ *Price Code C* ■

First floor — 1,289 sq. ft.
Second floor — 542 sq. ft.
Bonus room — 393 sq. ft.
Garage & storage — 521 sq. ft.

No. 99859

■ **This plan features:**

— Three bedrooms

— Two full and one half baths

■ Three-bedroom country cottage has lots of room to expand

■ Two-story Foyer contains palladian window in a clerestory dormer

■ Efficient Kitchen opens to Breakfast Area and Deck for outdoor dining

■ Columns separating the Great Room and Dining Room which have nine foot ceilings

■ Master Bedroom on the first level features a skylight above the whirlpool tub

■ An optional basement or crawl space foundation — please specify when ordering

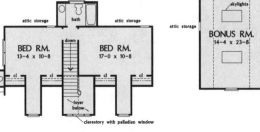

FIRST FLOOR PLAN

© 1990 Donald A Gardner Architects, Inc.

SECOND FLOOR PLAN

High Impact Family Home

No. 20111

This plan features:

- Four bedrooms
- Two full and one half baths
- A balcony linking the upstairs bedrooms and a skylit bath dividing a two-story Foyer
- A massive fireplace in the charming, open Living Room
- A well-situated Kitchen provides handy access to both the formal Dining Room and sunny Breakfast area
- A convenient, private first-floor Master Suite with a garden tub, step-in shower and walk-in closet

First floor — 1,701 sq. ft.
Second floor — 665 sq. ft.
Basement — 1,045 sq. ft.
Garage — 633 sq. ft.

An EXCLUSIVE DESIGN *By Karl Kreeger*

■ Total living area 2,366 sq. ft. ■ Price Code D ■

Rustic Warmth

No. 90440

This plan features:

- Three bedrooms
- Two full baths
- A fireplaced Living Room with built-in bookshelves
- A fully-equipped Kitchen with an island
- A sunny Dining Room with glass sliders to a wood deck
- A first floor Master Suite with walk-in closet and lavish master bath
- An optional basement or crawl space foundation — please specify when ordering

First floor — 1,100 sq. ft.
Second floor — 664 sq. ft.
Basement — 1,100 sq. ft.

■ Total living area 1,764 sq. ft. ■ Price Code B ■

Quality and Diversity

Total living area 2,022 sq. ft. ■ *Price Code C* ■

FIRST FLOOR

- Breakfast 11' x 9'10"
- Great Room 16'5" x 16'8"
- Master Bedroom 14'0" x 13'0"
- Kitchen 13' x 10'5"
- Laun. 9'6" x 8'1"
- Bath
- Garage 20'0" x 21'3"
- Dining Room 11'0" x 13'0"
- Foyer
- Porch
- Bath
- walk-in closet

55'4"
47'6"

SECOND FLOOR

- Bedroom 11'2" x 11'0"
- Great Room Below
- Bedroom 11'0" x 11'2"
- Hall
- Bath
- Bedroom 11'0" x 12'1"
- Foyer Below

No. 92629

■ This plan features:

— Four bedrooms

— Two full and one half baths

■ Elegant arched entrance from Porch into Foyer and Great Room beyond

■ Formal Dining Room for quiet entertaining

■ Corner fireplace and atrium door highlight Great Room

■ Hub Kitchen with walk-in Pantry and peninsula counter easily accesses glass Breakfast bay, backyard, Great Room, Dining Room, Laundry and Garage

■ Master Bedroom wing crowned by tray ceiling offers plush bath and walk-in closet

■ Three additional bedrooms with decorative windows and large closets share a full bath

■ No materials list is available for this plan

First floor — 1,401 sq. ft.
Second floor — 621 sq. ft.
Basement — 1,269 sq. ft.
Garage — 478 sq. ft.

One-Story Home Brimming With Amenities

Total living area 2,079 sq. ft. ■ *Price Code C* ■

No. 94805

■ This plan features:

— Three bedrooms

— Two full baths

■ Pleasant country look with double dormer windows and wrap-around Porch

■ Foyer opens to Dining Room and Activity Room enhanced by tray ceiling, corner fireplace and Sun Deck access

■ Kitchen/Breakfast Room topped by a sloped ceiling, offers an angular serving counter and lots of storage space

■ Secluded Master Bedroom graced with twin walk-in closets and a garden tub bath

■ Two additional bedrooms with easy access to full bath

Main floor — 2,079 sq. ft.
Basement — 2,079 sq. ft.
Garage — 438 sq. ft.

- SUN DECK 19'-0" x 12'-8"
- BREAKFAST ROOM 12'-6" x 10'-0"
- BED ROOM 20'-0" x 13'-6"
- KITCHEN
- ACTIVITY ROOM 15'-0" x 22'-0"
- BED ROOM 11'-0" x 11'-6"
- DINING ROOM 12'-0" x 13'-6"
- BED ROOM 11'-6" x 11'-0"
- FOYER
- PORCH
- GARAGE 20'-0" x 20'-6"

52'-6"
64'-0"
20'-6"

WHEELCHAIR ACCESSIBLE DETAILS FURNISHED

- BED ROOM
- WALK-IN CLOSET
- WALK-IN CLOSET
- BATH

WHEELCHAIR BATH (OPT.)

FIRST FLOOR

Towering Windows Enhance Elegance

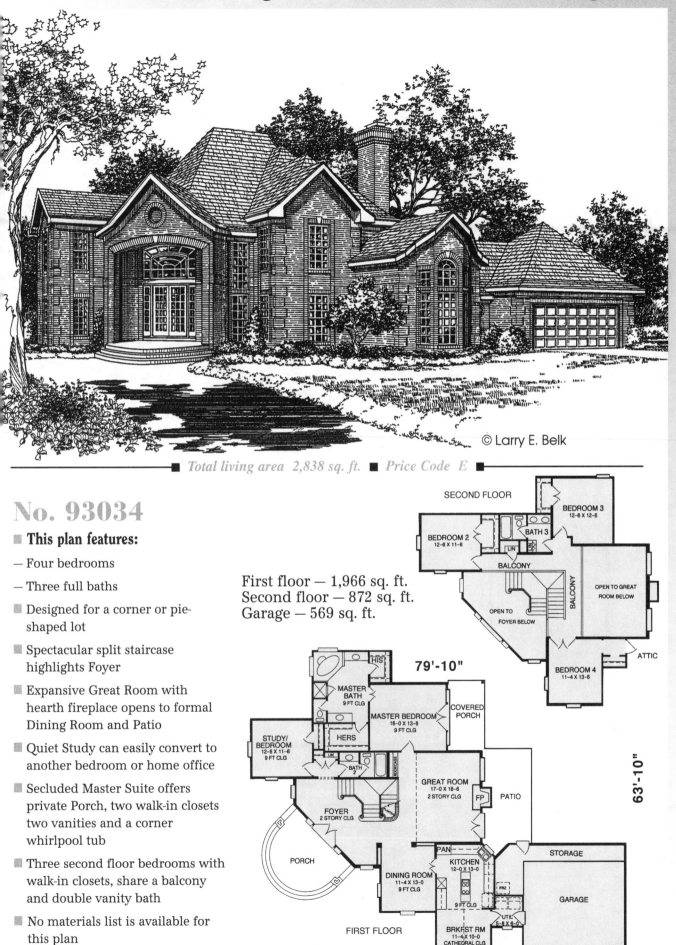

© Larry E. Belk

■ *Total living area 2,838 sq. ft.* ■ *Price Code E* ■

No. 93034

■ This plan features:

— Four bedrooms

— Three full baths

■ Designed for a corner or pie-shaped lot

■ Spectacular split staircase highlights Foyer

■ Expansive Great Room with hearth fireplace opens to formal Dining Room and Patio

■ Quiet Study can easily convert to another bedroom or home office

■ Secluded Master Suite offers private Porch, two walk-in closets two vanities and a corner whirlpool tub

■ Three second floor bedrooms with walk-in closets, share a balcony and double vanity bath

■ No materials list is available for this plan

First floor — 1,966 sq. ft.
Second floor — 872 sq. ft.
Garage — 569 sq. ft.

SECOND FLOOR

BEDROOM 3
12-6 X 12-6

BEDROOM 2
12-6 X 11-6

BATH 3

LIN

BALCONY

OPEN TO GREAT
ROOM BELOW

BALCONY

OPEN TO
FOYER BELOW

ATTIC

BEDROOM 4
11-4 X 13-6

79'-10"

63'-10"

HIS

MASTER
BATH
9 FT CLG

MASTER BEDROOM
16-0 X 13-6
9 FT CLG

COVERED
PORCH

STUDY/
BEDROOM
12-6 X 11-6
9 FT CLG

HERS

LIN

BATH
2

BOOKCASE

GREAT ROOM
17-0 X 18-6
2 STORY CLG

FP

PATIO

FOYER
2 STORY CLG

PORCH

DINING ROOM
11-4 X 13-0
9 FT CLG

PAN

KITCHEN
12-0 X 13-0

9 FT CLG

FRZ

UTIL
5-8 X 6-0

STORAGE

GARAGE

BRKFST RM
11-4 X 10-0
CATHEDRAL CLG

FIRST FLOOR

151

Cabin in the Country

■ *Total living area 928 sq. ft.* ■ *Price Code A* ■

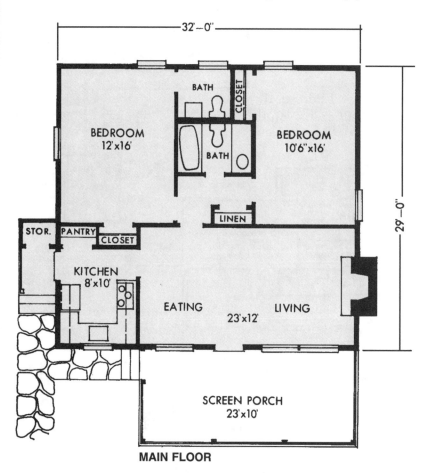

MAIN FLOOR

No. 90433 ⚒

■ **This plan features:**

— Two bedrooms

— One full and one half baths

■ A Screened Porch for enjoyment of your outdoor surroundings

■ A combination Living and Dining area with cozy fireplace for added warmth

■ An efficiently laid out Kitchen with a built-in pantry

■ Two large bedrooms located at the rear of the home

■ An optional slab or crawl space foundation — please specify when ordering

Main floor — 928 sq. ft.
Screened porch — 230 sq. ft.
Storage — 14 sq. ft.

Economical Three-Bedroom

No. 99849

■ **This plan features:**

— Three bedrooms

— Two full baths

■ Dormers above the covered Porch casting light into the Foyer

■ Columns punctuating the entrance to the open Great Room/Dining Room area with a shared cathedral ceiling and a bank of operable skylights

■ Kitchen with a breakfast counter is open to the Dining Area

■ Private Master Suite with a tray ceiling and luxurious bath featuring a double vanity, separate shower and skylights over the whirlpool tub

Main floor — 1,322 sq. ft.
Garage & Storage — 413 sq. ft.

■ *Total living area 1,322 sq. ft.* ■ *Price Code B* ■

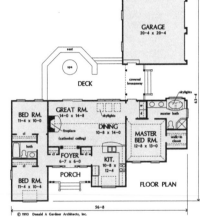

Kick it Up a Notch

No. 98819

■ **This plan features:**

— Four bedrooms

— Two full and one half baths

■ Columned, covered entry leads into a formal Foyer

■ The sunken Living Room is enhanced by a gas fireplace and decorative windows

■ The Dining Room is highlighted by a built-in china cabinet

■ The Kitchen/Nook and Family Room, are accented with a second fireplace and also include a built-in desk and a work island

■ The Master Suite includes a large walk-in closet and a whirlpool bath

■ Three additional bedrooms share a full hall bath

■ No materials list is available for this plan

First floor — 1,090 sq. ft.
Second floor — 1,126 sq. ft.
Basement — 1,067 sq. ft.
Garage — 418 sq. ft.

■ *Total living area 2,216 sq. ft.* ■ *Price Code D* ■

Outstanding Four-Bedroom

■ *Total living area 1,945 sq. ft.* ■ *Price Code C* ■

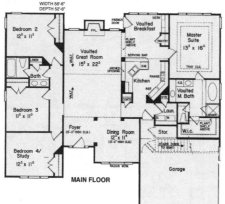

MAIN FLOOR

No. 98435

■ **This plan features:**

— Four bedrooms

— Two full baths

■ Radius window highlighting the exterior and the formal Dining Room

■ High ceiling topping the Foyer for a grand first impression

■ Vaulted ceiling enhances the Great Room accented by a fireplace framed by windows to either side

■ Arched opening to the Kitchen from the Great Room

■ Breakfast Room topped by a vaulted ceiling and enhanced by elegant French door to the rear yard

■ Tray ceiling and a five-piece compartmental bath gives luxurious presence to the Master Suite

■ Three additional bedrooms share a full, double vanity bath in the hall

■ An optional basement or crawl space foundation — please specify when ordering

Main floor — 1,945 sq. ft.

Quoin Accents Distinguish this Plan

■ *Total living area 1,142 sq. ft.* ■ *Price Code A* ■

© Larry E. Belk

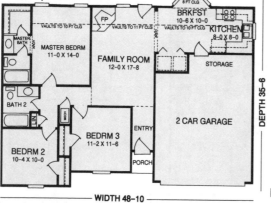

MAIN FLOOR

No. 93017

■ **This plan features:**

— Three bedrooms

— Two full baths

■ A traditional brick elevation with quoin accents

■ A large Family Room with a corner fireplace and direct access to the outside

■ An arched opening leading to the Breakfast Area

■ A bay window illuminating the Breakfast Area with natural light

■ An efficiently designed U-shaped kitchen with ample cabinet and counter space

■ A Master Suite with a private master bath

■ Two additional bedrooms that share a full hall bath

■ No materials list is available for this plan

Main floor — 1,142 sq. ft.
Garage — 428 sq. ft.

Rustic Exterior; Complete Home

■ *Total living area 1,328 sq. ft.* ● *Price Code A* ■

No. 34600

■ This plan features:

— Three bedrooms

— Two full baths

■ A two-story, fireplaced Living Room with exposed beams adds to the rustic charm

■ An efficient, modern Kitchen with ample work and storage space

■ Two first floor bedrooms with individual closet space share a full bath

■ A Master Bedroom secluded on the second floor with its own full bath

■ A welcoming front Porch adding to the living space

First floor — 1,013 sq. ft.
Second floor — 315 sq. ft.
Basement — 1,013 sq. ft.

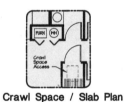

Crawl Space / Slab Plan

Upper Floor

Main Floor

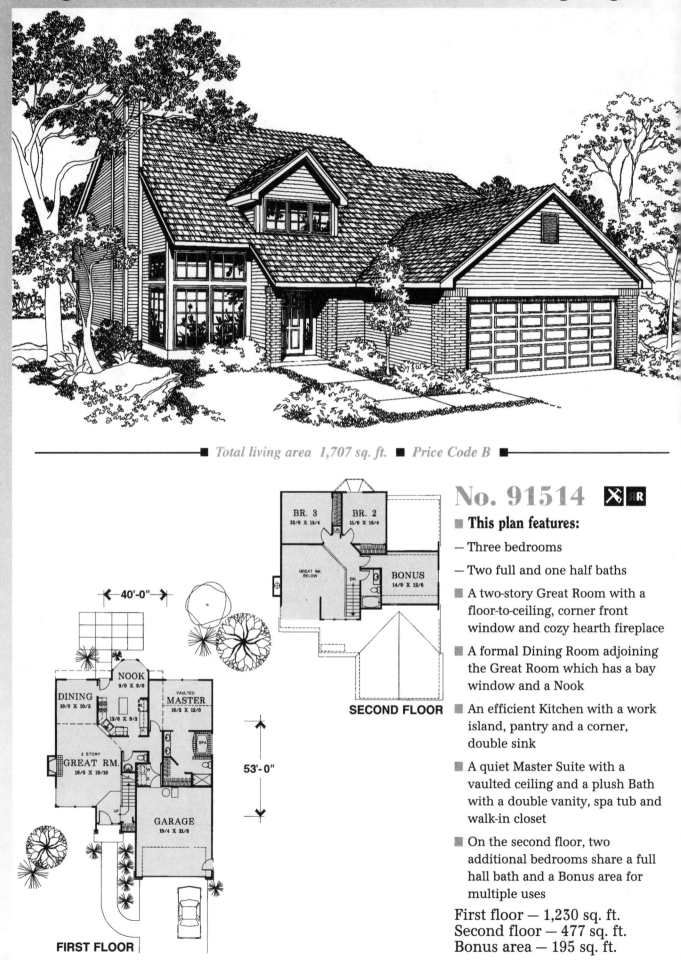

■ *Total living area 1,707 sq. ft.* ■ *Price Code B* ■

FIRST FLOOR

40'-0"

DINING
10/0 X 10/2

NOOK
9/0 X 9/0

VAULTED
MASTER
16/2 X 12/0

12/6 X 9/2

2 STORY
GREAT RM.
16/0 X 19/10

53'-0"

UP

GARAGE
19/4 X 21/8

SECOND FLOOR

BR. 3
12/6 X 12/4

BR. 2
11/0 X 12/4

GREAT RM.
BELOW

DN.

BONUS
14/0 X 12/6

No. 91514

■ **This plan features:**

— Three bedrooms

— Two full and one half baths

■ A two-story Great Room with a floor-to-ceiling, corner front window and cozy hearth fireplace

■ A formal Dining Room adjoining the Great Room which has a bay window and a Nook

■ An efficient Kitchen with a work island, pantry and a corner, double sink

■ A quiet Master Suite with a vaulted ceiling and a plush Bath with a double vanity, spa tub and walk-in closet

■ On the second floor, two additional bedrooms share a full hall bath and a Bonus area for multiple uses

First floor — 1,230 sq. ft.
Second floor — 477 sq. ft.
Bonus area — 195 sq. ft.

Stately Three Bedroom Home

No. 93175

■ This plan features:

— Three bedrooms

— Two full and one half baths

■ Columns astride the front door and window boxes for plants create a charming exterior

■ Extensive use of windows that flood this home with natural light

■ Great Room has a cathedral ceiling and a corner fireplace

■ Efficient U-shaped Kitchen features a breakfast counter and access to the formal Dining Room

■ First floor laundry area with storage and a half bath

■ Master Bedroom boasts a cathedral ceiling and a private bath with a double vanity

■ No materials list is available for this plan

■ This plan is not to be built within a 20 mile radius of Iowa City, IA

Main floor — 804 sq. ft.
Second floor — 746 sq. ft.
Basement — 804 sq. ft.

■ *Total living area 1,550 sq. ft.* ■ *Price Code B* ■

SECOND FLOOR PLAN

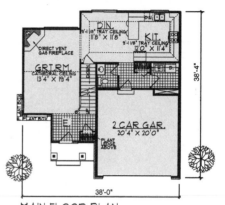

MAIN FLOOR PLAN

Family Room with a Fireplace

No. 93319

■ This plan features:

— Four bedrooms

— Two full and one half baths

■ An island Kitchen with a built-in pantry, double sink and a convenient Dinette area

■ A cozy fireplace enhancing the Family Room

■ A formal Living Room and Dining Room

■ A luxurious Master Suite with an ultra bath and walk-in closet

■ Three additional bedrooms that share a full hall bath

■ No materials list is available for this plan

First floor — 1,228 sq. ft.
Second floor — 1,191 sq. ft.
Basement — 1,228 sq. ft.
Garage — 528 sq. ft.

■ *Total living area 2,419 sq. ft.* ■ *Price Code D* ■

An
EXCLUSIVE DESIGN
By Patrick Morabito, A.I.A. Architect

157

Brick and Wood Highlighted by Sunbursts

Total living area 1,813 sq. ft. ■ *Price Code C* ■

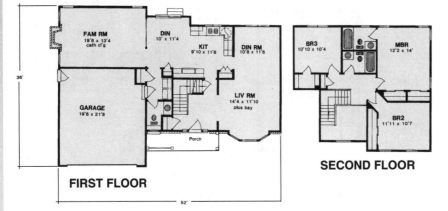

FIRST FLOOR

SECOND FLOOR

No. 94104

■ **This plan features:**

— Three bedrooms

— Two full and one half baths

■ Sheltered Porch entrance leads into two-story Foyer with lovely landing staircase

■ Beautiful bay window brightens Living Room, which opens into formal Dining Room

■ Efficient, L-shaped Kitchen with a built-in Pantry and Dining Area with sliding glass door to rear yard

■ Comfortable Family Room with focal point fireplace topped by cathedral ceiling

■ Corner Master Bedroom offers two closets and a private bath

■ Two additional bedrooms with large closets share a full bath

■ No materials list is available for this plan

First floor — 1,094 sq. ft.
Second floor — 719 sq. ft.
Basement — 1,078 sq. ft.
Garage — 432 sq. ft.

A Very Distinctive Ranch

Total living area 1,947 sq. ft. ■ *Price Code C* ■

MAIN FLOOR

No. 99115

■ **This plan features:**

— Three bedrooms

— Two full and one half baths

■ Hip roofed ranch with an exterior mixing brick and siding

■ Recessed entrance with sidelights which work to create a formal entry

■ Formal Dining Room has a butler's Pantry for added convenience

■ Great Room features a vaulted ceiling and a fireplace for added atmosphere

■ Large open Kitchen has ample cupboard space and a spacious Breakfast Area

■ Master Suite includes a walk-in closet, private bath and an elegant bay window

■ Laundry Room on the main level between the three-car Garage and Kitchen

■ No materials list is available for this plan

Main floor — 1,947 sq. ft.
Basement — 1,947 sq. ft.

For an Established Neighborhood

■ *Total living area 1,292 sq. ft.* ■ *Price Code A* ■

No. 93222

■ **This plan features:**

— Three bedrooms

— Two full baths

■ An expansive Living Room enhanced by natural light streaming in from the large front window

■ A bayed formal Dining Room with direct access to the Sun Deck and the Living Room for entertainment ease

■ An efficient, galley Kitchen, convenient to both formal and informal eating areas

■ An informal Breakfast Room with direct access to the Sun Deck

■ A large Master Suite equipped with a walk-in closet and a full private Bath

Main area — 1,276 sq. ft.
Finished staircase — 16 sq. ft.
Basement — 392 sq. ft.
Garage — 728 sq. ft.

SUNDECK 14'-0"X10'-0"

BREAKFAST 9'-6"X 8'-2"

KITCHEN 10'-0X8'-2"

REF

DINING RM. 12'-0"X9'-6"

BEDRM.3 10'-0"X11'-6"

LIN

M.BEDRM. 16'-0"X11'-6"

LIVING AREA 13'-8"X15'-0"

ENTRY

BEDRM.2 13'-6"X13'-0"

26'-0"

FLOOR PLAN

48'-0"

An **EXCLUSIVE DESIGN** *By Jannis Vann & Associates, Inc.*

159

French Flavor

■ *Total living area 2,490 sq. ft.* ■ *Price Code E* ■

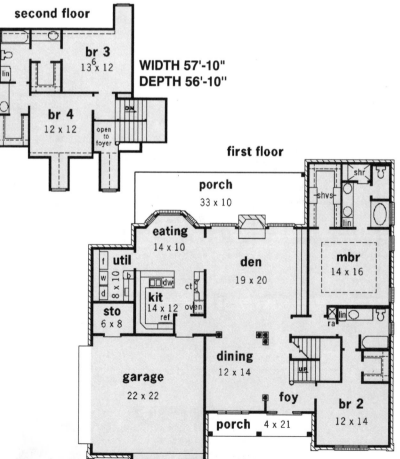

second floor

WIDTH 57'-10"
DEPTH 56'-10"

br 3
13⁶ x 12

br 4
12 x 12

open to foyer

lin

first floor

porch
33 x 10

eating
14 x 10

util
8 x 10

sto
6 x 8

kit
14 x 12

den
19 x 20

mbr
14 x 16

garage
22 x 22

dining
12 x 14

foy

br 2
12 x 14

porch 4 x 21

shr
shvs
lin

lin

No. 92549

■ **This plan features:**

— Four bedrooms

— Three full baths

■ Porch entry into open Foyer with a lovely, landing staircase

■ Elegant columns define Dining and Den area for gracious entertaining

■ Efficient, U-shaped Kitchen with a serving counter, Eating bay, and nearby Utility and Garage

■ Decorative ceiling tops Master Bedroom offering a huge walk-in closet and plush bath

■ An optional crawl space or slab foundation — please specify when ordering

First floor — 1,911 sq. ft.
Second floor — 579 sq. ft.
Garage — 560 sq. ft.

Charming with Drama

No. 96478

This plan features:

- Four bedrooms
- Three full baths
- Transom windows and gables charm the exterior
- Decorative columns and dramatic ceiling treatments highlighting the interior
- Sharing a cathedral ceiling, the Great Room and Kitchen are open to each other as well as the Breakfast Bay
- A sliding pocket door separates the Kitchen from the formal Dining Room, which is topped by a tray ceiling
- Master Suite also includes a tray ceiling and a luxurious bath with a skylit garden tub and a walk-in closet
- Three additional bedrooms, including one with a private bath and optional arrangement for the physically changed, are located on the opposite side of the home

Main floor — 2,203 sq. ft.
Garage & storage — 551 sq. ft.
Bonus room — 395 sq. ft.

Total living area 2,203 sq. ft. ■ Price Code D

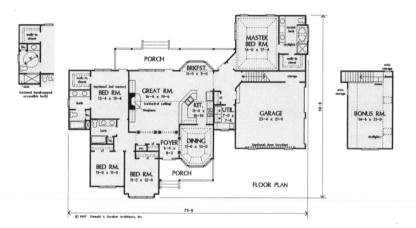

Small Yet Sophisticated

No. 92281

This plan features:

- Three bedrooms
- Two full baths
- Spacious Great Room highlighted by a fireplace and built-in shelving
- Efficient, U-shaped Kitchen with ample work and storage space, sliding glass door to Covered Patio and a Dining area with a window seat
- Spacious Master Suite enhanced by window seats, vaulted ceiling, a lavish bath and large walk-in closet
- Two additional bedrooms share a full bath
- Convenient Utility area and Garage entry
- No materials list is available for this plan

Main floor — 1,360 sq. ft.
Garage — 380 sq. ft.

Total living area 1,360 sq. ft. ■ Price Code A

Friendly Colonial

No. 90606

■ This plan features:

— Four bedrooms

— Two full and one half baths

■ A beautiful circular stair ascending from the central Foyer and flanked by the formal Living Room and Dining Room

■ Exposed beams, wood paneling, and a brick fireplace wall in the Family Room

■ A separate dinette opening to an efficient Kitchen

First floor — 1,099 sq. ft.
Second floor — 932 sq. ft.
Basement — 1,023 sq. ft.
Garage — 476 sq. ft.

■ Total living area 2,031 sq. ft. ■ Price Code C ■

Plenty of Room to Grow

No. 92647

■ This plan features:

— Three or four bedrooms

— Two full and one half baths

■ Fieldstone and wood siding accent Porch entrance into open Foyer with lovely landing staircase

■ Sunken Great Room with large fireplace, built-in entertainment center and access to rear yard

■ Hub Kitchen with built-in Pantry, serving counter, bright Breakfast area and adjoining Dining Room, Laundry and Garage entry

■ Corner Master bedroom with walk-in closet, pampering bath with double vanity and whirlpool tub topped by sloped ceiling

■ Two or three additional bedrooms share a full bath and a study/computer area

■ No materials list is available for this plan

First floor — 1,065 sq. ft.
Second floor — 833 sq. ft.
Bonus Room — 254 sq. ft.
Basement — 995 sq. ft.
Garage — 652 sq. ft.

■ Total living area 1,898 sq. ft. ■ Price Code C ■

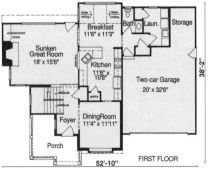

Total living area 3,443 sq. ft. ■ *Price Code F* ■

No. 91562

■ This plan features:

— Three bedrooms

— Two full and one half baths

■ Vaulted Living Room enhanced by French doors to balcony and sharing a see-thru fireplace with a corner Den

■ Elegant ceiling tops a decorative window in Dining Room

■ Kitchen with a cooktop island/snack bar, corner pantry and eating Nook

■ Corner fireplace and a triple window accent the Family Room

■ Master Bedroom offers a balcony, decorative ceiling and deluxe bathroom

■ No materials list available

First floor — 1,989 sq. ft.
Second floor — 1,349 sq. ft.
Lower floor — 105 sq. ft.
Bonus room — 487 sq. ft.

FIRST FLOOR

LOWER FLOOR

SECOND FLOOR

A Home for Today and Tomorrow

■ Total living area 1,583 sq. ft. ■ Price Code B ■

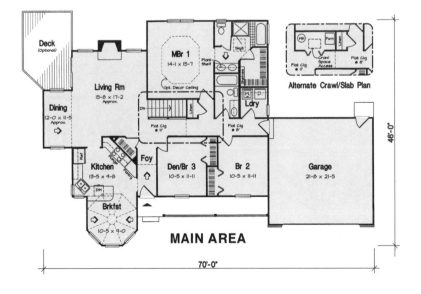

An
EXCLUSIVE DESIGN
By Karl Kreeger

MAIN AREA

No. 34043

■ This plan features:

— Three bedrooms

— Two full baths

■ An intriguing Breakfast Nook off the Kitchen

■ A wide open, fireplaced Living Room with glass sliders to an optional Deck

■ A step-saving arrangement of the Kitchen between the Breakfast Area and formal Dining Room

■ A handsome Master Bedroom with skylit compartmentalized bath

Main area — 1,583 sq. ft.
Basement — 1,573 sq. ft.
Garage — 484 sq. ft.

Classic Brick with One Floor Living

No. 24709

This plan features:

— Two or three bedrooms

— Two full baths

- Living room, enhanced by triple window and cozy fireplace opens to Dining Room through graceful columns

- Quiet Study, with convenient built-ins and a sloped ceiling, can convert to third bedroom

- Formal Dining Room highlighted by glass alcove and atrium door to rear yard

- Efficient, U-shaped Kitchen with laundry closet, Garage entry and extended counter/eating bar

- Corner Master Bedroom with double vanity bath

- Second bedroom with large closet and access to a full bath

- No materials list is available for this plan

Main floor — 1,330 sq. ft.
Garage — 523 sq. ft.

Total living area 1,330 sq. ft. • Price Code A

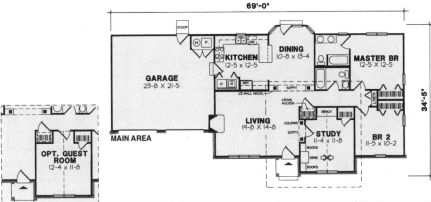

Natural Light Creates Bright Living Spaces

No. 24317

This plan features:

— Three bedrooms

— One full and one three-quarter baths

- A generous use of windows throughout the home, creating a bright living space

- A center work island and a built-in Pantry in the Kitchen

- A sunny Eating Nook for informal eating and a formal Dining Room for entertaining

- A large Living Room with a cozy fireplace to add atmosphere as well as warmth

- A Master Bedroom with a private bath and double closets

- Two additional bedrooms that share a full, compartmented hall bath

Main area — 1,620 sq. ft.

Total living area 1,620 sq. ft. • Price Code B

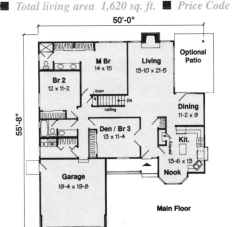

An
EXCLUSIVE DESIGN
By Marshall Associates

Isolated Master Suite

■ Total living area 2,473 sq. ft. ■ Price Code D ■

WIDTH 91'-8"
DEPTH 45'-8"

FIRST FLOOR

SECOND FLOOR

No. 90420

■ **This plan features:**

— Three bedrooms

— Two full and one half baths

■ A spacious, sunken Living Room with a cathedral ceiling

■ An isolated Master Suite with a private bath and walk-in closet

■ Two additional bedrooms with a unique bath-and-a-half and ample storage space

■ An efficient U-shaped Kitchen with a double sink, ample cabinets, counter space and a Breakfast Area

■ A second floor Studio overlooking the Living Room

■ An optional basement, slab or crawl space foundation — please specify when ordering

First floor — 2,213 sq. ft.
Second floor — 260 sq. ft.
Basement — 2,213 sq. ft.
Garage — 422 sq. ft.

Plan Yields Lots of Living Space

■ Total living area 1,355 sq. ft. ■ Price Code A ■

No. 10519

■ **This plan features:**

— Three bedrooms

— Two full and one half baths

■ Sloped ceilings and an open central stairway

■ An efficient, U-shaped Kitchen with easy access to the Dining Room and a laundry facility

■ Ample closet space throughout the home

First floor — 872 sq. ft.
Second floor — 483 sq. ft.

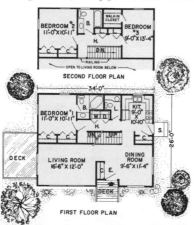

SECOND FLOOR PLAN

FIRST FLOOR PLAN

Two-Story Foyer Adds to Elegance

■ *Total living area 2,454 sq. ft.* ■ *Price Code D* ■

No. 93240 ✕

■ This plan features:

— Four bedrooms

— Two full and one half baths

■ Two-story entrance with lovely, curved staircase

■ Family Room enhanced by fireplace and access to Sundeck

■ Country-sized Kitchen with bright Breakfast area, adjoins Dining Room and Utility/Garage entry

■ French doors lead into plush Master Bedroom with decorative ceiling and large master bath

■ Three additional bedrooms with ample closets share a full bath and Bonus Room

■ An optional basement, crawl space or slab foundation — please specify when ordering

First floor — 1,277 sq. ft.
Second floor — 1,177 sq. ft.
Bonus room — 392 sq. ft.
Basement — 1,261 sq. ft.
Garage — 572 sq. ft.

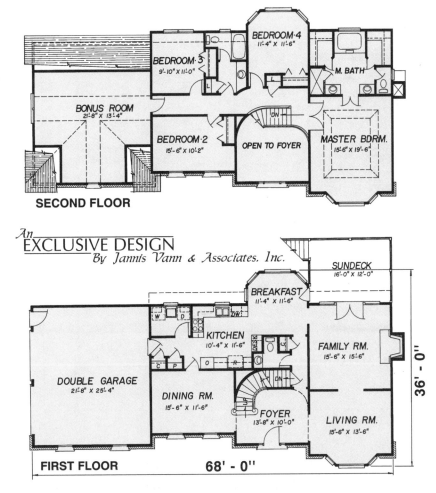

SECOND FLOOR

An EXCLUSIVE DESIGN
By Jannis Vann & Associates, Inc.

FIRST FLOOR 68' - 0"

Ten Foot Entry

■ *Total living area 1,604 sq. ft.* ■ *Price Code B* ■

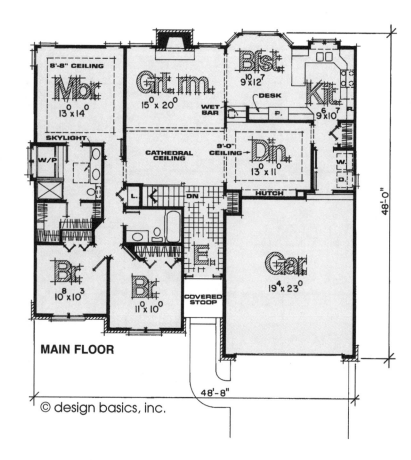

MAIN FLOOR

© design basics, inc.

No. 94986

■ **This plan features:**

— Three bedrooms

— Two full baths

■ Large volume Great Room highlighted by a fireplace flanked by windows

■ See-through wetbar enhancing the Breakfast Area and the Dining Room

■ Decorative ceiling treatment giving elegance to the Dining Room

■ Fully equipped Kitchen with a planning desk and a pantry

■ Roomy Master Suite has a skylighted dressing/bath area, plant shelf, a double vanity and a whirlpool tub

■ Secondary bedrooms share a convenient hall bath

Main floor — 1,604 sq. ft.
Garage — 466 sq. ft.

Brick Home with Four Bedrooms

No. 22004

This plan features:

— Four bedrooms

— Two full and one three-quarter baths

■ Four roomy bedrooms, including the Master Bedroom

■ A centrally located Family Room including a fireplace, wetbar and access to the patio

■ A large Dining Room at the front of the home for entertaining

■ An interesting Kitchen and Nook with an adjoining Utility room

Main floor — 2,070 sq. ft.
Garage — 474 sq. ft.

Total living area 2,070 sq. ft. ■ *Price Code C* ■

MAIN FLOOR

Country Exterior With Formal Interior

No. 90451

This plan features:

— Three bedrooms

— Two full and one half baths

■ Wrap-around Porch leads into central Foyer and formal Living and Dining rooms

■ Large Family Room with a cozy fireplace and Deck access

■ Convenient Kitchen opens to Breakfast Area with a bay window and built-in Pantry

■ Corner Master Bedroom with walk-in closet and appealing bath

■ Two additional bedrooms plus a Bonus Room share a full bath and Laundry

■ An optional basement or crawl space foundation — please specify when ordering

First floor — 1,046 sq. ft.
Second floor — 1,022 sq. ft.
Bonus — 232 sq. ft.
Basement — 1,046 sq. ft.

Total living area 2,068 sq. ft. ■ *Price Code C* ■

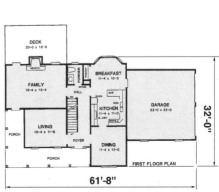

Unique Tower Creates Unique Spaces

■ Total living area 2,362 sq. ft. ■ Price Code D ■

◄ 50'-6" ►

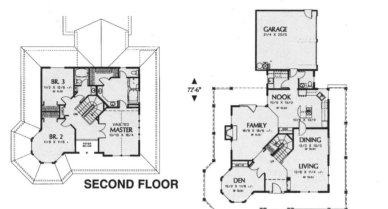

SECOND FLOOR

▲ 72'-6" ▼

BR. 3
11/2 X 12/6

VAULTED MASTER
13/10 X 16/4

BR. 2
11/8 X 11/6

GARAGE
21/4 X 20/0

NOOK
10/3 X 13/0

FAMILY
15/8 X 18/6

DINING
12/0 X 10/0

LIVING
13/8 X 11/4

DEN
15/2 X 11/6

FIRST FLOOR

No. 91565

■ This plan features:

— Three bedrooms

— Two full and one half baths

■ Extensive porch wraps around and accesses active areas of home

■ Combined Living and Dining area offers comfortable entertaining

■ Efficient Kitchen with a cooktop work island, built-in desk, nearby laundry and Garage entry

■ An expansive Family Room with a cozy fireplace and atrium door to Porch

■ Unique Den with loads of light and built-in shelves

■ Vaulted ceiling, walk-in closet and a luxurious bath enhance Master Suite

■ Two additional bedrooms, one with a unique shape, share a full bath

First floor — 1,337 sq. ft.
Second floor — 1,025 sq. ft.

Perfect Proportional Design

■ Total living area 2,131 sq. ft. ■ Price Code C ■

© design basics, inc.

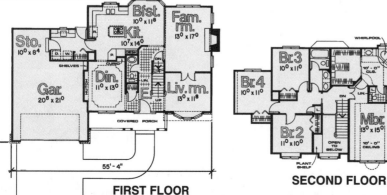

37'-8"

Sto.
10⁰ x 8⁴

Bfst.
10⁰ x 11⁸

Kit.
10⁷ x 14⁰

Fam. rm.
13⁰ x 17⁰

SHELVES

Gar.
20⁸ x 21⁰

Din.
11⁰ x 13⁰

Liv. rm.
13⁰ x 11⁸

COVERED PORCH

55'-4"

FIRST FLOOR

WHIRLPOOL

Br.3
10⁰ x 11⁰

Br.4
10⁰ x 11⁰

Br.2
11⁰ x 10⁰

Mbr.
13⁰ x 15⁰
10'-0" CEILING

OPEN TO BELOW

PLANT SHELF

SECOND FLOOR

No. 94941

■ This plan features:

— Four bedrooms

— Two full and one half baths

■ The large covered Porch is framed by a wood railing

■ The Living Room is enhanced by the warmth of a bay window and has a double French door to the Family Room

■ The Dining Room is crowned with a decorative ceiling treatment and is accented by a built-in curio cabinet

■ The efficient Kitchen is located steps away from the Dinette and the Dining Room

■ The Family Room is enhanced by a cozy fireplace

■ Double doors open to the luxurious Master Bedroom with a distinctive vaulted ceiling

■ Three additional bedrooms share the full bath in the hall

First floor — 1,093 sq. ft.
Second floor — 1,038 sq. ft.
Basement — 1,093 sq. ft.
Garage — 527 sq. ft.

Country Living in Any Neighborhood

■ *Total living area 2,181 sq. ft.* ■ *Price Code C* ■

No. 90436

■ **This plan features:**

— Three bedrooms

— Two full and two half baths

■ An expansive Family Room with fireplace

■ A Dining Room and Breakfast Nook lit by flowing natural light from bay windows

■ A first floor Master Suite with a double vanity bath that wraps around his-n-her closets

■ An optional basement, slab or crawl space foundation — please specify when ordering

First floor — 1,477 sq. ft.
Second floor — 704 sq. ft.
Basement — 1,374 sq. ft.

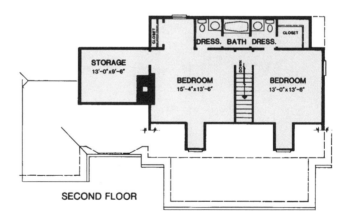

SECOND FLOOR

STORAGE
13'-0"x9'-6"

BEDROOM
15'-4"x13'-6"

BEDROOM
13'-0"x13'-6"

DRESS. BATH DRESS.

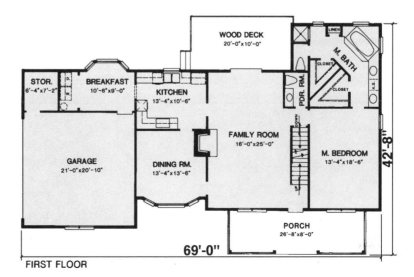

WOOD DECK
20'-0"x10'-0"

M. BATH

STOR.
6'-4"x7'-2"

BREAKFAST
10'-6"x9'-0"

KITCHEN
13'-4"x10'-6"

PDR. RM.

FAMILY ROOM
16'-0"x25'-0"

GARAGE
21'-0"x20'-10"

DINING RM.
13'-4"x13'-6"

M. BEDROOM
13'-4"x18'-6"

PORCH
26'-8"x8'-0"

42'-8"

69'-0"

FIRST FLOOR

Classic Exterior, Modern Interior

■ *Total living area 3,397 sq. ft.* ■ *Price Code F* ■

WIDTH 79'-0"
DEPTH 55'-0"

EATING AREA
SUNROOM
KITCHEN
FAMILY ROOM
MASTER BEDROOM
4 CAR GARAGE
SITTING AREA
DINING ROOM
STUDY
FOYER

MAIN FLOOR

OPEN TO
FAMILY RM.

BEDROOM #2
BEDROOM #4
OPEN TO
FOYER
BEDROOM #3

SECOND FLOOR

No. 93118 R

■ This plan features:

— Four bedrooms

— Three full and one half baths

■ Entry with arched window, sidelights and two-story Foyer

■ Dining Room and Study are highlighted by decorative windows

■ Convenient Kitchen with cooktop island opens to Eating Area with outdoor access

■ The Family Room is accented by cozy fireplace between built-ins

■ Secluded Master Bedroom offers a bright Sitting Area, large walk-in closet and deluxe bath

■ This plan cannot be built within a 75 mile radius of Cedar Rapids, IA

■ No materials list is available for this plan

First floor — 2,385 sq. ft.
Second floor — 1,012 sq. ft.
Garage — 846 sq. ft.
Basement — 2,385 sq. ft.

Modern Design Highlighted by Split Roofline

No. 90028

This plan features:

- Three bedrooms
- Two full baths
- An energy efficient solar hot water system with solar flat-plate collector panels and double glazed windows
- A Living/Dining area accentuated by massive stonefaced, heat-circulating fireplace
- An upstairs bedrooms sharing a lovely, sky-lit full bath

First floor — 960 sq. ft.
Second floor — 580 sq. ft.
Wood deck — 460 sq. ft.

■ *Total living area 1,540 sq. ft.* ■ *Price Code B* ■

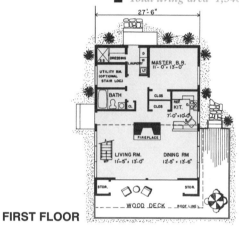

FIRST FLOOR

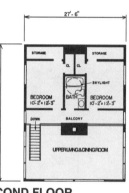

SECOND FLOOR

Wonderful Views

No. 20068

This plan features:

- Three bedrooms
- Two full and one half baths
- A fireplaced Living Room with sloped ceiling
- A second floor balcony
- A huge Master Bedroom featuring a lavish bath
- Walk-in closets for all bedrooms

First floor — 1,277 sq. ft.
Second floor — 616 sq. ft.
Basement — 1,265 sq. ft.
Garage — 477 sq. ft.

■ *Total living area 1,893 sq. ft.* ■ *Price Code C* ■

An
EXCLUSIVE DESIGN
By Karl Kreeger

173

Charming, Compact and Convenient

■ *Total living area 1,752 sq. ft.* ■ *Price Code B* ■

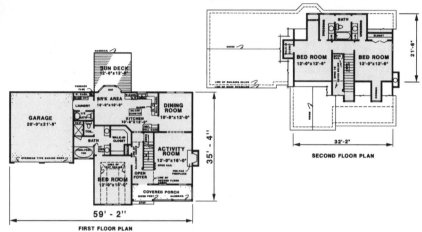

SECOND FLOOR PLAN

FIRST FLOOR PLAN

No. 94803

■ **This plan features:**

— Three bedrooms

— Two full and one half baths

■ Double dormer, arched window and covered Porch add light and space

■ Open Foyer graced by banister staircase and balcony

■ Spacious Activity Room with a pre-fab fireplace opens to formal Dining Room

■ Country-size Kitchen/Breakfast area with island counter and access to Sun Deck and Laundry/Garage entry

■ First floor bedroom highlighted by lovely arched window below a tray ceiling and a pampering bath

■ Two upstairs bedrooms share a twin vanity bath

■ An optional basement or crawl space foundation — please specify when ordering

First floor — 1,165 sq. ft.
Second floor — 587 sq. ft.
Basement — 1,165 sq. ft.
Garage — 455 sq. ft.

Drive Under Garage

■ *Total living area 1,208 sq. ft.* ■ *Price Code A* ■

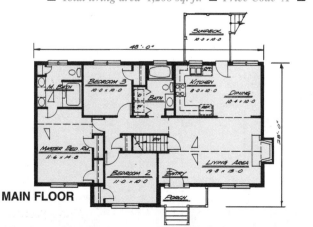

MAIN FLOOR

No. 98915

■ **This plan features:**

— Three bedrooms

— Two full baths

■ Porch shelters entry into Living Area with an inviting fireplace topped by a vaulted ceiling

■ Convenient Dining area opens to Living Room, Kitchen and Sundeck

■ Efficient, U-shaped Kitchen serves Dining area and Sundeck beyond

■ Pampering Master Bedroom with a vaulted ceiling, two closets and a double vanity bath

■ Two additional bedrooms share a full bath and convenient Laundry center

Main floor — 1,208 sq. ft.
Basement — 728 sq. ft.
Basement garage — 480 sq. ft.

An EXCLUSIVE DESIGN
By Jannis Vann & Associates, Inc.

■ *Total living area 2,162 sq. ft.* ■ *Price Code C* ■

No. 91343

■ This plan features:

— Three bedrooms

— Two full and one half baths

■ A stone-faced fireplace and vaulted ceiling in the Living Room

■ An island food preparation center with a sink and a Breakfast bar in the Kitchen

■ Sliding glass doors leading from the Dining Room to the adjacent deck

■ A Master Suite with a vaulted ceiling, a Sitting Room, and a lavish Master Bath with a whirlpool tub, skylights, double vanity and a walk-in closet

First floor — 1,338 sq. ft.
Second floor — 763 sq. ft.
Lower floor — 61 sq. ft.

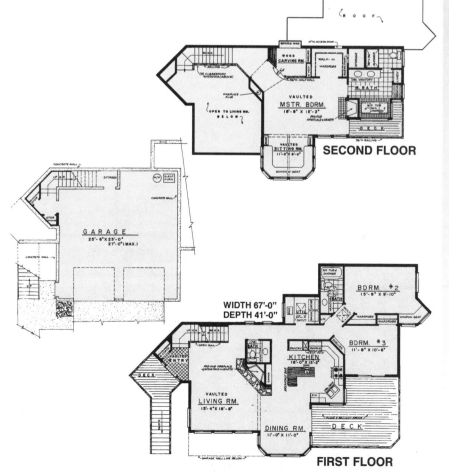

WIDTH 67'-0"
DEPTH 41'-0"

SECOND FLOOR

FIRST FLOOR

Simplicity at it's Finest

Total living area 1,694 sq. ft. ■ Price Code B

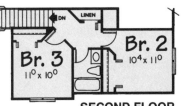

SECOND FLOOR

Br. 3
11⁰ x 10⁰

Br. 2
10⁴ x 11⁰

LINEN

DN

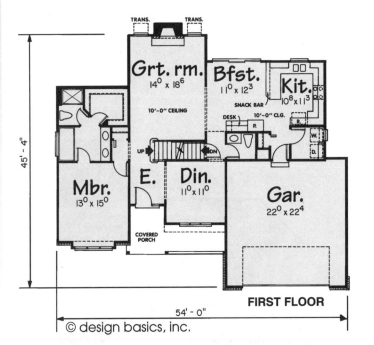

TRANS. TRANS.

Grt. rm.
14⁰ x 18⁶

10'-0" CEILING

Bfst.
11⁰ x 12³

SNACK BAR

Kit.
10⁸ x 11³

10'-0" CLG.

DESK

UP

DN

Mbr.
13⁰ x 15⁰

E.

Din.
11⁰ x 11⁰

Gar.
22⁰ x 22⁴

COVERED PORCH

W.

D.

FIRST FLOOR

45' - 4"

54' - 0"

© design basics, inc.

No. 99420

■ **This plan features:**

— Three bedrooms

— Two full and one half baths

■ A covered porch gives the home a nostalgic feel

■ The volume Great Room offers a fireplace with transom windows on either side

■ A built-in planning desk and Pantry in the Breakfast Area

■ A snack bar for informal meals highlights the Kitchen

■ The formal Dining Room overlooks the porch, which has easy access to the Kitchen

■ An isolated Master Suite has a five-piece bath and a walk-in closet

First floor — 1,298 sq. ft.
Second floor — 396 sq. ft.
Basement — 1,298 sq. ft.
Garage — 513 sq. ft.

Terrific Open Layout

No. 92160

This plan features:

- Four bedrooms
- Two full and one half baths
- An impressive entrance leads to an entry hall that has access to a Powder Room and both the formal and informal areas
- Generous corner Kitchen is open to the bayed Nook bringing in an abundance of natural sunlight
- Family Room including a focal point fireplace enjoyed from the Nook and Kitchen
- Large Master Suite with a luxurious bath and a walk-in closet
- Three additional bedrooms with a full bath located in proximity

First floor — 1,041 sq. ft.
Second floor — 954 sq. ft.

■ Total living area 1,995 sq. ft. ■ Price Code C ■

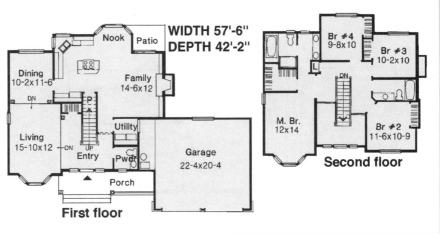

First floor

WIDTH 57'-6"
DEPTH 42'-2"

Second floor

Country Porch Shelters Entry

No. 93904

This plan features:

- Three bedrooms
- Two full and one half baths
- A two-story Foyer illuminated by an arched window above
- A formal Living Room adjoined to the Dining Room by an arched opening
- A second arched opening into the Family Room highlighted by a gas fireplace
- An efficient Kitchen equipped with an island and a bayed Breakfast Area
- A lavish master bath with a garden tub and a walk-in closet adding pampering features to the Master Suite
- Two additional bedrooms that share the full hall bath
- A Bonus Room for future expansion
- No materials list is available for this plan

First floor — 1,121 sq. ft.
Second floor — 748 sq. ft.

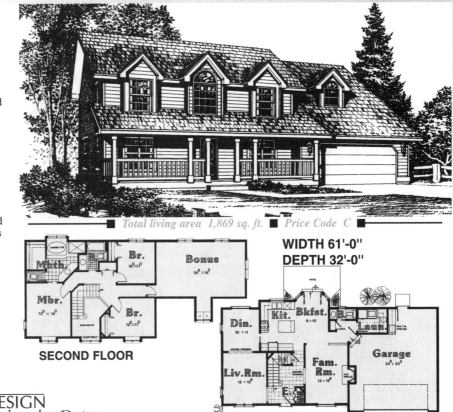

■ Total living area 1,869 sq. ft. ■ Price Code C ■

SECOND FLOOR

WIDTH 61'-0"
DEPTH 32'-0"

FIRST FLOOR

An EXCLUSIVE DESIGN
By Independent Designs

177

Expansive, Not Expensive

Total living area 1,474 sq. ft. ■ Price Code A ■

No. 90623 ⚒

■ **This plan features:**

— Three bedrooms

— Two full baths

■ A Master Suite with his-n-her closets and a private master bath

■ Two additional bedrooms that share a full hall closet

■ A pleasant Dining Room that overlooks a rear garden

■ A well-equipped Kitchen with a built-in planning corner and eat-in space

Main floor — 1,474 sq. ft.

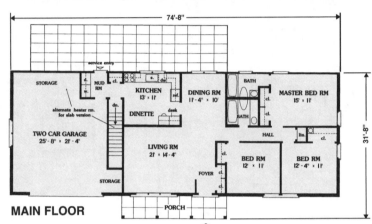

74'-8"

31'-8"

STORAGE

MUD RM

KITCHEN 13' × 11'

DINING RM 11'-4" × 10'

BATH

MASTER BED RM 15' × 11'

alternate heater rm. for slab version

DINETTE

desk

BATH

TWO CAR GARAGE 25'-8" × 21'-4"

LIVING RM 21' × 14'-4"

HALL

STORAGE

FOYER

BED RM 12' × 11'

BED RM 12'-4" × 11'

MAIN FLOOR

PORCH

Demonstrative Detail

Total living area 1,854 sq. ft. ■ Price Code C ■

No. 93410 ⚒

■ **This plan features:**

— Three bedrooms

— Two full and one half baths

■ Keystone arched windows, stone and stucco combine with shutters and a flower box to create an eye-catching elevation

■ The Foyer accesses the Dining Room, Family Room or the Master Suite

■ The Family Room has a sloped ceiling and is accented by a fireplace with windows to either side

■ The Kitchen/Breakfast area has easy access to the rear Porch

■ Two roomy bedrooms on the second floor share the full hall bath

■ An optional Bonus Area over the Garage offers possibilities for future expansion

First floor — 1,317 sq. ft.
Second floor — 537 sq. ft.
Bonus — 312 sq. ft.
Basement — 1,317 sq. ft.
Garage — 504 sq. ft.

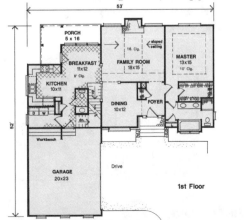

53'

52'

PORCH 5 × 16

BREAKFAST 11x12

FAMILY ROOM 18x15

MASTER 13x15

KITCHEN 10x11

DINING 10x12

FOYER

Workbench

GARAGE 20x23

Drive

1st Floor

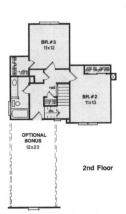

BR.#3 11x12

BR.#2 11x13

OPTIONAL BONUS 12x23

2nd Floor

An EXCLUSIVE DESIGN *By Greg Marquis*

Fireplace-Equipped Family Room

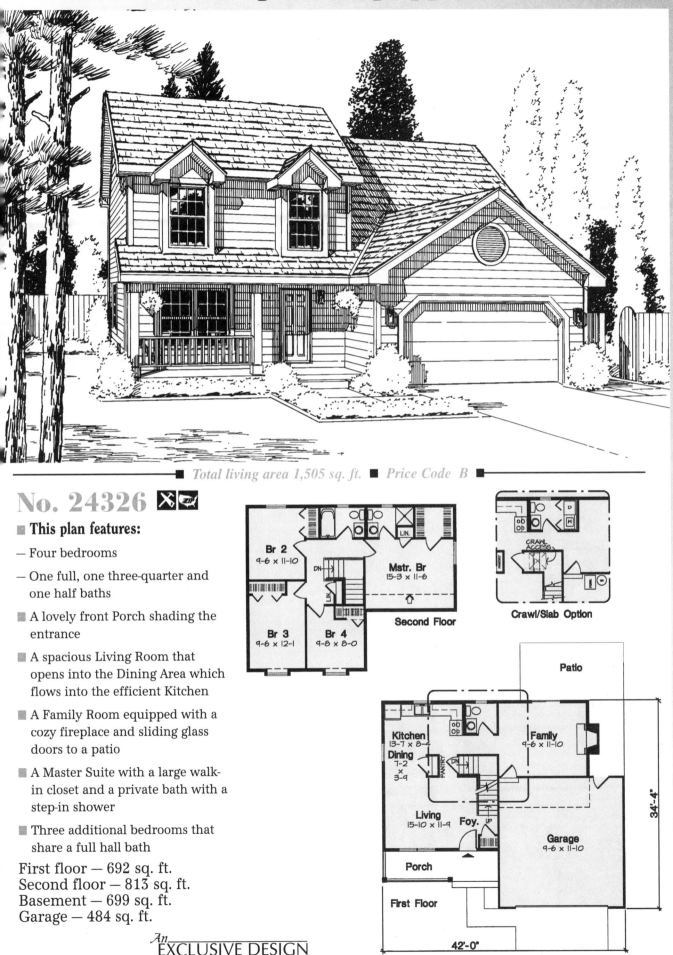

■ *Total living area 1,505 sq. ft.* ■ *Price Code B* ■

No. 24326

■ This plan features:

— Four bedrooms

— One full, one three-quarter and one half baths

■ A lovely front Porch shading the entrance

■ A spacious Living Room that opens into the Dining Area which flows into the efficient Kitchen

■ A Family Room equipped with a cozy fireplace and sliding glass doors to a patio

■ A Master Suite with a large walk-in closet and a private bath with a step-in shower

■ Three additional bedrooms that share a full hall bath

First floor — 692 sq. ft.
Second floor — 813 sq. ft.
Basement — 699 sq. ft.
Garage — 484 sq. ft.

An EXCLUSIVE DESIGN *By Marshall Associates*

Br 2 9-6 x 11-10
Mstr. Br 15-3 x 11-6
Br 3 9-6 x 12-1
Br 4 9-8 x 8-0
LIN.
DN
Second Floor

CRAWL ACCESS
Crawl/Slab Option

Patio
Kitchen 13-7 x 8-4
Dining 7-2 x 3-9
PANTRY
DN
Family 9-6 x 11-10
Living 15-10 x 11-9
Foy.
UP
Garage 9-6 x 11-10
Porch
First Floor
34'-4"
42'-0"

Timeless Beauty

■ *Total living area 2,957 sq. ft.* ■ *Price Code E* ■

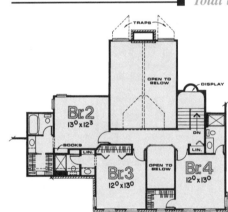

SECOND FLOOR

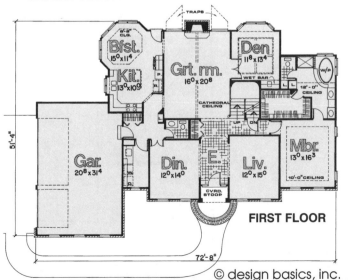

FIRST FLOOR

72'-8"

51'-4"

No. 94994

■ This plan features:

— Four bedrooms

— Two full, two three-quarter and one half baths

■ Two-story Entry hall accesses formal Dining and Living room

■ Spacious Great Room with cathedral ceiling, fireplace between floor-to-ceiling windows and French doors into private Den

■ Ideal Kitchen with built-in desk and pantry, work island, glass Breakfast area, and nearby laundry and Garage entry

■ Master Bedroom with a decorative ceiling, dressing/bath area with a walk-in closet and whirlpool tub

■ Three second floor bedrooms with roomy closets and private baths

First floor — 2,063 sq. ft.
Second floor — 894 sq. ft.
Basement — 2,063 sq. ft.
Garage — 666 sq. ft.

© design basics, inc.

Thoroughly Modern Split Level

No. 99123

■ This plan features:

— Three bedrooms

— One full, one three-quarter and one half baths

■ The covered entry leads to the Foyer and on into the Living Room

■ The formal Living Room is topped by a vaulted ceiling and adjoins the Nook

■ The Kitchen includes a Pantry and is designed in an efficient U-shape

■ The Family Room is complemented by a fireplace

■ The Master Bedroom includes a three-quarter bath and a walk-in closet

■ Two additional bedrooms share a full bath

■ No materials list is available for this plan

Upper floor — 1,289 sq. ft.
Lower floor — 443 sq. ft.
Basement — 553 sq. ft.

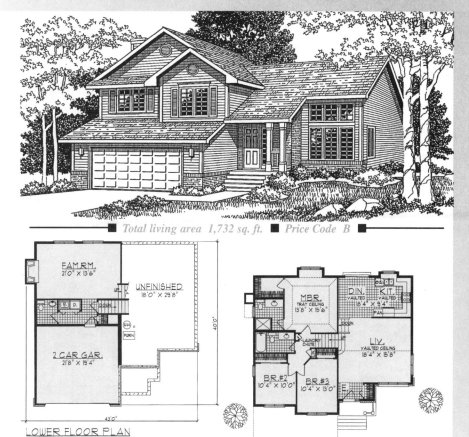

■ Total living area 1,732 sq. ft. ■ Price Code B ■

First Floor Master Suite

No. 98357

■ This plan features:

— Three bedrooms

— Two full and one half baths

■ Front porch and dormer add to the country appeal of this home

■ Elegant Dining Room is topped by a decorative ceiling and has direct Kitchen access

■ Kitchen/Breakfast Room includes a cooktop island, a double corner sink, a walk-in pantry, a built-in desk and a vaulted ceiling

■ Great Room accented by a vaulted ceiling and a fireplace

■ A double door entrance, a box bay window, a vaulted ceiling and a plush five-piece bath are all features of the Master Suite

■ Two additional bedrooms share use of the full bath in the hall

Main floor — 1,490 sq. ft.
Upper floor — 436 sq. ft.
Basement — 1,490 sq. ft.
Garage — 400 sq. ft.

■ Total living area 1,926 sq. ft. ■ Price Code C ■

Elegant Elevation

Total living area 2,428 sq. ft. ■ *Price Code D* ■

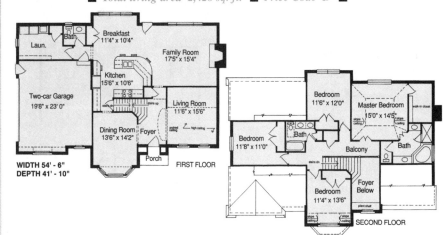

Breakfast 11'4" x 10'4"
Laun.
Bath
Family Room 17'5" x 15'4"
Kitchen 15'6" x 10'6"
Two-car Garage 19'8" x 23' 0"
Living Room 11'6" x 15'6"
Dining Room 13'6" x 14'2"
Foyer
Porch

WIDTH 54' - 6"
DEPTH 41' - 10"

FIRST FLOOR

Bedroom 11'6" x 12'0"
Master Bedroom 15'0" x 14'5"
walk-in closet
Bedroom 11'8" x 11'0"
Bath
Balcony
Bath
Bedroom 11'4" x 13'6"
Foyer Below
plant shelf

SECOND FLOOR

No. 92634

■ **This plan features:**
— Four bedrooms
— Two full and one half baths
■ A wide-apron staircase and plant shelf highlight the open Foyer
■ An arched entrance frames formal Living Room with high ceiling
■ Decorative bay window enhances formal Dining Room
■ Expansive Family Room with focal point fireplace and view of rear yard
■ Hub Kitchen with Breakfast Area, Garage entry, Laundry, and peninsula counter/ snackbar
■ Comfortable Master Bedroom with sloped ceiling, large walk-in closet and plush bath
■ Three additional bedrooms share a double vanity bath with skylight
■ No materials list is available for this plan

First floor — 1,309 sq. ft.
Second floor — 1,119 sq. ft.
Basement — 1,277 sq. ft.
Garage — 452 sq. ft.

Wide Open Spaces

Total living area 2,408 sq. ft. ■ *Price Code D* ■

No. 92676

■ **This plan features:**
— Four bedrooms
— Two full and one half baths
■ A half-circle window above the entrance enhances the impressive two-story Foyer
■ The Great Room boasts imposing windows, a fireplace and direct access to the Porch and Kitchen/Breakfast area
■ The Breakfast Area is central to the Great Room, Porch, Kitchen and Family area
■ The formal Dining Room is brightened by a lovely bay window
■ A bath, pantry, closet and Laundry Room are located near the two-car Garage
■ On the upper level find the Master Suite with a walk-in closet and a private full bath
■ The three other bedrooms share a hallway bath
■ No materials list is available for this plan

First floor — 1,294 sq. ft.
Second floor — 1,114 sq. ft.
Basement — 1294 sq. ft.
Garage — 458 sq. ft.

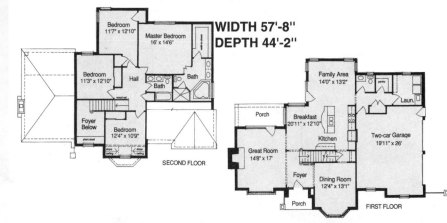

Bedroom 11'7" x 12'10"
Master Bedroom 16' x 14'6"
Bedroom 11'3" x 12'10"
Hall
Bath
Bath
Foyer Below
Bedroom 12'4" x 10'9"

SECOND FLOOR

WIDTH 57'-8"
DEPTH 44'-2"

Family Area 14'0" x 13'2"
pantry
Laun.
Porch
Breakfast 20'11" x 12'10"
Kitchen
Two-car Garage 19'11" x 26'
Great Room 14'8" x 17'
Foyer
Dining Room 12'4" x 13'1"
Porch

FIRST FLOOR

Modern Luxury

■ *Total living area 2,686 sq. ft.* ■ *Price Code E* ■

No. 98457

■ This plan features:

— Four bedrooms

— Three full and one half baths

■ A feeling of spaciousness is created by the two-story Foyer in this home

■ Arched openings and decorative windows enhance the Dining and Living rooms

■ The efficient Kitchen has a work island, pantry and a Breakfast area

■ The plush Master Suite features a tray ceiling, an alcove of windows and a whirlpool bath

■ An optional basement or a crawl space foundation — please specify when ordering

First floor — 1,883 sq. ft.
Second floor — 803 sq. ft.
Basement — 1,883 sq. ft.
Garage — 495 sq. ft.

Distinctive Windows Add to Curb Appeal

■ *Total living area 2,735 sq. ft.* ■ *Price Code F* ■

No. 92550

■ **This plan features:**

— Four bedrooms

— Three full baths

■ A private Master Bedroom with a raised ceiling and attached bath with a spa tub

■ A wing of three bedrooms on the right side of the home sharing two full baths

■ An efficient Kitchen is straddled by an Eating Nook and a Dining Room

■ A cozy Den with a raised ceiling and a fireplace that is the focal point of the home

■ A two-car garage with a storage area

■ An optional crawl space or slab foundation — please specify when ordering

Main floor — 2,735 sq. ft.
Garage — 561 sq. ft.

WIDTH 68'-10"
DEPTH 67'-4"

MAIN FLOOR

Elegant Executive Home

No. 96448

This plan features:

— Four bedrooms

— Two full and one half baths

■ Understated elegance with arched clerestory window lighting the two-story Foyer

■ With a cathedral ceiling topping it, the Great Room has an arched transom window above the slider to Deck, and a fireplace

■ Open and efficient, the Kitchen with adjacent Breakfast area accesses the Deck, Dining Room and Garage

■ First floor Master Bedroom offers twin closets and vanities, plus a skylight over the garden tub

■ Second floor boasts three bedrooms and a full bath

First floor — 1,639 sq. ft.
Second floor — 662 sq. ft.
Bonus Room — 336 sq. ft.
Garage & storage — 520 sq. ft.

Total living area 2,301 sq. ft. ■ Price Code D

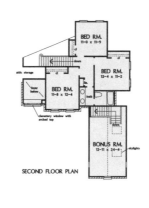

SECOND FLOOR PLAN

FIRST FLOOR PLAN

Secluded Master Suite

No. 24720

This plan features:

— Three bedrooms

— Two full and one half baths

■ Arched Porch shelters entry into an open Foyer with a cascading staircase

■ Great Room highlighted by a vaulted ceiling, sunburst window and hearth fireplace

■ Columns frame entrance to formal Dining Room with decorative ceiling

■ Efficient Kitchen with breakfast bar, Breakfast area with Screened Porch access and nearby Utility/Garage entry

■ Master Bedroom offers an angled ceiling, private Deck, a large walk-in closet and plush bath

■ Two additional bedrooms with ample closets, share a full bath

■ No materials list is available for this plan

First floor — 900 sq. ft.
Second floor — 841 sq. ft.
Basement — 891 sq. ft.
Garage — 609 sq. ft.

Total living area 1,741 sq. ft. ■ Price Code B

First Floor

Crawl/Slab Plan

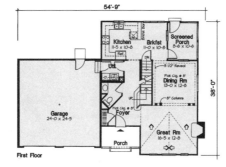

Second Floor

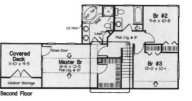

185

Vacation Retreat or Year Round Living

No. 1078 ⚒

■ **This plan features:**

— Two bedrooms

— One full bath

■ A long hallway dividing bedrooms and living areas assuring privacy

■ A centrally located Utility Room and bath

■ An open Living/Dining Room area with exposed beams, sloping ceilings and optional fireplace

Main floor — 1,024 sq. ft.
Carport & Storage — 387 sq. ft.
Deck — 411 sq. ft.

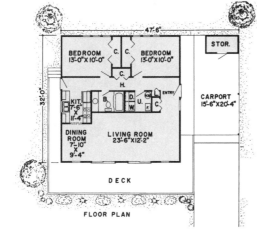

■ *Total living area 1,024 sq. ft.* ■ *Price Code A* ■

FLOOR PLAN

Elegant Elevation

No. 92622

■ **This plan features:**

— Three bedrooms

— Two full and one half baths

■ Brick trim, sidelights and a transom window give a warm welcome to this home

■ High ceilings continue from Foyer into Great Room which counts among it's amenities a fireplace and entertainment center

■ The Kitchen serves the formal and informal dining areas with ease

■ The Master Suite is positioned for privacy on the first floor

■ The second floor has loads of possibilities with a Bonus space and a Study

■ Two bedrooms, each with walk-in closet, share a full bath

■ No materials list is available for this plan

First floor — 1,134 sq. ft.
Second floor — 1,083 sq. ft.
Basement — 931 sq. ft.
Garage — 554 sq. ft

■ *Total living area 2,217 sq. ft.* ■ *Price Code D* ■

FIRST FLOOR

SECOND FLOOR

Bay Windows and a Terrific Front Porch

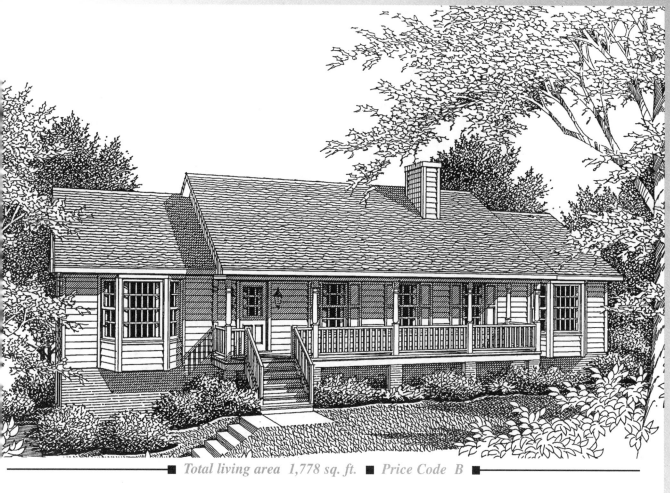

■ *Total living area 1,778 sq. ft.* ■ *Price Code B* ■

No. 93261

■ This plan features:

— Three bedrooms

— Two full baths

■ A country front porch

■ An expansive Living Area that includes a fireplace

■ A Master Suite with a private Master Bath and a walk-in closet, as well as a bay window view of the front yard

■ An efficient Kitchen that serves the sunny Breakfast Area and the Dining Room with equal ease

■ A built-in pantry and a desk add to the conveniences in the Breakfast Area

■ Two additional bedrooms that share the full hall bath

■ A convenient main floor Laundry Room

An EXCLUSIVE DESIGN
By Jannis Vann & Associates, Inc.

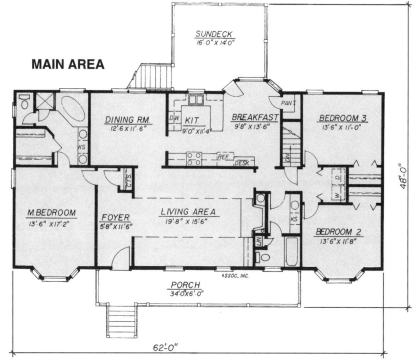

Main area — 1,778 sq. ft.
Basement — 1,008 sq. ft.
Garage — 728 sq. ft.

Country Style For Today

■ *Total living area 2,406 sq. ft.* ■ *Price Code D* ■

DECK

BEDROOM 2
14⁰ x 15⁶

OPEN TO BELOW

DN BRIDGE

LINEN
WH

OPEN TO
BELOW

BEDROOM 3
14⁰ x 11⁸

SECOND FLOOR

No. 91700

■ This plan features:

— Three bedrooms

— Two full and one half baths

■ A wide wrap-around porch for a farmhouse style

■ A spacious Living Room with double doors and a large front window

■ A garden window over the double sink in the huge, country Kitchen with two islands, one a butcher block and the other an eating bar

■ A corner fireplace in the Family Room enjoyed throughout the Nook and Kitchen, thanks to an open layout

■ A Master Suite with a spa tub, and a huge walk-in closet as well as a shower and double vanity

First floor — 1,785 sq. ft.
Second floor — 621 sq. ft.

55'-0"

DN

DECK

DN

NOOK
12⁶ x 10⁰

FIREPLACE

FAMILY ROOM
21⁰ x 15⁶

MASTER SUITE
14⁰ x 14⁸

GARDEN WINDOW

ISLAND

KITCHEN
15⁶ x 14⁸

BUTCHER BLOCK

DESK

WALK-IN CLOSET

SHOWER

42'-0"

SPA

R & O

PANTRY

UP

DINING ROOM
11⁶ x 11⁰

DN

UTILITY

WSH DRY

LIVING ROOM
14⁰ x 14²

PORCH

DN

FIRST FLOOR

Compact Classic

No. 91413

This plan features:

— Three bedrooms

— Two full and one half baths

■ A spacious Family Room with a cozy fireplace and direct access to the patio

■ A well-appointed Kitchen with an eating bar peninsula, double sink and sunny Eating Nook

■ A formal Living Room and Dining Room located at the front of the house

■ A Master Suite equipped with a walk-in closet, a double vanity and a full master bath

■ An optional basement, slab or crawl space foundation — please specify when ordering

First floor — 963 sq. ft.
Second floor — 774 sq. ft.

Total living area 1,737 sq. ft. ■ Price Code B

SECOND FLOOR

BR 10 X 12
WI CLO
MB
BR 11 X 11
MBR 11/8 X 19
OPEN TO FOYER

FIRST FLOOR

54'-6"
33'
GARAGE 22 X 21
NOOK 8 X 8
PATIO
KIT 15/6 X 6/4
FAMILY RM 16 X 13/8
DINE 11 X 10
LIVING RM 12 X 14

Four-Bedroom Stucco

No. 94240

This plan features:

— Three bedrooms

— Two full baths

■ Fits easily on narrow depth lots

■ Grand Room layout has vaulted ceiling that includes the Foyer and Dining Room

■ Grand Room is highlighted by a built-in entertainment center and access to Lanai

■ Compact Kitchen opens to glass Nook and formal Dining area

■ Private Master Suite has glass doors to the Lanai area and a plush bath

■ Two bedrooms and a Study or third bedroom located on the opposite side have ample closet space

■ Guest bath has outdoor access for the pool area

■ No materials list is available for this plan

Main floor — 1,647 sq. ft.
Garage — 427 sq. ft.

Total living area 1,647 sq. ft. ■ Price Code B

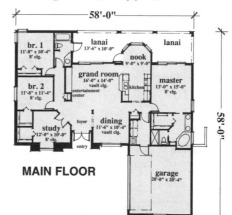

58'-0"
58'-0"

br. 1 11'-8" x 10'-4" 8' clg.
br. 2 11'-8" x 11'-4" 8' clg.
study 12'-0" x 10'-0" 8' clg.
lanai 13'-6" x 10'-0"
nook 9'-0" x 9'-0"
grand room 16'-0" x 14'-0" vault clg. entertainment center
foyer
dining 11'-6" x 10'-4" vault clg.
entry
lanai
master 13'-0" x 15'-0" 8' clg.
kitchen
garage 20'-0" x 20'-4"

MAIN FLOOR

Perfect Plan for Busy Family

Total living area 1,756 sq. ft. ■ **Price Code B** ■

MAIN FLOOR

No. 93191

■ **This plan features:**

— Three bedrooms

— Two full baths

■ Covered entry opens to vaulted Foyer and Family Room

■ Spacious Family Room with a vaulted ceiling, central fireplace and expansive backyard views

■ Angular and efficient Kitchen with an eating bar, built-in desk, Dining area with outdoor access, and nearby Laundry and Garage entry

■ Secluded Master Bedroom with a large walk-in closet and double vanity bath

■ Two additional bedrooms with ample closets and easy access to a full bath

■ Plenty of room for growing family to expand on lower level

■ No materials list is available for this plan

Main floor — 1,756 sq. ft.
Basement — 1,756 sq. ft.

Sophisticated European Stucco

Total living area 1,856 sq. ft. ■ **Price Code C** ■

No. 92562

■ **This plan features:**

— Three bedrooms

— Two full baths

■ A raised ceiling in Master Suite and in the Den add architectural interest to the plan

■ A spacious Kitchen serves the Breakfast Area and Dining Room with efficiency and ease

■ A Breakfast Bar for snacks or meals on the go

■ The vaulted ceiling in the Dining Room adds elegance to the room

■ The luxurious master bath with a separate tub and shower pampers you in the Master Suite

■ Secondary bedrooms are in close proximity to the full bath in the hall

■ An optional crawl space or slab foundation —please specify when ordering

Main floor — 1,856 sq. ft.
Garage & storage — 521 sq. ft.

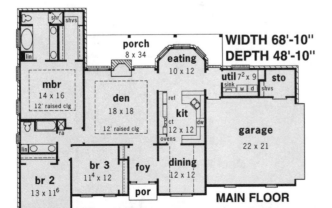

WIDTH 68'-10"
DEPTH 48'-10"

MAIN FLOOR

European Styling with a Georgian Flair

■ *Total living area 1,873 sq. ft.* ■ *Price Code D* ■

No. 92552

■ This plan features:

— Four bedrooms

— Two full baths

■ Elegant European styling spiced with Georgian Styling

■ Arched windows, quoins and shutters on the exterior, a columned covered front and a rear porch

■ Formal foyer gives access to the Dining Room to the left and spacious Den straight ahead

■ Kitchen flows into the informal eating area and is separated from the Den by an angled extended counter eating bar

■ An optional crawl space or slab foundation — please specify when ordering

Main floor — 1,873 sq. ft.
Bonus area — 145 sq. ft.
Garage — 613 sq. ft.

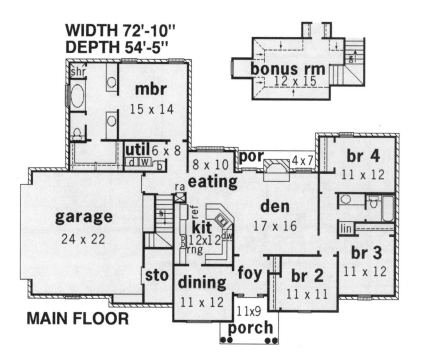

WIDTH 72'-10"
DEPTH 54'-5"

bonus rm
12 x 15

mbr
15 x 14

util 6 x 8
d w

8 x 10

por
4 x 7

br 4
11 x 12

eating

ra

garage
24 x 22

ref

den
17 x 16

kit
12x12

rng

dw

lin

br 3
11 x 12

sto

dining
11 x 12

foy

11x9

br 2
11 x 11

MAIN FLOOR

porch

Country Style Charm

■ *Total living area 1,857 sq. ft.* ■ *Price Code B* ■

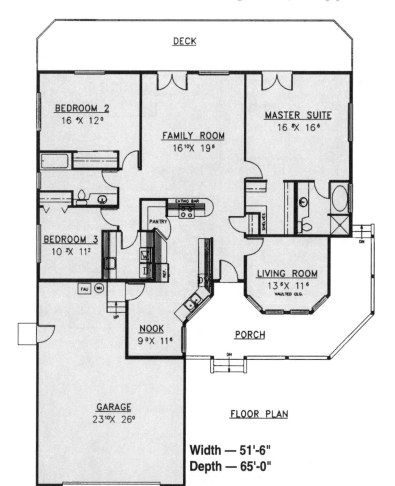

DECK

BEDROOM 2
16⁴X 12⁰

FAMILY ROOM
16¹⁰X 19⁶

MASTER SUITE
16⁶X 16⁶

EATING BAR

PANTRY

BEDROOM 3
10³X 11²

SHELVES

FAU

DN

LIVING ROOM
13⁶X 11⁶
VAULTED CLG.

UP

NOOK
9⁰X 11⁶

PORCH

DN

GARAGE
23¹⁰X 26⁰

FLOOR PLAN

Width — 51'-6"
Depth — 65'-0"

No. 91731

■ **This plan features:**

— Three bedrooms

— Two full baths

■ Brick accents, front facing gable, and railed wrap-around covered porch

■ A built-in range and oven in a dog-leg shaped Kitchen

■ A Nook with garage access for convenient unloading of groceries and other supplies

■ A bay window wrapping around the front of the formal Living Room

■ A Master Suite with French doors opening to the deck

Main area — 1,857 sq. ft.
Garage — 681 sq. ft.

No. 99610 ✕

■ This plan features:

— Three bedrooms

— Two full baths

■ A large front porch with pediment and columns

■ A stunning, heat-circulating fireplace flanked by cabinetry and shelves in the Living Room

■ A formal Dining Room enhanced by a bay window

■ An efficient, U-shaped Kitchen with a peninsula counter and informal Dinette area

■ A Master Suite with a private Master Bath and direct access to the private terrace

■ Two additional bedrooms sharing a full hall bath

Main floor — 1,528 sq. ft.
Basement — 1,367 sq. ft.
Garage & storage — 494 sq. ft.

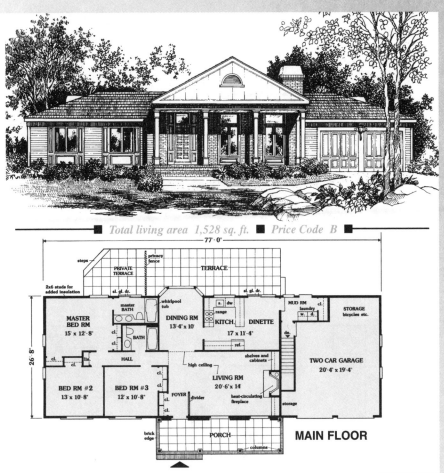

■ Total living area 1,528 sq. ft. ■ Price Code B

MAIN FLOOR

Two Choices for Courtyard Home

No. 94302

■ This plan features:

— Two or Three bedrooms

— One full and one three quarter baths

■ A tiled Entry leading to an open Dining/Living Room area with hearth fireplace and a wall of windows with an atrium door to Terrace

■ An efficient Kitchen with a corner window and eating bar adjoins Dining area, Garage and Terrace

■ A Master Bedroom with walk-in closet and private bath featuring either recessed, decorative window or atrium door to Terrace

■ One or two additional bedrooms with ample closets near full bath

■ No materials list is available for this plan

Main floor — 1,137 sq. ft.
Garage — 390 sq. ft.

An EXCLUSIVE DESIGN *By Marshall Associates*

■ Total living area 1,137 sq. ft. ■ Price Code A

MAIN FLOOR

A Decorative Widows Walk

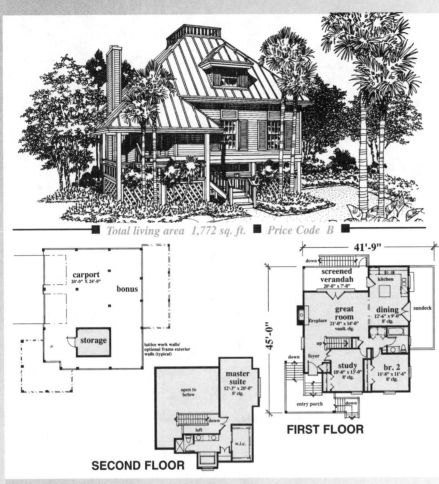

Total living area 1,772 sq. ft. ■ *Price Code B* ■

SECOND FLOOR

FIRST FLOOR

No. 94203

■ **This plan features:**

— Two bedrooms

— Two full baths

■ Living area above the Carport and Storage/Bonus areas offering a "piling" design for coastal, waterfront or low-lying terrain

■ A covered Entry Porch leading into a spacious Great Room

■ A Great Room with a vaulted ceiling, cozy fireplace and double glass door to the screened Veranda

■ An efficient, L-shaped Kitchen with a work island and Dining area with a double door to a Sundeck

■ A Study and secondary Bedroom with ample closet space sharing a full bath and laundry area

■ A private, second floor Master Suite with an oversized walk-in closet and luxurious bath

■ No materials list is available for this plan

First floor — 1,136 sq. ft.
Second floor — 636 sq. ft.
Garage — 526 sq. ft.

Spread Out Ranch

Total living area 1,870 sq. ft. ■ *Price Code C* ■

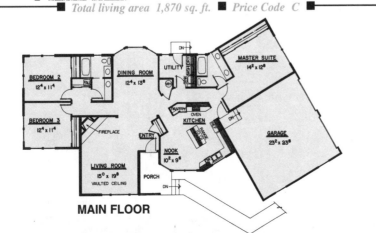

MAIN FLOOR

No. 91720 ✖

■ **This plan features:**

— Three bedrooms

— Two full baths

■ The covered front Porch protects from the elements

■ The Living room has a vaulted ceiling, bright windows, and a corner fireplace

■ The dining room features a bay with windows

■ The Kitchen has an island with a range, and adjoins the unique angled Nook

■ The Master suite has a closet that spans the entire rear wall, plus a private bath

■ Two additional bedrooms share a full bath with dual vanities

Main floor — 1,870 sq. ft.
Garage — 588 sq. ft.
Width — 84'-7"
Depth — 46'-8"

Total living area 1,660 sq. ft. ▪ Price Code C

No. 92560 ✕

▪ This plan features:

—Three bedrooms

—Two full baths

▪ Traditional country styling with front and rear covered porches

▪ Peninsula counter/eating bar in Kitchen for meals on the go

▪ Formal Dining room with built-in cabinet

▪ Vaulted ceiling and cozy fireplace highlighting Den

▪ Private Master Bedroom suite pampered by five-piece bath

▪ Two bedrooms at the opposite of home sharing a full bath

▪ An optional slab or crawl space foundation available — please specify when ordering

Main floor — 1,660 sq. ft.
Garage — 544 sq. ft.

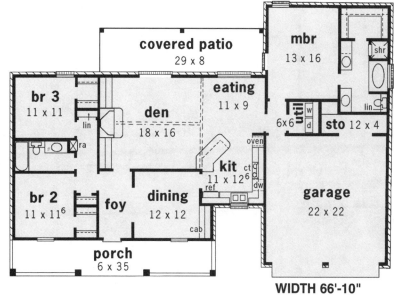

WIDTH 66'-10"
DEPTH 46'-10"

Attractive Exterior

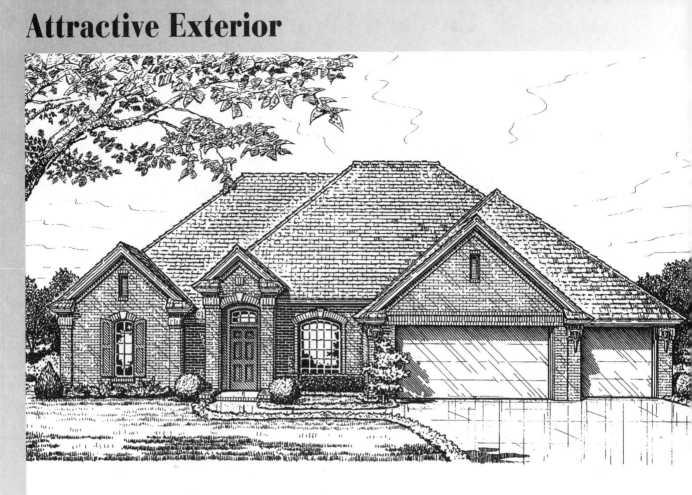

■ *Total living area 2,167 sq. ft.* ■ *Price Code C* ■

No. 98512

■ **This plan features:**

— Three bedrooms

— Two full baths

■ In the Gallery, columns separate space between the Great Room and the Dining Room

■ Access to backyard covered Patio from bayed Breakfast Nook

■ The large Kitchen is a chef's dream with lots of counter space and a Pantry

■ The Master Bedroom is removed from traffic areas and contains a luxurious master bath

■ A hall connects the two secondary bedrooms which share a full skylit bath

■ No materials list is available for this plan

Main floor — 2,167 sq. ft.
Garage — 690 sq. ft.

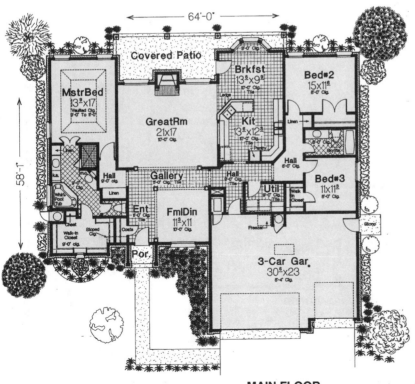

MAIN FLOOR

Outdoor-Lovers' Delight

No. 10748

This plan features:

— Three bedrooms

— Two full baths

■ A roomy Kitchen and Dining Room

■ A massive Living Room with a fireplace and access to the wrap-around porch via double French doors

■ An elegant Master Suite and two additional spacious bedrooms closely located to the laundry area

Main Area — 1,540 sq. ft.
Porches — 530 sq. ft.

■ *Total living area 1,540 sq. ft.* ■ *Price Code B* ■

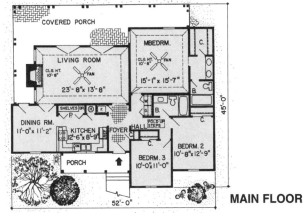

MAIN FLOOR

Polished & Poised

No. 96471

This plan features:

— Three bedrooms

— Two full and one half baths

■ Hip roof, gables and brick accents add poise and polish to this traditional home

■ Curved transom window and sidelights illuminate the gracious Foyer

■ A curved balcony overlooks the Great Room which has a cathedral ceiling, fireplace and a wall of windows overlooking the Patio

■ Hub Kitchen easily serves the Dining Room, Breakfast area and the Patio beyond

■ Master Bedroom wing is enhanced by a tray ceiling, walk-in closet and a deluxe bath

First floor — 1,577 sq. ft.
Second floor — 613 sq. ft.
Bonus room — 360 sq. ft.
Garage & storage — 634 sq. ft.

■ *Total living area 2,190 sq. ft.* ■ *Price Code D* ■

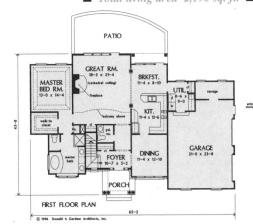

FIRST FLOOR PLAN

SECOND FLOOR PLAN

Didn't Waste An Inch of Space

© 1994 Donald A. Gardner Architects, Inc.

■ Total living area 1,575 sq. ft. ■ Price Code C ■

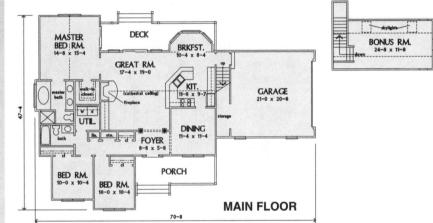

MAIN FLOOR

No. 99834

■ **This plan features:**

— Three bedrooms

— Two full baths

■ Great Room with fireplace and built-in cabinets sharing a cathedral ceiling with angled Kitchen

■ Separate Dining Room allows for more formal entertaining

■ Master Bedroom topped by a cathedral ceiling, walk-in closet, and well-appointed bath

■ Front and rear covered Porches encourage relaxation

■ Skylit Bonus Room making a great Recreation Room or Office in the future

Main floor — 1,575 sq. ft.
Bonus room — 276 sq. ft.
Garage — 536 sq. ft.

Columns Accentuate Southern Flair

■ Total living area 2,400 sq. ft. ■ Price Code D ■

MAIN FLOOR

No. 94641

■ **This plan features:**

— Four bedrooms

— Two full baths

■ Four columns accentuating the warm Southern welcome alluded to by the front porch

■ Foyer leading to the Living Room, or the Dining Room to the right

■ Efficient Kitchen including a peninsula counter, plenty of counter and storage space and an easy flow into the Breakfast Room

■ Master Bedroom topped by a decorative ceiling treatment and pampered by a compartmental master bath with a whirlpool tub

■ Two additional bedrooms with walk-in closets share a double vanity bath in the hall

■ No materials list is available for this plan

Main floor — 2,400 sq. ft.
Garage — 534 sq. ft.
Width — 61'-10"
Depth — 66'-6"

An Affordable Floor Plan

■ *Total living area 1,410 sq. ft.* ■ *Price Code A* ■

No. 91807 ⚒

■ **This plan features:**

— Three bedrooms

— One full and one three quarter baths

■ A covered porch entry

■ An old-fashioned hearth fireplace in the vaulted ceiling Living Room

■ An efficient Kitchen with U-shaped counter that is accessible from the Dining Room

■ A Master Bedroom with a large walk-in closet and private bath

■ An optional crawl space and slab foundation available — please specify when ordering

Main floor — 1,410 sq. ft.
Garage — 484 sq. ft.

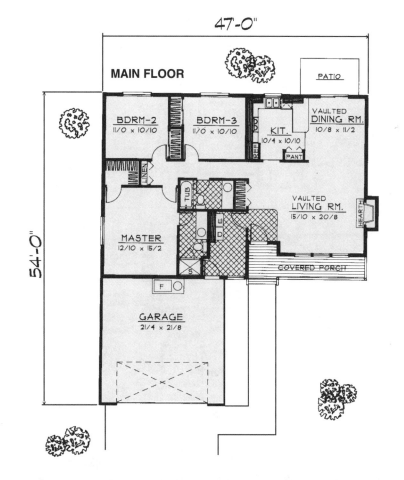

Impressive Two-Story Entrance

■ *Total living area 2,957 sq. ft.* ■ *Price Code E* ■

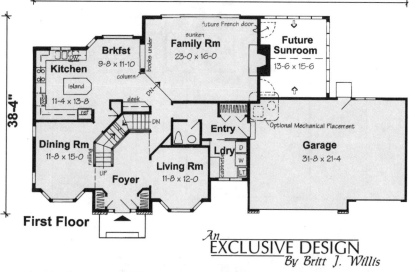

Br 2
11-0 x 12-2

Master Suite
14-0 x 17-4

whirlpool

Lin

Lin

railing

DN

ldry chute

Study
19-8 x 9-4

Br 3
11-8 x 12-0

open to foyer

Br 4
11-8 x 11-10

Second Floor

76'-0"

38'-4"

future French door

Brkfst
9-8 x 11-10

sunken

Family Rm
23-0 x 16-0

Future Sunroom
13-6 x 15-6

Kitchen
11-4 x 13-8

island

books under

column

desk

ref

DN

DN

Optional Mechanical Placement

Entry

Dining Rm
11-8 x 15-0

railing

UP

Foyer

Ldry

D

W

LT

cabinets

Living Rm
11-8 x 12-0

Garage
31-8 x 21-4

First Floor

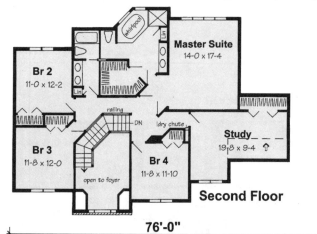

No. 24594

■ This plan features:

— Four bedrooms

— Two full and one half baths

■ Two-story Foyer highlighted by lovely, angled staircase and decorative window

■ Bay windows enhance Dining and Living rooms

■ Kitchen with work island and an open Breakfast area

■ Family Room with a fireplace and Future Sunroom access

■ Private Master Suite offers a walk-in closet and pampering bath

■ Three additional bedrooms share a double vanity bath and large Study

First floor — 1,497 sq. ft.
Second floor — 1,460 sq. ft.
Future Sunroom — 210 sq. ft.
Basement — 1,456 sq. ft.
Garage — 680 sq. ft.

An
EXCLUSIVE DESIGN
By Britt J. Willis

Striking Structure

No. 99431

This plan features:

— Four bedrooms

— Two full and one half baths

■ Wrap-around covered porch and windows create a striking appearance

■ Great Room features a cathedral ceiling, transom windows, and huge fireplace

■ Center-island kitchen has a lazy Susan and an ample pantry

■ Double doors access the Master Bedroom which is enhanced by a decorative boxed ceiling

■ Upstairs are three more bedrooms and a full bath

First floor — 1,570 sq. ft.
Second floor — 707 sq. ft.
Basement — 1,570 sq. ft.
Garage — 504 sq. ft.

■ Total living area 2,277 sq. ft. ■ Price Code D ■

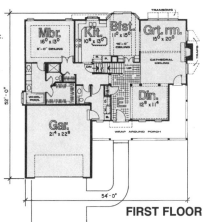

© design basics, inc.

SECOND FLOOR

FIRST FLOOR

Larger Feeling Than Square Footage Indicates

No. 96419

This plan features:

— Three bedrooms

— Two full baths

■ Arched windows, dormers, front and side porches, rear deck, and an open interior give this home a larger feeling

■ Elegant columns define the Dining Room, while the Great Room gains an open and airy feeling from the cathedral ceiling and arched window above the sliding door

■ Master Suite pampers the owner with a private bath which includes a whirlpool tub, separate shower, double vanity, linen closet, and walk-in closet

■ Please specify crawl space or basement when ordering

Main floor — 1,541 sq. ft.
Garage & Storage — 446 sq. ft.

■ Total living area 1,541 sq. ft. ■ Price Code C ■

© 1991 Donald A. Gardner Architects, Inc.

ALTERNATE PLAN
FOR BASEMENT

FLOOR PLAN

Welcoming Entry Porch

■ Total living area 1,685 sq. ft. ■ Price Code B ■

FIRST FLOOR

SECOND FLOOR

No. 94924 ⊠

■ **This plan features:**

— Three bedrooms

— Two full and one half baths

■ The entry views the formal Dining Room that is accented with a boxed window while the Great Room is beyond

■ An open Kitchen/Dinette area with a pantry, desk and a snack counter

■ The elegant Master Suite includes a formal ceiling detail and a window seat

■ The skylight above the whirlpool tub in the Master Suite provides natural illumination

■ Secondary bedrooms share a centrally located bathroom

First floor — 1,297 sq. ft.
Second floor — 388 sq. ft.
Basement — 1,297 sq. ft.
Garage — 466 sq. ft.

Spacious Family Areas

■ Total living area 1,749 sq. ft. ■ Price Code B ■

SECOND FLOOR

FIRST FLOOR

No. 93220 ⊠ ◪

■ **This plan features:**

— Three bedrooms

— Two full and one half baths

■ Two-story Foyer with landing staircase leads to formal Living and Dining Rooms

■ Open layout for Kitchen/Breakfast area and Family Room offers a spacious feeling and easy interaction

■ Efficient Kitchen with cooktop peninsula, built-in pantry and a glassed Breakfast area

■ Comfortable Family Room with a focal point fireplace and a wall of windows with access to Sundeck

■ Master Bedroom enhanced by decorative ceiling and French doors into private bath and walk-in closet

■ Two additional bedrooms, full bath, laundry closet and Bonus Room complete second floor

■ An optional basement, crawl space or slab foundation — please specify when ordering

First floor — 902 sq. ft.
Second floor — 819 sq. ft.
Finished staircase — 28 sq. ft.
Bonus room — 210 sq. ft.
Basement — 874 sq. ft.
Garage — 400 sq. ft.

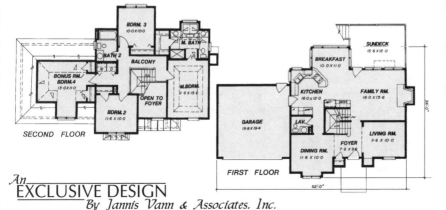

An EXCLUSIVE DESIGN
By Jannis Vann & Associates, Inc.

Exciting Three-Bedroom

© 1994 Donald A Gardner Architects, Inc.

■ *Total living area 1,787 sq. ft.* ■ *Price Code C* ■

No. 99805

This plan features:

- Three bedrooms

- Two full baths

■ A Great Room enhanced by a fireplace, cathedral ceiling and built-in bookshelves

■ A Kitchen designed for efficiency with a food preparation island and a Pantry

■ A Master Suite topped by a cathedral ceiling and pampered by a luxurious bath and a walk-in closet

■ Two additional bedrooms, one with a cathedral ceiling and a walk-in closet, sharing a skylit bath

■ A second floor Bonus Room, perfect for a study or a play area

■ An optional basement or crawl space foundation — please specify when ordering

Main floor — 1,787 sq. ft.
Garage & storage — 521 sq. ft.
Bonus room — 326 sq. ft.

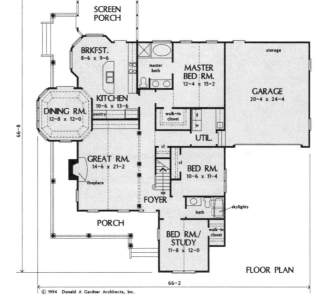

FLOOR PLAN

© 1994 Donald A Gardner Architects, Inc.

Unusual and Dramatic

■ *Total living area 3,500 sq. ft.* ■ *Price Code F* ■

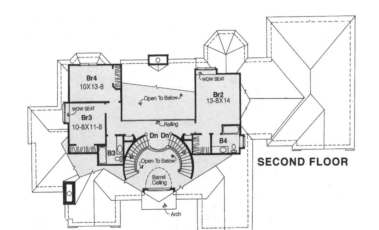

SECOND FLOOR

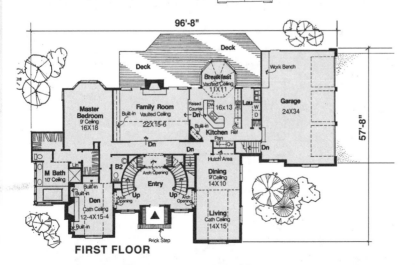

FIRST FLOOR

No. 92048

■ This plan features:

— Four bedrooms

— Three full and one half baths

■ Elegant Entry with decorative windows, arched openings and a double curved staircase

■ Cathedral ceilings crown arched windows in the Den and Living Room

■ Family Room with a vaulted ceiling and a large fireplace

■ Hub Kitchen with a work island/serving counter, Breakfast alcove and nearby Garage entry

■ Secluded Master Suite with a lovely bay window, two walk-in closets and a plush bath

■ Three second floor bedrooms, one with a private bath

First floor — 2,646 sq. ft.
Second floor — 854 sq. ft.
Basement — 2,656 sq. ft.

Classic Blend of Brick and Stucco

No. 92555

This plan features:

- Three bedrooms
- Two full baths
- Arch top windows on the front of this home combining with brick and stucco, brick quoins and dentil molding
- Foyer giving access to the formal dining room accented by columns, the Den or secondary bedrooms
- Den includes a raised ceiling and a focal point fireplace
- Kitchen and breakfast nook open into the den creating a feeling of spaciousness
- Master suite is situated to the left, rear corner and features a five piece bath and walk-in closet
- Two secondary bedrooms sharing a full bath located in the hall between the two rooms
- Rear covered porch extends the living space outdoors
- An optional slab or crawl space foundation — please specify when ordering

Main floor — 1,668 sq. ft.
Garage — 537 sq. ft.
Width — 51'-10"
Depth — 62'-10"

Total living area 1,668 sq. ft. ■ Price Code C

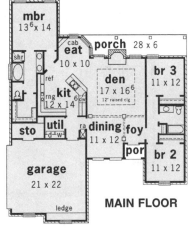

MAIN FLOOR

Farmhouse Flavor

No. 90685

Total living area 1,770 sq. ft. ■ Price Code B

This plan features:

- Three bedrooms
- Two full baths
- An octagonal stair tower
- A Foyer opening to a Living and Dining Room combination, enhanced by a striking glass wall
- A heat-circulating fireplace adding welcome warmth
- A galley-style Kitchen including a large pantry, snackbar, and laundry area
- A Master Suite with a private Deck overlooking the backyard

First floor — 1,073 sq. ft.
Second floor — 604 sq. ft.
Retreat tower — 93 sq. ft.
Garage — 428 sq. ft.

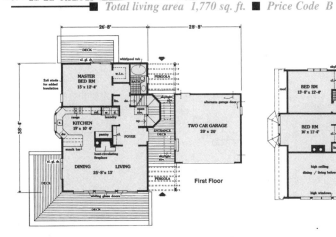

No Wasted Space

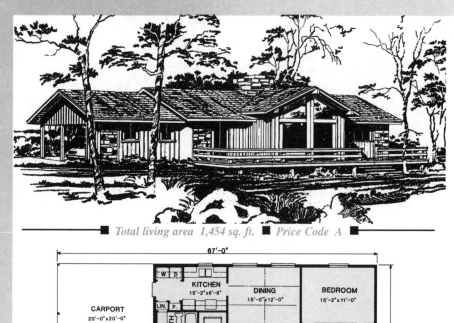

■ *Total living area 1,454 sq. ft.* ■ *Price Code A* ■

No. 90412

■ This plan features:

— Three bedrooms

— Two full baths

■ A centrally located Great Room with a cathedral ceiling, exposed wood beams, and large areas of fixed glass

■ The Living and Dining areas separated by a massive stone fireplace

■ A secluded Master Suite with a walk-in closet and private master bath

■ An efficient Kitchen with a convenient laundry area

■ An optional basement, slab or crawl space foundation — please specify when ordering

Main area — 1,454 sq. ft.

67'-0"

MAINFLOOR

CARPORT
20'-0"x20'-0"

STORAGE STORAGE

KITCHEN
15'-2"x8'-8"

W D

LIN. P.

BATH

CL.

M. BEDROOM
15'-2"x13'-6"

DINING
15'-0"x12'-0"

CATHEDRAL CEILING

LIVING
15'-0"x21'-10"

BEDROOM
15'-2"x11'-0"

BATH

CL.

CL.

BEDROOM
12'-8"x11'-0"

34'-10"

DECK

Attractive Combination of Brick and Siding

No. 24259

■ This plan features:

— Three bedrooms

— Two full baths

■ A Great Room sunny bayed area, fireplace and built-in entertainment center

■ A private Master Bedroom with luxurious master bath and walk-in closet

■ Dining Room has a Butler Pantry

■ Two additional bedrooms have use of hall full bath

Main floor — 2,010 sq. ft.
Basement — 2,010 sq. ft.

■ *Total living area 2,010 sq. ft.* ■ *Price Code C* ■

An
EXCLUSIVE DESIGN
By Energetic Enterprises

Spectacular Curving Stairway

■ *Total living area 3,172 sq. ft.* ■ *Price Code E* ■

No. 94995

■ This plan features:

— Four bedrooms

— Two full, one three-quarter and one half baths

■ Spacious formal entry with arched transom and further enhanced by curved staircase

■ Great Room is inviting with a cozy fireplace, a wetbar and triple arched windows

■ Open Kitchen, Breakfast and Hearth area combine efficiency and comfort for all

■ Master Bedroom retreat offers a private back door, a double walk-in closet and a whirlpool bath

■ Generous closets and baths enhance the three second floor bedrooms

First floor — 2,252 sq. ft.
Second floor — 920 sq. ft.
Basement — 2,252 sq. ft.
Garage — 646 sq. ft.

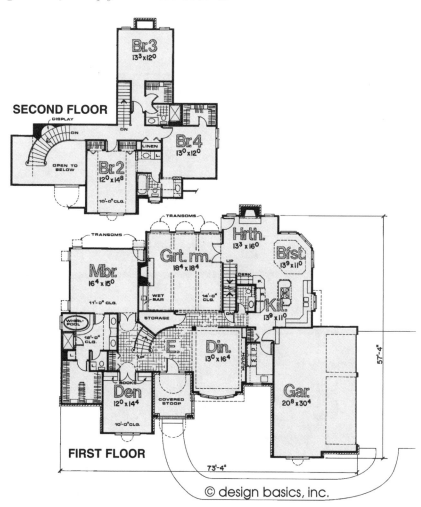

© design basics, inc.

European Classic

■ *Total living area 2,846 sq. ft.* ■ *Price Code E* ■

No. 92613

■ **This plan features:**

— Three bedrooms

— Two full and two half baths

■ Decorative stucco, keystone arches and boxed windows

■ A sloped ceiling in the Great Room accenting a wall of windows

■ An elegant formal Dining Room with a tray ceiling

■ An efficient, island Kitchen opening to the Patio through atrium doors

■ Master Bedroom Suite with a luxurious Bath, walk-in closet and a raised, corner window tub

■ A second floor with two additional bedrooms sharing a full hall bath

■ No materials list is available for this plan

First floor — 2,192 sq. ft.
Second floor — 654 sq. ft.
Bonus — 325 sq. ft.
Basement — 1,922 sq. ft.
Garage — 706 sq. ft.

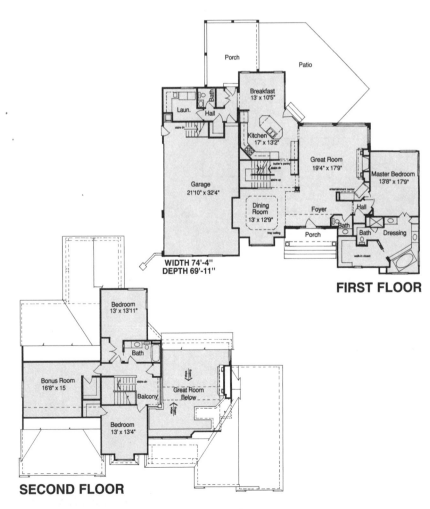

FIRST FLOOR

WIDTH 74'-4"
DEPTH 69'-11"

SECOND FLOOR

Recreation Room Houses Fireplace

No. 9964 ℞ ⚒

■ This plan features:

— Four bedrooms

— Two full baths

■ A wood-burning fireplace warming the Living/Dining Room, which is accessible to the large wooden sun deck

■ Two first-floor bedrooms with access to a full hall bath

■ Two ample-sized second floor bedrooms

■ A Recreation Room with a cozy fireplace and convenient half bath

Main floor — 906 sq. ft.
Upper floor — 456 sq. ft.
Basement — 279 sq. ft.
Lower — 594 sq. ft.

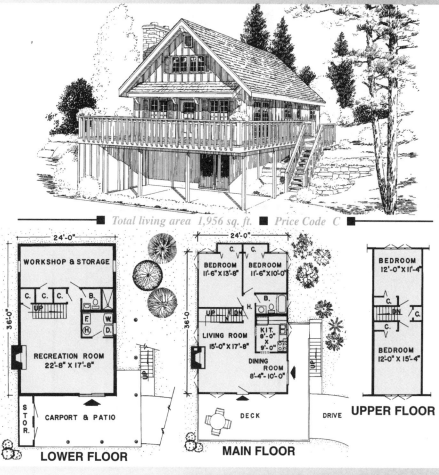

■ Total living area 1,956 sq. ft. ■ Price Code C ■

WORKSHOP & STORAGE

RECREATION ROOM 22'-8" X 17'-8"

STOR.

CARPORT & PATIO

LOWER FLOOR

BEDROOM 11'-6" X 13'-8"   **BEDROOM** 11'-6" X 10'-0"

LIVING ROOM 15'-0" X 17'-8"

KIT. 8'-0" X 9'-0"

DINING ROOM 8'-4"-10'-0"

DECK   **DRIVE**

MAIN FLOOR

BEDROOM 12'-0" X 11'-4"

BEDROOM 12'-0" X 15'-4"

UPPER FLOOR

Expandable Home

No. 34077 ⚒ 🍃

■ This plan features:

— Four bedrooms

— Three full baths

■ Front Entry into open Living Room highlighted by double window

■ Bright Dining area with sliding glass door to optional Patio

■ Compact, efficient Kitchen with peninsula serving/snackbar, laundry closet and outdoor access

■ Two first floor bedrooms with ample closet share a full bath

■ Second floor Master Bedroom and additional bedroom feature dormer windows, private baths and walk-in closets

First floor — 957 sq. ft.
Second floor — 800 sq. ft.

■ Total living area 1,757 sq. ft. ■ Price Code B ■

optional **Patio**

40'-0"

Kit 10 x 10-5

Dining 10-3 x 10-5

Br 3 11-2 x 10-5

Living Rm 17-3 x 12-7

Entry

Br 4 14-6 x 10-2

First Floor

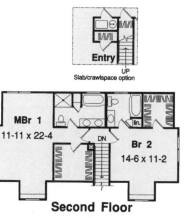

Entry

Slab/crawlspace option

MBr 1 11-11 x 22-4

Br 2 14-6 x 11-2

Second Floor

Versatile Chalet

■ *Total living area 1,360 sq. ft.* ■ *Price Code A* ■

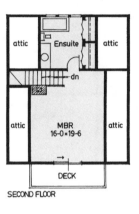

SECOND FLOOR

MAIN FLOOR

No. 90847

■ **This plan features:**

— Two bedrooms

— Two full baths

■ A Sun deck entry into a spacious Living Room/Dining Room with a fieldstone fireplace, a large window and a sliding glass door

■ A well-appointed Kitchen with extended counter space and easy access to the Dining Room and the Utility area

■ A first floor bedroom adjoins a full hall bath

■ A spacious Master Bedroom, with a private Deck, a Suite bath and plenty of storage

Main floor — 864 sq. ft.
Second floor — 496 sq. ft.
Width — 27'-0"
Depth — 32'-0"

An
EXCLUSIVE DESIGN
By Westhome Planners, Ltd.

A Home for Today's Lifestyle

■ *Total living area 2,787 sq. ft.* ■ *Price Code E* ■

MAIN FLOOR

No. 92902

■ **This plan features:**

— Four bedrooms

— Three full baths

■ Family living area comprised of a family room, breakfast area, and island kitchen

■ Formal Dining Room with easy access from the Kitchen

■ Pampering Master Suite with private Master Bath and an abundance of storage space

■ Two additional baths, have ample closet space

■ Screened porch and covered patio extending living space outdoors

■ No materials list is available for this plan

Main floor — 2,787 sq. ft.
Garage — 685 sq. ft.
Width — 78'-0"
Depth — 78'-6"

An
EXCLUSIVE DESIGN
By Kent & Kent, Inc.

Covered Porches Front and Back

© 1993 Donald A. Gardner Architects, Inc.

■ *Total living area 2,301 sq. ft.* ■ *Price Code D* ■

No. 96404

■ This plan features:

— Three bedrooms

— Two full and one half baths

■ Open floor plan plus Bonus Room, great for today's family needs

■ Two-story Foyer with palladian, clerestory window and balcony overlooking Great Room

■ Great Room with cozy fireplace provides perfect gathering place

■ Columns visually separate Great Room from Breakfast area and smart, U-shaped kitchen

■ Privately located Master Bedroom accesses Porch and luxurious Master Bath with separate shower and double vanity

First floor — 1,632 sq. ft.
Second floor — 669 sq. ft.
Bonus room — 528 sq. ft.
Garage & storage — 707 sq. ft.

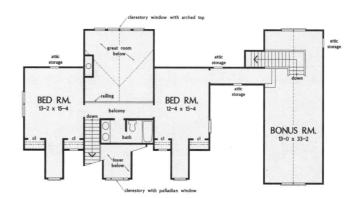

SECOND FLOOR PLAN

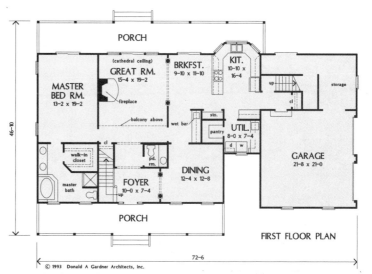

FIRST FLOOR PLAN

© 1993 Donald A Gardner Architects, Inc.

Luxury Personified

■ Total living area 2,653 sq. ft. ■ Price Code E ■

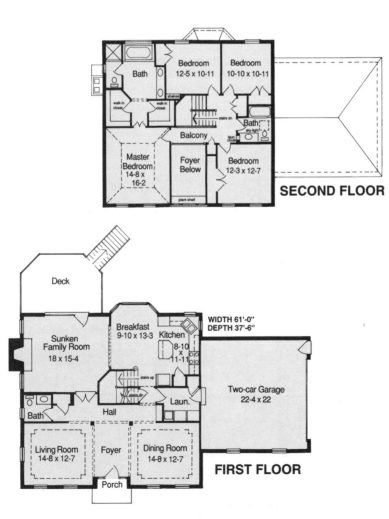

SECOND FLOOR

- Bath
- Bedroom 12-5 x 10-11
- Bedroom 10-10 x 10-11
- walk-in closet
- shelves
- walk-in closet
- stairs dn
- Bath
- Balcony
- Master Bedroom 14-8 x 16-2
- Foyer Below
- Bedroom 12-3 x 12-7
- plant shelf

FIRST FLOOR

- Deck
- Sunken Family Room 18 x 15-4
- Breakfast 9-10 x 13-3
- Kitchen 8-10 x 11-11
- WIDTH 61'-0"
- DEPTH 37'-6"
- stairs up
- Laun.
- Two-car Garage 22-4 x 22
- Bath
- Hall
- Living Room 14-8 x 12-7
- Foyer
- Dining Room 14-8 x 12-7
- Porch

No. 92623

■ This plan features:

— Four bedrooms

— Two full and one half baths

■ A tray ceiling in the formal Living Room and Dining Room with corner columns

■ An island Kitchen with a corner sink with windows to either side

■ A sunken Family Room with a cozy fireplace

■ A luxurious Master Suite with double walk-in closets, sloped ceiling and private Master Bath

■ Three additional bedrooms that share a skylit full bath with laundry chute located close by

■ A balcony overlooking the foyer with a plant shelf, arched window and skylight

■ No materials list is available for this plan

First floor — 1,365 sq. ft.
Second floor — 1,288 sq. ft.
Basement — 1,217 sq. ft.
Garage — 491 sq. ft.

A Modern Look At Colonial Styling

No. 93287

■ This plan features:

— Three bedrooms

— Two full and one half baths

■ Brick detailing and keystones highlight elevation

■ Two-story Foyer opens to formal Living and Dining rooms

■ Expansive Family Room with a hearth fireplace between built-in shelves and Deck access

■ U-shaped Kitchen with serving counter, Breakfast alcove, and nearby Garage entry

■ Elegant Master Bedroom with a decorative ceiling, large walk-in closet and a double vanity bath

■ Two additional bedrooms share a full bath, laundry and Bonus area

First floor — 987 sq. ft.
Second floor — 965 sq. ft.
Bonus — 272 sq. ft.
Finished staircase — 72 sq. ft.
Basement — 899 sq. ft.

An
EXCLUSIVE DESIGN
By Jannis Vann & Associates, Inc.

■ Total living area 2,024 sq. ft. ■ Price Code C ■

Comfortable and Relaxed Environment

No. 92639

■ This plan features:

— Three bedrooms

— Two full and one half baths

■ A covered porch and boxed window enhancing the exterior

■ An easy flow traffic pattern creating step saving convenience in the interior

■ An open stairway adding elegances to the Foyer

■ A spacious Great Room and Breakfast Area forming an area large enough for real family enjoyment

■ A U-shaped Kitchen highlighted by a corner sink and ample counter and storage space

■ A half bath and a Laundry Room rounding out the first floor

■ A Master Suite with a walk-in closet plus a compartmented bath

■ Two additional bedrooms sharing use of a bath with skylight

■ A full basement providing the option of creating expanded play area in the lower level

■ No materials list is available for this plan

First floor — 748 sq. ft.
Second floor — 705 sq. ft.
Basement — 744 sq. ft.

■ Total living area 1,453 sq. ft. ■ Price Code A ■

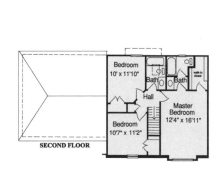

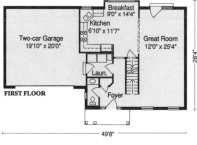

Appealing Brick Elevation

■ *Total living area 2,172 sq. ft.* ■ *Price Code C* ■

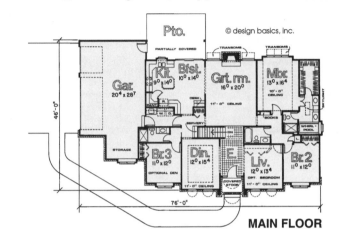

MAIN FLOOR

No. 94971

■ This plan features:

— Three bedrooms

— Two full and one three-quarter bath

■ Formal Living and Dining Room flanking the Entry

■ Impressive Great Room topped by an eleven foot ceiling and enhanced by picture windows framing the raised hearth fireplace

■ Attractive Kitchen/Dinette Area includes an island, desk, wrapping counters, a walk-in pantry and access to the covered Patio

■ Pampering Master Suite with a skylit dressing area, a walk-in closet, double vanity, a whirlpool tub and a decorative plant shelf

Main floor — 2,172 sq. ft.
Garage — 680 sq. ft.

With All the Amenities

■ *Total living area 1,884 sq. ft.* ■ *Price Code C* ■

Main floor

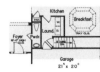

OPT. BASEMENT STAIRS LOCATION

No. 98430

■ This plan features:

— Three bedrooms

— Two full and one half baths

■ A sixteen foot high ceiling over the Foyer

■ Arched openings highlight the hallway accessing the Great Room which is further enhanced by a fireplace

■ A French door to the rear yard and decorative columns at its arched entrance

■ Another vaulted ceiling topping the dining room, convenient to both the living room and the kitchen

■ An expansive kitchen features a center work island, a built-in pantry and a breakfast area defined by a tray ceiling

■ A Master Suite also has a tray ceiling treatment and includes a lavish private bath and a huge walk-in closet

■ Secondary bedrooms have private access to a full bath

■ An optional basement, slab or crawl space foundation — please specify when ordering

Main floor — 1,884 sq. ft.
Basement — 1,908 sq. ft.
Garage — 495 sq. ft.

Moderate Ranch Has Features of a Larger Plan

■ *Total living area 1,811 sq. ft.* ■ *Price Code C* ■

No. 90441

■ This plan features:

— Three bedrooms

— Two full baths

■ A large Great Room with a vaulted ceiling and a stone fireplace with bookshelves on either side

■ A spacious Kitchen with ample cabinet space conveniently located next to the large Dining Room

■ A Master Suite having a large bath with a garden tub, double vanity and a walk-in closet

■ Two other large bedrooms, each with a walk-in closet and access to the full bath

■ An optional basement, slab or crawl space combination — please specify when ordering

Main floor — 1,811 sq. ft.

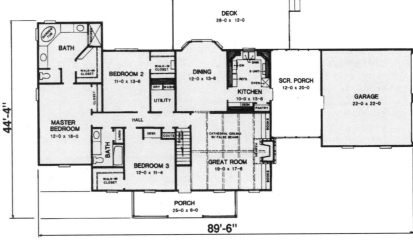

MAIN FLOOR

European Flair

■ *Total living area 1,544 sq. ft.* ■ *Price Code B* ■

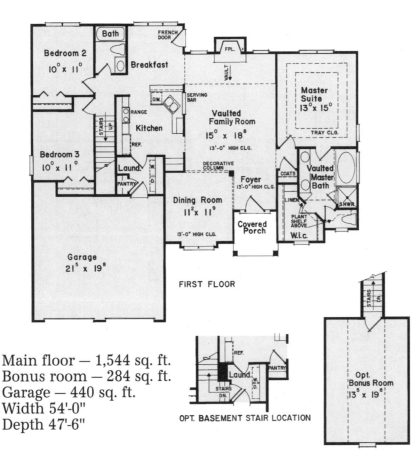

FIRST FLOOR

Main floor — 1,544 sq. ft.
Bonus room — 284 sq. ft.
Garage — 440 sq. ft.
Width 54'-0"
Depth 47'-6"

OPT. BASEMENT STAIR LOCATION

OPTIONAL BONUS ROOM

No. 98460

■ **This plan features:**

— Three bedrooms

— Two full baths

■ Large fireplace serving as an attractive focal point for the vaulted Family Room

■ Decorative column defining the elegant Dining Room

■ Kitchen including a serving bar for the Family Room and a Breakfast Area

■ Master Suite topped by a tray ceiling over the bedroom and a vaulted ceiling over the five-piece master bath

■ Optional bonus room for future expansion

■ An optional basement or crawl space foundation — please specify when ordering

■ No materials list is available for this plan

Split Bedroom Floor Plan

No. 96519

This plan features:

- Three bedrooms
- Two full baths
- A split bedroom floor plan gives the Master Bedroom ultimate privacy
- The Great room is highlighted by a fireplace and a vaulted ten foot ceiling
- A snackbar peninsula counter is one of the many conveniences of the Kitchen
- The Patio is accessed from the Dining Room and expands dining to the outdoors
- Two additional bedrooms share the full bath in the hall
- No materials list is available for this plan

Main floor — 1,243 sq. ft.
Garage — 523 sq. ft.

Total living area 1,243 sq. ft. ■ Price Code A

MAIN FLOOR

A Nest for Empty-Nesters

No. 90934

This plan features:

- Two bedrooms
- One full bath
- An economical design
- A covered sun deck adding outdoor living space
- A mudroom/laundry area inside the side door, trapping dirt before it can enter the house
- An open layout between the Living Room with fireplace, Dining Room and Kitchen

Main floor — 884 sq. ft.
Width — 34'-0"
Depth — 28'-0"

An EXCLUSIVE DESIGN
By Westhome Planners, Ltd.

Total living area 884 sq. ft. ■ Price Code A

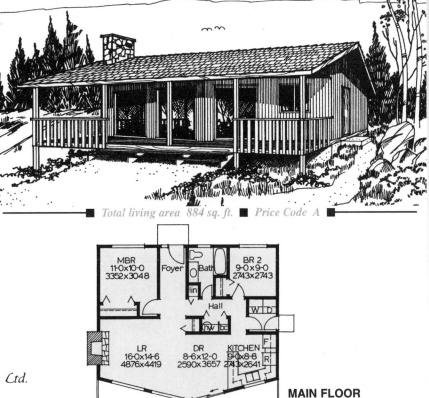

MAIN FLOOR

Compact Ranch Loaded with Living Space

No. 34328

This plan features:

— Three bedrooms

— One full bath

■ A central entrance, opening to the Living Room with ample windows

■ A Kitchen, featuring a Breakfast area with sliding doors to the backyard and an optional deck

Main area — 1,092 sq. ft.
Basement — 1,092 sq. ft.

■ Total living area 1,092 sq. ft. ■ Price Code A ■

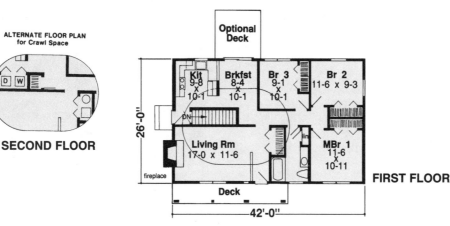

ALTERNATE FLOOR PLAN for Crawl Space

SECOND FLOOR

Optional Deck

Kit 9-8 x 10-1

Brkfst 8-4 x 10-1

Br 3 9-1 x 10-1

Br 2 11-6 x 9-3

Living Rm 17-0 x 11-6

MBr 1 11-6 x 10-11

fireplace

Deck

26'-0"

42'-0"

FIRST FLOOR

Zoned for Harmony

No. 20209

This plan features:

— Three bedrooms

— Two and one half baths

■ A lofty vaulted ceiling over the entire living level

■ A spacious, efficient Kitchen with a peninsula counter separating it from the Breakfast Room

■ A formal Living and Dining Room that efficiently flow into each other for ease in entertaining

■ A Family Room with a fireplace and built-in bookshelves

■ A Master Suite with a romantic window seat, a large walk-in closet and a lavish Master Bath

■ Two additional bedrooms, with walk-in closets, that share a full hall bath

First floor — 1,861 sq. ft.
Lower floor — 526 sq. ft.
Basement — 874 sq. ft.
Garage — 574 sq. ft.

■ Total living area 2,387 sq. ft. ■ Price Code D ■

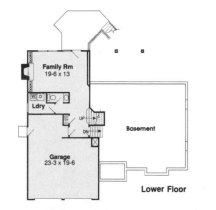

Family Rm 19-6 x 13

Ldry

Basement

Garage 23-3 x 19-6

Lower Floor

54'-0"

win. seat

MBr 14 x 15

Deck

Brkfst 9 x 9

Kitchen 11-6 x 13-6

Dining Rm 12 x 13-6

Hall

Foyer

Br 2 11 x 11-6

Br 3 12 x 11

Living Rm 20-3 x 13-6

50'-0"

Main Floor

driveway

An EXCLUSIVE DESIGN
By Karl Kreeger

Country Estate Home

■ *Total living area 3,480 sq. ft.* ■ *Price Code F* ■

No. 98508

■ This plan features:

— Four bedrooms

— Three full and one half baths

■ Formal Living and Dining rooms gracefully defined with columns and decorative windows

■ Wood plank flooring and a massive fireplace accent the Great Room

■ Hub Kitchen with brick pavers and extended serving counter

■ Private Master Bedroom offers a Private Lanai and plush dressing area

■ Three second floor bedrooms with walk-in closets and private access to a full bath

■ No materials list is available for this plan

Main floor — 2,441 sq. ft.
Upper floor — 1,039 sq. ft.
Bonus — 271 sq. ft.
Garage — 660 sq. ft.

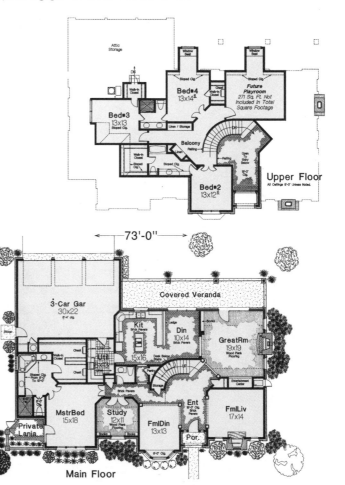

Relaxed Country Living

© 1997 Donald A. Gardner Architects, Inc.

■ *Total living area 2,027 sq. ft.* ■ *Price Code D* ■

No. 96402

■ **This plan features:**

— Three bedrooms

— Two full baths

■ Comfortable country home with deluxe Master Suite, front and back Porches and dual-sided fireplace

■ Vaulted Great Room brightened by two clerestory dormers and fireplace shared with Breakfast bay

■ Dining Room and front Bedroom/Study dressed up with tray ceilings

■ Master Bedroom features vaulted ceiling, and luxurious bath with over-sized, walk-in closet

■ Skylit Bonus Room over Garage provides extra room for family needs

Main floor — 2,027 sq. ft.
Bonus room — 340 sq. ft.
Garage & storage — 532 sq. ft.

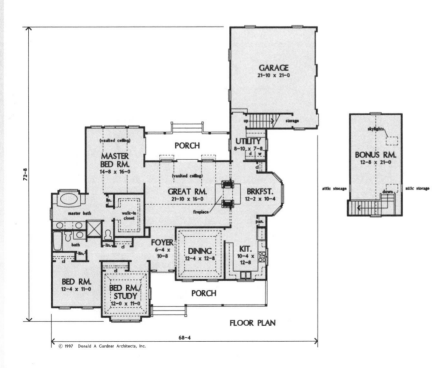

FLOOR PLAN

© 1997 Donald A Gardner Architects, Inc.

Living Room Features Vaulted Ceiling

No. 90353

This plan features:

— Three bedrooms

— Two full baths

■ A vaulted ceiling in the Living Room and the Dining Room, with a clerestory above

■ A Master Bedroom with a walk-in closet and private full bath

■ An efficient Kitchen, with a corner double sink and peninsula counter

■ A Dining Room with sliding doors to the deck

■ A Living Room with a fireplace that adds warmth to open areas

■ Two additional bedrooms that share a full hall bath

Main floor — 846 sq. ft.
Upper floor — 400 sq. ft.

■ Total living area 1,246 sq. ft. ■ Price Code A ■

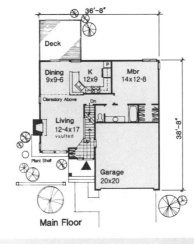

Main Floor

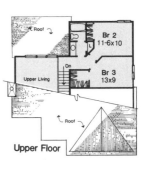

Upper Floor

European Styling

No. 90467

This plan features:

— Three bedrooms

— Two full and one half baths

■ The large foyer leads to the open Living and Dining rooms

■ A large informal area includes the Kitchen, Gathering, and Breakfast rooms

■ The Kitchen features an island bar, double sink, pantry, desk, and a wall oven

■ The home has two fireplaces, one in the Great room the other in the Gathering room

■ Decorative ceiling can be found in the Dining room, the Master suite, and the Breakfast nook

■ The Master suite features dual walk-in closets and a five piece bath

■ Two additional bedrooms share a linen closet and a full bath

■ An optional basement or a crawl space foundation — please specify when ordering

Main floor — 2,290 sq. ft.
Basement — 2,290 sq. ft.
Bonus — 304 sq. ft.
Garage — 544 sq. ft.

■ Total living area 2,290 sq. ft. ■ Price Code D ■

221

Elegant and Efficient

No. 92515

This plan features:

— Three bedrooms

— Two full baths

■ Covered entrance into the Foyer leads to a spacious Den with a decorative ceiling above a hearth fireplace and French doors to the patio area

■ Decorative window and ceiling highlight the formal Dining Room

■ Large, country Kitchen with double ovens, a cooktop and a peninsula snackbar serving the bright Breakfast area

■ Large Master Bedroom suite with a decorative ceiling, a walk-in closet and a plush bath with a double vanity and a whirlpool tub

■ Two additional bedrooms with walk-in closets share a full bath

■ This plan is available with a Slab or Crawlspace foundation — please specify when ordering

Main floor — 1,959 sq. ft.
Garage — 512 sq. ft.
Width — 65'-0"
Depth — 51'-0"

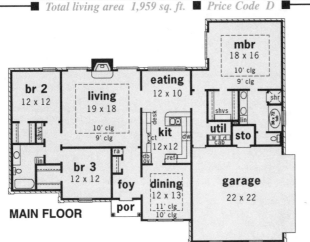

■ *Total living area 1,959 sq. ft.* ■ *Price Code D* ■

Convenient and Efficient Ranch

■ *Total living area 1,810 sq. ft.* ■ *Price Code C* ■

No. 93311

This plan features:

— Three bedrooms

— Two full and one half baths

■ A barrel vault ceiling in the Foyer

■ A stepped ceiling in both the Dinette and the formal Dining Room

■ An expansive Gathering Room with a large focal point fireplace and access to the wood deck

■ An efficient Kitchen that includes a work island and a built-in pantry

■ A luxurious Master Suite with a private bath that includes a separate tub and step-in shower

■ Two additional bedrooms that share a full hall bath

■ No materials list is available for this plan

Main floor — 1,810 sq. ft.
Garage — 528 sq. ft.

An
EXCLUSIVE DESIGN
By Patrick Morabito, A.I.A. Architect

Total living area 3,292 sq. ft. ■ *Price Code F*

No. 92209

■ This plan features:

— Four bedrooms

— Three full baths

■ Entry opens to Gallery, formal Dining and Living rooms with decorative ceilings

■ Spacious Kitchen with a work island opens to Dining alcove, Family Room and Patio beyond

■ Comfortable Family Room offers vaulted ceiling above fireplace, and a wetbar

■ Corner Master Bedroom suite enhanced by a vaulted ceiling, double vanity bath and huge walk-in closet

■ Three additional bedrooms with walk-in closets have access to full baths

■ No materials list is available for this plan

Main floor – 3,292 sq. ft.
Garage – 670 sq. ft.

Main Floor
WIDTH — 101'-1"
DEPTH — 73'-10"

Count Your Options

Total living area 2,472 sq. ft. ■ Price Code D

FIRST FLOOR PLAN

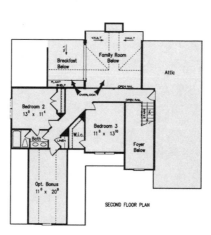

SECOND FLOOR PLAN

First floor — 1,860 sq. ft.
Second floor — 612 sq. ft.
Opt. Bonus Room — 244 sq. ft.
Basement — 1,860 sq. ft.
Garage — 460 sq. ft.

No. 97258

■ This plan features:

— Three bedrooms

— Three full baths

■ An elegant formal Dining Room accesses the covered Porch

■ The formal Living Room has the option of becoming a sitting room for the Master Suite

■ The Master Suite is topped by a tray ceiling in the bedroom and a vaulted ceiling in the bath

■ The Family Room is adorned by a vaulted ceiling

■ The Kitchen with a large pantry and center island opens into the Breakfast Room

■ An optional basement or crawl space foundation — please specify when ordering

■ No materials list is available for this plan

Beckoning Country Porch

No. 34603

This plan features:

- Three bedrooms
- Two full and one half baths
- Country styled exterior with dormer windows above friendly front Porch
- Vaulted ceiling and central fireplace accent the spacious Great Room
- L-shaped Kitchen/Dining Room with work island and atrium door to backyard
- First floor Master Suite with vaulted ceiling, walk-in closet, private bath and optional private Deck with hot tub
- Two additional bedrooms on the second floor with easy access to full bath

First floor — 1,061 sq. ft.
Second floor — 499 sq. ft.
Basement — 1,061 sq. ft.

Total living area 1,560 sq. ft. ■ *Price Code B* ■

FIRST FLOOR

Alternate Foundation Plan

SECOND FLOOR

Cathedral Ceilings Add Impact In Key Places

No. 24402

This plan features:

- Three bedrooms
- Two full baths
- A spacious Living Room with a cathedral ceiling and elegant fireplace
- A Dining Room that adjoins both the Living Room and the Kitchen
- An efficient Kitchen, with double sinks, ample cabinet space and peninsula counter that doubles as an eating bar
- A convenient hallway laundry center
- A Master Suite with a cathedral ceiling and a private Master Bath

Main area — 1,346 sq. ft.
Garage — 449 sq. ft.

Total living area 1,346 sq. ft. ■ *Price Code A* ■

MAIN FLOOR

An EXCLUSIVE DESIGN By Upright Design

Stone and Stucco Gives this House Class

■ *Total living area 4,097 sq. ft.* ■ *Price Code F* ■

LOWER FLOOR

MAIN FLOOR

No. 10540

■ **This plan features:**

— Four bedrooms

— Three full and one half baths

■ A large, majestic foyer flowing into the formal Dining Room

■ A Great Room accented by a wetbar, a stone fireplace, and access to a spacious deck

■ A spacious Kitchen highlighted by a writing area, work area, and a beamed Breakfast Room

■ A huge Master Bedroom with a dressing room and a separate whirlpool bath

■ A lower level featuring a recreation area and two additional bedrooms

Main floor — 2,473 sq. ft.
Lower floor — 1,624 sq. ft.
Basement — 732 sq. ft.
Garage & storage — 686 sq. ft.

An
EXCLUSIVE DESIGN
By Karl Kreeger

Charming Gabled Porch

■ *Total living area 1,642 sq. ft.* ■ *Price Code B* ■

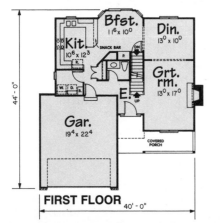

FIRST FLOOR

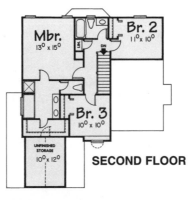

SECOND FLOOR

No. 94908

■ **This plan features:**

— Three bedrooms

— Two full and one half baths

■ Formal Dining Room expands into the Great Room for easy entertaining

■ Kitchen snackbar and Breakfast alcove provide two informal eating options

■ A corner Master Bedroom suite has a double vanity bath, a large walk-in closet and an Unfinished Storage area beyond

■ Two additional bedrooms share a full hall bath and linen closet

First floor — 862 sq. ft.
Second floor — 780 sq. ft.
Basement — 862 sq. ft.
Garage — 454 sq. ft.
Bonus — 132 sq. ft.

© design basics, inc.

■ *Total living area 3,783 sq. ft.* ■ *Price Code F* ■

No. 92237

■ This plan features:

— Four bedrooms

— Three full and one half baths

■ A stone hearth fireplace and built-in book shelves enhance the Living Room

■ Family Room with a huge fireplace, cathedral ceiling and access to Covered Veranda

■ Spacious Kitchen with cooktop island/snackbar, built-in pantry and Breakfast Room

■ Master Bedroom with a pullman ceiling, sitting area, private Covered Patio, two walk-in closets and a whirlpool tub

■ No materials list is available for this plan

Lower level — 2,804 sq. ft.
Upper level — 979 sq. ft.
Basement — 2,804 sq. ft.
Garage — 802 sq. ft.

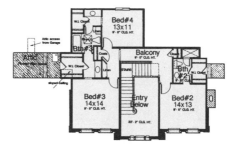

Upper Level

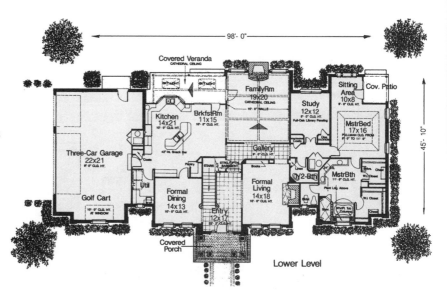

Lower Level

Columns Punctuate the Interior Space

© 1997 Donald A Gardner Architects, Inc.

B. NATHAN

■ *Total living area 2,188 sq. ft.* ■ *Price Code D* ■

No. 99801

■ **This plan features:**

— Three bedrooms

— Two full and one half baths

■ A two-story Great Room and Foyer, both with dormer windows

■ Large Kitchen, featuring a center cooking island with counter and large Breakfast Area

■ Columns punctuate interior spaces

■ Master Bedroom suite, privately situated on the first floor, has a double vanity, garden tub and separate shower

First floor — 1,618 sq. ft.
Second floor — 570 sq. ft.
Bonus room — 495 sq. ft.
Garage & storage — 649 sq. ft.

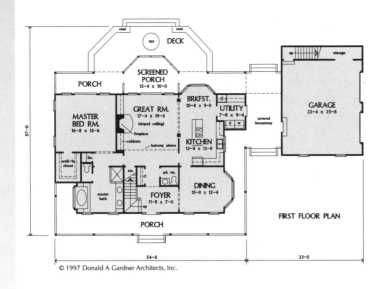

© 1997 Donald A Gardner Architects, Inc.

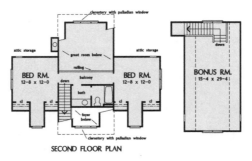

SECOND FLOOR PLAN

Compact Country Cottage

No. 99856

■ **This plan features:**

— Three bedrooms

— Two full baths

■ Foyer opening to a large Great Room with a fireplace and a cathedral ceiling

■ Efficient U-shaped Kitchen with peninsula counter extending work space and separating it from the Dining Room

■ Two front bedrooms, one with a bay window, the other with a walk-in closet, sharing a full bath in the hall

■ Master Suite located to the rear with a walk-in closet and a private bath with a double vanity

■ Partially covered Deck with skylights accessible from the Dining Room, Great Room and the Master Bedroom

Main floor — 1,310 sq. ft.
Garage & storage — 455 sq. ft.

■ *Total living area 1,310 sq. ft.* ■ *Price Code B* ■

Two-Story Charmer

No. 99112

■ **This plan features:**

— Three bedrooms

— Two full and one half baths

■ Covered front Porch and vaulted entry provide a warm welcome

■ Living Room has a vaulted ceiling and a corner fireplace

■ The Dining Doom has sliding doors to the backyard

■ The U-shaped Kitchen features a pantry, serving bar and a double sink

■ The first floor Master Suite spans the width of the home and includes a private bath

■ Upstairs find two bedrooms, one with a massive closet and a full bath

■ No materials list is available for this plan

First floor — 1,498 sq. ft.
Second floor — 626 sq. ft.
Basement — 1,485 sq. ft.

■ *Total living area 2,124 sq. ft.* ■ *Price Code C* ■

SECOND FLOOR PLAN

MAIN FLOOR PLAN

For the Young at Heart

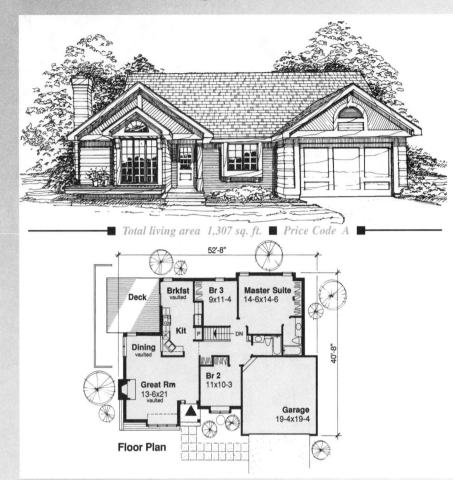

Total living area 1,307 sq. ft. ■ *Price Code A*

Floor Plan

52'-8"

Deck

Brkfst vaulted

Br 3 9x11-4

Master Suite 14-6x14-6

Kit

P   DN

Dining vaulted

40'-8"

Great Rm 13-6x21 vaulted

Br 2 11x10-3

Garage 19-4x19-4

No. 99324

■ This plan features:

— Three bedrooms

— Two full baths

■ Half-round transom windows, divided-light windows, bay windows and a covered entry porch

■ A Great Room with a vaulted ceiling, a fireplace and a transom window

■ A Kitchen with a vaulted ceiling and a Breakfast area with sliding doors to the deck

■ A Master Suite with ample closet space and a private full Master Bath

Main floor — 1,307 sq. ft.
Basement — 1,307 sq. ft.
Garage — 374 sq. ft.

Abundance of Windows for Natural Lighting

Total living area 1,931 sq. ft. ■ *Price Code C*

No. 94902

■ This plan features:

— Four bedrooms

— Two full and one half baths

■ Interesting staircase with landing in volume Entry

■ Ten foot ceiling above transom windows and hearth fireplace accent the Great Room

■ Island counter/snackbar, pantry and desk featured in Kitchen/Breakfast area

■ Kitchen conveniently accesses laundry area and Garage

■ Beautiful arched window under volume ceiling in Bedroom two

■ Master Bedroom suite features decorative ceiling to walk-in closets and double vanity bath with a whirlpool tub

■ Two additional bedrooms with ample closets share a full bath

First floor — 944 sq. ft.
Second floor — 987 sq. ft.
Basement — 944 sq. ft.
Garage — 557 sq. ft.

TRANSOMS

Bfst. 12⁰x13⁰

Kit. 12⁰x11⁰

DESK

SNACK BAR

Grt. rm. 14⁰x18⁰

10'-0" CEILING

PANT.

STORAGE

42'-0"

UP

E

Din. 11⁰x12⁰

Gar. 20⁸x28⁰

TRANSOMS

TRANS.

COVERED PORCH

54'-0"

FIRST FLOOR

Br3 10⁰x11⁰

Br4 10⁰x11⁰

DN

OPEN TO BELOW

LIN.

Mbr. 14⁸x13⁵

9'-0" CEILING

Br2 11⁰x11³ 10'-0" CEILING

10'-0" CEILING

TRANSOM

SECOND FLOOR

■ Total living area 2,759 sq. ft. ■ Price Code E ■

No. 90443

■ This plan features:

— Three bedrooms

— Three full and two half baths

■ A Master Suite with two closets and bath with separate shower, corner tub and dual vanity

■ A large Dining Room with a bay window, adjacent to the Kitchen

■ A formal Living Room for entertaining and a cozy Family Room with fireplace

■ Two upstairs bedrooms with walk-in closets and private baths

■ A Bonus Room to allow the house to grow with your needs

■ An optional basement or crawl space foundation — please specify when ordering

First floor — 1,927 sq. ft.
Second floor — 832 sq. ft.
Bonus room — 624 sq. ft.
Basement — 1,674 sq. ft.

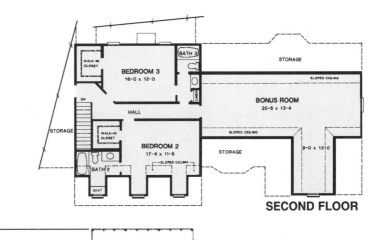

SECOND FLOOR

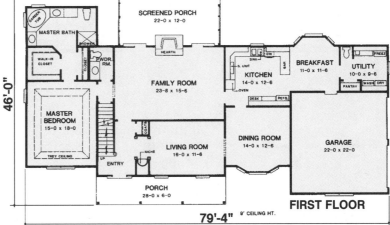

FIRST FLOOR

For the Discriminating Buyer

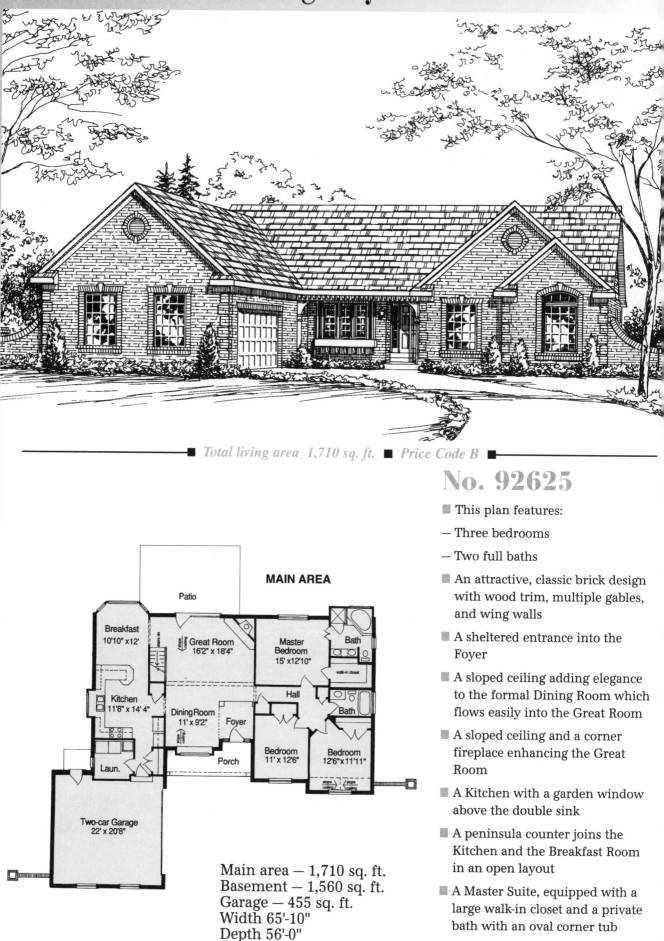

■ *Total living area 1,710 sq. ft.* ■ *Price Code B* ■

MAIN AREA

Patio

Breakfast
10'10" x12'

Great Room
16'2" x 18'4"

Master
Bedroom
15' x12'10"

Bath

walk-in closet

Kitchen
11'8" x 14' 4"

Dining Room
11' x 9'2"

Foyer

Hall

Bath

Laun.

Porch

Bedroom
11' x 12'6"

Bedroom
12'6"x11'11"

slope ceiling / slope ceiling

Two-car Garage
22' x 20'8"

Main area — 1,710 sq. ft.
Basement — 1,560 sq. ft.
Garage — 455 sq. ft.
Width 65'-10"
Depth 56'-0"

No. 92625

■ This plan features:

— Three bedrooms

— Two full baths

■ An attractive, classic brick design with wood trim, multiple gables, and wing walls

■ A sheltered entrance into the Foyer

■ A sloped ceiling adding elegance to the formal Dining Room which flows easily into the Great Room

■ A sloped ceiling and a corner fireplace enhancing the Great Room

■ A Kitchen with a garden window above the double sink

■ A peninsula counter joins the Kitchen and the Breakfast Room in an open layout

■ A Master Suite, equipped with a large walk-in closet and a private bath with an oval corner tub

■ No materials list is available for this plan

Wonderful One Level Living

No. 93193

■ This plan features:

– Three bedrooms

– Two full and one half baths

■ Charming front porch accesses easy-care Entry with archway to Dining Room

■ Central Great Room enhanced by a cathedral ceiling over a cozy fireplace set in a wall of windows

■ Large and convenient Kitchen with work island/snackbar, eating Nook with sliding glass door to back yard, and nearby Laundry/Garage entry

■ Corner Master Bedroom features a walk-in closet and plush bath with a double vanity and spa tub

■ Two additional bedrooms with ample closets and double windows, share a full bath

■ No materials list is available for this plan

Main floor — 1,802 sq. ft.
Basement — 1,802 sq. ft.

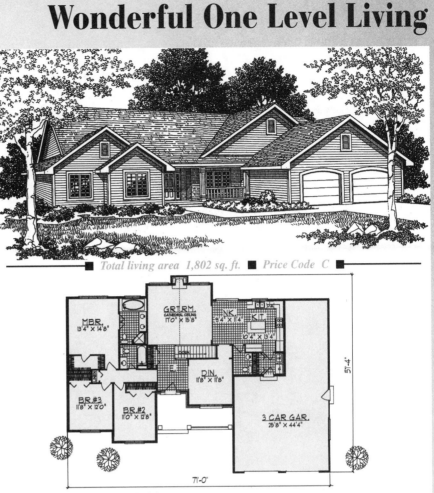

Total living area 1,802 sq. ft. ■ Price Code C ■

MAIN FLOOR PLAN

Warm and Inviting

No. 92528

■ This plan features:

– Three bedrooms

– Two full baths

■ A Den with a cozy fireplace and vaulted ceiling

■ A well-equipped Kitchen with a windowed double sink and built-in pantry

■ A spacious Master Bedroom with a private Master Bath and walk-in closet

■ Additional bedrooms sharing full hall bath

■ An optional slab or crawlspace foundation — please specify when ordering

Main floor — 1,363 sq. ft.
Garage — 434 sq. ft.

Total living area 1,363 sq. ft. ■ Price Code B ■

MAIN FLOOR

Beautiful Stucco & Stone

Total living area 1,913 sq. ft. ■ Price Code C

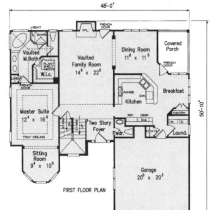

FIRST FLOOR PLAN

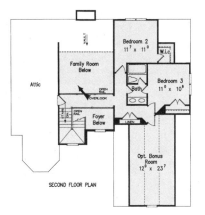

SECOND FLOOR PLAN

No. 98445

■ **This plan features:**

— Three bedrooms

— Two full and one half baths

■ This home is accented by keystone arches and a turret styled roof

■ The two-story Foyer includes a half bath

■ The vaulted Family Room is highlighted by a fireplace and French doors to the rear yard

■ The Dining Room adjoins the Family Room which has access to the covered porch and the Kitchen

■ The Master Bedroom is crowned by a tray ceiling, while Master Bath has a vaulted ceiling

■ Two additional bedrooms share a full double vanity bath

■ A Balcony overlooks the Family Room and Foyer below

■ An basement, slab or crawl space foundation — please specify when ordering

■ No materials list is available for this plan

First floor — 1,398 sq. ft.
Second floor — 515 sq. ft.
Basement — 1,398 sq. ft.
Garage — 421 sq. ft.
Bonus — 282 sq. ft.

For the Growing Family

Total living area 1,862 sq. ft. ■ Price Code C

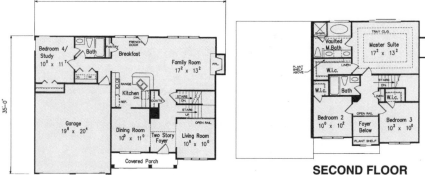

FIRST FLOOR

SECOND FLOOR

No. 98473

■ **This plan features:**

— Three bedrooms

— Three full baths

■ Formal areas are located to either side of the impressive two-story Foyer

■ An open rail staircase adorning the living room while the Dining Room features easy access to the Kitchen

■ Kitchen equipped with a corner double sink and a wrap-around snack bar is open to the Family Room and Breakfast Area

■ Fireplace in the Family Room giving warmth and atmosphere to living space

■ Secondary bedroom or study privately located in the left rear corner of the home with direct access to a full bath

■ Master Suite decorated by a tray ceiling in the bedroom and a vaulted ceiling in the master bath

■ No materials list is available for this plan

■ An optional basement or crawl space foundation — please specify when ordering

First floor — 1,103 sq. ft.
Second floor — 759 sq. ft.
Basement — 1,103 sq. ft.
Garage — 420 sq. ft.

© 1997 Donald A. Gardner Architects, Inc.

■ *Total living area 1,903 sq. ft.* ■ *Price Code D* ■

No. 96405

■ **This plan features:**

— Four bedrooms

— Two full baths

■ This home combines Victorian charm with today's lifestyle needs

■ Ceilings vaulted in Great Room and ten feet height in Foyer, Dining Room, Kitchen/Breakfast bay and Bedroom/Study

■ Secluded Master Bedroom suite features tray ceiling, walk-in closet and private, skylit bath

■ Two additional bedrooms, located in separate wing, share a full bath

■ Front and rear Porches extend living area outdoors

Main floor — 1,903 sq. ft.
Garage & storage — 531 sq. ft.

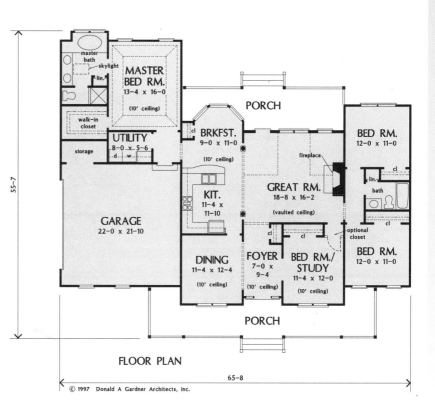

FLOOR PLAN

© 1997 Donald A Gardner Architects, Inc.

Country Porch Topped by Dormer

■ *Total living area 1,470 sq. ft.* ■ *Price Code A* ■

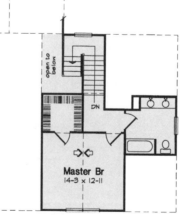

SECOND FLOOR

open to below

DN

Master Br
14-3 x 12-11

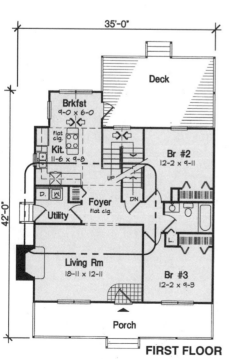

35'-0"

Deck

Brkfst
9-0 x 6-0

flat clg.

Kit.
11-6 x 9-8

Foyer
flat clg.

Utility

UP

DN

D.

W

Living Rm
18-11 x 12-11

Br #2
12-2 x 9-11

Br #3
12-2 x 9-3

42'-0"

Porch

FIRST FLOOR

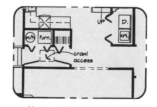

crawl access

UP

D.

W

furn.

Alternate Foundation Plan

No. 24706

■ **This plan features:**

— Three bedrooms

— Two full baths

■ Front Porch leads into tiled entry and spacious Living Room with focal point fireplace

■ Side entrance leads into Utility Room and central Foyer with a landing staircase

■ Kitchen with cooktop island, and a bright Breakfast area

■ Second floor Master Bedroom offers dormer window, vaulted ceiling, walk-in closet and double vanity bath

■ Two additional bedrooms with ample closets, share a full bath

First floor — 1,035 sq. ft.
Second floor — 435 sq. ft.
Basement — 1,018 sq. ft.

Clever Use of Interior Space

No. 99844 ⚒

This plan features:

- Three bedrooms
- Two full baths
- Efficient interior with cathedral and tray ceilings create feeling of space
- Great Room boasts cathedral ceiling above cozy fireplace, built-in shelves and columns
- Octagon Dining Room and Breakfast alcove bathed in light and easily access Porch
- Open Kitchen features island counter sink and pantry
- Master Bedroom suite enhance by tray ceiling and plush bath

Main floor — 1,737 sq. ft.
Garage & storage — 517 sq. ft.

© 1994 Donald A. Gardner Architects, Inc.

■ Total living area 1,737 sq. ft. ■ Price Code C ■

FLOOR PLAN

Impressive Entry

No. 98812 ⚒

This plan features:

- Three bedrooms
- Two full and one half baths
- High arched entry as a prelude to impressive floor plan
- Living Room topped by a vaulted ceiling and enhanced by a gas fireplace
- Dining Room topped by a vaulted ceiling adjoins the living room to create a large living space
- Pocket doors opening to the Kitchen/Nook area from the Dining Room
- A work island and a walk-in pantry add to the convenience and efficiency of the Kitchen
- An attractive French door accesses the covered patio from Nook area
- Family Room contains another gas fireplace
- Master Suite includes a whirlpool bath and a separate shower
- Two additional bedrooms share the full bath in the hall

First floor — 1,212 sq. ft.
Second floor — 922 sq. ft.
Basement — 1,199 sq. ft.
Garage — 464 sq. ft.

■ Total living area 2,134 sq. ft. ■ Price Code C ■

FIRST FLOOR

SECOND FLOOR

237

Stunning First Impression

Total living area 2,464 sq. ft. ■ **Price Code D**

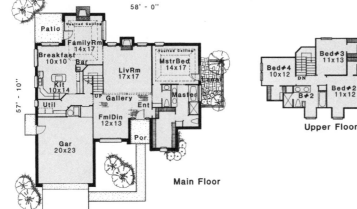

58' - 0"

Patio
Vaulted Ceiling
FamilyRm 14x17
Breakfast 10x10
Bar
Kit 10x14
Util
LivRm 17x17
MstrBed 14x17
Master
UP Gallery
Ent
FmlDin 12x13
Por
Gar 20x23

57' - 10"

Main Floor

Bed#4 10x12
DN
Bed#3 11x13
B#2
Bed#2 11x12

Upper Floor

No. 98540

■ **This plan features:**

— Four bedrooms

— Two full and one half baths

■ Dormer windows on the second floor, arched windows and entrance, brick quoin corners come together for a stunning first impression

■ Large Living Room with a fireplace and an open formal Dining Area

■ Family Room at the rear of home containing a bar

■ Huge island Kitchen with a Breakfast area and plenty of work and storage space

■ Luxurious Master Suite occupying an entire wing of the home and providing a quiet retreat

■ Three additional bedrooms on the second floor sharing a large bath

■ No materials list is available for this plan

First floor — 1,805 sq. ft.
Second floor — 659 sq. ft.
Basement — 1,800 sq. ft.
Garage — 440 sq. ft

Celebrate the Outdoors

© 1990 Donald A. Gardner Architects, Inc.

Total living area 2,218 sq. ft. ■ **Price Code D**

seat
DECK
spa
seat
skylights
SUN RM. 16-2 x 8-10
GREAT RM. 15-4 x 21-0 (cathedral ceiling)
fireplace pass-thru
balcony above
walk-in closet
master bath
MASTER BED RM. 12-8 x 16-4
FOYER 11-10 x 7-2 (sloped ceiling)
BRKFST. 9-10 x 9-10
UTILITY 8-0 x 7-10
KITCHEN 12-8 x 13-0
DINING 14-8 x 12-8
PORCH
FIRST FLOOR PLAN
55-0
© 1992 Donald A Gardner Architects, Inc.

clerestory window with arched top
(cathedral ceiling)
great room below
attic storage
railing
attic storage
BED RM. 12-8 x 12-0
balcony
BED RM. 12-8 x 12-0
down
bath
foyer below
clerestory with palladian window

SECOND FLOOR PLAN

No. 96423 ⚒

■ **This plan features:**

— Three bedrooms

— Two full and one half baths

■ Country classic celebrating the outdoors with a wrap-around Porch, Sun Room and spacious rear Deck

■ Palladian window in front, a grand arched window in the rear and skylights in the Sun Room letting the sun shine in

■ Second floor balcony overlooking the generous Great Room with a cathedral ceiling and clerestory

■ Large country Kitchen with a pass-through to the Great Room and a center island for easy food preparation

■ Private Master Suite with access to the Sun Room through a luxurious master bath

■ An optional basement or crawl space foundation — please specify when ordering

First floor — 1,651 sq. ft.
Second floor — 567 sq. ft.

Grand Columned Entrance

■ *Total living area 3,335 sq. ft.* ■ *Price Code F* ■

No. 92219

■ This plan features:

- Four bedrooms

- Two full, one three-quarter and one half baths

■ Entry hall with a graceful landing staircase, flanked by formal areas

■ Fireplaces highlight the Living Room/Parlor and Dining Room

■ Kitchen with an island cooktop, built-in pantry and Breakfast area

■ Cathedral ceiling crowns Family Room and is accented by a fireplace

■ Lavish Master Bedroom wing with plenty of storage space

■ Three bedrooms, one with a private bath

■ No materials list available

Main floor — 2,432 sq. ft.
Upper floor — 903 sq. ft.
Basement — 2,432 sq. ft.
Garage — 742 sq. ft.

Upper Floor

Main Floor

Small, But Not Lacking

■ *Total living area 1,546 sq. ft.* ■ *Price Code C* ■

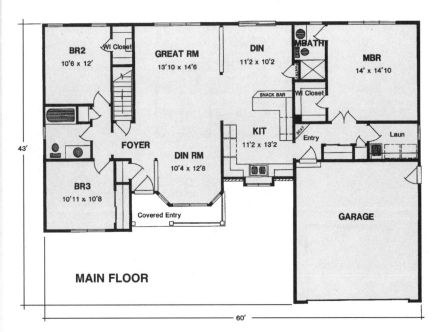

MAIN FLOOR

No. 94116

■ **This plan features:**

— Three bedrooms

— One full and one three-quarter baths

■ Great Room adjoining the Dining Room for ease in entertaining

■ Kitchen highlighted by a peninsula counter/snack bar extending work space and offering convenience in serving informal meals or snacks

■ Split bedroom plan allowing privacy for the Master Bedroom with a private bath and a walk-in closet

■ Two additional bedrooms sharing the full family bath in the hall

■ Garage entry convenient to the kitchen

Main floor — 1,546 sq. ft.
Garage — 440 sq. ft.
Basement — 1,530 sq. ft.

Classic Style and Comfort

No. 94105

This plan features:

— Three bedrooms

— Two full and one half bath

■ Covered Entry into two-story Foyer with a dramatic landing staircase brightened by decorative window

■ Spacious Living/Dining Room combination with hearth fireplace and decorative windows

■ Hub Kitchen with built-in pantry and informal Dining area with sliding glass door to rear yard

■ First floor Master Bedroom offers a walk-in closet, dressing area and full bath

■ Two additional bedrooms on second floor share a full bath

■ No materials list is available for this plan

First floor — 1,281 sq. ft.
Second floor — 511 sq. ft.
Garage — 481 sq. ft.
Basement — 1,281 sq. ft.
Width — 58'-0"
Depth — 44'-0"

Total living area 1,792 sq. ft. ■ *Price Code B*

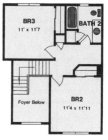

FIRST FLOOR

SECOND FLOOR

Elegant Brick Exterior

No. 92557

This plan features:

— Three bedrooms

— Two full baths

■ Detailing and accenting columns highlight the covered front porch

■ Den is enhanced by a corner fireplace and adjoins with Dining Room

■ Efficient Kitchen is well-appointed and has easy access to the utility/laundry room

■ Master Bedroom is topped by a vaulted ceiling and pampered by a private bath and a walk-in closet

■ Two secondary bedrooms are located at the opposite end of home share a full bath located between the two rooms

■ An optional slab or crawl space foundation — please specify when ordering

Main floor — 1,390 sq. ft.
Garage — 590 sq. ft.
Width — 67'-4"
Depth — 32'-10"

Total living area 1,390 sq. ft. ■ *Price Code B*

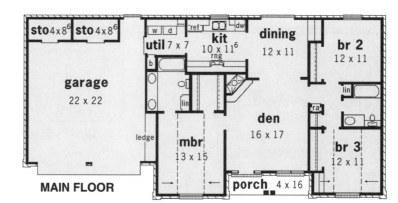

MAIN FLOOR

Affordable Living

Total living area 984 sq. ft. ■ **Price Code A**

Optional Basement Plan

Kitchen 8-0 x 8-3

Mstr. Br. 13-7 x 11-8

Kitchen 8-0 x 8-3

Dining 8-10 x 8-3

Covered Patio

Br 2 9-8 x 11-8

Br 3 11-0 x 10-2

Living Rm 15-8 x 11-7

Garage 13-9 x 19-5

54'-0"

28'-0"

Main Floor Plan # 24303

No. 24303

This plan features:
— Three bedrooms
— Two full baths
■ A simple, yet gracefully designed exterior
■ A sheltered entrance into a roomy Living Room graced with a large front window
■ A formal Dining Room flowing from the Living Room, allowing for ease in entertaining
■ A well-appointed U-shaped Kitchen with double sinks and adequate storage
■ A Master Bedroom equipped with a full Bath
■ Two additional bedrooms that share a full hall bath complete with a convenient laundry center
■ A covered Patio, tucked behind the garage, perfect for a cook out or picnic

Main area — 984 sq. ft.
Basement — 960 sq. ft.
Garage — 280 sq. ft.
Opt. 2-car Garage — 400 sq. ft.

An EXCLUSIVE DESIGN *By Marshall Associates*

First Floor Master Suite is Special

Total living area 1,973 sq. ft. ■ **Price Code C**

No. 90624

This plan features:
— Three bedrooms
— Two and one half baths
■ Access to the terrace or Garage through the Family Room
■ A heat-circulating fireplace
■ A Master Suite with vaulted ceilings and spectacular windows

First floor — 1,360 sq. ft.
Second floor — 613 sq. ft.
Basement — 1,340 sq. ft.
Garage — 462 sq. ft.

TERRACE

DINING RM 14'-4" x 11'-6"

KITCHEN 13'-4"x8'-10"

FAMILY RM 14'-0" x 13'-4"

MASTER SUITE 21'-0" x 13'-0"

LIVING RM 19'-0" x 13'-4"

TWO CAR GARAGE 21'-4" x 20'-4"

FOYER

PORTICO

32'-4"

75'-0"

FIRST FLOOR

BED RM 3 12'-8" x 10'-0"

BED RM 2 15'-8" x 14'-0"

HALL

STORAGE

SECOND FLOOR

■ *Total living area 1,388 sq. ft.* ■ *Price Code A* ■

No. 93279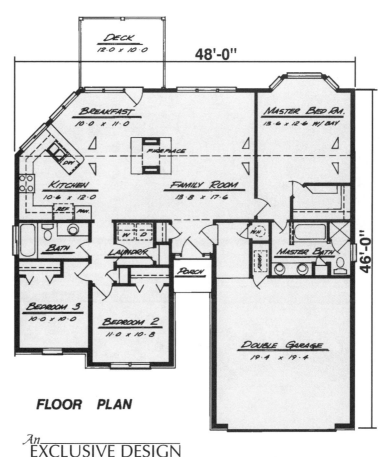

■ This plan features:

— Three bedrooms

— Two full baths

■ A central, double fireplace adding warmth and atmosphere to the Family Room, Kitchen and the Breakfast area

■ An efficient Kitchen highlighted by a peninsula counter that doubles as a snack bar

■ A Master Suite that includes a walk-in closet, a double vanity, separate shower and tub in the bath

■ Two additional bedrooms sharing a full hall bath

■ A wooden Deck that can be accessed from the Breakfast Area

■ An optional crawl space or slab foundation — please specify when ordering

Main floor — 1,388 sq. ft.
Garage — 400 sq. ft.

FLOOR PLAN

An EXCLUSIVE DESIGN
By Jannis Vann & Associates, Inc.

DECK
12·0 x 10·0

48'-0"

BREAKFAST
10·0 x 11·0

MASTER BED RM.
13·6 x 12·6 W/ BAY

FIREPLACE

KITCHEN
10·6 x 12·0

FAMILY ROOM
13·8 x 17·6

REF. PAN.

W D

BATH

LAUNDRY

PORCH

MASTER BATH

46'-0"

BEDROOM 3
10·0 x 10·0

BEDROOM 2
11·0 x 10·8

DOUBLE GARAGE
19·4 x 19·4

Southern Hospitality

■ *Total living area 1,830 sq. ft.* ■ *Price Code C* ■

No. 92220

■ **This plan features:**

— Three bedrooms

— Two full baths

■ Covered Veranda catches breezes

■ Tiled Entry leads into Great Room with fieldstone fireplace, a cathedral ceiling and atrium door to another Covered Veranda

■ A bright Kitchen/Dining Room includes a stovetop island/ snackbar, built-in pantry and desk

■ Vaulted ceiling crowns Master Bedroom that offers a plush bath and huge walk-in closet

■ Two additional bedrooms with ample closets share a double vanity bath

■ No materials list is available for this plan

Main floor — 1,830 sq. ft.
Garage — 759 sq. ft.

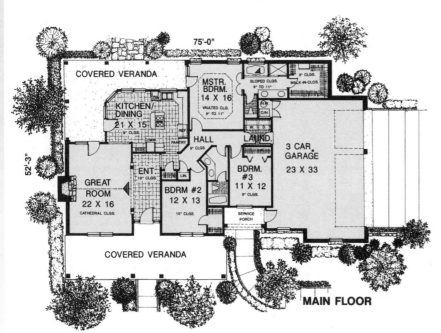

MAIN FLOOR

A Hint of Victorian Nostalgia

No. 90909

This plan features:

— Three bedrooms

— Two full and one half baths

A classic center stairwell

A Kitchen with full bay window and built-in eating table

A spacious Master Suite including a large walk-in closet and full bath

Main floor — 1,206 sq. ft.
Second floor — 969 sq. ft.
Garage — 471 sq. ft.
Basement — 1,206 sq. ft.
Width — 61'-0"
Depth — 44'-0"

An EXCLUSIVE DESIGN
By Westhome Planners, Ltd.

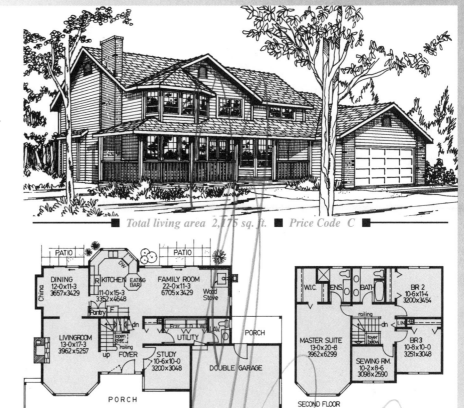

■ Total living area 2,175 sq. ft. ■ Price Code C ■

Style and Convenience

No. 92283

This plan features:

— Three bedrooms

— Two full baths

A sheltered Porch leads into an easy-care tile Entry

Spacious Living Room offers a cozy fireplace, triple window and access to Patio

An efficient Kitchen with a skylight, work island, Dining area, walk-in pantry and Utility/Garage entry

Secluded Master Bedroom highlighted by a vaulted ceiling, access to Patio and a lavish bath

Two additional bedrooms, one with a cathedral ceiling, share a full bath

No materials list is available for this plan

Main floor — 1,653 sq. ft.
Garage — 420 sq. ft.

■ Total living area 1,653 sq. ft. ■ Price Code B ■

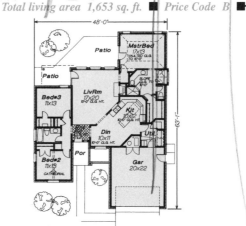

Main Floor

A Lovely Small Home

■ Total living area 1,402 sq. ft. ■ Price Code A ■

WIDTH 59–10

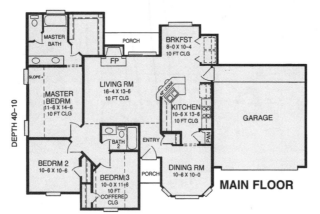

MAIN FLOOR

No. 93026

■ **This plan features:**

— Three bedrooms

— Two full baths

■ A large Living Room with a ten foot ceiling

■ A Dining Room with a distinctive bay window

■ A Breakfast Room located off the Kitchen

■ A Kitchen with an angled eating bar to open that opens the room to the Living Room

■ A Master Suite with ten foot ceiling and his-n-her vanities, a combination whirlpool tub and shower, plus a huge walk-in closet

■ Two additional bedrooms that share a full bath

■ No materials list is available for this plan

Main area — 1,402 sq. ft.
Garage — 437 sq. ft.

An Established Feeling

■ Total living area 2,495 sq. ft. ■ Price Code D ■

No. 93337

■ **This plan features:**

— Four bedrooms

— Two full and one half baths

■ A sheltered entrance with an attractive doorway using side lights and an arched window above the door

■ A Foyer graces a staircase with a wooden railing and rounded step

■ A formal Living Room using a tray ceiling treatment and pocket doors as accents

■ A half wall separating the Family Room form the informal Dining area

■ An island Kitchen, with a built-in pantry and ample storage, that efficiently serves both the formal and informal eating areas

■ A stepped ceiling topping the first floor Master Suite

■ Three additional bedrooms and a full bath on the second floor

■ No materials list is available for this plan

First floor — 1,788 sq. ft.
Second floor — 707 sq. ft.

FIRST FLOOR

SECOND FLOOR

An
EXCLUSIVE DESIGN
By Patrick Morabito, A.I.A. Architect

Mind Your Manor

■ Total living area 3,381 sq. ft. ■ Price Code F ■

No. 98514

■ **This plan features:**

— Five bedrooms

— Two full, one three-quarter and one half baths

■ The Entry/Gallery features a grand spiral staircase

■ The Study has built-in bookcases

■ Formal Living and Dining rooms each have palladian windows

■ The large Family Room has a fireplace

■ The first floor Master Bedroom contains a luxurious bath with a cathedral ceiling

■ An optional slab or crawl space foundation — please specify when ordering

■ No materials list is available for this plan

Main floor — 2,208 sq. ft.
Upper floor — 1,173 sq. ft.
Bonus — 224 sq. ft.
Garage — 520 sq. ft.

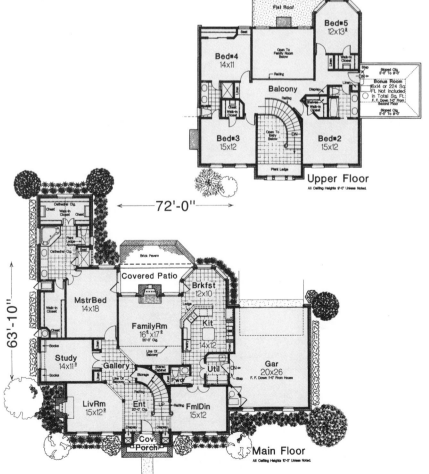

Main Floor

Traditional Ranch has Many Modern Features

■ Total living area 2,301 sq. ft. ■ Price Code D ■

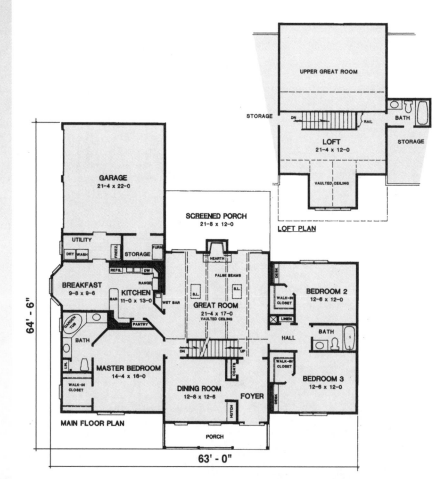

GARAGE
21-4 x 22-0

SCREENED PORCH
21-8 x 12-0

UTILITY

DRY | WASH

STORAGE | FURN.

FREEZ.

BREAKFAST
9-8 x 9-6

REFG. | DW

RANGE

KITCHEN
11-0 x 13-0

BAR

WET BAR

HEARTH

FALSE BEAMS

B.I. | B.I.

GREAT ROOM
21-4 x 17-0
VAULTED CEILING

DESK

WALK-IN CLOSET

BEDROOM 2
12-6 x 12-0

LINEN

HALL

BATH

WALK-IN CLOSET

DESK

BEDROOM 3
12-6 x 12-0

GARDEN TUB

PANTRY

BATH

LIN.

MASTER BEDROOM
14-4 x 16-0

DN

CLOSET

WALK-IN CLOSET

DINING ROOM
12-6 x 12-6

HUTCH

FOYER

PORCH

MAIN FLOOR PLAN

64' - 6"

63' - 0"

UPPER GREAT ROOM

STORAGE

DN | RAIL | BATH

LOFT
21-4 x 12-0

STORAGE

VAULTED CEILING

LOFT PLAN

No. 90444

■ **This plan features:**

— Three bedrooms

— Three full baths

▪ A vaulted-ceiling Great Room with skylights and a fireplace

▪ A double L-shaped Kitchen with an eating bar opening to a bayed Breakfast Room

▪ A Master Suite with a walk-in closet, corner garden tub, separate vanities and a linen closet

▪ Two additional bedrooms each with a walk-in closet and built-in desk, sharing a full hall bath

▪ A loft that overlooks the Great Room which includes a vaulted ceiling and open rail balcony

▪ An optional basement or crawl space foundation — please specify when ordering

Main floor — 1,996 sq. ft.
Loft — 305 sq. ft.

Contemporary Cape

No. 93501

■ This plan features:

— Four bedrooms

— Two full baths

■ Covered Entry leads into Living Room with barrel vault ceiling, arched window and cozy fireplace dividing Family/Dining area

■ Skylight highlights compact Kitchen with open snackbar serving Dining area and Patio/Optional Sunspace beyond

■ Private Master Bedroom offers a wall of closets, a double vanity bath with skylight and nearby bedroom or multi-purpose room

■ Two first floor bedrooms with ample closets, share a full bath

First floor — 1,154 sq. ft.
Second floor — 585 sq. ft.
Garage — 516 sq. ft.

■ Total living area 1,739 sq. ft. ■ Price Code B ■

Country Style for Today

No. 99620

■ This plan features:

— Four bedrooms

— Two full and one half baths

■ Two bay windows in the formal Living Room with a heat-circulating fireplace to enhance the mood and warmth

■ A spacious formal Dining Room with a bay window and easy access to the Kitchen

■ An octagon-shaped Dinette defined by columns, dropped beams and a bay window

■ An efficient island Kitchen with ample storage and counter space

■ A Master Suite equipped with a large whirlpool tub plus a double vanity

■ Three additional bedrooms that share a full hall bath

First floor — 1,192 sq. ft.
Second floor — 1,020 sq. ft.
Basement — 1,026 sq. ft.
Garage & storage — 469 sq. ft.

■ Total living area 2,212 sq. ft. ■ Price Code D ■

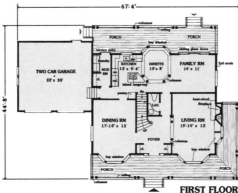

Grace with an Elegant Front Porch

Total living area 1,750 sq. ft. ■ **Price Code B**

No. 98462

■ **This plan features:**

— Three bedrooms

— Two full and one half baths

■ The two-story Foyer accesses the Dining Room, Living Room and Family Room with ease

■ The Kitchen opens to the Breakfast Area and in turn the Breakfast Area is open to the Family Room

■ The Family Room is enhanced by a fireplace

■ A work island adds counter space to the Kitchen

■ The Master Suite with a private bath is topped by a vaulted ceiling

■ The front secondary bedroom is highlighted by a window seat

■ Please specify a basement, a slab, or a crawl space foundation when ordering

■ There is no materials list available for this plan

First floor — 926 sq. ft.
Second floor — 824 sq. ft.
Bonus room — 282 sq. ft.
Basement — 926 sq. ft.
Garage — 440 sq. ft.

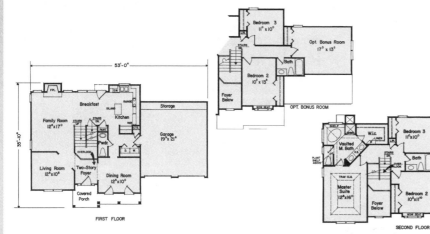

Conventional and Classic Comfort

Total living area 1,961 sq. ft. ■ **Price Code C**

No. 93349

■ **This plan features:**

— Three bedrooms

— Two full and one half baths

■ Cozy Porch accesses two-story Foyer with decorative window highlighting a landing staircase

■ Formal Dining Room accented by a recessed window adjoins Kitchen

■ Spacious Family Room crowned by a vaulted ceiling over a hearth fireplace surrounded by more decorative windows

■ Efficient Kitchen with an extended counter/eating bar and bright Dinette area with bay window and access to Deck

■ Convenient Laundry, Powder Room and Garage entry near Kitchen

■ First floor Master Bedroom with walk-in closet and Master Bath with double vanity

■ Two additional bedrooms and a full bath complete second floor

■ No materials list is available for this plan

First floor — 1,454 sq. ft.
Second floor — 507 sq. ft.
Basement — 1,454 sq. ft.
Garage — 624 sq. ft.

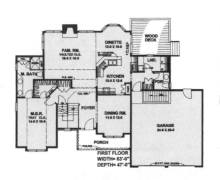

An
EXCLUSIVE DESIGN
By Patrick Morabito, A.I.A. Architect

250

A Whisper of Victorian Styling

■ *Total living area 3,198 sq. ft.* ■ *Price Code E* ■

No. 93333

■ This plan features:

— Four bedrooms

— Two full and one half baths

■ Formal Living Room features wrap-around windows and direct access to the front Porch

■ An elegant, formal Dining Room accented by a stepped ceiling

■ Efficient Kitchen is equipped with a cooktop island/eating bar and a double sink

■ A bright, all-purpose Sun Room with glass on four sides adjoining an expansive Deck

■ A private Master Suite with a decorative ceiling and a luxurious bath with a raised, atrium tub, oversized walk-in shower, two vanities and an oversized walk-in closet

■ Three additional bedrooms sharing a full, hall bath with double vanity

■ No materials list is available for this plan

First floor — 1,743 sq. ft.
Second floor — 1,455 sq. ft.

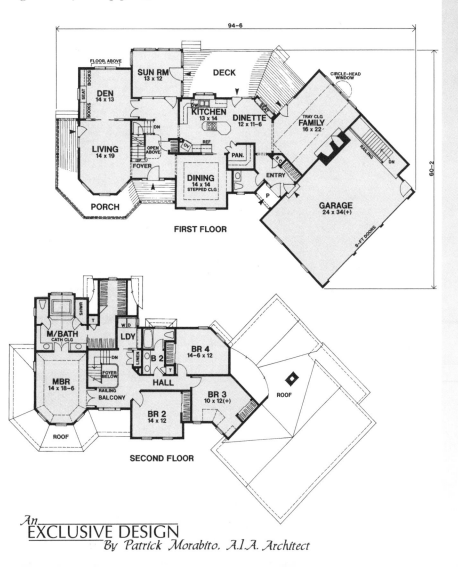

An
EXCLUSIVE DESIGN
By Patrick Morabito, A.I.A. Architect

251

Just Picture It

■ *Total living area 1,995 sq. ft.* ■ *Price Code C* ■

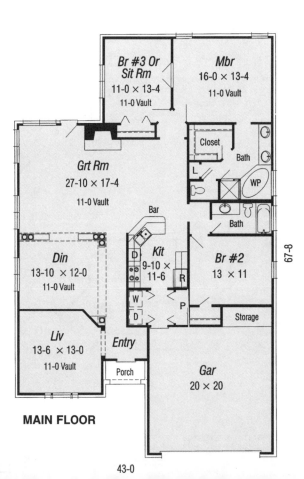

MAIN FLOOR

43-0

No. 91125

■ **This plan features:**

— Three bedrooms

— Two full baths

■ Three front gables and a brick archway achieve terrific curb appeal

■ Columns dividing wall thereby defining Dining Room

■ Expansive Great Room topped by a vaulted ceiling and highlighted by a fireplace

■ Formal Living Room enhanced by a paladian window

■ Master Suite can be adjoined to the adjacent room resulting in a Sitting Room, home Office or a Nursery

■ Kitchen equipped with an open bar for meals on the go

■ No materials list is available for this plan

Main floor — 1,995 sq. ft.
Garage & storage — 469 sq. ft.

Expansive Windows Compliment Leisure Living

No. 99645

This plan features:

- Three bedrooms
- Three full baths
- Wrap-around Deck expands Living outdoors and provides multiple access to Living Room
- Impressive fieldstone fireplace with log holder warms Living/Dining Room below cathedral ceiling
- Efficient L-shaped Kitchen with built-in counter table and Laundry with built-in pantry
- Master Bedroom suite with double windows and plush, double vanity bath
- Second bedroom on first floor and another bedroom on second floor each have access to full baths
- Side entrance into Vestibule with Gear Equipment area and Foyer with two closet

First floor — 1,361 sq. ft.
Loft floor — 453 sq. ft.
Basement — 694 sq. ft.

Total living area 1,814 sq. ft. ■ Price Code C

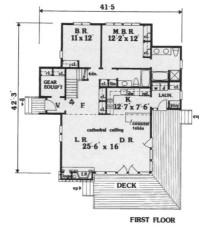

FIRST FLOOR

LOFT FLOOR

Vaulted Ceilings and Skylights

No. 98733

This plan features:

- Three bedrooms
- Two full baths
- A sheltered entrance leading to a large Living Room topped by a vaulted ceiling and enhanced by a large bay window and a fireplace
- A formal Dining Room with arched openings and a vaulted ceiling
- A large fireplace warms the mood and the temperature in the Family Room which is conveniently equipped with a built-in entertainment center
- A cooktop island/eating bar and a walk-in pantry adding to the efficiency of the Kitchen that is open to the Nook
- A privately situated Master Suite including an ultra bath, his-n-her walk-in closets and direct access to the side porch that is equipped with a hot tub
- Two additional bedrooms with bay windows sharing a hall bath that includes two skylights

Main floor — 2,496 sq. ft.
Garage — 827 sq. ft.
Basement — 2,401 sq. ft.
Width — 96'-0"
Depth — 54'-0"

Total living area 2,496 sq. ft. ■ Price Code D

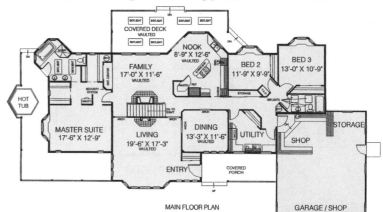

MAIN FLOOR PLAN

Attractive Styling

No. 98338

This plan features:

— Three bedrooms

— Two full and one half baths

■ Columns highlighting the sheltered entrance

■ Living Room crowned in a vaulted ceiling and flowing effortlessly into the Dining Room

■ Kitchen/Breakfast room highlighted by a work island, large bay window and access to the rear deck

■ Fireplace accenting the Family Room with a cozy atmosphere

■ Master Suite topped by a vaulted ceiling and enhanced by a bay window, a private bath and a walk-in closet

■ Two secondary bedrooms sharing a full bath in the hall

First floor — 945 sq. ft.
Second floor — 808 sq. ft.
Basement — 945 sq. ft.

■ *Total living area 1,753 sq. ft.* ■ *Price Code B* ■

FIRST FLOOR

SECOND FLOOR

Rear of Home as Attractive as Front

No. 90413

This plan features:

— Three bedrooms

— Two full and one half baths

■ A sunken Family Room with a cathedral ceiling and a massive stone fireplace

■ Two front bedrooms having ample closet space and sharing a unique bath-and-a-half arrangement

■ A Master Bedroom with a walk-in closet and compartmentalized bath with double vanity and linen closet

■ A U-shaped Kitchen, well-equipped and efficient, serving the Breakfast Nook and the formal Dining Room with ease

■ A second floor with a large Studio

■ An optional basement or crawl space foundation — please specify when ordering

First floor — 2,192 sq. ft.
Second floor — 248 sq. ft.
Basement — 2,192 sq. ft.

■ *Total living area 2,440 sq. ft.* ■ *Price Code D* ■

FIRST FLOOR

SECOND FLOOR

Cozy Front Porch

■ *Total living area 1,735 sq. ft.* ■ *Price Code B* ■

No. 93269

■ This plan features:

— Three bedrooms

— Two full and one half baths

■ A Living Room enhanced by a large fireplace

■ A formal Dining Room that is open to the Living Room

■ An efficient Kitchen that includes ample counter and cabinet space as well as double sinks and pass-thru window

■ Breakfast Area with vaulted ceiling and a door to the Sundeck

■ First floor Master Suite with separate tub & shower stall, plus a walk-in closet

■ Two additional bedrooms that share a full hall bath

First floor — 1,045 sq. ft.
Second floor — 690 sq. ft.
Basement — 465 sq. ft.
Garage — 580 sq. ft.

SECOND FLOOR

BATH 2

BDRM.2
12'-2"X14'-4"

BDRM.3
13'-2"X14'-4"

LIN.

SITTING AREA

FIRST FLOOR

SUNDECK
16'-0"X12'-0"

BREAKFAST
9'-0"X7'-8"

KIT.
9'-0"X9'-6"

DINING
10'-0"X11'-4"

REF.

W D

LIVING AREA
18'-0"X13'-6"

M.BDRM.
15'-6"X13'-6"

LIN.

PORCH

40'-4"

32'-0"

An
EXCLUSIVE DESIGN
By Jannis Vann & Associates, Inc.

Easy Everyday Living and Entertaining

■ *Total living area 1,664 sq. ft.* ■ • *Price Code B* ■

No. 92238

■ **This plan features:**

— Three bedrooms

— Two full baths

■ Front entrance accented by segmented arches, sidelight and transom windows

■ Open Living Room with focal point fireplace, wetbar and access to Patio

■ Dining area open to both the Living Room and the Kitchen

■ Efficient Kitchen with a cooktop island, walk-in pantry and Utility area with a Garage entry

■ Large walk-in closet, double vanity bath and access to Patio featured in the Master Bedroom suite

■ No materials list is available for this plan

Main floor — 1,664 sq. ft.
Basement — 1,600 sq. ft.
Garage — 440 sq. ft

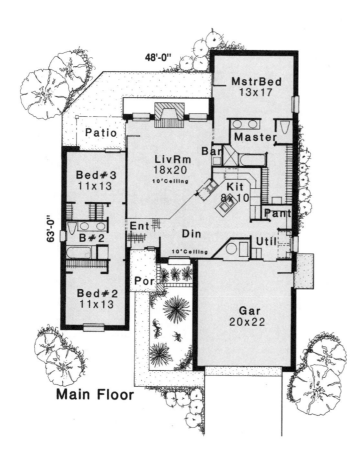

Main Floor

Bedrooms Sliders Open Onto Wooden Deck

No. 10220

This plan features:

— Two bedrooms

— One full bath

■ A fifty foot deck setting the stage for a relaxing lifestyle encouraged by this home

■ A simple, yet complete floor plan centering around the large Family Area, warmed by a prefab fireplace and sliders to the deck

■ An efficient L-shaped Kitchen that includes a double sink with a window above, and direct access to the rear yard and the Laundry Room

■ Two bedrooms privately located, each outfitted with sliding doors to the deck and a large window for plenty of light

Main area — 888 sq. ft.

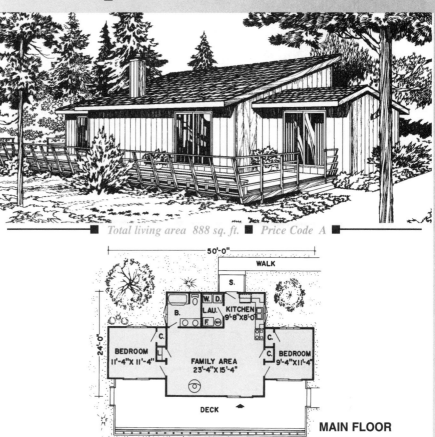

Total living area 888 sq. ft. ■ *Price Code A*

MAIN FLOOR

Living Areas Gather Around Fireplace

No. 94979

This plan features:

— Three bedrooms

— Two full and one half baths

■ A see-through fireplace situated between the hearth room and the Great Room

■ Open layout between the Kitchen, Hearth Room and the Breakfast Room creating a terrific informal living space

■ Built-in pantry, work island and a peninsula counter/snackbar highlighting the Kitchen

■ Great Room is directly across the hall from the Dining Room and is at the heart of the home

■ Master Bedroom features two-walk-in closets and a five piece bath

■ Two additional bedrooms have private access to a full bath

Main floor — 2,404 sq. ft.
Garage — 696 sq. ft.

© design basics, inc.

Total living area 2,404 sq. ft. ■ *Price Code D*

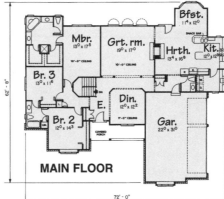

MAIN FLOOR

Compact Design Packs Much In

Total living area 1,372 sq. ft. ■ Price Code A ■

MAIN FLOOR

No. 98804

■ **This plan features:**

— Three bedrooms

— Two full baths

■ The covered front porch leads into a foyer that contains a coat closet

■ The U-shaped Kitchen has it all, including a corner double sink, a Pantry, a desk, and a nook with a bay window

■ Direct access to the formal Dining Room from the Kitchen is provided

■ The Living Room is large and features access to the rear deck, and a open railed staircase to the basement

■ The Master Bedroom has double closets, a private bath, and a French door out to the deck

■ Two bedrooms, identical in size share a bath in the hall with a skylight above it.

■ his home has a Laundry/Utility room on the way out to the two-car garage

■ No materials list is available for this plan

Main floor — 1,372 sq. ft.
Basement — 1,372 sq. ft.
Garage — 484 sq. ft.

Rustic Three Bedroom

© 1992 Donald A. Gardner Architects, Inc.

Total living area 1,622 sq. ft. ■ Price Code C ■

FIRST FLOOR

SECOND FLOOR PLAN

No. 96436 ✖

■ **This plan features:**

— Three bedrooms

— Two full baths

■ Spacious covered Porches on the front of the home and on the rear of the home

■ Openness in the Great Room to the Kitchen/Dining Area provides a spacious feeling of a much large home

■ Cooktop island Kitchen includes L-shaped counter for ample work space

■ Master Suite, with a generous walk-in closet and pampering master bath

■ Two second floor bedrooms, one over looking the Great Room for added drama

First floor — 1,039 sq. ft.
Second floor — 583 sq. ft.

■ *Total living area 3,423 sq. ft.* ■ *Price Code F* ■

No. 98536

■ This plan features:

— Four bedrooms

— Two full and one half baths

■ Vaulted Master Bedroom has a private skylit bath

■ Three more bedrooms have walk-in closets and share a full bath

■ A loft and bonus room above the Living Room

■ Family Room has built-in book shelves, a fireplace, and overlooks the covered verandah

■ The huge three-car garage has a separate shop area

■ An optional slab or a crawl space foundation — please specify when ordering

■ No materials list is available for this plan

Main floor — 2,787 sq. ft.
Upper floor — 636 sq. ft.
Garage — 832 sq. ft.

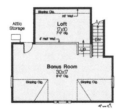

Upper Floor
Optional Bonus Room & Loft

Upper Floor

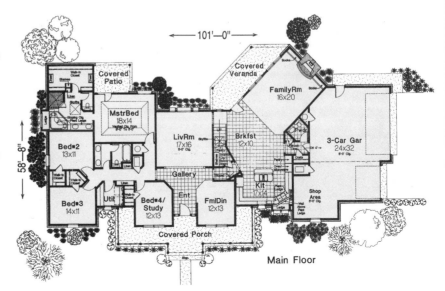

Main Floor

A Little Drama

■ *Total living area 1,768 sq. ft.* ■ *Price Code B* ■

No. 92609

■ **This plan features:**

— Three bedrooms

— Two full and one half baths

■ A 12' high Entry with transom and sidelights, multiple gables and a box window

■ A sunken Great Room with a fireplace and access to a rear Porch

■ A Breakfast Bay and Kitchen flowing into each other and accessing a rear Porch

■ A Master Bedroom with a tray ceiling, walk-in closet and a private master bath

■ No materials list is available for this plan

First floor — 960 sq. ft.
Second floor — 808 sq. ft.
Basement — 922 sq. ft.
Garage — 413 sq. ft.

SECOND FLOOR

Bedroom 11-4 x 11-4
Bath
Hall
Great Room Below 12' ceiling
Foyer Below 12' ceiling
stairs dn
Master Bedroom 12 x 16 tray ceiling
Bath
Bedroom 11-4 x 9-6
walk-in closet

FIRST FLOOR

Porch
Breakfast 10 x 13-4
Kitchen 8-6 x 11
Bath
Laundry
Sunken Great Room 13 x 17-4
stairs up
stairs dn
walk-in closet
Foyer
Dining Room 11-4 x 12
furniture alcove
Porch
Two-car Garage 20-4 x 20

WIDTH 55'-4"
DEPTH 40'-4"

Surprisingly Spacious for a Smaller Home

No. 98743

■ **This plan features:**

— Three bedrooms

— Two full baths

■ A vaulted ceiling in the richly illuminated Foyer, which presents three choices of direction

■ An eye-catching Great Room with a vaulted ceiling, a corner fireplace and a bank of windows on the rear wall showering the room with light

■ An efficient U-shaped Kitchen with an angled eating bar, built-in pantry and a double sink that views the Great Room

■ A luxurious Master Suite that includes a roomy walk-in closet, access to the rear deck and a private bath

■ A Mini-Master Suite that includes a walk-in closet with a vanity right outside and private access to the hall bath

■ A third bedroom that shares the use of the hall bath

■ No materials list is available for this plan

Main floor — 1,958 sq. ft.
Width — 58'-0"
Depth — 68'-6"

■ *Total living area 1,958 sq. ft.* ■ *Price Code C* ■

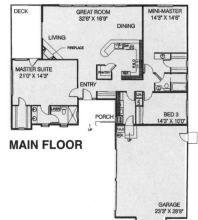

MAIN FLOOR

First Floor Master Suite

No. 94613

■ **This plan features:**

— Four bedrooms

— Three full and one half baths

■ Welcoming country porch adds to appeal and living space

■ Central Foyer provides ventilation and access to all areas of home

■ Spacious Living Room enhanced by fireplace and access to Covered Porch

■ Efficient Kitchen with work island, built-in pantry, Utility room, Garage entry and Breakfast Area

■ Spacious Master Bedroom suite with a pampering, private bath

■ Three second floor bedrooms with walk-in closets, share two full baths and a Game Room

■ No materials list is available for this plan

■ An optional crawl space or slab foundation — please specify when ordering

First floor — 1,492 sq. ft.
Second floor — 865 sq. ft.
Bonus — 303 sq. ft.
Garage — 574 sq. ft.
Width — 66'-10"
Depth — 49'-7"

■ *Total living area 2,357 sq. ft.* ■ *Price Code D* ■

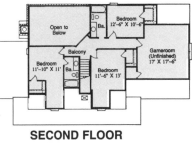

FIRST FLOOR

SECOND FLOOR

Beautiful Arched Window

■ Total living area 1,911 sq. ft. ■ Price Code C ■

MAIN FLOOR

© design basics, inc.

No. 94966 ✖

■ **This plan features:**

— Three bedrooms

— Two full baths

■ Ten foot ceilings topping the Entry and the Great Room

■ A see-through fireplace is shared between the Great Room and the Hearth Room

■ Built-in entertainment center and a bayed window highlighting the Hearth Room

■ Breakfast Room and Hearth Room in an open layout separated by only a snackbar in the kitchen

■ Built-in pantry and corner sinks enhancing efficiency in the Kitchen

■ Split bedroom plan assuring homeowner's privacy in the Master Suite which includes a decorative ceiling, private bath and a large walk-in closet

■ Two additional bedrooms at the opposite side of the home sharing a full, skylit bath in the hall

Main floor — 1,911 sq. ft.
Garage — 481 sq. ft.

Colonial Charmer

■ Total living area 1,920 sq. ft. ■ Price Code C ■

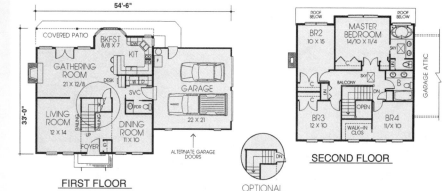

FIRST FLOOR

OPTIONAL BASEMENT

SECOND FLOOR

No. 93523 ✖

■ **This plan features:**

— Four bedrooms

— Two full and one half baths

■ An oversized Family Room that opens into the Kitchen/Nook area creating a feeling of space

■ A large fireplace and access to the patio in the Family Room

■ A peninsula counter and double sinks as well as an abundance of counter and cupboard space in the Kitchen

■ A formal Living Room and Dining Room for entertaining

■ A Master Suite that includes two closets, a jacuzzi and double vanity

■ Three additional bedrooms, one with a walk-in closet, that share a full hall bath

First floor — 970 sq. ft.
Second floor — 950 sq. ft.
Basement — 970 sq. ft.
Garage — 462 sq. ft.

Essence of Style & Grace

■ *Total living area 1,883 sq. ft.* ■ *Price Code C* ■

No. 98524

■ This plan features:

— Four bedrooms

— Three full and one half baths

■ French doors introduce Study and columns define the Gallery and formal areas

■ The expansive Family Room with an inviting fireplace and a cathedral ceiling opens to the Kitchen

■ The Kitchen features a cooktop island, butler's Pantry, Breakfast Area and Patio access

■ The first floor Master Bedroom offers a private Patio, vaulted ceiling, twin vanities and a walk-in closet

■ No materials list is available for this plan

■ An optional basement or slab foundation — please specify when ordering

First floor — 2,036 sq. ft.
Second floor — 866 sq. ft.
Garage — 720 sq. ft.

Elegant and Inviting

■ *Total living area 2,744 sq. ft.* ■ *Price Code E* ■

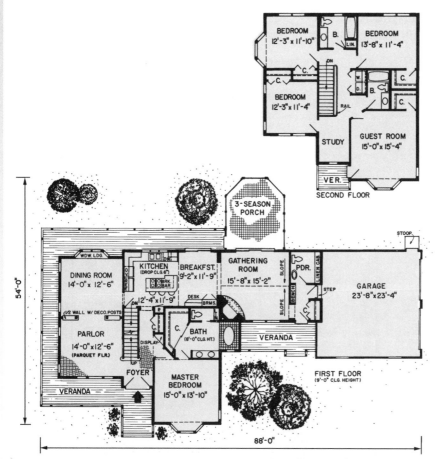

3-SEASON PORCH

SECOND FLOOR

BEDROOM 12'-3" x 11'-10"

BEDROOM 13'-8" x 11'-4"

BEDROOM 12'-3" x 11'-4"

STUDY

GUEST ROOM 15'-0" x 15'-4"

VER.

DINING ROOM 14'-0" x 12'-6"

KITCHEN (DROP CLG. 6")

BREAKFST. 9'-2" x 11'-9"

GATHERING ROOM 15'-8" x 15'-2"

GARAGE 23'-8" x 23'-4"

PDR.

12'-4" x 11'-9"

BATH (8'-0" CLG. HT.)

VERANDA

PARLOR 14'-0" x 12'-6" (PARQUET FLR.)

FOYER

MASTER BEDROOM 15'-0" x 13'-10"

VERANDA

FIRST FLOOR (9'-0" CLG. HEIGHT)

54'-0"

88'-0"

No. 10689

■ **This plan features:**

— Five bedrooms

— Three full and one half baths

■ Wrap-around verandas and a three-season porch

■ An elegant Parlor with a parquet floor and a formal Dining Room separated by a half-wall

■ An adjoining Kitchen with a Breakfast bar and Nook

■ A Gathering Room with a fireplace, soaring ceilings and access to the 3-Season Porch

First floor — 1,580 sq. ft.
Second floor — 1,164 sq. ft.
Basement — 1,329 sq. ft.
Garage — 576 sq. ft.

Mid-Sized Country Style

No. 98748

This plan features:

- Three bedrooms
- Two full baths
- A vaulted ceiling over the Entry, Living Room, Dining Room, Family Room and Master Suite
- Wide window bay expanding the Living Room
- Wide garden window expanding the Kitchen while the cooktop, L-shaped island/eating bar adds convenience
- A walk-in closet, oversized shower, a spa tub and a double vanity outside the bath area highlight the Master Suite
- Two roomy additional bedrooms share the full bath in the hall

Main floor — 2,126 sq. ft.

Total living area 2,126 sq. ft. Price Code C

WIDTH 64'-0"
DEPTH 64'-0"

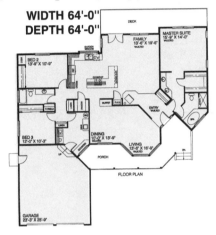

Farmhouse Flavor

No. 10785

This plan features:

- Three bedrooms
- Two full and one half baths
- A inviting wrap-around Porch with old-fashioned charm
- Two-story foyer
- A wood stove in the Living Room that warms the entire house
- A modern Kitchen flowing easily into the bayed Dining Room
- A first floor Master Bedroom with private master bath
- Two additional bedrooms with walk-in closets and cozy gable sitting nooks

First floor — 1,269 sq. ft.
Second floor — 638 sq. ft.
Basement — 1,269 sq. ft.

An EXCLUSIVE DESIGN
By Karl Kreeger

Total living area 1,907 sq. ft. Price Code C

Slab/Crawl Space Option

SECOND FLOOR

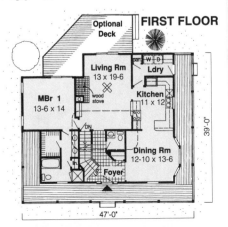

FIRST FLOOR

265

Letting the Light In

■ *Total living area 1,525 sq. ft.* ■ *Price Code B* ■

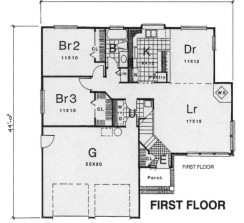

FIRST FLOOR

SECOND FLOOR

No. 91081

■ **This plan features:**

– Four bedrooms

– Two full baths

■ Covered Porch leads into easy-care tile Entry with angled staircase

■ Vaulted Ceiling tops decorative corner windows and cozy wood stove in Living Room

■ Sliding glass door to rear yard brightens Dining Room and adjoining Living Room and Kitchen

■ Efficient Kitchen with built-in pantry, pass-through counter and plant shelf window

■ Two first floor bedrooms with ample closets, share a full bath and Utility area

■ French doors lead into private Master Bedroom with skylight bath and walk-in closet

■ Loft/Bedroom overlooking Living Room offers many options

■ No materials list is available for this plan

First floor – 1076 sq. ft.
Second floor – 449 sq. ft.

Country Ranch

■ *Total living area 1,485 sq. ft.* ■ *Price Code A* ■

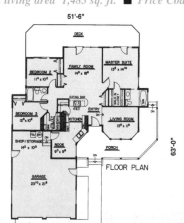

FLOOR PLAN

No. 91797

■ **This plan features:**

– Three bedrooms

– Two full baths

■ A railed and covered wrap-around porch, adding charm to this country-styled home

■ A high vaulted ceiling in the Living Room

■ A smaller Kitchen with ample cupboard and counter space, that is augmented by a large pantry

■ An informal Family Room with access to the wood deck

■ A private Master Suite with a spa tub and a walk-in closet

■ Two family bedrooms that share a full hall bath

■ A shop and storage area in the two-car garage

Main area – 1,485 sq. ft.
Garage – 701 sq. ft.

Stately Colonial Home

■ *Total living area 2,959 sq. ft.* ■ • *Price Code E* ■

No. 98534

■ This plan features:

— Four bedrooms

— Three full and one half baths

■ Stately columns and lovely arched windows

■ The Entry is highlighted by a palladian window, a plant shelf and an angled staircase

■ The formal Living and Dining Rooms located off the Entry for ease in entertaining

■ Great Room has a fireplace and opens to Kitchen/Breakfast area and the Patio

■ The Master Bedroom wing offers Patio access, a luxurious bath and a walk-in closet

■ No materials list is available for this plan

First floor — 1,848 sq. ft.
Second floor — 1,111 sq. ft.
Garage & shop — 722 sq. ft.

WIDTH 73'-4"
DEPTH 44'-1"

SECOND FLOOR

FIRST FLOOR

Four Bedroom Country Classic

© 1994 Donald A. Gardner Architects, Inc.

R. NATHAN

■ *Total living area 2,164 sq. ft.* ■ *Price Code D* ■

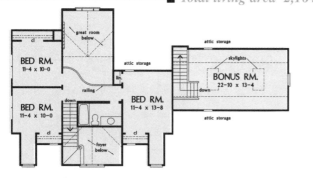

SECOND FLOOR PLAN

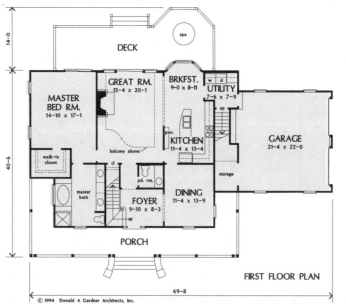

FIRST FLOOR PLAN

No. 96408

■ This plan features:

— Four bedrooms

— Two full and one half baths

■ Foyer open to the Dining Room creating a hall with a balcony over the vaulted Great Room

■ Great Room opens to the Deck and to the island Kitchen with convenient pantry

■ Nine foot ceilings on the first floor expand volume

■ Master Suite pampered by a whirlpool tub, double vanity, separate shower and Deck access

■ Bonus room to be finished now or later

First floor — 1,499 sq. ft.
Second floor — 665 sq. ft.
Garage & storage — 567 sq. ft.
Bonus room — 380 sq. ft.

© 1994 Donald A Gardner Architects, Inc.

No. 96457

This plan features:

— Three bedrooms

— Two full and one half baths

■ The large common area combines the Great Room and the Dining Room under a vaulted ceiling that is punctuated with skylights

■ The Kitchen/Breakfast Bay includes a peninsula counter/snackbar

■ From the Great Room extend entertaining outdoors to the covered back porch

■ The Master Suite has a generous bath and ample closet space

■ The front bedroom/study doubles as a Guest Room

■ On the second floor the loft/study makes a terrific office or play room

First floor — 1,234 sq. ft.
Second floor — 609 sq. ft.
Garage — 496 sq. ft.

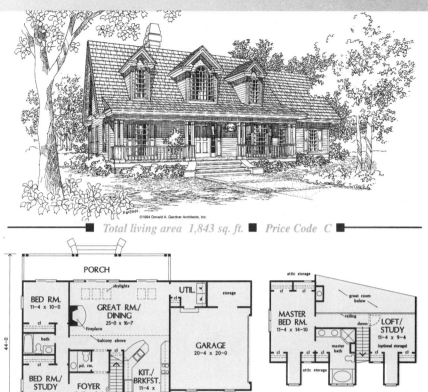

■ Total living area 1,843 sq. ft. ■ Price Code C ■

FIRST FLOOR PLAN

SECOND FLOOR PLAN

© 1994 Donald A Gardner Architects, Inc.

Colonial Facade Disguises Split Foyer

No. 93297

This plan features:

— Three bedrooms

— Two full baths

■ Stylish colonial facade disguising a split Foyer design

■ Spacious Kitchen offering all the amenities including a built-in pantry

■ Bright Breakfast Area and formal Dining Room for informal and formal gatherings

■ Split bedroom design giving Master Suite privacy

■ Spacious Master Bedroom includes a large walk-in closet and a dual vanity master bath

■ Split Foyer design offering an expandable lower level for a growing family

Main floor — 1,672 sq. ft.
Bonus room — 352 sq. ft.
Finished staircase — 32 sq. ft.
Future bedroom — 224 sq. ft.
Basement — 192 sq. ft.
Garage — 720 sq. ft.

An EXCLUSIVE DESIGN
By Jannis Vann & Associates, Inc.

■ Total living area 1,704 sq. ft. ■ Price Code B ■

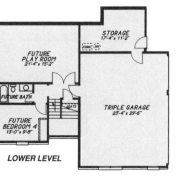

LOWER LEVEL

FLOOR PLAN

Yesterday's Style for Today's Lifestyle

■ Total living area 2,306 sq. ft. ■ Price Code D ■

Main Level Floor Plan
10' Ceilings

Upper Level Floor Plan
8' Ceilings

No. 93704

■ **This plan features:**

— Three bedrooms

— Two full and one half baths

■ Front Porch shelters entrance into Foyer, Great Room and Study

■ Great Room with inviting fireplace opens to formal Dining Room

■ Spacious Kitchen with work island, built-in pantry and serving/snackbar for Breakfast area and Porch

■ Master Bedroom adjoins Study, pampering bath and Utility area

■ Two second floor bedrooms with double closets, share a double vanity bath and study alcove

■ No materials list is available for this plan

First floor — 1,748 sq. ft.
Second floor — 558 sq. ft.
Garage — 528 sq. ft.

An EXCLUSIVE DESIGN
By Building Science Associates

Perfect for Your Corner Lot

■ Total living area 1,868 sq. ft. ■ Price Code C ■

MAIN FLOOR PLAN

No. 93192

■ **This plan features:**

— Three bedrooms

— Two full and one half baths

■ Pillars and decorative windows highlight front entrance into Foyer with cathedral ceiling and a large closet

■ Spacious Living Room enhanced by a central fireplace and decorative window

■ Convenient Kitchen with a work island, Dining area with outdoor access, and nearby laundry/Garage entry

■ Corner Master Suite offers direct access to back yard, a large walk-in closet and a pampering bath

■ Two additional bedrooms with ample closet space and easy access to a full bath

■ No materials list is available for this plan

Main floor — 1,868 sq. ft.
Basement — 1,868 sq. ft.

Four Bedroom with One Floor Convenience

■ *Total living area 2,675 sq. ft.* ■ *Price Code E* ■

No. 92275

■ **This plan features:**

— Four bedrooms

— Three full baths

■ A distinguished brick exterior adds curb appeal

■ Formal Entry/Gallery opens to large Living Room with hearth fireplace set between windows overlooking Patio and rear yard

■ Efficient Kitchen with angled counters and serving bar easily serves Breakfast Room, Patio and formal Dining Room

■ Corner Master Bedroom enhanced by a vaulted ceiling and pampering bath with a large walk-in closet

■ Three additional bedrooms with walk-in closets have access to full baths

■ No materials list is available for this plan

Main floor —2,675 sq. ft.
Garage — 638 sq. ft.

Main Floor

Quaint Starter Home

■ *Total living area 1,050 sq. ft.* ■ *Price Code A* ■

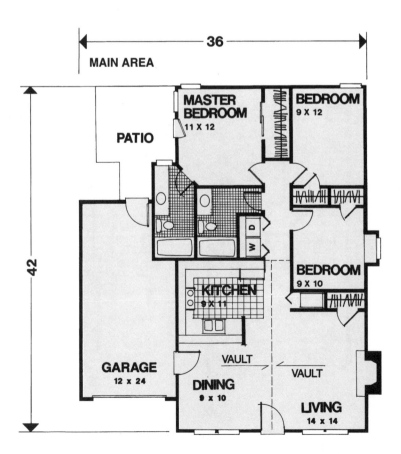

MAIN AREA

36

42

MASTER BEDROOM 11 X 12

BEDROOM 9 X 12

PATIO

BEDROOM 9 X 10

W D

GARAGE 12 X 24

KITCHEN 9 X 11

VAULT

VAULT

DINING 9 X 10

LIVING 14 X 14

No. 92400

■ **This plan features:**

— Three bedrooms

— Two full baths

■ A vaulted ceiling giving an airy feeling to the Dining and Living Rooms

■ A streamlined Kitchen with a comfortable work area, a double sink and ample cabinet space

■ A cozy fireplace in the Living Room

■ A Master Suite with a large closet, French doors leading to the patio and a private bath

■ Two additional bedrooms sharing a full bath

■ No materials list is available for this plan

Main area — 1,050 sq. ft.

Offering an Inviting Welcome

No. 96472

This plan features:

— Three bedrooms

— Two full and one half baths

- Triple gables and a wrapping front Porch
- Cathedral ceiling highlights the Great Room which also includes defining columns and a cozy fireplace
- Octagonal Dining Room with a tray ceiling and easy access to the Porch for summer dining outdoors
- Kitchen equipped with a pantry and a work island
- Master Suite with a roomy walk-in closet and bath located downstairs for privacy
- Upstairs, two bedrooms sharing a full bath and access to a skylit bonus room

First floor — 1,512 sq. ft.
Second floor — 477 sq. ft.
Bonus room — 347 sq. ft.
Garage & storage — 636 sq. ft.

■ Total living area 1,989 sq. ft. ■ Price Code C ■

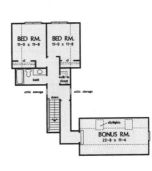

Perfect for a First Home

No. 92405

This plan features:

— Three bedrooms

— Two full baths

- A spacious Master Suite including a separate Master Bath with a garden tub and shower
- A Dining Room and Family Room highlighted by vaulted ceilings
- An oversized patio accessible from the Master Suite, Family Room and Breakfast Room
- A well-planned Kitchen measuring 12' x 11'
- No materials list available for this plan

Main floor — 1,564 sq. ft.
Garage & Storage — 476 sq. ft

■ Total living area 1,564 sq. ft. ■ Price Code B ■

MAIN FLOOR

Country Classic

Total living area 1,838 sq. ft. ■ Price Code C

©1995 Donald A. Gardner Architects, Inc.

No. 96461 ✕

■ This plan features:

— Three bedrooms

— Two full and one half baths

■ Casually elegant exterior with dormers, gables and a charming front porch

■ U-shaped Kitchen easily serves both adjacent eating areas

■ Nine foot ceilings amplify the first floor

■ Master Suite highlighted by a vaulted ceiling and dormer

■ Garden tub with a double window are focus of the master bath

■ Two bedrooms with walk-in closets sharing a hall bath, while back stairs lead to a spacious bonus room

First floor — 1,313 sq. ft.
Second floor — 525 sq. ft.
Bonus room — 367 sq. ft.
Garage — 513 sq. ft.

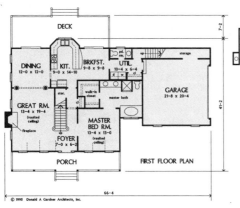

Spacious Country Charm

Total living area 1,887 sq. ft. ■ Price Code C

No. 94107

■ This plan features:

— Three bedrooms

— Two full and one half baths

■ Comfortable front Porch leads into bright, two-story Foyer

■ Pillars frame entrance to formal Dining Room highlighted by bay window

■ Expansive Great Room accented by hearth fireplace and triple window opens to Kitchen/Dining area

■ Efficient Kitchen with loads of counter and storage space and Dining area with window access to rear yard

■ Corner Master Bedroom offers triple window and luxurious master bath

■ Two additional bedrooms with ample closets, share a full bath

■ No materials list is available for this plan

First floor — 961 sq. ft.
Second floor — 926 sq. ft.
Garage — 548 sq. ft.
Basement — 928 sq. ft.

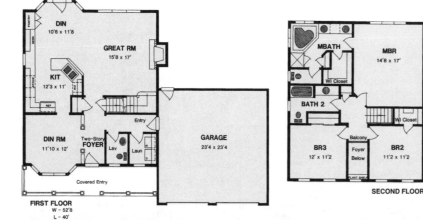

■ *Total living area 3,220 sq. ft.* ■ *Price Code F* ■

No. 93505 ⚒

■ **This plan features:**

— Four bedrooms

— Two full and one three-quarter baths

■ A vaulted ceiling foyer

■ A Living Room with a vaulted ceiling and elegant fireplace

■ A formal Dining Room that adjoins the Living Room, with a built-in buffet

■ An island cooktop in the well-appointed Kitchen with a walk-in pantry and an open layout to the Family Room

■ A vaulted ceiling in the Family Room with a, corner fireplace

■ A huge walk-in closet, built-in entertainment center, and a full bath with every amenity in the Master Suite

First floor — 2,125 sq. ft.
Second floor — 1,095 sq. ft.
Basement — 2,125 sq. ft.
Garage — three-car

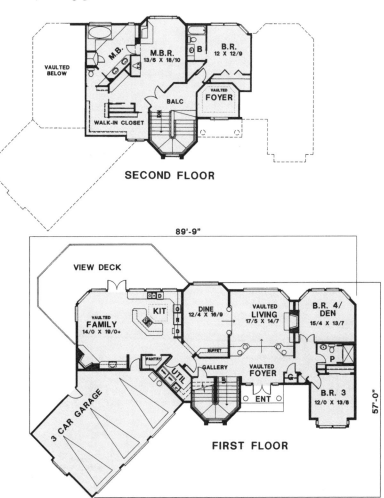

SECOND FLOOR

FIRST FLOOR

Elegant Brick Two-Story

■ *Total living area 2,398 sq. ft.* ■ *Price Code D* ■

SECOND FLOOR PLAN

MAIN FLOOR PLAN

No. 90450

■ This plan features:

— Four bedrooms

— Two or three full and one half baths

■ A two-story Great Room with a fireplace and access to a deck

■ Master Suite with two walk-in closets and a private master bath

■ A large island Kitchen serving the formal Dining Room and the sunny Breakfast Nook with ease

■ Three additional bedrooms, two with walk-in closets, sharing a full hall bath

■ An optional Bonus Room with a private entrance from below

■ An optional basement or crawl space foundation — please specify when ordering

First floor — 1,637 sq. ft.
Second floor — 761 sq. ft.
Opt. bath & closet — 106 sq. ft.
Opt. bonus — 347 sq. ft.

Flexible Plan Creates Many Options

No. 90324

This plan features:

— Two bedrooms with optional third bedroom/den

— Two full baths

■ A Great Room featuring vaulted ceiling, fireplace, and built-in bookcase

■ An eat-in Kitchen opening onto a partially enclosed deck through sliding doors

■ An L-shaped design of the Kitchen providing for easy meal preparation

■ A Master Bedroom with private bath, large walk-in closet, and window seat

Main floor — 1,016 sq. ft.

■ *Total living area 1,016 sq. ft.* ■ *Price Code A* ■

MAIN FLOOR

Compact Victorian Ideal for Narrow Lot

No. 90406

This plan features:

— Three bedrooms

— Three full baths

■ A large, front Parlor with a raised hearth fireplace

■ A Dining Room with a sunny bay window

■ An efficient galley Kitchen serving the formal Dining Room and informal Breakfast Room

■ A beautiful Master Suite with two closets, an oversized tub and double vanity, plus a private sitting room with a bayed window and vaulted ceiling

■ An optional basement, slab or crawl space foundation — please specify when ordering

First floor — 954 sq. ft.
Second floor — 783 sq. ft.

■ *Total living area 1,737 sq. ft.* ■ *Price Code B* ■

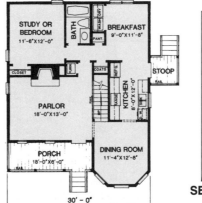

FIRST FLOOR

SECOND FLOOR

Impressive Two-Sided Fireplace

Total living area 1,580 sq. ft. ■ Price Code B

MAIN FLOOR

© design basics, inc.

No. 94972

■ **This plan features:**

— Three bedrooms

— Two full baths

■ Foyer directs traffic flow into the Great Room enhanced by an impressive two-sided fireplace

■ Formal Dining Area is open to the Great Room offering a view of the fireplace

■ French doors off entry access Kitchen with a large Pantry, a planning desk and a snackbar

■ Dinette accesses a large comfortable screen Porch

■ Laundry Room is strategically located off the Kitchen providing direct access from the Garage

■ French doors provide access to the Master Ssuite topped by an elegant, decorative ceiling and highlighted by a pampering bath

Main floor — 1,580 sq. ft.
Garage — 456 sq. ft.

Simple and Practical

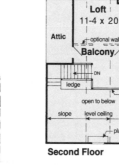

Total living area 1,003 sq. ft. ■ Price Code A

Slab/ Crawl Space Option

Second Floor

First Floor

No. 35009

■ **This plan features:**

— One bedroom

— One full bath

■ A large front Deck area

■ A U-shaped Kitchen with an efficient layout, double sink and ample workspace

■ A Dining area that views the front deck and yard

■ A Living Room with a built-in entertainment center and view of the front deck and yard

■ A large Bedroom that includes a double closet

■ A Loft overlooking the Dining and Living Room, that can be expanded as future needs arise

First floor — 763 sq. ft.
Second floor — 240 sq. ft.

278

Dramatic Windows and Gables

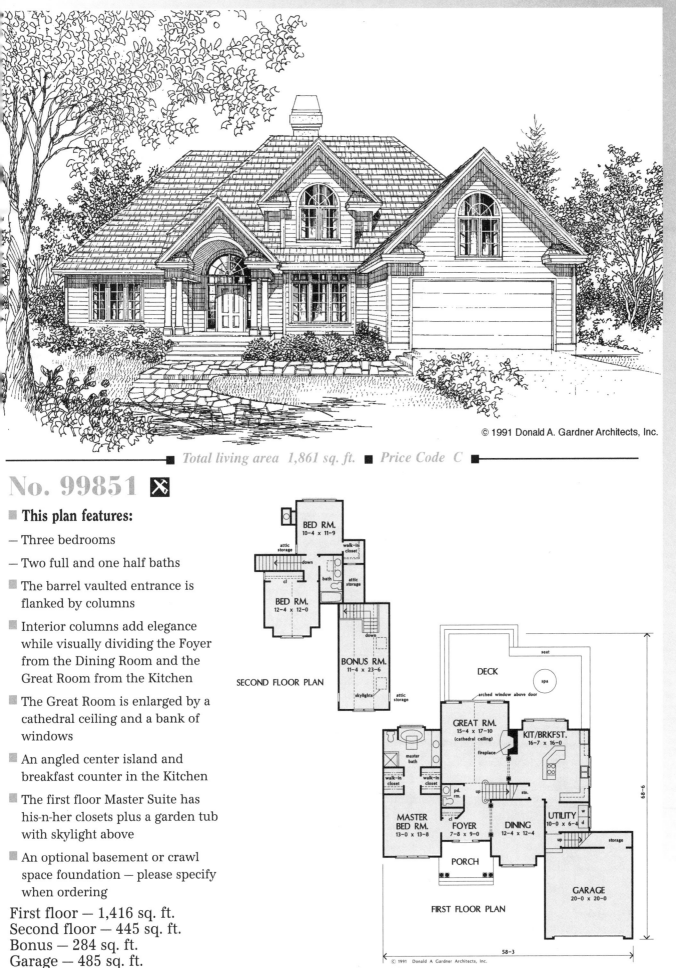

© 1991 Donald A. Gardner Architects, Inc.

■ *Total living area 1,861 sq. ft.* ■ *Price Code C* ■

No. 99851

■ **This plan features:**

— Three bedrooms

— Two full and one half baths

■ The barrel vaulted entrance is flanked by columns

■ Interior columns add elegance while visually dividing the Foyer from the Dining Room and the Great Room from the Kitchen

■ The Great Room is enlarged by a cathedral ceiling and a bank of windows

■ An angled center island and breakfast counter in the Kitchen

■ The first floor Master Suite has his-n-her closets plus a garden tub with skylight above

■ An optional basement or crawl space foundation — please specify when ordering

First floor — 1,416 sq. ft.
Second floor — 445 sq. ft.
Bonus — 284 sq. ft.
Garage — 485 sq. ft.

SECOND FLOOR PLAN

BED RM.
10-4 x 11-9

attic storage

walk-in closet

attic storage

bath

down

cl

BED RM.
12-4 x 12-0

down

BONUS RM.
11-4 x 23-6

skylights

attic storage

FIRST FLOOR PLAN

DECK

seat

spa

arched window above door

GREAT RM.
15-4 x 17-10
(cathedral ceiling)

fireplace

KIT/BRKFST.
16-7 x 16-0

master bath

walk-in closet

walk-in closet

pd. rm.

cl

up

sto.

up

UTILITY
10-0 x 6-4

w
d

MASTER BED RM.
13-0 x 13-8

FOYER
7-8 x 9-0

DINING
12-4 x 12-4

storage

PORCH

GARAGE
20-0 x 20-0

68-6

58-3

© 1991 Donald A Gardner Architects, Inc.

279

Exciting Arched Accents Give Impact

■ *Total living area 2,209 sq. ft.* ■ *Price Code D* ■

Great Room Below skylight walk-in closet

Study 10'3" 13'6"

Bedroom 13'10" x 10'8"

wood rail stairs dn

Hall linen

Bath

Bedroom 11'0" x 13'0" walk-in closet

slope ceiling

Bonus Room 11'1" x 20'

slope ceiling slope ceiling

SECOND FLOOR

Great Room 15'6" x 18'1" high ceiling

Breakfast 11'7" x 12'0"

Laun. hanging space

Bath walk-in closet

wood rail island stove

Kitchen 11'9" x 11' walk-in pantry

Hall

Foyer Dining Room 11' x 13'

Bath

Master Bedroom 13' x 13'11"

Porch

Two-car Garage 20' x 21'

FIRST FLOOR

58'6"

49'

No. 92643

■ This plan features:

— Three bedrooms

— Two full and one half baths

■ Keystone arch accents entrance

■ Great Room enhanced by an entertainment center, a hearth fireplace and a wall of windows

■ Efficient, angled Kitchen offers work island/snackbar, Breakfast area with access to backyard, Laundry, a bath and Garage

■ Master Bedroom wing features a lavish Bath with two vanities and corner window tub

■ No materials list available

First floor — 1,542 sq. ft.
Second floor — 667 sq. ft.
Bonus — 236 sq. ft.
Basement — 1,470 sq. ft.
Garage — 420 sq. ft.

Sunny Two-story Foyer

No. 96476

This plan features:

- Three bedrooms
- Two full and one half baths
- The two-story Foyer off the formal Dining Room sets an elegant mood in this one-and-a-half story, dormered home
- The Great Room and Breakfast Area are both topped by a vaulted ceiling
- The screened porch has a relaxing atmosphere
- The Master Suite on the first floor includes a cathedral ceiling and an elegant bath with whirlpool tub and separate shower
- There is plenty of attic and garage storage space available

First floor — 1,335 sq. ft.
Second floor — 488 sq. ft.
Garage & Storage — 465 sq. ft.

© 1994 Donald A. Gardner Architects, Inc.

■ *Total living area* 1,823 sq. ft. ■ *Price Code C* ■

FIRST FLOOR PLAN

SECOND FLOOR PLAN

First Floor Master Suite

No. 93411

This plan features:

- Three bedrooms
- Two full and one half baths
- Children have their own floor, while adults receive the privacy they deserve in the first floor Master Suite
- An open layout between the Kitchen and Dining Room adds a spacious feeling to the home
- The cooktop island/snack bar expands work space in the Kitchen
- A pass-through into the Family Room offers convenience
- The Family Room includes a fireplace and views to the front yard
- Two secondary bedrooms share the full bath in the hall
- There is no materials list available for this plan

First floor — 1,229 sq. ft.
Second floor — 551 sq. ft.
Basement — 1229 sq. ft.
Garage — 569 sq. ft.

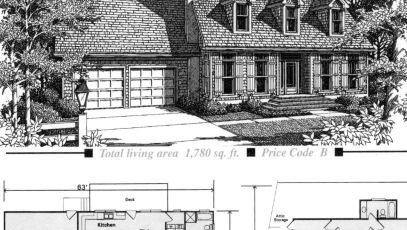

■ *Total living area* 1,780 sq. ft. ■ *Price Code B* ■

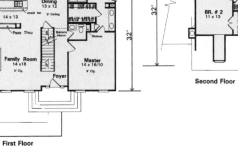

First Floor

Second Floor

An EXCLUSIVE DESIGN
By Greg Marquis

Modern with a Touch of Yesterday

■ Total living area 1,342 sq. ft. ■ Price Code A ■

No. 93121 ℞

■ **This plan features:**

— Three bedrooms

— Two full and one half baths

■ A modern open floor plan with the look of yesterday

■ Living Room accented by a vaulted ceiling and fireplace

■ Open layout between the island Kitchen and Dining Room

■ Main floor Master Suite has a large walk-in closet and a double vanity bath

■ Second floor bedrooms are joined by a single full bath

■ No materials list is available for this plan

First floor — 927 sq. ft.
Second floor — 415 sq. ft.
Basement — 927 sq. ft.
Garage — 446 sq. ft.
Width — 42'-0"
Depth — 44'-0"

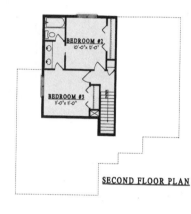

SECOND FLOOR PLAN

MAIN FLOOR PLAN

Comfortable and Charming

No. 92660

■ **This plan features:**

— Three bedrooms

— Two full baths

■ Front entry into an open Foyer and spacious Great Room with massive fireplace between built-ins, and lots of windows with Patio access

■ Formal Dining Room with sloped ceiling and expansive view of back yard

■ Cooktop island and pantry in Kitchen efficiently serve Breakfast area and Dining Room

■ Corner Master Bedroom offers a sloped ceiling, huge walk-in closet and pampering bath with whirlpool tub and two vanities

■ Two additional bedrooms, one with an arched window, share full bath

■ No materials list is available for this plan

Main floor — 1,964 sq. ft.
Garage — 447 sq. ft.
Basement — 1,809 sq. ft.

■ Total living area 1,964 sq. ft. ■ Price Code C ■

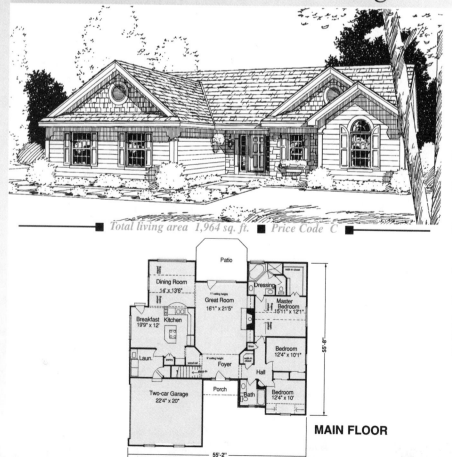

MAIN FLOOR

Brick Opulence and Grandeur

■ Total living area 3,921 sq. ft. ■ Price Code F ■

No. 92248

■ **This plan features:**

— Four bedrooms

— Three full and one half baths

■ Dramatic two-story glass Entry with a curved staircase

■ Both Living and Family rooms offer high ceilings, decorative windows and large fireplaces

■ Large, efficient Kitchen with a cooktop serving island, walk-in pantry, bright Breakfast Area and Patio access

■ Lavish Master Bedroom with a cathedral ceiling, two walk-in closets and large bath

■ Two additional bedrooms with ample closets share a double vanity bath

■ No materials list available

First floor — 2,506 sq. ft.
Second floor — 1,415 sq. ft.
Basement — 2,400 sq. ft.
Garage — 660 sq. ft.

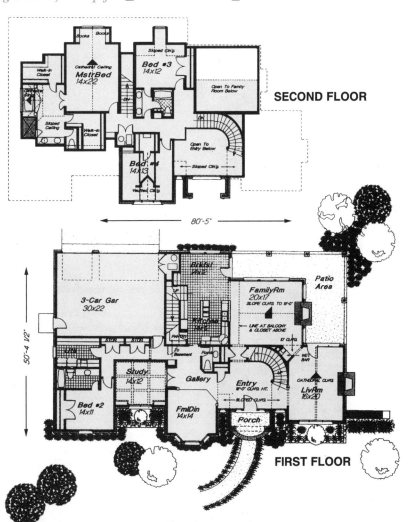

Impressive Fieldstone Facade

Total living area 3,110 sq. ft. ■ Price Code E

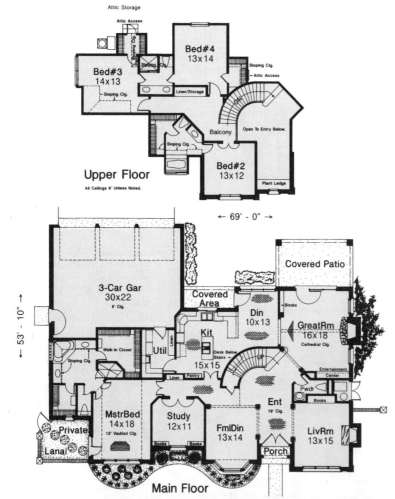

Upper Floor

Attic Storage

Attic Access

Bed#3
14x13

Bed#4
13x14

Linen/Storage

Balcony

Open To Entry Below.

Bed#2
13x12

Plant Ledge

All Ceilings 8' Unless Noted.

← 69' - 0" →

← 53' - 10" →

Main Floor

3-Car Gar
30x22
8' Clg.

Covered Patio

Covered Area

Din
10x13

GreatRm
16x18
Cathedral Clg.

Kit
15x15

Walk-in Closet

Util

Linen
Pantry

Entertainment Center

Pwdr

Ent

MstrBed
14x18
12' Vaulted Clg.

Study
12x11

FmlDin
13x14

LivRm
13x15

Private

Lanai

Porch

No. 92277

■ This plan features:

— Four bedrooms

— Three full and one half baths

■ Double door leads into two-story entry with an exquisite curved staircase

■ Formal Living Room features a marble hearth fireplace, triple window and built-in book shelves

■ Formal Dining Room defined by columns and a lovely bay window

■ Expansive Great Room with entertainment center, fieldstone fireplace and cathedral ceiling

■ Vaulted ceiling crowns Master Bedroom suite offering a plush bath and two walk-in closets

■ No materials list is available for this plan

Main floor — 2,190 sq. ft.
Upper floor — 920 sq. ft.
Garage — 624 sq. ft.

Great Room With Cathedral Ceiling

No. 94970

This plan features:

- Three bedrooms
- One full and one three-quarter baths
- A convenient split ranch design with three steps up from the entry to the Great Room
- Bay window, fireplace and an outstanding volume ceiling highlight the Great Room
- Dinette's angled shape is accentuated by windows on the corner angles and a vaulted ceiling
- Efficient family Kitchen with snackbar/island counter plus a corner sink and built-in pantry
- Master bedroom is enhanced by a tiered ceiling, three quartered bath and a boxed window
- Two additional bedrooms share a full bath in the hall

Main floor — 1,385 sq. ft.
Garage — 658 sq. ft.

Total living area 1,385 sq. ft. ■ Price Code A

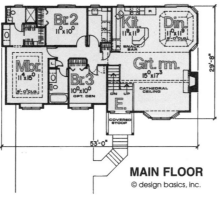

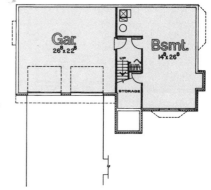

MAIN FLOOR
© design basics, inc.

Carefree Comfort

No. 91418

This plan features:

- Three bedrooms
- Two full baths
- A dramatic vaulted Foyer
- A range top island Kitchen with a sunny eating Nook surrounded by a built-in planter
- A vaulted ceiling in the Great Room with a built-in bar and corner fireplace
- A bayed Dining Room that combines with the Great Room for a spacious feeling
- A Master Bedroom with a private reading nook, vaulted ceiling, walk-in closet, and a well-appointed private Bath
- Two additional bedrooms sharing a full hall bath
- An optional basement, crawl space or slab foundation — please specify when ordering

Main area — 1,665 sq. ft.
Garage — 2-car

Total living area 1,665 sq. ft. ■ Price Code B

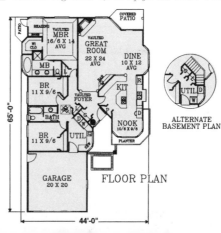

FLOOR PLAN

ALTERNATE BASEMENT PLAN

Exciting Exterior and Impressive Entry

Total living area 1,744 sq. ft. ■ Price Code B

FIRST FLOOR

Garage 19⁹ x 25⁴

Breakfast

Kitchen

Family Room 18⁵ x 13⁹

Dining Room 11⁶ x 10⁵

Two Story Foyer

Bath

Study/Bdrm. 4 11³ x 10⁵

Covered Porch

OPT. BONUS ROOM

Opt. Bonus Room 14⁴ x 14³

Master Bath

Bath

W.i.c.

Bedroom 3 11⁸ x 11²

SECOND FLOOR

Vaulted M.Bath

Master Suite 18² x 13⁰ TRAY CEILING

Bath

W.i.c.

W.i.c.

Bedroom 3 11⁸ x 11²

Foyer Below

Bedroom 2 11³ x 10²

No. 98474

■ This plan features:

— Four bedrooms

— Three full baths

■ A triple arched front porch, segmented arched window keystones and shutters accent the exterior

■ An impressive two-story Foyer adjoins the elegant Dining Room

■ The Family Room, Breakfast Room and Kitchen have an open layout

■ The Study/Bedroom Four is topped by a vaulted ceiling and is located close to a full bath

■ The Master Suite is topped by a tray ceiling while there is a vaulted ceiling over the Bath

■ An optional Bonus Room offers expansion for future needs

■ An optional basement or crawl space foundation — please specify when ordering

■ No materials list is available for this plan

First floor — 972 sq. ft.
Second floor — 772 sq. ft.
Bonus room — 358 sq. ft.
Basement — 972 sq. ft.
Garage — 520 sq. ft.

Entertaining is No Problem

Total living area 2,346 sq. ft. ■ Price Code D

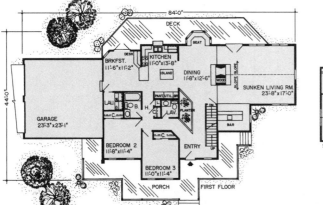

DECK

SEAT

BRKFST. 11⁶ x 11²

KITCHEN 11⁰ x 13⁸

ISLAND

DINING 11⁸ x 12⁶

WOOD

SUNKEN LIVING RM. 23⁸ x 17⁴

LAU.

PANT/UTIL.

LAV.

PLANTER

GARAGE 23³ x 23¹

BAR

BEDROOM 2 11⁸ x 11⁴

ENTRY

BEDROOM 3 11⁰ x 11⁴

PORCH

FIRST FLOOR

SECOND FLOOR

C.

B.

SITTING 11⁸ x 13⁶

M. BEDROOM 11⁰ x 13⁶

No. 10610

■ This plan features:

— Three bedrooms

— Two full and one half baths

■ A Master Bedroom privately set with a sitting area, full bath and walk-in closet

■ An island Kitchen centered between the Dining Room and Breakfast area

■ A sunken Living Room with vaulted ceilings and a two-way fireplace

■ A covered porch and enormous deck

First floor — 1,818 sq. ft.
Second floor — 528 sq. ft.
Basement — 1,818 sq. ft.
Garage — 576 sq. ft.

Elegant Victorian

■ *Total living area 2,455 sq. ft.* ■ *Price Code D* ■

No. 98518

This plan features:

— Three bedrooms

— Two full and one half baths

■ Serve guests dinner in the bayed Dining Room and then gather in the Living Room which features a cathedral ceiling

■ The Family Room is accented by a fireplace

■ The Master Bedroom has a Sitting Area, walk-in closet, and a private bath

■ There is a Bonus Room upstairs for future expansion

■ An optional basement or slab foundation — please specify when ordering

■ No materials list is available for this plan

First floor — 1,447 sq. ft.
Second floor — 1,008 sq. ft.
Garage — 756 sq. ft.

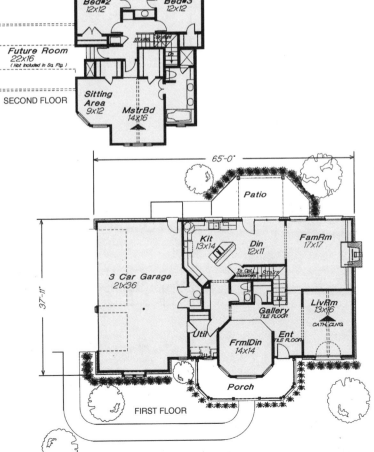

Country Elegance

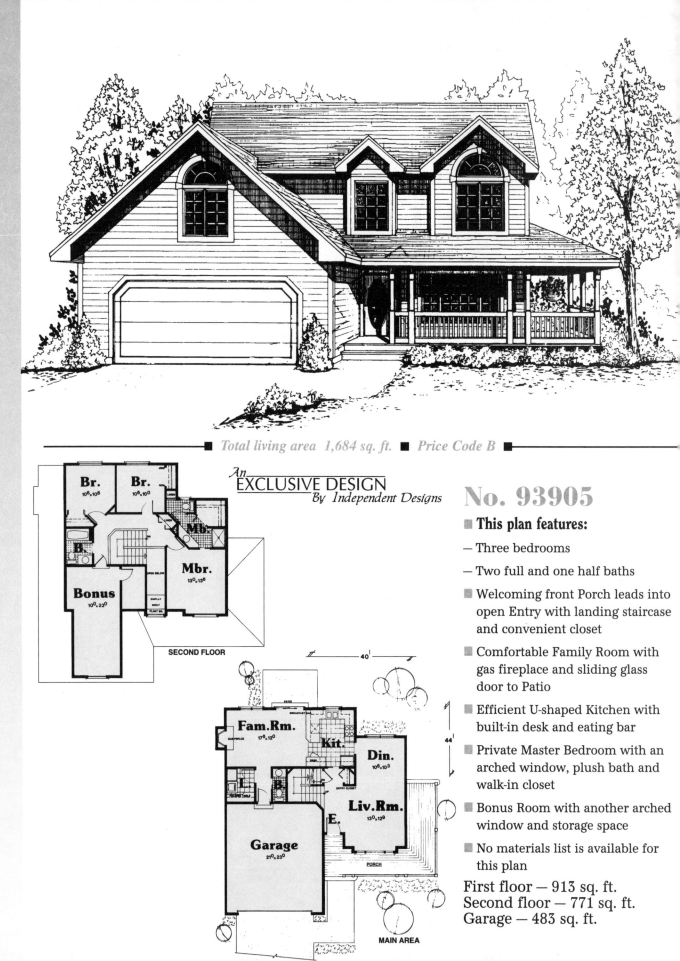

■ *Total living area 1,684 sq. ft.* ■ *Price Code B* ■

An
EXCLUSIVE DESIGN
By Independent Designs

No. 93905

■ **This plan features:**

— Three bedrooms

— Two full and one half baths

■ Welcoming front Porch leads into open Entry with landing staircase and convenient closet

■ Comfortable Family Room with gas fireplace and sliding glass door to Patio

■ Efficient U-shaped Kitchen with built-in desk and eating bar

■ Private Master Bedroom with an arched window, plush bath and walk-in closet

■ Bonus Room with another arched window and storage space

■ No materials list is available for this plan

First floor — 913 sq. ft.
Second floor — 771 sq. ft.
Garage — 483 sq. ft.

Split Bedroom Ranch

No. 90476

This plan features:

- Three bedrooms
- Two full baths
- The formal Foyer opens into the Great room which features a vaulted ceiling and a hearth fireplace
- The U-shaped Kitchen is located between the Dining room and the Breakfast nook
- The secluded Master bedroom is spacious and includes amenities such as walk-in closets and a full bath
- Two secondary Bedrooms have ample closet space and share a full bath
- The covered front Porch and rear Deck provide additional space for entertaining
- An optional basement, slab or a crawl space foundation — please specify when ordering

Main Floor — 1,804 sq. ft.
Basement — 1,804 sq. ft.
Garage — 506 sq. ft.

■ *Total living area 1,804 sq. ft.* ■ *Price Code C* ■

MAIN FLOOR

High Impact Angles

No. 90357

This plan features:

- Three bedrooms
- Two full baths
- Soaring ceilings to give the house a spacious, contemporary feeling
- A fireplaced Great Room adjoining a convenient Kitchen, with a sunny Breakfast Nook
- Sliding glass doors opening onto an angular deck
- A Master Suite with vaulted ceilings and a private bath

Main area — 1,368 sq. ft.

■ *Total living area 1,368 sq. ft.* ■ *Price Code A* ■

Main Floor Plan

Family Favorite

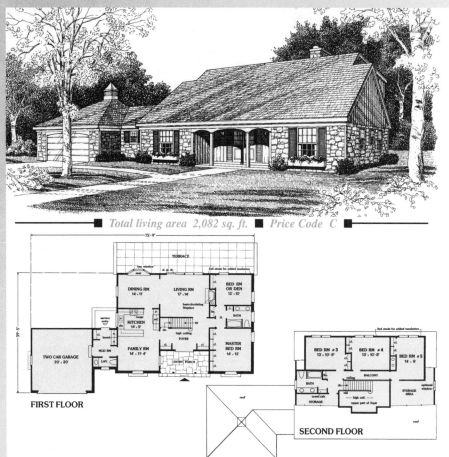

■ Total living area 2,082 sq. ft. ■ Price Code C ■

FIRST FLOOR

SECOND FLOOR

No. 90690

■ **This plan features:**

– Five bedrooms

– Two full and one half baths

■ An efficient Kitchen with a peninsula counter opening into the Family Room

■ A cozy bay window seat in the formal Dining Room

■ A first floor Master Bedroom with an adjoining private Bath including double vanities

■ A heat-circulating fireplace in the Living Room which has sliding glass doors to the Terrace

■ Three bedrooms located on the second floor that share a full bath

First floor — 1,407 sq. ft.
Second floor — 675 sq. ft.
Basement — 1,304 sq. ft.
Garage — 421 sq. ft.

Steep Pitched Roof with Quoins

■ Total living area 1,556 sq. ft. ■ Price Code C ■

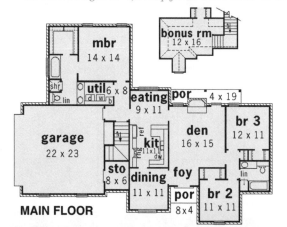

MAIN FLOOR

No. 92556

■ **This plan features:**

– Three bedrooms

– Two full baths

■ Classic brick exterior features a steep pitched roof, and decorative quoins

■ The Foyer leads into the Den which is highlighted by a fireplace

■ The Kitchen is centered between the Dining Room and the Eating Nook

■ Two secondary bedrooms each have walk-in closets and share a full hall bath

■ The isolated Master Bedroom has a walk-in closet and a full bath

■ There is a Bonus Room over the two-car Garage for future expansion

■ An optional slab or crawl space foundation — please specify when ordering

Main floor — 1,556 sq. ft.
Bonus — 282 sq. ft.
Garage — 565 sq. ft.
Width — 66'-10"
Depth — 50'-10"

Keystones, Arches and Gables

■ *Total living area 1,642 sq. ft.* ■ *Price Code B* ■

No. 93171

■ **This plan features:**

— Three bedrooms

— Two full and one half baths

■ Tiled Entry opens to Living Room with focal point fireplace

■ U-shaped Kitchen with a built-in pantry, eating bar and nearby laundry/Garage entry

■ Comfortable Dining Room with bay window and French doors to Screen Porch expanding living area outdoors

■ Corner Master Bedroom offers a great walk-in closet and private bath

■ Two additional bedrooms with ample closets and double windows share a full bath

■ No materials list is available for this plan

Main floor — 1,642 sq. ft.
Basement — 1,642 sq. ft.

MAIN FLOOR PLAN

Cozy Country Ranch

■ *Total living area 1,576 sq. ft.* ■ *Price Code B* ■

No. 24708

■ This plan features:

— Three bedrooms

— Two full baths

■ Front Porch shelters outdoor visiting and entrance into Living Room

■ Expansive Living Room highlighted by a boxed window and hearth fireplace between built-ins

■ Columns frame entrance to Dining Room which has access to backyard

■ Efficient, U-shaped Kitchen with direct access to the Screened Porch and the Dining Room

■ Master Bedroom wing enhanced by a large walk-in closet and a double vanity bath with a whirlpool tub

■ Two additional bedrooms with large closets share a double vanity bath with laundry center

■ No materials list is available for this plan

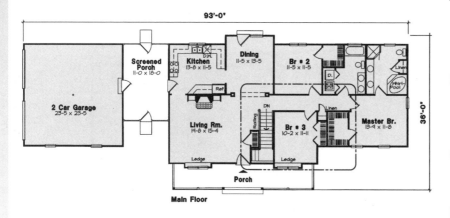

Main Floor

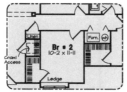

Alternate Crawl/Slab Plan

Main floor — 1,576 sq. ft.
Garage — 576 sq. ft.
Basement — 1,454 sq. ft.

Colonial Home with All the Traditional Comforts

No. 34705

■ Total living area 2,224 sq. ft. ■ Price Code D ■

■ This plan features:

— Four bedrooms

— Two full and one half baths

■ A formal Living Room and Dining Room flanking a spacious entry

■ Family areas flowing together into an open space at the rear of the home

■ An island Kitchen with a built-in pantry centrally located for easy service to the Dining Room and Breakfast area

■ A Master Suite including large closets and double vanities in the bath

First floor — 1,090 sq. ft.
Second floor — 1,134 sq. ft.
Basement — 1,090 sq. ft.
Garage — 576 sq. ft.

Basement Option

Second Floor

MBr 1 13-8 x 15-6
Br 2 11-8 x 16
Br 3 11-4 x 10-8
Br 4 11-4 x 10-8

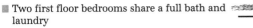

First Floor

66'-0"
27'-0"

Garage 21-8 x 23-4

Kitchen 10-4 x 12-6
Brkfst 10-8 x 10-2
island
pan
Family Rm 20 x 12-6

Dining Rm 13-8 x 12-6
Living 15 x 12-6
UP

Charming Country Home

No. 24711

■ This plan features:

— Three bedrooms

— Two full baths

■ A welcoming front Porch invites visiting and shelters entrance

■ Cozy fireplace below a vaulted ceiling and dormer window in Living Room

■ Country Kitchen with a peninsula counter/snackbar, built-in pantry and access to laundry and Screened Area-way and Garage beyond

■ Two first floor bedrooms share a full bath and laundry

■ Private second floor Master Suite offers a dormer window, walk-in closet and private bath

■ No materials list is available for this plan

First floor — 1,018 sq. ft.
Second floor — 416 sq. ft.
Garage — 624 sq. ft.
Basement — 1,008 sq. ft.

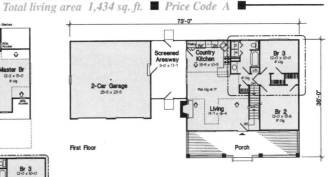

■ Total living area 1,434 sq. ft. ■ Price Code A ■

Second Floor

Master Br 12-2 x 15-0

First Floor

73'-0"
38'-0"

2-Car Garage 25-5 x 23-5

Screened Areaway 11-0 x 17-7

Country Kitchen 15-4 x 10-5

Br 3 12-0 x 10-0

Br 2 12-0 x 10-6

Living 14-1 x 16-4

Porch

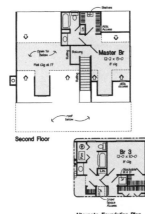

Br 3 12-0 x 10-0

Alternate Foundation Plan

Year Round Retreat

■ Total living area 1,432 sq. ft. ■ Price Code A ■

No. 90613

■ **This plan features:**

— Three bedrooms

— Two full baths

■ A Living Room with a dramatic sloping ceiling and a wood burning stove

■ A Kitchen and Living Room opening onto the rear deck

■ A Master Suite with a full bath, linen closet and ample closet space

■ Two bedrooms and a full bath upstairs with open views from the balcony to the living room

First floor — 967 sq. ft.
Second floor — 465 sq. ft.
Basement — 811 sq. ft
Garage — 234 sq. ft.

FIRST FLOOR

SECOND FLOOR

Amenity-Packed Affordability

■ Total living area 1,484 sq. ft. ■ Price Code B ■

No. 92525

■ **This plan features:**

— Three bedrooms

— Two full baths

■ A sheltered entrance inviting your guests onward

■ A fireplace in the Den offering a focal point, while the decorative ceiling adds definition to the room

■ A well-equipped Kitchen flowing with ease into the Breakfast bay or Dining Room

■ A Master Bedroom, having two closets and a private Master Bath

■ An optional crawlspace or slab foundation — please specify when ordering

Main area — 1,484 sq. ft.
Garage — 544 sq. ft.
Width — 65'-6"
Depth — 38'-0"

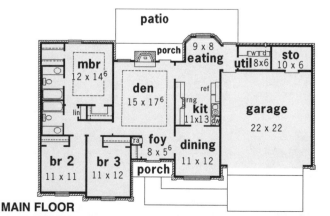

MAIN FLOOR

Traditional Ranch Plan

■ *Total living area 2,218 sq. ft.* ■ *Price Code D* ■

No. 90454 ⚒

■ This plan features:

— Three bedrooms

— Two full baths

■ Large Foyer set between the formal Living and Dining rooms

■ Spacious Great Room adjacent to the open Kitchen/Breakfast area

■ Secluded Master Bedroom highlighted by the master bath with a garden tub, separate shower and his-n-her vanities

■ Bay window allows bountiful natural light into the Breakfast Area

■ Two additional bedrooms sharing a full bath

■ An optional basement or crawl space foundation — please specify when ordering

Main floor — 2,218 sq. ft.
Basement — 1,658 sq. ft.
Garage — 528 sq. ft.

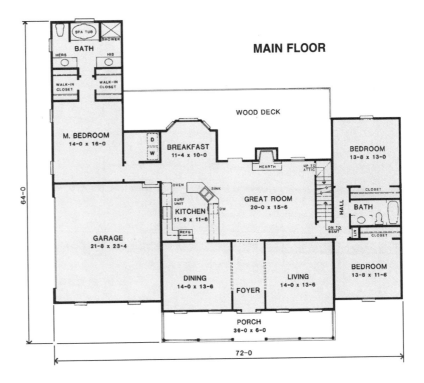

MAIN FLOOR

Traditional Ranch

■ *Total living area 2,275 sq. ft.* ■ *Price Code D* ■

MAIN FLOOR

No. 92404

■ **This plan features:**

— Three bedrooms

— Two full baths

■ A tray ceiling in the Master Suite that is equipped with his -n- her walk-in closets and a private Master Bath with a cathedral ceiling

■ A formal Living Room with a cathedral ceiling

■ A decorative tray ceiling in the elegant formal Dining Room

■ A spacious Family Room with a vaulted ceiling and a fireplace

■ A modern, well-appointed Kitchen with snack bar and bayed Breakfast area

■ Two additional bedrooms that share a full hall bath each having a walk-in closet

Main floor — 2,275 sq. ft.
Basement — 2,207 sq. ft.
Garage — 512 sq. ft.

Great Room Heart of Home

No. 93015

■ This plan features:

— Three bedrooms

— Two full baths

■ Sheltered porch leads into the Entry with arches and a Great Room

■ Spacious Great Room with a ten foot ceiling above a wall of windows and rear yard access

■ Efficient Kitchen with a built-in pantry, a laundry closet and a Breakfast area accented by a decorative window

■ Bay of windows enhances the Master Bedroom suite with a double vanity bath and a walk-in closet

■ Two additional bedrooms with ample closets, share a full bath

■ This plan is available with a Slab foundation only

■ No materials list is available for this plan

Main floor — 1,087 sq. ft.

■ *Total living area 1,087 sq. ft.* ■ *Price Code A* ■

MAIN FLOOR

Arches Grace Classic Facade

No. 10677

■ This plan features:

— Three bedrooms

— Two full and one half baths

■ Built-in planters and half walls to define rooms

■ A balcony that connects three upstairs bedrooms

■ Double sinks and built-in vanities in the Master Bath

■ Ample closet space

First floor — 932 sq. ft.
Second floor — 764 sq. ft.
Garage — 430 sq. ft.
Basement — 920 sq. ft.

■ *Total living area 1,696 sq. ft.* ■ *Price Code B* ■

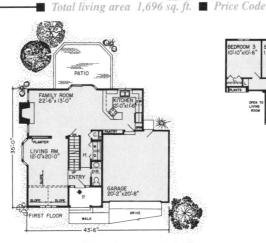

Rustic Retreat

Total living area 897 sq. ft. ■ **Price Code A**

Loft
9 x 12

railing

38'-0"

Br 1
14-8 x 9-6

line of loft above

Nook   Kit.
8x 11-6
pantry

Living
14 x 17

linen

ladder

Br 2
14-8 x 9-6

grill

26'-0"

Deck

Main Floor

No. 24309

■ **This plan features:**

— Two bedrooms

— One full bath

■ A wrap-around deck equipped with a built-in bar-b-que for easy outdoor living

■ An entry, in a wall of glass, opens the Living area to the outdoors

■ A large fireplace in the Living area opens into an efficient Kitchen, with a built-in pantry, that serves the Nook area

■ Two bedrooms share a centrally located full bath with a window tub

■ A loft area ready for multiple uses

Main floor — 789 sq. ft.
Loft — 108 sq. ft.

An
EXCLUSIVE DESIGN
By Marshall Associates

Good Things Come in Small Packages

Total living area 1,253 sq. ft. ■ **Price Code A**

36'-5"

DN

BRK.

KITCHEN
16'-8" x 8'-0"

SKLT.

BEDRM.3
11'-8" x 10'-4"

B.

LIVING RM.
16'-0"
x
14'-6"

UP

BEDRM.2
11'-6" x 10'-4"

30'-0"

SEAT   SL. SL.

DN

COAT/BOOT
STOR.

FIRST FLOOR

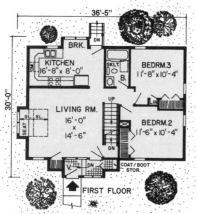

VAN.

B.

SKYLT.

SH

TO ATTIC   SHELVES

MBEDRM.
11'-6" x 15'-4"

LIN

DN

SLOPE
CLG.

LEVEL
CLG.

SLOPE
CLG.

SECOND FLOOR

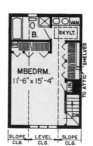

No. 20303

■ **This plan features:**

— Three bedrooms

— Two full baths

■ An air-lock vestibule entry that keeps the chill outside

■ A cozy sitting nook in the Living Room

■ A well-equipped Kitchen with a Breakfast nook

■ A sky-lit hall bath shared by two of the bedrooms

■ A Master Suite with his-n-her closets and a private, sky lit full bath

First floor — 885 sq. ft.
Second floor — 368 sq. ft.
Basement — 715 sq. ft.

One-Story Country Home

■ Total living area 1,367 sq. ft. ■ Price Code A ■

No. 99639

■ This plan features:

— Three bedrooms

— Two full baths

■ A Living Room with an imposing high ceiling that slopes down to a normal height of eight feet, focusing on the decorative heat-circulating fireplace at the rear wall

■ An efficient Kitchen that adjoins the Dining Room

■ A Dinette Area for informal eating in the Kitchen that can comfortably seat six people

■ A Master Suite arranged with a large dressing area that has a walk-in closet plus two linear closets and space for a vanity

Main area — 1,367 sq. ft.
Basement — 1,267 sq. ft.
Garage — 431 sq. ft.

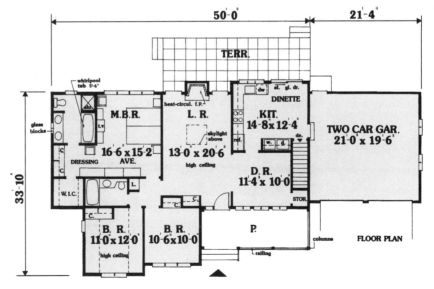

FLOOR PLAN

Distinctive Detail and Design

■ *Total living area 1,897 sq. ft.* ■ *Price Code C* ■

walk-in closet

Master Bedroom
12' x 14'11"

Bedroom
10'6" x 11'2"

Great Room Below

Bath

Bath

computer desk

Balcony

Bedroom
11' x 12'

stairs dn

window seat

SECOND FLOOR

Laun.

hanging space

Bath

Breakfast
10'8" x 11'

10'6" x 13'6"
Kitchen

pantry

French doors w/ arched window above

Great Room
14'10" x 17'1"

high ceiling

wood rail

Two-car Garage
20' x 21'

furniture alcove

Dining Room
11' x 13'7"

Foyer

stairs up

stairs dn

FIRST FLOOR

38'

48'

No. 92644

■ This plan features:

— Three bedrooms

— Two full and one half baths

■ Impressive pilaster entry into open Foyer with landing staircase

■ Great Room accented by hearth fireplace and French doors

■ Formal Dining Room enhanced by furniture alcove

■ Efficient, L-shaped Kitchen with work island, walk-in pantry and bright Breakfast Area

■ Quiet Master Bedroom offers a walk-in closet, and plush bath with two vanities and whirlpool tub

■ Two additional bedrooms share a full bath and computer desk

■ No materials list available

First floor — 1,036 sq. ft.
Second floor — 861 sq. ft.
Garage — 420 sq. ft.

Designed for Sloping Lot

No. 91517

This plan features:

— Three bedrooms

— Two full and one half baths

■ An impressive elevation accented by palladium windows and a raised entrance

■ Two-story Living Room with corner fireplace opens to Dining area and Kitchen for ease in entertaining

■ Expansive Dining area with atrium door to rear yard

■ Efficient Kitchen with built-in pantry and angled serving counter

■ Comfortable Family Room with French doors to raised Deck and easy access to laundry and half bath

■ Secluded Master suite with arched window below vaulted ceiling, walk-in closet and double vanity bath

■ Two additional bedrooms with ample closets share a full bath

Main floor — 1,022 sq. ft.
Upper floor — 813 sq. ft.
Basement — 1077 sq. ft.

Total living area 1,835 sq. ft. ■ Price Code C

◀ 36' ▶

33'

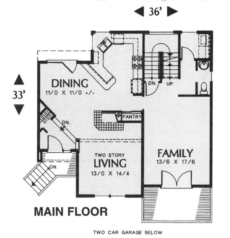

MAIN FLOOR

TWO CAR GARAGE BELOW

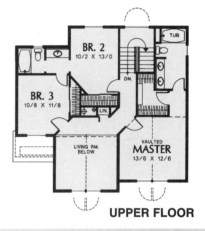

UPPER FLOOR

Timeless Appeal

No. 93075

This plan features:

— Three bedrooms

— Two full baths

■ Ten foot ceilings giving the Living Room an open feel

■ Cozy corner fireplace and access to the rear yard highlight the Living Room

■ Dining area enhanced by a sunny bay window and is open to the Kitchen

■ Bedrooms conveniently grouped and include roomy closets

■ Master Bedroom features a private bath

■ Garage is located on the rear and not visible from the front

■ An optional slab or crawl space foundation — please specify when ordering

■ No materials list is available for this plan

Main floor — 1,170 sq. ft.
Garage — 478 sq. ft.

Total living area 1,170 sq. ft. ■ Price Code A

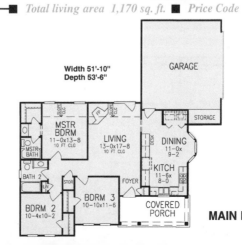

Width 51'-10"
Depth 53'-6"

MAIN FLOOR

Fieldstone with Flexible Floor Plan

■ *Total living area 2,234 sq. ft.* ■ *Price Code D* ■

FIRST FLOOR

ALTERNATE 2-BEDROOM

SECOND FLOOR

No. 90600 ✖

■ **This plan features:**

— Four or five bedrooms

— Two full and two half baths

■ Unique design expands from a cozy five room cottage to an eight room home

■ Portico leads into an open Foyer with a landing staircase

■ Spacious Living/Dining Room with a hearth fireplace and sliding glass door to back yard

■ Hub Kitchen with peninsula snackbar and nearby Dining Room, Family Room, Laundry/Mud Room with Garage entry

■ Master Suite offers a fireplace, Porch access and dressing area with built-in desk/vanity

■ Alternative floor plan offers two bedrooms on first floor, one with a fireplace

■ Three second floor bedrooms with loads of closets, share one and a half baths

First floor — 1,409 sq. ft.
Second floor — 825 sq. ft.
Basement — 1,038 sq. ft.
Garage — 511 sq. ft.

Half-Round Window Graces Attractive Exterior

■ *Total living area 1,452 sq. ft.* ■ *Price Code A* ■

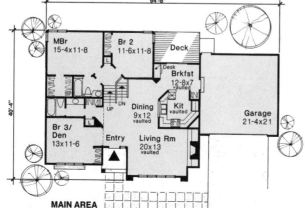

MAIN AREA

No. 90395 ✖

■ **This plan features:**

— Three bedrooms

— Two full baths

■ Soaring ceilings in the Kitchen, Living Room, Dining, and Breakfast Rooms

■ An efficient, well-equipped Kitchen with a pass-through to the Dining room

■ Built-in bookcases flanking the fireplace in the Living Room

■ A Master Suite with a private Master Bath and walk-in closet

Main floor — 1,452 sq. ft
Basement — 1,452 sq. ft.
Garage — 448 sq. ft.

302

© 1995 Donald A. Gardner Architects, Inc.

■ *Total living area 1,561 sq. ft.* ■ *Price Code C* ■

No. 96417

■ This plan features:

— Three bedrooms

— Two full baths

■ Arched windows, dormers and charming front and back porches with columns creating country flavoring

■ Central Great Room topped by a cathedral ceiling, a fireplace and a clerestory window

■ Breakfast bay for casual dining is open to the Kitchen

■ Columns accenting the entryway into the formal Dining Room

■ Cathedral ceiling crowning the Master Bedroom

■ Master Bath with skylights, whirlpool tub, shower, and a double vanity

Main floor — 1, 561 sq. ft.
Garage & Storage — 346 sq. ft.

© 1995 Donald A Gardner Architects, Inc.

European Style

■ *Total living area* 2,727 sq. ft. ■ *Price Code F* ■

No. 92501 ✖

■ This plan features:

— Four bedrooms

— Three full and one half baths

■ Central Foyer between spacious Living and Dining rooms with arched windows

■ Hub Kitchen with extended counter and nearby Utility/Garage entry, easily serves Breakfast Area and Dining Room

■ Spacious Den with a hearth fireplace between built-ins and sliding glass doors to Porch

■ Master Bedroom wing with decorative ceiling, plush bath with two walk-in closets

■ Three additional bedrooms with ample closets and private access to a full bath

■ An optional slab or crawl space foundation — please specify when ordering

WIDTH 70'-10'
DEPTH 64'-5"

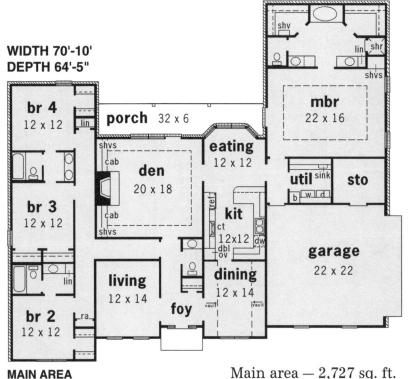

MAIN AREA

Main area — 2,727 sq. ft.
Garage — 569 sq. ft.

Carefree Living on One Level

No. 20089

This plan features:

— Three bedrooms

— Two full baths

■ A full basement and an oversized two-car Garage

■ A spacious Master Suite with a walk-in closet

■ A fireplaced Living Room, an open Dining Room and Kitchen for convenience

Main floor— 1,588 sq. ft.
Basement — 780 sq. ft.
Garage — 808 sq. ft.

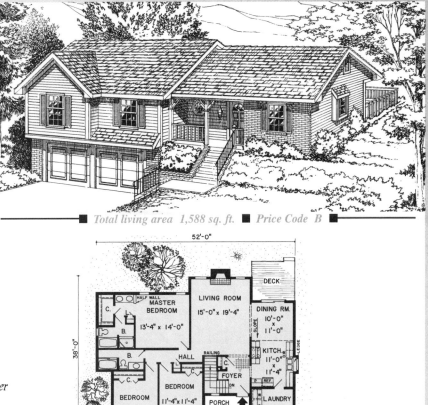

■ Total living area 1,588 sq. ft. ■ Price Code B ■

An EXCLUSIVE DESIGN
By Karl Kreeger

MAIN FLOOR

Stately Entrance Adds to Home's Exterior

No. 24268

This plan features:

— Three or four bedrooms

— Two full and one half baths

■ A vaulted ceiling in the Living Room adding to its spaciousness

■ A formal Dining Room with easy access to both the Living Room and the Kitchen

■ An efficient Kitchen with double sinks, and ample storage and counter space

■ An informal Eating Nook with a built-in pantry

■ A large Family Room with a fireplace

■ A plush Master Suite with a vaulted ceiling and luxurious Master Bath plus two walk-in closets

■ Two additional bedrooms share a full bath with a convenient laundry chute

First floor — 1,115 sq. ft.
Second floor — 1,129 sq. ft.
Basement — 1,096 sq. ft.
Garage — 415 sq. ft.

■ Total living area 2,244 sq. ft. ■ Price Code D ■

An EXCLUSIVE DESIGN
By Energetic Enterprises

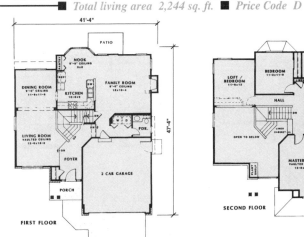

FIRST FLOOR

SECOND FLOOR

Step Saving, One Floor Convenience

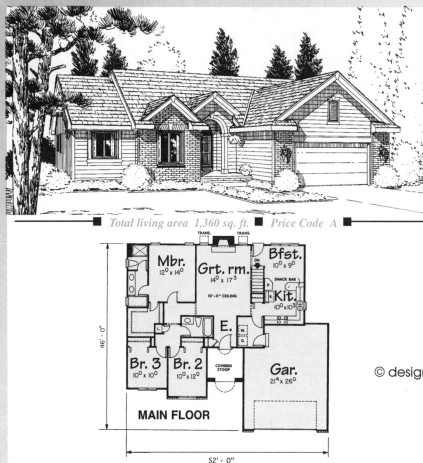

Total living area 1,360 sq. ft. ■ **Price Code A**

MAIN FLOOR

- Mbr. 12⁰ x 14⁰
- Grt. rm. 14⁰ x 17³ — 10'-0" CEILING
- Bfst. 10⁰ x 9⁰
- Kit. 10⁰ x 10³
- SNACK BAR
- Br. 3 10⁰ x 10⁰
- Br. 2 10⁰ x 12⁰
- COVERED STOOP
- Gar. 21⁴ x 26⁰
- 46'-0"
- 52'-0"
- TRANS. TRANS.
- DN
- E.
- W. D.

No. 94982

■ This plan features:

— Three bedrooms

— One full and one three quarter baths

■ The covered Porch leads to a short entry way with a convenient coat closet

■ The fireplace with transoms to either side highlights the Great Room

■ The Kitchen/Breakfast area features a pantry, an extended counter/snackbar and a double sink

■ The Laundry Room doubles as a Mud Room from the garage

■ The Master Suite includes a private bath and a large walk-in closet

■ Two secondary bedroom are located in close proximity to a full bath

Main floor — 1,360 sq. ft.
Garage — 544 sq. ft.

© design basics, inc.

Inviting Front Porch

Total living area 1,683 sq. ft. ■ **Price Code B**

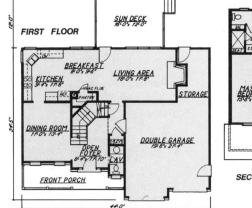

FIRST FLOOR

- SUN DECK 16⁰ x 12⁰
- BREAKFAST 8⁰ x 9⁶
- KITCHEN 9⁴ x 7⁸
- LIVING AREA 16⁰ x 17⁸
- STORAGE
- PANTRY
- DINING ROOM 11⁰ x 13⁴
- OPEN FOYER 8⁴ x 7'10"
- DOUBLE GARAGE 19⁸ x 21⁴
- LAV.
- FRONT PORCH

SECOND FLOOR

- M. BATH
- BEDROOM 3 13⁰ x 9⁶
- LINEN
- HVAC FLUE
- BATH 2
- MASTER BEDROOM 13⁶ x 17⁰
- BEDROOM 2 13⁰ x 9⁶
- OPEN TO FOYER

No. 93298

■ This plan features:

— Three bedrooms

— Two full and one half baths

■ Detailed gables and inviting front porch create a warm welcoming facade

■ Open foyer features an angled staircase, a half bath and a coat closet

■ The expansive, informal Living Area at the rear of the home features a fireplace and opens onto the sundeck

■ The efficient Kitchen has easy access to both the formal and informal dining areas

■ Master Bedroom includes a walk-in closet and compartmented private bath

■ Two secondary bedrooms share a bath with a double vanity

■ No materials list is available for this plan

First floor — 797 sq. ft.
Second floor — 886 sq. ft.
Basement — 797 sq. ft.
Garage — 414 sq. ft.

An
EXCLUSIVE DESIGN
By Jannis Vann & Associates, Inc.

Wide Open and Convenient

■ *Total living area 1,737 sq. ft.* ■ *Price Code B* ■

No. 20100

■ This plan features:

— Three bedrooms

— Two full baths

■ Vaulted ceilings in the Dining Room and Master Bedroom

■ A sloped ceiling in the fireplaced Living Room

■ A skylight illuminating the master bath

■ A large Master Bedroom with a walk-in closet

Main floor — 1,737 sq. ft.
Basement — 1,727 sq. ft.
Garage — 484 sq. ft.

An
EXCLUSIVE DESIGN
By Karl Kreeger

MAIN FLOOR

Compact Three Bedroom

© 1990 Donald A. Gardner Architects, Inc.

■ *Total living area 1,452 sq. ft.* ■ *Price Code B* ■

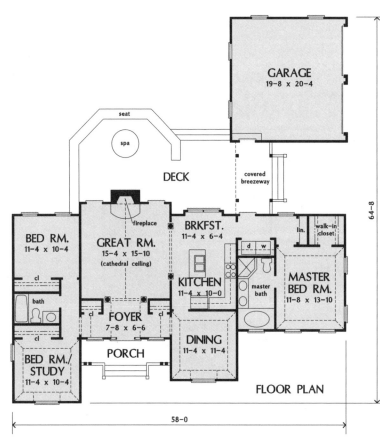

GARAGE
19-8 x 20-4

seat

spa

DECK

covered breezeway

fireplace

BED RM.
11-4 x 10-4

GREAT RM.
15-4 x 15-10
(cathedral ceiling)

BRKFST.
11-4 x 6-4

lin.

walk-in closet

KITCHEN
11-4 x 10-0

d w

master bath

MASTER BED RM.
11-8 x 13-10

cl

bath

cl

FOYER
7-8 x 6-6

cl

DINING
11-4 x 11-4

BED RM./
STUDY
11-4 x 10-4

PORCH

FLOOR PLAN

58-0

64-8

© 1990 Donald A. Gardner Architects, Inc.

No. 96418

■ **This plan features:**

— Three bedrooms

— Two full baths

■ Contemporary interior punctuated by elegant columns

■ Dormers above the covered Porch light the Foyer leading to the dramatic Great Room crowned in a cathedral ceiling and enhanced by a fireplace

■ Great Room opens to the island Kitchen with Breakfast area and access to a spacious rear Deck

■ Tray ceilings adding interest to the Bedroom/Study, Dining Room and the Master Bedroom

■ Luxurious Master Bedroom highlighted by a walk-in closet and a bath with dual vanity, shower and whirlpool tub

Main floor — 1,452 sq. ft.
Garage & storage — 427 sq. ft.

Large Living in a Small Space

No. 24304 ✖

■ This plan features:

— Three bedrooms

— Two full baths

■ A sheltered entrance leads into an open Living Room with a corner fireplace and a wall of windows

■ A well-equipped Kitchen features a peninsula counter with a Nook, a laundry and clothes closet, and a built-in pantry

■ A Master Bedroom with a private bath

■ Two additional bedrooms that share full hall bath

Main floor — 993 sq. ft.
Garage — 390 sq. ft.
Basement — 987 sq. ft.

An EXCLUSIVE DESIGN
By Marshall Associates

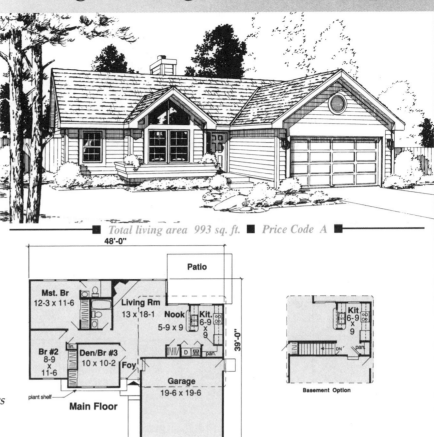

■ *Total living area 993 sq. ft.* ■ *Price Code A* ■

Main Floor

Basement Option

Fireplace Center of Circular Living Area

No. 10274 ✖

■ This plan features:

— Three bedrooms

— Two full baths

■ A dramatically positioned fireplace as a focal point for the main living area

■ The Kitchen, Dining and Living Rooms form a circle that allows work areas to flow into living areas

■ Sliding glass doors accessible to wood a Deck

■ A convenient Laundry Room located off the Kitchen

■ A double Garage providing excellent storage

Main area— 1,783 sq. ft.
Garage — 576 sq. ft.

■ *Total living area 1,783 sq. ft.* ■ *Price Code B* ■

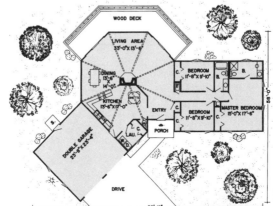

MAIN FLOOR

Country Styled Duplex

■ Total living area 1,288 sq. ft. ■ Price Code G ■

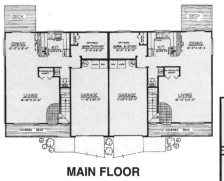

MAIN FLOOR

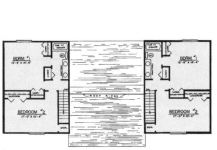

SECOND FLOOR

No. 91335

■ This plan features(per unit):

— Two or three bedrooms

— One and a half baths

■ Covered sitting porch, cedar shingles on gable ends, wood shutters and window boxes add to country flavor

■ Tiled entry into spacious Living area with decorative window, opens to Dining area

■ Efficient, U-shaped Kitchen with a serving counter/snackbar

■ First floor Study/Bedroom with closet and access to a half bath

■ Large second floor bedrooms offer maximum privacy with separating roof

■ Rear bedroom enhanced by two closets and private access to double vanity bath

Main floor — 700 sq. ft.
Second floor — 588 sq. ft.
Width — 66'-0"
Depth — 32'-0"

Arches are Appealing

■ Total living area 1,642 sq. ft. ■ Price Code B ■

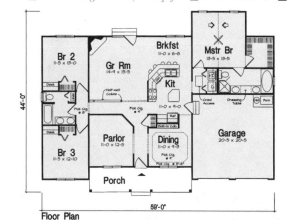

Floor Plan

No. 24717

■ This plan features:

— Three bedrooms

— Two full baths

■ Welcoming front Porch enhanced by graceful columns and curved windows

■ Parlor and Dining Room frame entry hall

■ Expansive Great Room accented by a corner fireplace and outdoor access

■ Open and convenient Kitchen with a work island, angled, peninsula counter/eating bar, and nearby laundry and Garage entry

■ Secluded Master Bedroom with a large walk-in closet and luxurious bath with a dressing table

■ Two additional bedrooms with ample closets, share a double vanity bath

■ No materials list is available for this plan

Main floor — 1,642 sq. ft.
Garage — 430 sq. ft.

Double Gables and Exciting Entry

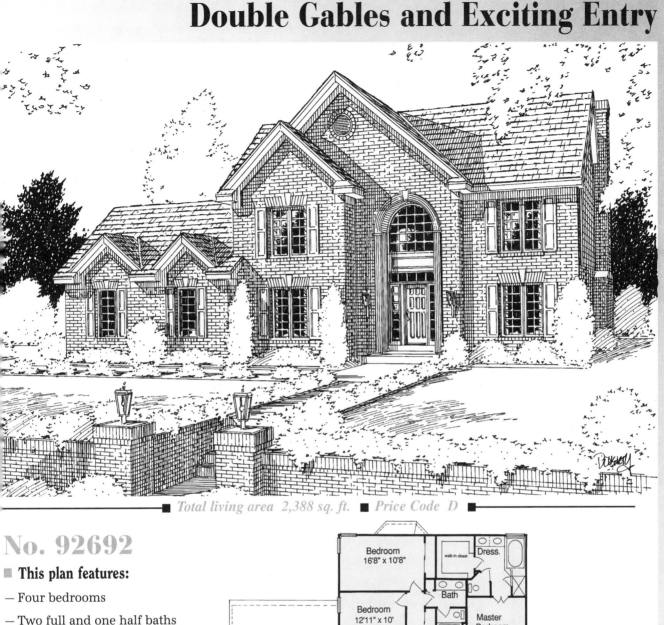

■ *Total living area 2,388 sq. ft.* ■ *Price Code D* ■

No. 92692

■ **This plan features:**

— Four bedrooms

— Two full and one half baths

■ Impressive exterior features double gables and arched window

■ Foyer separates the Dining Room and Living Room

■ Roomy Kitchen and Breakfast Bay are adjacent to the large Family Room which has a fireplace

■ Spacious Master Bedroom features private bath with dual vanity, shower stall and whirlpool tub

■ Three additional bedrooms share a full hall bath

■ No materials list is available for this plan

First floor — 1,207 sq. ft.
Second floor — 1,181 sq. ft.
Basement — 1,207 sq. ft.
Garage — 484 sq. ft.

SECOND FLOOR

FIRST FLOOR

Dramatic Design

■ *Total living area 2,607 sq. ft.* ■ *Price Code E* ■

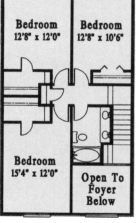

Bedroom 12'8" x 12'0"

Bedroom 12'8" x 10'6"

Bedroom 15'4" x 12'0"

Open To Foyer Below

Upper Level Floor Plan

An
EXCLUSIVE DESIGN
By Building Science Associates

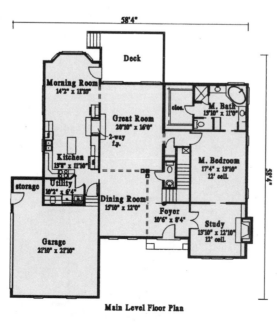

Main Level Floor Plan

No. 93709

■ **This plan features:**

— Four bedrooms

— Two full and one half baths

■ Dramatic two-story Foyer flows into the formal dining area which is defined by a cluster of columns

■ Great Room shares a two-way fireplace with the Morning Room that opens onto the deck

■ The Kitchen features a built-in pantry, island and a planning desk

■ The Master Bedroom has a private, double vanity bath and a walk-in closet

■ Three upstairs bedrooms contain abundant closet space and share an oversized bath

■ No materials list is available for this plan

First floor — 1,910 sq. ft.
Second floor — 697 sq. ft.
Garage — 536 sq. ft.

Cozy and Comfortable

No. 93306

This plan features:

– Three bedrooms

– Two full and one half baths

■ Center Foyer leads into formal Living and Dining rooms

■ Open Family Room accented by hearth fireplace

■ Efficient Kitchen with peninsula counter, nearby Laundry and Garage entry, and Dinette with access to rear yard

■ Corner Master Bedroom offers a plush bath with a double vanity and whirlpool tub

■ Two additional bedrooms with ample closets share a full bath

■ No materials list is available for this plan

First floor — 884 sq. ft.
Second floor — 788 sq. ft.
Basement — 884 sq. ft.
Garage — 450 sq. ft.

An
EXCLUSIVE DESIGN
By Patrick Morabito, A.I.A. Architect

Total living area 1,672 sq. ft. ■ *Price Code B*

FIRST FLOOR PLAN

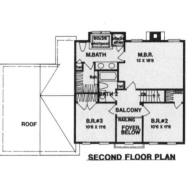

SECOND FLOOR PLAN

Deck Surrounds House on Three Sides

No. 91304 ✖

This plan features:

– Three bedrooms

– One full, one three-quarter and one half baths

■ A sunken, circular Living Room with windows on four sides and a vaulted clerestory for a wide-open feeling

■ Back-to-back fireplaces in the Living Room and the adjoining Great Room

■ A convenient, efficient Kitchen with a sunny Eating Nook

■ A Master Suite with a walk-in closet and a private master bath

■ Two additional bedrooms that share a full hall bath

First floor — 1,439 sq. ft.
Second floor — 873 sq. ft.

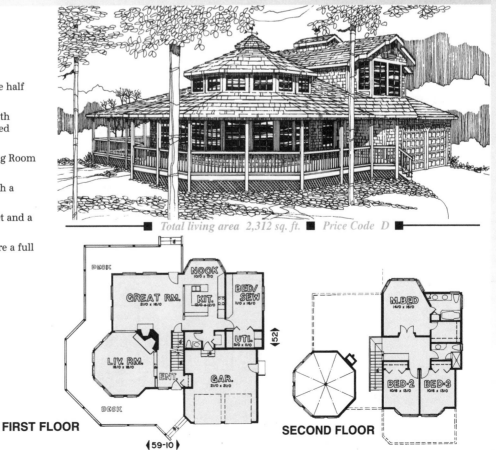

Total living area 2,312 sq. ft. ■ *Price Code D*

FIRST FLOOR

SECOND FLOOR

313

One-Floor Living

Total living area 2,020 sq. ft. ■ *Price Code C*

No. 20099

This plan features:

— Three bedrooms

— Two full and one half baths

■ Angular windows and recessed ceilings separating the two dining areas from the adjoining island Kitchen

■ A window wall flanking the fireplace in the soaring, sky-lit Living Room

■ A Master Suite with a bump-out window and a double-vanity bath

Main floor — 2,020 sq. ft.
Basement — 2,020 sq. ft.
Garage — 534 sq. ft.

MAIN FLOOR

An EXCLUSIVE DESIGN *By Karl Kreeger*

Stucco and Stone

Total living area 2,176 sq. ft. ■ *Price Code C*

No. 10555

This plan features:

— Three bedrooms

— Two full and one half baths

■ A formal foyer leading through double doors into a well-designed library

■ A Master Bedroom offering vaulted ceilings and a huge bath area

■ An oversized Living Room with a fireplace

■ A utility room and half bath located next to the Garage

First floor — 1,671 sq. ft.
Second floor — 505 sq. ft.
Basement — 1,661 sq. ft.
Garage — 604 sq. ft.
Screened porch — 114 sq. ft.

An EXCLUSIVE DESIGN *By Karl Kreeger*

Delightful Detailing

■ *Total living area 2,622 sq. ft.* ■ *Price Code E* ■

No. 98426

This plan features:

— Three bedrooms

— Two full and one half baths

■ The vaulted ceiling extends from the Foyer into the Living Room

■ The Dining Room is delineated by columns with a plant shelf above

■ Family Room has a vaulted ceiling, and a fireplace with radius windows on either side

■ The Kitchen equipped with an island serving bar, a desk, a wall oven, a Pantry and a Breakfast Bay

■ The Master Suite is highlighted by a Sitting Room, a walk-in closet and a private bath with a vaulted ceiling

■ An optional Bonus Room over the Garage

■ An optional basement or crawl space foundation — please specify when ordering

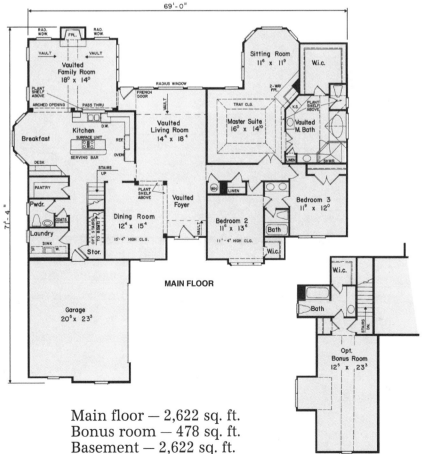

Main floor — 2,622 sq. ft.
Bonus room — 478 sq. ft.
Basement — 2,622 sq. ft.
Garage — 506 sq. ft.

315

Inviting Porch Adorns Affordable Home

■ *Total living area 1,243 sq. ft.* ■ *Price Code A* ■

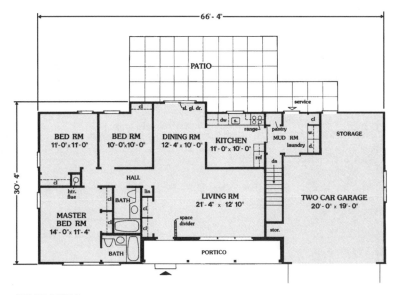

MAIN AREA

No. 90682 ✕

■ **This plan features:**

— Three bedrooms

— Two full baths

■ A large and spacious Living Room that adjoins the Dining Room for ease in entertaining

■ A private bedroom wing offering a quiet atmosphere

■ A Master Bedroom with his-n-her closets and a private bath

■ An efficient Kitchen with a walk-in pantry

Main area — 1,243 sq. ft.

oped Ceiling Attractive Feature of Ranch Design

No. 10548

■ This plan features:

- Three bedrooms
- Two full and one half baths
- ■ A fireplace and sloped ceiling in the Living Room
- ■ A Master Bedroom complete with a full bath, shower and dressing area
- ■ A decorative ceiling in the Dining Room

Main area — 1,688 sq. ft.
Basement — 1,688 sq. ft.
Screened porch — 120 sq. ft.
Garage — 489 sq. ft.

An EXCLUSIVE DESIGN *By Karl Kreeger*

■ Total living area 1,688 sq. ft. ■ Price Code B ■

MAIN FLOOR

Snug Retreat With A View

No. 91031

■ This plan features:

- One bedroom plus loft
- One full bath
- ■ A large front Deck providing views and an expansive entrance
- ■ A two-story Living/Dining area with double glass doors leading out to the Deck
- ■ An efficient, U-shaped Kitchen with a pass through counter to the Dining area
- ■ A first floor Bedroom, with ample closet space, located near a full shower bath
- ■ A Loft/Bedroom on the second floor offering multiple uses

Main floor — 572 sq. ft.
Loft — 308 sq. ft.

■ Total living area 880 sq. ft. ■ Price Code A ■

MAIN FLOOR

LOFT

Expansive Family Living Area

Total living area 2,462 sq. ft. ■ *Price Code D* ■

An EXCLUSIVE DESIGN
By Patrick Morabito, A.I.A. Architect

No. 93340

■ **This plan features:**

— Four bedrooms

— Two full and one half baths

■ Vaulted ceiling tops the Foyer adding extra volume

■ Living Room has a tray ceiling and a boxed bay window

■ Kitchen adjoins the Living Room and Dining Room providing a perfect arrangement for entertaining

■ The Kitchen is enhanced by a cooktop island and accesses the rear wood Deck

■ Family Room includes a fireplace framed by windows

■ Posh, pampering Master Suite includes a large walk-in closet and a tray ceiling

■ Three additional bedrooms share the full hall bath

■ No materials list is available for this plan

First floor — 1,378 sq. ft.
Second floor — 1,084 sq. ft.
Basement — 1,378 sq. ft.
Garage — 448 sq. ft.

Stately Manor

Total living area 2,380 sq. ft. ■ *Price Code D* ■

No. 90966 ✖

■ **This plan features:**

— Three bedrooms

— Two full and one half baths

■ A porch serving as a grand entrance

■ A very spacious Foyer with an open staircase and lots of angles

■ A beautiful Kitchen equipped with a cooktop island and a full bay window wall that includes a roomy Breakfast Nook

■ A Living Room with a vaulted ceiling that flows into the formal Dining Room for ease in entertaining

■ A grand Master Suite equipped with a walk-in closet and five-piece private bath

Main floor — 1,383 sq. ft.
Second floor — 997 sq. ft.
Basement — 1,374 sq. ft.
Garage — 420 sq. ft.
Width — 54'-0"
Depth — 47'-0"

An EXCLUSIVE DESIGN
By Westhome Planners, Ltd

Spectacular Traditional

■ *Total living area 1,237 sq. ft.* ■ *Price Code B* ■

No. 92502 ⚒

■ This plan features:

– Three bedrooms

– Two full baths

■ The use of gable roofs and the blend of stucco and brick to form a spectacular exterior

■ A high vaulted ceiling and a cozy fireplace, with built-in cabinets in the Den

■ An efficient, U-shaped Kitchen with an adjacent Dining Area

■ A Master Bedroom, with a raised ceiling, that includes a private bath and a walk-in closet

■ Two family bedrooms that share a full hall bath

■ An optional crawl space or slab foundation available — please specify when ordering

Main area — 1,237 sq. ft.
Garage — 436 sq. ft.

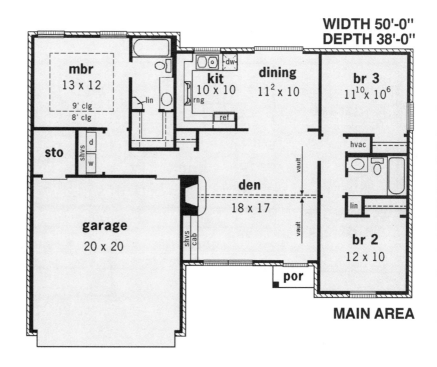

WIDTH 50'-0"
DEPTH 38'-0"

mbr 13 x 12 — 9' clg — 8' clg

sto

garage 20 x 20

kit 10 x 10 — rng

dining 11² x 10

br 3 11¹⁰ x 10⁶

hvac

den 18 x 17

br 2 12 x 10

por

MAIN AREA

Charming Southern Traditional

■ *Total living area 1,271 sq. ft.* ■ *Price Code B* ■

No. 92503

■ **This plan features:**

— Three bedrooms

— Two full baths

■ A covered front porch with striking columns, brick quoins, and dentil molding

■ A spacious Great Room with vaulted ceilings, a fireplace, and built-in cabinets

■ A Utility Room adjacent to the Kitchen which leads to the two-car Garage and Storage Rooms

■ A Master Bedroom including a large walk-in closet and a compartmentalized bath

■ An optional crawl space or slab foundation available — please specify when ordering

Main area — 1,271 sq. ft.
Garage — 506 sq. ft.

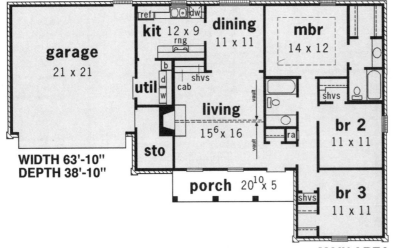

WIDTH 63'-10"
DEPTH 38'-10"

MAIN AREA

Towering Windows

No. 91071

This plan features:

- Three bedrooms
- Two full baths
- A wrap-around Deck above a three-car garage with plenty of work/storage space
- Both the Dining and Living areas claim vaulted ceilings above French doors to the Deck
- A octagon-shaped Kitchen with a view, a cooktop peninsula and an open counter to the Dining area
- A Master Bedroom on the upper level, with an over-sized closet, a private bath and an optional Loft
- Two additional bedrooms sharing a full hall bath
- An optional crawlspace or slab foundation — please specify when ordering
- No materials list is available for this plan

Main floor — 1,329 sq. ft.
Upper floor — 342 sq. ft.
Garage — 885 sq. ft.
Deck — 461 sq. ft.

Total living area 1,671 sq. ft. ■ Price Code B

LOWER FLOOR

UPPER FLOOR

MAIN FLOOR PLAN

Decorative Detailing Adds Charm

No. 34005

This plan features:

- Three bedrooms
- One and one half baths
- A Living Room with a cozy fireplace and sloped ceiling
- An efficient Kitchen equipped with a plant shelf easily accessible to the Dining Room
- A Master Bedroom with a decorative ceiling and a private bath
- A second bath equipped with a washer and dryer

Main area — 1,441 sq. ft.
Garage — 672 sq. ft.
Basement — 769 sq. ft.

An EXCLUSIVE DESIGN
By Karl Kreeger

Total living area 1,441 sq. ft. ■ Price Code A

Floor Plan

Ultimate Master Suite

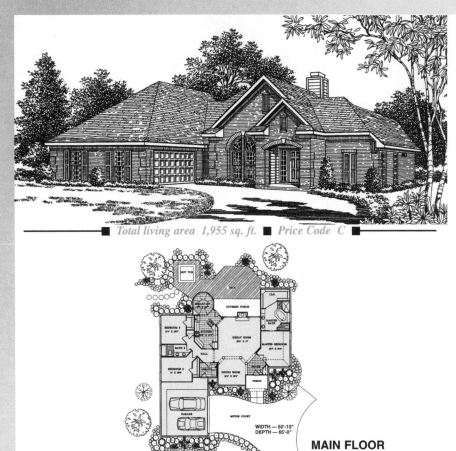

Total living area 1,955 sq. ft. ■ Price Code C

WIDTH — 60'-10"
DEPTH — 65'-0"

MAIN FLOOR

No. 93030

■ **This plan features:**

– Three bedrooms

– Two full baths

■ A covered Porch leading into the tiled Foyer, a columned Dining Room and an expansive Great Room

■ A large hearth fireplace between sliding glass doors to a covered Porch and a Deck with hot tub

■ A spacious Kitchen with a built-in Pantry, a peninsula sink and an octagon-shaped Breakfast Area

■ A Master Bedroom wing with French doors, a vaulted ceiling, a plush master bath with a huge walk-in closet, a double vanity and a window tub

■ Two additional bedrooms with walk-in closets, sharing a full hall bath

■ No materials list is available for this plan

Main floor — 1,995 sq. ft.
Garage — 561 sq. ft.

Comfort Zone

Total living area 1,908 sq. ft. ■ Price Code C

MAIN FLOOR

SECOND FLOOR

No. 91105

■ **This plan features:**

– Three bedrooms

– Two full baths

■ The stunning brick veneer, arched windows, gabled roof lines and herringbone patterns add plenty of character

■ The efficient master bath includes a double vanity with knee space, a corner whirlpool tub, and a separate shower

■ Bonus Area for future expansion is provided over the Garage and is accessed by a stairway near the Kitchen

■ Extra features include a Kitchen snackbar, a back Porch, an abundance of closets, and a large Living Room

■ No materials list is available for this plan

Main floor — 1,908 sq. ft.
Second floor bonus — 262 sq. ft.
Garage — 562 sq. ft.

Out of the English Countryside

■ *Total living area 2,524 sq. ft.* ■ *Price Code D* ■

No. 98519

■ This plan features:

- Four bedrooms

- Three full and one half baths

■ From the Entry, is the Living Room/Study with a cozy fireplace, or left into the Dining Room, both rooms have lovely bay windows

■ The Family Room has a fireplace and a door that leads out onto a covered patio

■ The Breakfast Area is adjacent to the Family Room and the Kitchen which features a center island

■ The first floor Master Bedroom has two walk-in closets and an attached bath with a spa tub

■ Upstairs bedrooms each have walk-in closets and use of two full baths

■ Also located upstairs is a Bonus Room that would be a perfect Playroom

■ No materials list is available for this plan

First floor — 1,735 sq. ft.
Second floor — 789 sq. ft.
Bonus — 132 sq. ft.
Garage — 482 sq. ft.

A Touch of Old World Charm

■ *Total living area 2,320 sq. ft.* ■ *Price Code D* ■

SECOND FLOOR

FIRST FLOOR

No. 92646

■ This plan features:

— Four bedrooms

— Two full and one half baths

■ Authentic balustrade railings and front courtyard greet one and all

■ High ceiling in Great Room tops corner fireplace and French doors

■ Formal Dining Room enhanced by a decorative window and furniture alcove

■ Country Kitchen with work island, two pantries, Breakfast area with French door to rear yard, Laundry and Garage entry

■ Master Bedroom wing offers a sloped ceiling, and a plush bath

■ No materials list available

First floor — 1,595 sq. ft.
Second floor — 725 sq. ft.
Basement — 1,471 sq. ft.
Garage — 409 sq. ft.

Pleasing to the Eye

No. 93073

This plan features:

— Three Bedrooms

— Two full baths

■ A large covered front porch opening to a foyer with nine foot ceilings

■ Kitchen with a dining area with a bay window, built-in desk and a sunny window over the sink

■ Living room including a corner fireplace and ten foot ceilings

■ Bedrooms grouped for homeowner convenience

■ Master suite topped by a sloped ceiling pampered by a private bath and walk-in closet

■ Two-car garage with optional door locations located at the rear of the home

■ An optional slab or crawlspace foundation — please specify when ordering

■ No materials list is available for this plan

Main floor — 1,202 sq. ft.
Garage — 482 sq. ft.

■ *Total living area 1,202 sq. ft.* ■ *Price Code A* ■

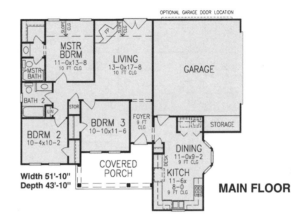

MAIN FLOOR

Cozy Traditional

No. 93000

— Three bedrooms

— Two full baths

■ An angled eating bar separating the Kitchen, Breakfast Room and Great Room, while leaving these areas open for easy entertaining

■ An efficient, well-appointed Kitchen that is convenient to both the formal Dining Room and the sunny Breakfast Room

■ A spacious Master Suite with oval tub, step-in shower, double vanity and walk-in closet

■ Two additional bedrooms with ample closet space that share a full hall bath

■ No materials list is available for this plan

Main floor — 1,862 sq. ft.
Garage — 520 sq. ft.

■ *Total living area 1,862 sq. ft.* ■ *Price Code C* ■

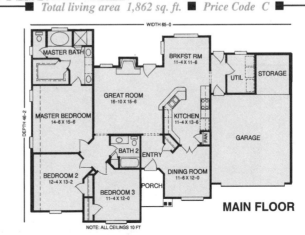

MAIN FLOOR

Contemporary Ranch Design

■ *Total living area 1,512 sq. ft.* ■ *Price Code B* ■

MAIN FLOOR

No. 26740 ⚒

■ **This plan features:**

— Three bedrooms

— Two full baths

■ Sloping cathedral ceilings

■ An efficient, U-shaped Kitchen

■ A Daylight Room for dining pleasure

■ A secluded Master Bedroom with Master Bath and access to private Deck

■ A Great Hall with fireplace

■ Two-car garage conveniently accesses the kitchen

■ Two secondary bedrooms share a full bath

Main floor — 1,512 sq. ft.
Garage — 478 sq. ft.

Ranch with Handicapped Access

■ *Total living area 1,734 sq. ft.* ■ *Price Code B* ■

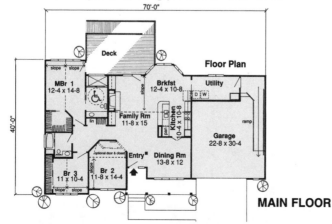

MAIN FLOOR

No. 20403 ⚒ ✈

■ **This plan features:**

— Three bedrooms

— One full and one three-quarter baths

■ Ramps into the front Entry from the Porch; the Utility area and the Kitchen from the Garage; and the Family Room from the Deck

■ An open area topped by a sloped ceiling for the Family Room, the Dining Room, the Kitchen and the Breakfast alcove

■ An efficient Kitchen with a built-in pantry and an open counter connecting to the Family Room, easily serves both the Breakfast nook and the Dining Room

■ A Master Bedroom suite accented by a sloping ceiling above a wall of window,s offering access to the Deck, and an oversized closet and a bath

■ Two front bedrooms with sloped ceilings share a full hall bath

Main floor — 1,734 sq. ft.
Porch — 118 sq. ft.
Deck — 354 sq. ft.
Garage — 606 sq. ft.

© 1991 Donald A. Gardner Architects, Inc.

■ *Total living area 1,778 sq. ft.* ■ *Price Code C* ■

No. 99873 ✂

■ This plan features:

— Three bedrooms

— Two full and one half baths

■ An exterior porch giving the home a traditional flavor

■ Great Room highlighted by a fireplace and a balcony above as well as a pass-through into the Kitchen

■ Kitchen eating area with skylights and bow windows overlooking the deck with spa

■ Two additional bedrooms with a full bath on the second floor

■ Master Suite on the first floor is naturally illuminated by two skylights

■ An optional basement or crawl space foundation — please specify when ordering

First floor — 1,325 sq. ft.
Second floor — 453 sq. ft.

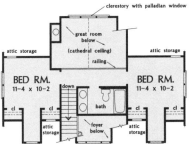

clerestory with palladian window

great room below
(cathedral ceiling)
railing

attic storage   attic storage

BED RM.
11-4 x 10-2

BED RM.
11-4 x 10-2

down

cl   cl   cl   cl

bath

attic storage   attic storage

foyer below

SECOND FLOOR PLAN

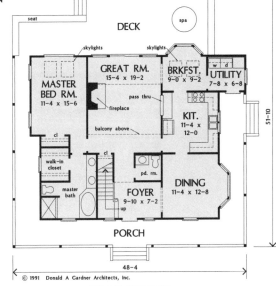

seat

DECK   spa

seat

skylights   skylights

GREAT RM.
15-4 x 19-2

BRKFST.
9-0 x 9-2

UTILITY
7-8 x 6-8

w d

MASTER
BED RM.
11-4 x 15-6

pass thru

fireplace

KIT.
11-4 x 12-0

balcony above

cl

walk-in closet

cl

pd. rm.

DINING
11-4 x 12-8

master bath

FOYER
9-10 x 7-2
up

51-10

PORCH

48-4

© 1991 Donald A Gardner Architects, Inc.

FIRST FLOOR PLAN

327

Formal Balance

■ *Total living area 1,476 sq. ft.* ■ *Price Code A* ■

No. 90689 ✖

■ **This plan features:**

— Three bedrooms

— Two full baths

■ A cathedral ceiling in the Living Room with a heat-circulating fireplace as the focal point

■ A bow window in the Dining Room that adds elegance as well as natural light

■ A well-equipped Kitchen that serves both the Dinette and the formal Dining Room efficiently

■ A Master Bedroom with three closets and a private master bath with sliding glass doors to the Master Deck with a hot tub

Main floor — 1,476 sq. ft.
Basement — 1,361 sq. ft.
Garage — 548 sq. ft.

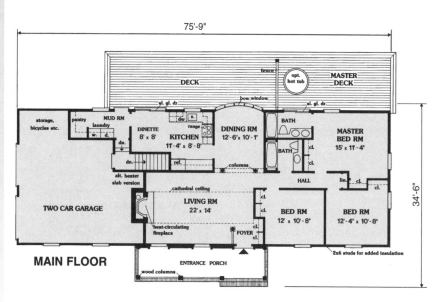

MAIN FLOOR

75'-9"

34'-6"

DECK

MASTER DECK

opt. hot tub

fence

bow window

storage, bicycles etc.

pantry

MUD RM

laundry

w. d.

DINETTE 8' x 8'

KITCHEN 11'-4" x 8'-8"

dw

range

sl. gl. dr.

s.

DINING RM 12'-6" x 10'-1"

BATH

BATH

MASTER BED RM 15' x 11'-4"

sl. gl. dr.

cl.

cl.

dn.

ref.

columns

HALL

lin.

cl.

cl.

alt. heater slab version

cathedral ceiling

TWO CAR GARAGE

LIVING RM 22' x 14'

heat-circulating fireplace

cl.

cl.

cl.

BED RM 12' x 10'-8"

BED RM 12'-4" x 10'-8"

FOYER

cl.

2x6 studs for added insulation

ENTRANCE PORCH

wood columns

328

Master Suite with Private Sun Deck

No. 91411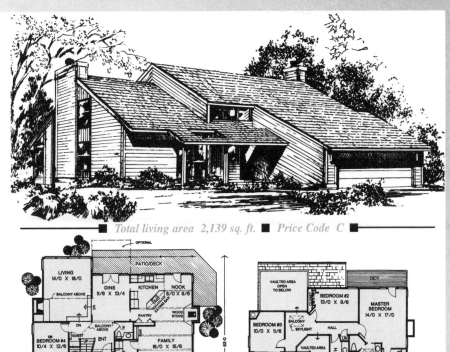

This plan features:

– Four bedrooms

– Two full and one half baths

■ A sunken Living Room, formal Dining Room, and island Kitchen enjoying an expansive view of the patio and backyard

■ A fireplaced Living Room keeping the house toasty after the sun goes down

■ Skylights brightening the balcony and Master Bath

■ An optional basement, slab or crawlspace foundation — please specify when ordering

Main floor — 1,249 sq. ft.
Upper floor — 890 sq. ft.
Garage — 462 sq. ft.

■ Total living area 2,139 sq. ft. ■ Price Code C ■

Enchanting Entry

No. 34679

This plan features:

– Three bedrooms

– Two full and one half baths

■ Split Entry leads down to Family Room, Utility Room, Den, half bath and two-car Garage

■ Up a half-flight of stairs leads to the large Living Room highlighted by a double window

■ Dining Room convenient to Living Room and Kitchen

■ Efficient Kitchen with rear yard access and room for eating

■ Corner Master Bedroom offers an over-sized closet and private bath

■ Two additional bedrooms with double windows, share a full bath

Upper floor — 1,331 sq. ft.
Lower floor — 663 sq. ft.
Garage — 584 sq. ft.

■ Total living area 1,994 sq. ft. ■ Price Code C ■

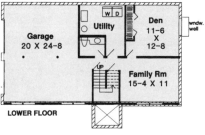

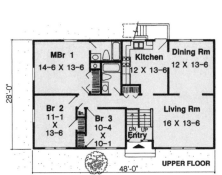

Elegant Elevation

No. 92662

■ **This plan features:**

— Three bedrooms

— Two full baths

■ Brick trim, sidelights, and a transom window give a warm welcome to this home

■ High ceilings continue from foyer into Great Room which counts among it's amenities a fireplace and entertainment center

■ The Kitchen serves the formal and informal dining areas with ease

■ The Master Suite is positioned for privacy on the first floor

■ The second floor has loads of possibilities with a Bonus space and a Study

■ Two bedrooms each with walk in closest share a full bath

■ There is no materials list available for this plan

First floor — 1,542 sq. ft.
Second floor — 667 sq. ft.
Bonus — 236 sq. ft.
Basement — 1,367 sq. ft.
Garage — 420 sq. ft

■ *Total living area 2,209 sq. ft.* ■ *Price Code D* ■

Sunny Character

No. 20158

■ **This plan features:**

— Three bedrooms

— Two full and one half baths

■ A Kitchen with easy access to screened porch

■ A Master suite including walk-in closet and luxury bath

■ A second story balcony linking two bedrooms

First floor — 1,293 sq. ft
Second floor — 526 sq. ft.
Basement — 1,286 sq. ft.
Garage — 484 sq. ft.

■ *Total living area 1,819 sq. ft.* ■ *Price Code C* ■

An
EXCLUSIVE DESIGN
By Karl Kreeger

French Influenced One-Story

© 1990 Donald A. Gardner Architects, Inc.

■ *Total living area 2,045 sq. ft.* ■ *Price Code D* ■

No. 96421 ☒

■ This plan features:

— Three bedrooms

— Two full baths

■ Elegant details, arched windows, round columns and rich brick veneer creating curb appeal

■ Arched clerestory window in the foyer introduces natural light to a large Great Room with cathedral ceiling and built-in cabinets

■ Great Room adjoins a skylit Sun Room with a wetbar which then opens onto a spacious Deck

■ Kitchen with cooking island centrally located with easy access to a large pantry and utility room

■ Large Master Bedroom opening to the deck and featuring a garden tub, separate shower and dual vanity

■ An optional basement or crawl space foundation — please specify when ordering

Main floor — 2,045 sq. ft.
Garage & storage — 563 sq. ft.

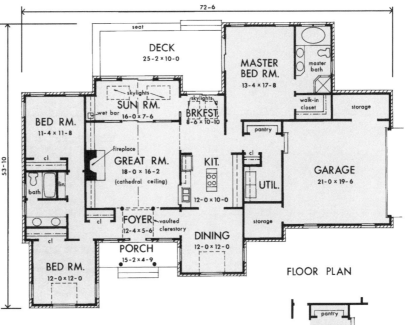

FLOOR PLAN

ALTERNATE PLAN
FOR BASEMENT

Secluded Master Suite

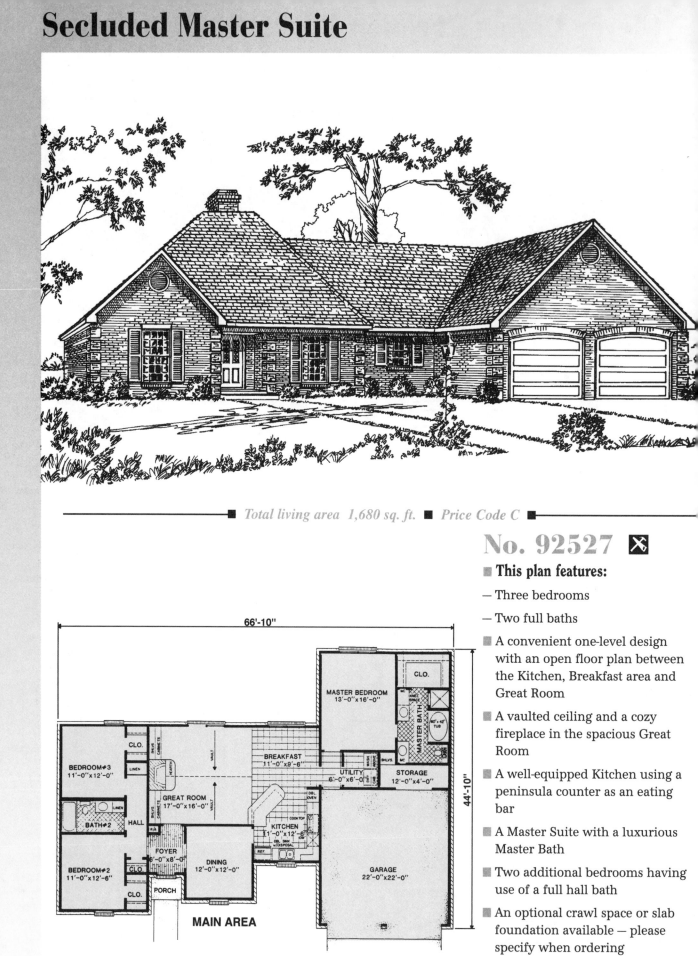

■ *Total living area 1,680 sq. ft.* ■ *Price Code C* ■

No. 92527

■ **This plan features:**

— Three bedrooms

— Two full baths

■ A convenient one-level design with an open floor plan between the Kitchen, Breakfast area and Great Room

■ A vaulted ceiling and a cozy fireplace in the spacious Great Room

■ A well-equipped Kitchen using a peninsula counter as an eating bar

■ A Master Suite with a luxurious Master Bath

■ Two additional bedrooms having use of a full hall bath

■ An optional crawl space or slab foundation available — please specify when ordering

Main area — 1,680 sq. ft.
Garage — 538 sq. ft.

Clever Design Packs in Plenty of Living Space

No. 24250

■ This plan features:

– Three bedrooms

– Two full baths

■ Custom, volume ceilings

■ A sunken Living Room that includes a vaulted ceiling and a fireplace with oversized windows framing it

■ A center island and an eating nook in the Kitchen that has more than ample counter space

■ A formal Dining Room that adjoins the Kitchen, allowing for easy entertaining

■ A spacious Master Suite including a vaulted ceiling and lavish bath

■ Secondary bedrooms with custom ceiling treatments and use of full hall bath

Main area — 1,700 sq. ft.

An
EXCLUSIVE DESIGN
By Energetic Enterprises

■ *Total living area 1,700 sq. ft.* ■ *Price Code B* ■

Main Floor

Delightful, Compact Home

No. 34003

■ This plan features:

– Three bedrooms

– Two full baths

■ A fireplaced Living Room brightened by a wonderful picture window

■ A counter island featuring double sinks separating the Kitchen and Dining areas

■ A Master Bedroom that includes a private Master Bath and double closets

■ Two additional bedrooms with ample closet spacethat share a full bath

Main floor — 1,146 sq. ft.

■ *Total living area 1,146 sq. ft.* ■ *Price Code A* ■

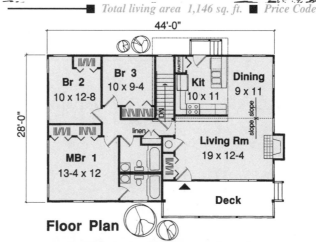

slab/crawlspace option

Floor Plan

Two-Sink Baths Ease Rush

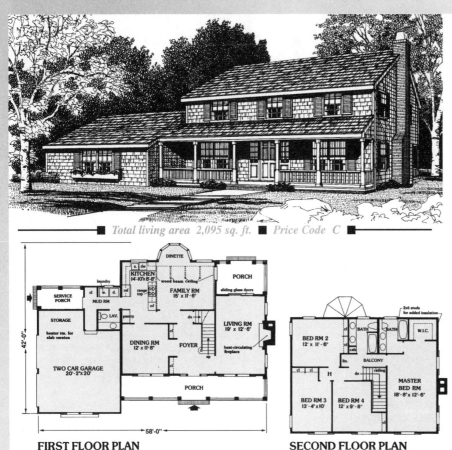

Total living area 2,095 sq. ft. ■ Price Code C

FIRST FLOOR PLAN

SECOND FLOOR PLAN

No. 90622

■ **This plan features:**

— Four bedrooms

— Two full and one half baths

■ A wood beam ceiling in the spacious Family Room

■ An efficient, island Kitchen with a sunny bay window dinette

■ A formal Living Room with a heat-circulating fireplace

■ A large Master Suite with a walk-in closet and a private Master Bath

■ Three additional bedrooms sharing a full hall bath

First floor — 1,082 sq. ft.
Second floor — 1,013 sq. ft.
Garage — 481 sq. ft.

Vaulted Ceilings Add Impact

Total living area 1,565 sq. ft. ■ Price Code B

MAIN FLOOR

No. 91527

■ **This plan features:**

— Three bedrooms

— Two full baths

■ A formal Living Room with a vaulted ceiling that flows into the formal Dining Room

■ An efficient Kitchen with a built-in pantry and a peninsula counter that doubles as an eating bar and adjoins the sunny Eating Nook

■ A Family Room with a cozy fireplace and a vaulted ceiling

■ A Master Suite that includes a walk-in closet and a private bath with a spa tub and double vanity

■ Two additional bedrooms that share a full bath

Main floor — 1,565 sq. ft.
Garage — 440 sq. ft.

Arched Windows Accent Sophisticated Design

■ *Total living area 2,551 sq. ft.* ■ *Price Code E* ■

No. 92509 ✖

■ **This plan features:**

– Four bedrooms

– Two full and one half baths

■ Graceful columns and full-length windows highlight front Porch

■ Spacious Great Room with decorative ceiling over hearth fireplace between built-in cabinets

■ Kitchen with peninsula counter and Breakfast alcove

■ Secluded Master Bedroom offers access to back Porch, and has a decorative ceiling and plush bath

■ Three additional bedrooms with loads of closets space share double vanity bath

■ An optional crawl space or slab foundation — please specify when ordering

Main floor — 2,551 sq. ft.
Garage — 532 sq. ft.

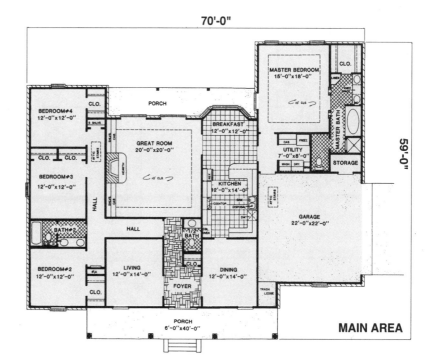

Farmhouse Charm

©1995 Donald A. Gardner Architects, Inc.

B. NATHAN.

■ *Total living area 1,846 sq. ft.* ■ *Price Code C* ■

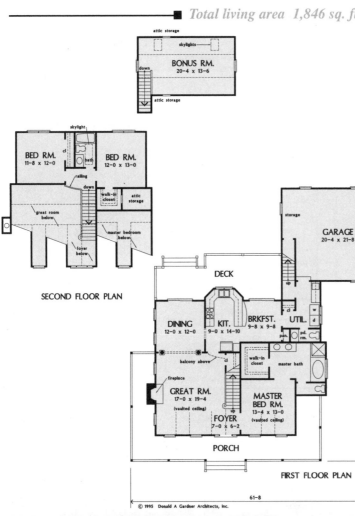

attic storage

skylights

BONUS RM.
20-4 x 13-6

down

attic storage

SECOND FLOOR PLAN

skylight

BED RM.
11-8 x 12-0

bath

BED RM.
12-0 x 13-0

railing

down

walk-in closet

attic storage

great room below

master bedroom below

foyer below

DECK

storage

GARAGE
20-4 x 21-8

up

DINING
12-0 x 12-0

KIT.
9-0 x 14-10

BRKFST.
9-8 x 9-8

UTIL.

pan.

pd. rm.

w
d

balcony above

walk-in closet

master bath

fireplace

GREAT RM.
17-0 x 19-4
(vaulted ceiling)

FOYER
7-0 x 6-2

MASTER BED RM.
13-4 x 13-0
(vaulted ceiling)

65-0

PORCH

FIRST FLOOR PLAN

61-8

© 1995 Donald A Gardner Architects, Inc.

No. 96462

■ **This plan features:**

— Three bedrooms

— Two full and one half baths

■ Nine foot ceilings and vaulted ceilings in Great Room and Master Bedroom add spaciousness

■ Dining Room accented by columns and accesses Deck for outdoor living

■ Efficient Kitchen features peninsula counter with serving bar for Breakfast area

■ Master Bedroom includes walk-in closet, garden tub, shower and double vanity

■ Two bedrooms, one with walk-in closet, share a full, skylit bath

First floor — 1,380 sq. ft.
Second floor — 466 sq. ft.
Bonus room — 326 sq. ft.
Garage — 523 sq. ft.

Spacious Stucco

No. 20368

This plan features:

- Three bedrooms
- Two full and one half baths
- A vaulted foyer flanked by a soaring Living Room with huge palladium windows
- A Family Room with a massive two-way fireplace
- A Master Suite with garden spa, private deck access, and a walk-in closet

First floor — 1,752 sq. ft.
Second floor — 620 sq. ft.
Basement — 1,726 sq. ft.
Garage — 714 sq. ft

■ *Total living area 2,372 sq. ft.* ■ *Price Code D* ■

First Floor

64'-0"
52'-0"

Deck
Family Rm 15-6 x 19-2 vaulted
MBr 1 15 x 13-2 pan vault
spa
Living Rm 13 x 13-8 vaulted
Foyer vaulted
Dining Rm 11 x 13-8
Dinette/Kitchen 22 x 13-8 bench
Balcony above
desk
pantry
UP DN
ov
Garage 21-4 x 31-4

Second Floor

Br 2 13-2 x 13-10
shelves
Loft
linen
DN
lin.
Br 3 12-6 x 10-8

Home on a Hill

No. 20501

This plan features:

- Three bedrooms
- Two full baths
- Window walls combining with sliders to unite active areas with a huge outdoor deck
- Interior spaces flowing together for an open feeling, that is accentuated by the sloping ceilings and towering fireplace in the Living Room
- An island Kitchen with easy access to the Dining Room
- A Master Suite complete with a garden spa, abundant closet space, and a balcony

First floor — 1,316 sq. ft.
Second floor — 592 sq. ft.

■ *Total living area 1,908 sq. ft.* ■ *Price Code C* ■

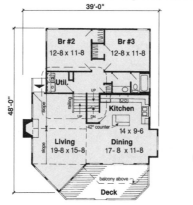

39'-0"
48'-0"

Br #2 12-8 x 11-8
Br #3 12-8 x 11-8
Util.
Kitchen 14 x 9-6
42" counter
Living 19-8 x 15-8
Dining 17-8 x 11-8
balcony above
Deck

First Floor

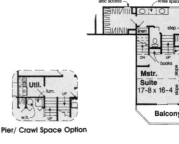

Util. furn.
w.h.

Pier/ Crawl Space Option

attic access
knee space
linen
step
shelf
DN UP
36" wall
books
Mstr. Suite 17-8 x 16-4
8'-0" ceiling
slope
Balcony

Second Floor

Unique A-Frame

No. 90025

This plan features:

— Three bedrooms

— Two full baths

■ Exterior highlighted by fieldstone chimney, red cedar roof, vertical siding and a redwood sun deck

■ Open Living Room, Dining and Kitchen layout provides a spacious feeling

■ Efficient, U-shaped Kitchen with built-in pantry and serving bar

■ Spacious first floor bedroom convenient to full bath and laundry

■ Two second floor bedrooms with ample closet space share a full bath

First floor — 867 sq. ft.
Second floor — 442 sq. ft.
Deck — 364 sq. ft.

Total living area 1,309 sq. ft. ■ *Price Code A*

FIRST FLOOR

SECOND FLOOR

Another Nice Ranch Design

No. 90354

This plan features:

— Three bedrooms

— One full and one three-quarter baths

■ A vaulted ceiling in the Great Room, that includes a fireplace and access to the rear deck

■ Double door entrance into the Den/third bedroom

■ A Kitchen and breakfast area with a vaulted ceiling and an efficient layout

■ A Master Suite crowned by a vaulted ceiling and pampered by a private bath and dressing area

■ A full hall bath that serves the two additional bedrooms

Main area — 1,360 sq. ft.

Total living area 1,360 sq. ft. ■ *Price Code A* ■

MAIN FLOOR

Inviting Wrap-Around Porch

■ *Total living area 1,716 sq. ft.* ■ *Price Code B* ■

No. 93909

■ **This plan features:**

— Three bedrooms

— Two full baths

■ A warm and inviting welcome, achieved by a wrap-around porch

■ A corner gas fireplace and two skylights highlighted in the Great Room

■ Flowing from the Great Room, the Dining Room naturally lighted by the sliding glass doors leads to a rear Deck and a skylight above

■ A well-appointed, U-shaped Kitchen separated from the Dining Room by a breakfast bar contains another skylight

■ A luxurious Master Bedroom equipped with a plush bath

■ Two additional bedrooms sharing the full bath in the hall and receiving light from the dormers

■ No materials list is available for this plan

Main floor — 1,716 sq. ft.

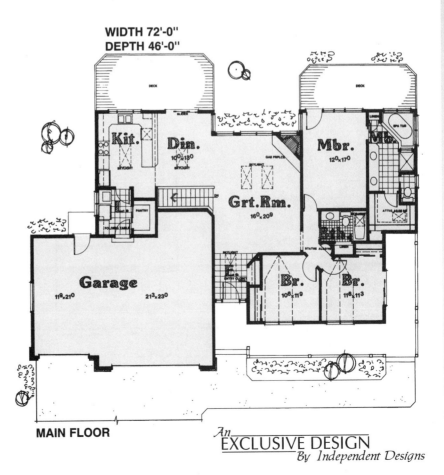

WIDTH 72'-0"
DEPTH 46'-0"

MAIN FLOOR

An EXCLUSIVE DESIGN
By Independent Designs

Exciting Ceilings Add Appeal

©1994 Donald A. Gardner Architects, Inc.

■ *Total living area 1,475 sq. ft.* ■ *Price Code B* ■

No. 96452

■ This plan features:

— Three bedrooms

— Two full baths

■ Open design enhanced by cathedral and tray ceilings above arched windows

■ Foyer with columns defining Great Room with central fireplace and Deck access

■ Cooktop island in Kitchen provides great cooks with convenience and company

■ Ultimate Master Bedroom suite offers walk-in closet, tray ceiling, and whirlpool bath

■ Front Bedroom/Study offers multiple uses with tray ceiling and arched window

Main floor — 1,475 sq. ft.
Garage & storage — 478 sq. ft.

Stylish Bay Window

No. 93004

This plan features:

- Three bedrooms
- Two full baths
- A stylish bay window and a covered porch highlight the exterior elevation
- The Great Room has a corner fireplace and a ten foot ceiling
- The Breakfast Bay is brightened by three windows
- The Kitchen is set up in a convenient U-shape and features a walk-in Pantry
- The large Master Bedroom has its own bath and a walk-in closet with built-in shelves
- Two additional bedrooms share a full bath in the hall
- No materials list is available for this plan

Main floor —1,260 sq. ft.
Width — 37'-6"
Depth — 44'-2"

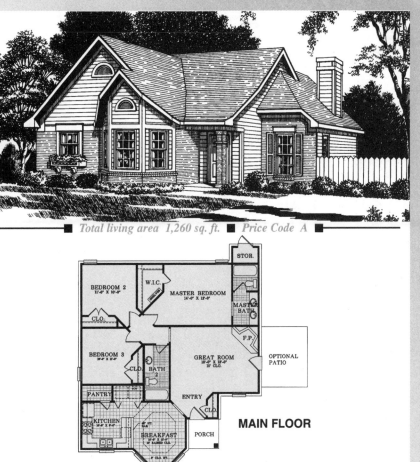

Total living area 1,260 sq. ft. ■ *Price Code A* ■

MAIN FLOOR

Distinctive European Design

No. 92516

This plan features:

- Three bedrooms
- Two full baths
- A spacious Foyer leading into a grand Living Room, topped by a vaulted ceiling, with a fireplace between built-in cabinets and a wall of glass leading to a covered Porch
- A gourmet Kitchen with a peninsula counter/snackbar and a built-in pantry, that is central to the Dining Room, the bay window Breakfast area, the Utility Room and the Garage
- A large Master Bedroom, crowned by a raised ceiling, with French doors leading to a covered Porch, a luxurious bath and a walk-in closet
- Two additional bedrooms with decorative windows and over-sized closets share a full hall bath
- An optional slab or crawl space foundation — please specify when ordering

Main floor — 1,887 sq. ft.
Garage & Storage — 524 sq. ft.
Width — 57'-10"
Depth — 54'-5"

Total living area 1,887 sq. ft. ■ *Price Code D* ■

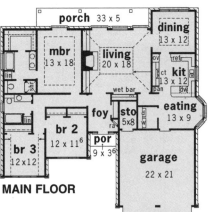

MAIN FLOOR

Built-In Beauty

Total living area 1,687 sq. ft. ■ Price Code B

MAIN FLOOR

FAMILY
13/0 X 17/0

MASTER
13/0 X 18/0

SPA

PANTRY

13/4 X 10/0

SKYLITE

LIVING
13/4 X 16/0

BR. 2
12/6 X 10/0

BR. 3
10/10 X 13/0

GARAGE
19/2 X 21/6

50'

52'

No. 91507

This plan features:

— Three bedrooms

— Two full baths

■ A sky-lit Foyer

■ A bump-out window enhancing the wide-open arrangement in the Living/Dining Room

■ An efficient island Kitchen with a built-in pantry, and a corner double sink

■ An informal Family Room with a lovely fireplace

■ A Master Suite with elegant double doors, and a luxurious private master bath

■ Two additional bedrooms flanking the laundry area

■ An optional basement or crawl space foundation — please specify when ordering

Main floor — 1,687 sq. ft.
Garage — 419 sq. ft.

Columns Enhance Entry

Total living area 2,107 sq. ft. ■ Price Code C

◄ 49' ►

40'

MAIN FLOOR

DINING
10/4 X 11/10

NOOK
7/8 X 10/0

FAMILY
13/6 X 15/2

PAN. O. DESK

LIVING
13/0 X 16/2

GARAGE
19/4 X 21/4

UP

W.

PORCH

UPPER FLOOR

SPA

DEN/BR. 2
10/3 X 9/10

BR. 3
11/6 X 13/4

LIN.

DN.

LINEN

MASTER
13/0 X 16/8

FOYER
BELOW

BR. 4
11/0 X 12/6

No. 91537

This plan features:

— Four bedrooms

— Two full and one half baths

■ The formal areas flow into each other while a fireplace accents the Living Room

■ A spacious, island kitchen efficiently serves both the Dining Room and the Nook

■ The Family Room conveniently flows from the Kitchen/Nook and includes a second fireplace

■ The second floor Master Suite has a private bath and a walk-in closet

■ Three additional bedrooms have ample closet space and easy access to the full bath in the hall

Main floor — 1,032 sq. ft.
Upper floor — 1,075 sq. ft.

Elegant Window Treatment

■ *Total living area 1,492 sq. ft.* ■ *Price Code A* ■

No. 34150

An
EXCLUSIVE DESIGN
By Karl Kreeger

■ This plan features:

— Two bedrooms (optional third)

— Two full baths

■ An arched window that floods the front room with light

■ A homey, well-lit Office or Den

■ Compact, efficient use of space

■ The Kitchen has easy access to the Dining Room

■ A fireplaced Living Room with a sloping ceiling and a window wall

■ The Master Bedroom sports a private master bath and a roomy walk-in closet

Main floor — 1,492 sq. ft.
Basement — 1,486 sq. ft.
Garage — 462 sq. ft.

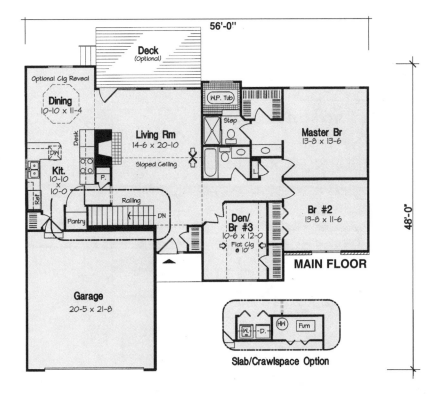

Traditional Elegance

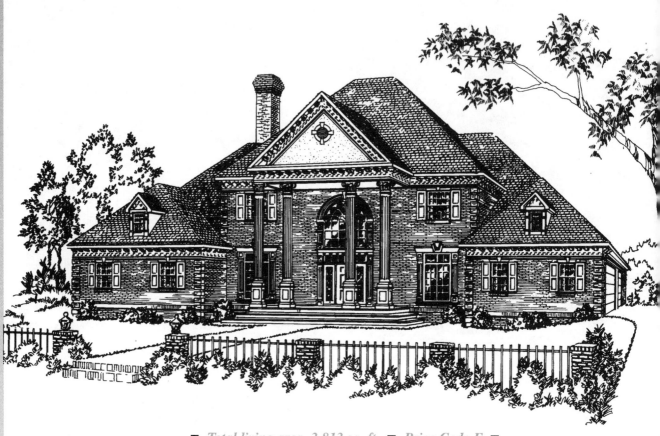

■ *Total living area 3,813 sq. ft.* ■ *Price Code F* ■

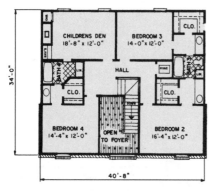

SECOND FLOOR PLAN

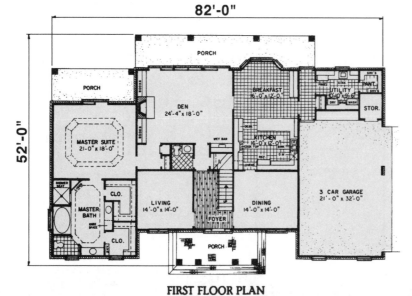

FIRST FLOOR PLAN

No. 92504 ✖

■ **This plan features:**

— Four bedrooms

— Three full and one half baths

■ A elegant entrance leading into a two-story Foyer

■ Floor-to-ceiling windows in the formal Living and Dining Rooms

■ A spacious Den with a hearth fireplace, built-in book shelves, a wetbar and a wall of windows

■ A Kitchen equipped with a bright Breakfast area and a walk-in pantry

■ A grand Master Suite with decorative ceilings, a private Porch and two walk-in closets

■ An optional crawl space or slab foundation — please specify when ordering

First floor — 2,553 sq. ft.
Second floor — 1,260 sq. ft.
Garage — 714 sq. ft.

Modest Tudor with a Massive Look

No. 90012

This plan features:

— Three bedrooms

— Two full and one half baths

■ A large log-burning fireplace centrally located on the far wall of the Living Room

■ A formal Dining Room with access to either the screen porch, terrace, or Kitchen

■ A Kitchen with a cooktop island and a built-in Breakfast Nook

■ A Family Room with French door access to another porch

■ A Master Suite with lounge area, private Master Bath, and a walk-in closet

■ Two additional bedrooms with access to the full hall bath

First floor — 1,078 sq. ft.
Second floor — 1,131 sq. ft.
Basement — 785 sq. ft.
Garage — 445 sq. ft.

Total living area 2,209 sq. ft. ■ Price Code D

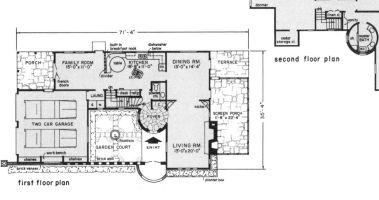

second floor plan

first floor plan

Vacation Cottage

No. 90821

This plan features:

— Two bedrooms

— One full bath

■ An economical, neat and simple design

■ Two picture windows in the Living/Dining Room

■ An efficient Kitchen design

■ A large, cozy loft bedroom flanked by big storage rooms

■ This plan is available with a basement or crawl space foundation — please specify when ordering

First floor — 616 sq. ft.
Loft — 180 sq. ft.
Width — 22'-0"
Depth — 28'-0"

Total living area 796 sq. ft. ■ Price Code A

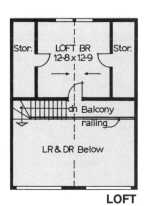

FIRST FLOOR

LOFT

An **EXCLUSIVE DESIGN** *By Westhome Planners, Ltd.*

345

Open Air Ranch

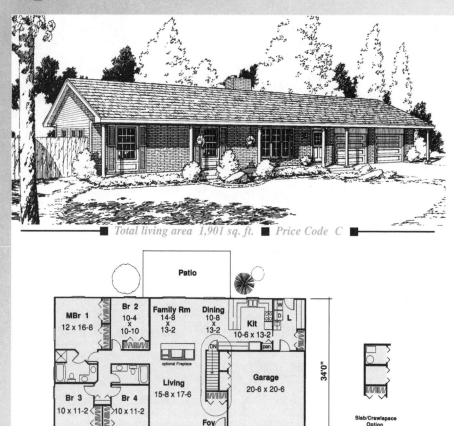

■ *Total living area 1,901 sq. ft.* ■ *Price Code C* ■

MAIN FLOOR

No. 84014

■ **This plan features:**

— Four bedrooms

— Two full baths

■ Stone fireplace, wood storage and bookshelves separate the Living room from the Family room

■ The Dining room features doors to the rear patio

■ A convenient U-shaped kitchen is highlighted by a double sink, a pantry, and ample counter space

■ A Laundry/Utility room is located off of the two-car Garage

■ Three bedrooms share a full bath

■ The Master bedroom has two closets and a private bath with dual vanities

■ There is no materials list available for this plan

Main floor — 1,901 sq. ft.
Garage — 420 sq. ft.

Contemporary Design With Sunken Living Room

■ *Total living area 1,487 sq. ft.* ■ *Price Code A* ■

No. 26112

■ **This plan features:**

— Two bedrooms, with possible third bedroom/den

— One and one half baths

■ A solar design with southern glass doors, windows, and an air-lock entry

■ R-26 insulation used for floors and sloping ceilings

■ A deck rimming the front of the home

■ A Dining Room separated from the Living Room by a half wall

■ An efficient Kitchen with an eating bar

First floor — 911 sq. ft.
Second floor — 576 sq. ft.
Basement — 911 sq. ft.

FIRST FLOOR

SECOND FLOOR

Windows Add Warmth To All Living Areas

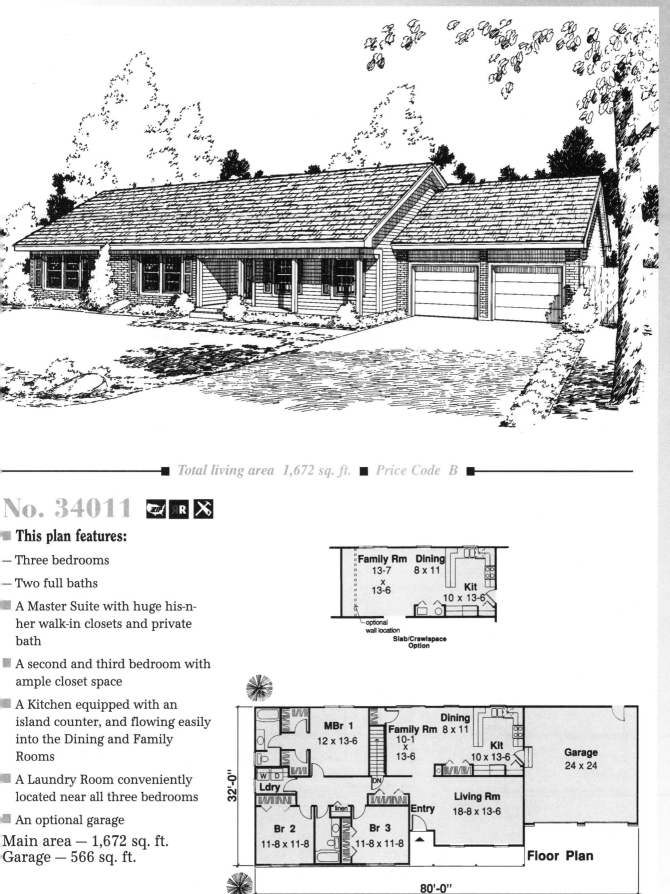

■ *Total living area   1,672 sq. ft.* ■ *Price Code   B* ■

No. 34011

This plan features:

— Three bedrooms

— Two full baths

■ A Master Suite with huge his-n-her walk-in closets and private bath

■ A second and third bedroom with ample closet space

■ A Kitchen equipped with an island counter, and flowing easily into the Dining and Family Rooms

■ A Laundry Room conveniently located near all three bedrooms

■ An optional garage

Main area — 1,672 sq. ft.
Garage — 566 sq. ft.

Family Rm
13-7
x
13-6

Dining
8 x 11

Kit
10 x 13-6

optional
wall location

Slab/Crawlspace Option

MBr 1
12 x 13-6

Family Rm
10-1
x
13-6

Dining 8 x 11

Kit
10 x 13-6

Garage
24 x 24

W D

Ldry

DN

Living Rm
18-8 x 13-6

linen

Entry

Br 2
11-8 x 11-8

Br 3
11-8 x 11-8

32'-0"

80'-0"

Floor Plan

Multiple Gables and a Cozy Front Porch

■ *Total living area 1,508 sq. ft.* ■ *Price Code B* ■

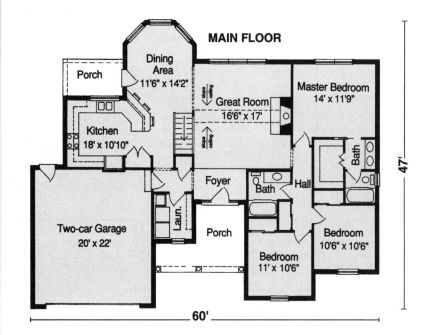

MAIN FLOOR

Porch

Dining Area
11'6" x 14'2"

Great Room
16'6" x 17'

Master Bedroom
14' x 11'9"

Bath

Kitchen
18' x 10'10"

slope ↓   ↓ slope

Foyer

Bath   Hall

Two-car Garage
20' x 22'

Laun.

Porch

Bedroom
10'6" x 10'6"

Bedroom
11' x 10'6"

47'

60'

Main floor — 1,508 sq. ft.
Basement — 1,429 sq. ft.
Garage — 440 sq. ft.

No. 92649

■ **This plan features:**

— Three bedrooms

— Two full baths

■ Multiple gables and a cozy front porch

■ A Foyer area that leads to a bright and cheery Great Room capped by a sloped ceiling and highlighted by a fireplace

■ The Dining Area includes double hung windows and angles adding light and dimension to the room

■ Kitchen with additional room provided by a breakfast bar

■ A Master Bedroom Suite with a private bath

■ Two additional bedrooms share a full bath in the hall

■ No materials list is available for this plan

Affordable Style

No. 91753

■ This plan features:

– Three bedrooms

– Two full baths

■ A country porch welcomes you to an Entry hall with a convenient closet

■ A well-appointed Kitchen boasts a double sink, ample counter and storage space, a peninsula eating bar and a built-in hutch

■ A terrific Master Suite including a private bath and a walk-in closet

■ A Dining Room that flows from the Great Room and into the Kitchen that includes sliding glass doors to the deck

■ A Great Room with a cozy fireplace that can also be enjoyed from the Dining area

■ Two additional bedrooms share a full hall bath

■ No materials list is available for this plan

Main area— 1,490 sq. ft.
Covered porch — 120 sq. ft.
Basement — 1,490 sq. ft.
Garage — 579 sq. ft.
Width — 58'-0"
Depth — 61"-0"

■ Total living area 1,490 sq. ft. ■ Price Code A ■

MAIN FLOOR

Attractive Roof Lines

No. 90983 ✗

■ This plan features:

– Three bedrooms

– One full and one three quarter baths

■ An open floor plan shared by the sunken Living Room, Dining and Kitchen areas

■ An unfinished daylight Basement which will provide future bedrooms, a bathroom and laundry facilities

■ A Master Suite with a big walk- in closet and a private bath featuring a double shower

Main floor — 1,396 sq. ft.
Basement — 1,396 sq. ft.
Garage — 389 sq. ft.
Width — 48'-0"
Depth — 54'-0"

An
EXCLUSIVE DESIGN
By Westhome Planners, Ltd.

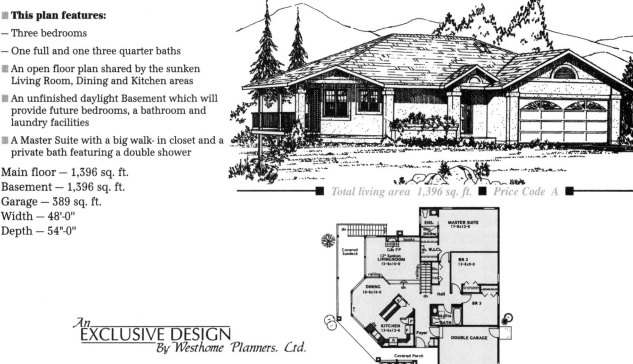

■ Total living area 1,396 sq. ft. ■ Price Code A ■

MAIN FLOOR

Enchanting Elevation

■ Total living area 1,704 sq. ft. ■ Price Code B ■

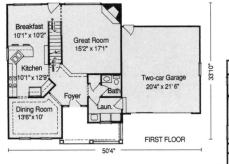

FIRST FLOOR

50'4"

33'10"

SECOND FLOOR

No. 92695

■ **This plan features:**

– Three bedrooms

– One full, one three-quarter, and one half baths

■ The covered front Porch provides a warm dry welcome

■ The large Foyer showcases interesting angled entries to the rooms beyond

■ The Dining Room has a tray ceiling and is directly connected to the Kitchen

■ The Great Room has a corner fireplace

■ The Kitchen is well-equipped and features a serving bar

■ The Breakfast Nook has an access door to the rear yard and stairs to the second floor

■ Upstairs find three bedrooms, all with ample closet space and two baths

■ No materials list is available for this plan

First floor — 906 sq. ft.
Second floor — 798 sq. ft.
Garage — 437 sq. ft.
Basement — 906 sq. ft.

Beautiful Combination of Old and New

■ Total living area 2,108 sq. ft. ■ Price Code C ■

MAIN LEVEL

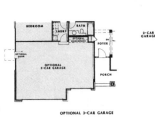

OPTIONAL 3-CAR GARAGE

OPTIONAL DEN

No. 24256 ✗

■ **This plan features:**

– Three bedrooms

– Two full baths

■ Vaulted ceilings in the family living areas; Living Room, Dining Room, Family Room and Eating Nook

■ An open layout between the Kitchen, Nook, and Family Room, making the rooms appear even more spacious

■ A corner fireplace in the Family Room, which also has access to the patio

■ A peninsula counter in the island Kitchen that doubles as an eating bar

■ A lavish Master Suite that is equipped with a private bath and walk-in closet

■ Two family bedrooms that share a full hall bath

Main area — 2,108 sq. ft.

An EXCLUSIVE DESIGN
By Energetic Enterprises

Private Master Suite

■ *Total living area 1,293 sq. ft.* ■ *Price Code B* ■

No. 92523

This plan features:

- Three bedrooms
- Two full baths
- A spacious Great Room enhanced by a vaulted ceiling and fireplace
- A well-equipped Kitchen with windowed double sink
- A secluded Master Suite with decorative ceiling, private master bath and walk-in closet
- Two additional bedrooms sharing hall bath
- Optional crawl space or slab foundation — please specify when ordering

Main floor — 1,293 sq. ft.
Garage — 433 sq. ft.

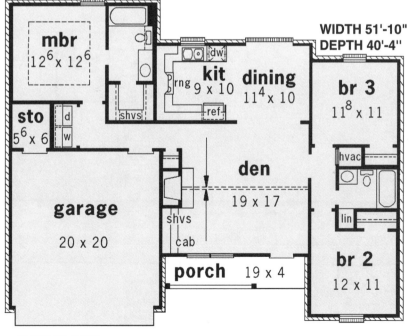

WIDTH 51'-10"
DEPTH 40'-4"

mbr
12⁶ x 12⁶

sto
5⁶ x 6

kit
9 x 10

dining
11⁴ x 10

br 3
11⁸ x 11

garage
20 x 20

den
19 x 17

br 2
12 x 11

porch   19 x 4

MAIN FLOOR

Eye-Catching Turret Adds to Master Suite

■ *Total living area 2,403 sq. ft.* ■ *Price Code D* ■

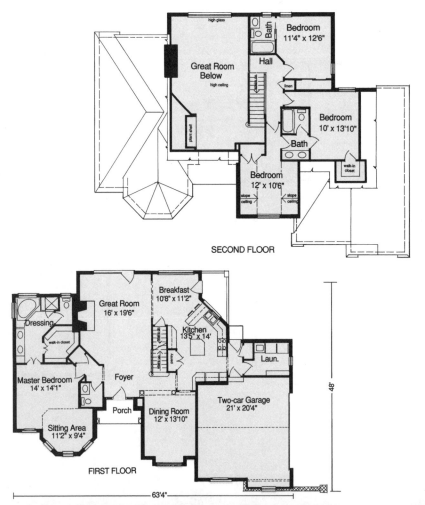

SECOND FLOOR

FIRST FLOOR

No. 92651

■ **This plan features:**

— Four bedrooms

— Three full and one half baths

■ Sheltered entry surrounded by glass leads into open Foyer and Great Room with high ceiling, hearth fireplace and atrium door to backyard

■ Columns frame entrance to Dining Room

■ Kitchen with built-in pantry, work island and bright Breakfast area

■ Master Bedroom wing with sitting area, walk-in closet and private bath with corner window tub and double vanity

■ Three bedrooms, one with a private bath

■ No materials list is available for this plan

First floor — 1,710 sq. ft.
Second floor — 693 sq. ft.
Basement — 1,620 sq. ft.
Garage — 467 sq. ft.

Dining in a Greenhouse Bay

No. 90620

This plan features:

- Three bedrooms
- Two full baths
- Covered entrance into a bright Foyer highlighted by a skydome
- Formal Living Room accented by a heat-circulating fireplace and sliding glass doors to the Terrace
- Greenhouse Dining Room feels like eating outdoors
- Efficient Kitchen with a peninsula counter and a bay window Dinette area convenient to the Laundry and Garage
- Comfortable Master Bedroom with a private bath and walk-in closet
- Two additional bedrooms share a full bath
- This plan is available with a Basement or Slab foundation — please specify when ordering

Main floor — 1,476 sq. ft.
Basement — 1,476 sq. ft.
Garage — 480 sq. ft.
Porch — 70 sq. ft.

Total living area 1,476 sq. ft. ■ *Price Code A*

MAIN FLOOR

Compact Home is Surprisingly Spacious

No. 90905

This plan features:

- Three bedrooms
- One full and one three-quarter baths
- A spacious Living Room warmed by a fireplace
- A Dining Room flowing off the Living Room, with sliding glass doors to the deck
- An efficient, well-equipped Kitchen with a snack bar, double sink, and ample cabinet and counter space
- A Master Suite with a walk-in closet and private full bath
- Two additional, roomy bedrooms with ample closet space and protection from street noise by the two-car garage

Main area — 1,314 sq. ft.
Basement — 1,488 sq. ft.
Garage — 484 sq. ft.
Width — 50'-0"
Depth — 54'-0"

Total living area 1,314 sq. ft. ■ *Price Code A*

MAIN FLOOR

An
EXCLUSIVE DESIGN
By Westhome Planners, Ltd.

Great Starter or Empty Nester

No. 91545 ✂

This plan features:

— Two bedrooms

— Two full baths

■ A formal Living Room or a cozy Den, the front room to the right of the Entry Hall adapts to your lifestyle

■ An efficient Kitchen with ample counter and storage space

■ A formal Dining Room situated next to the Kitchen and flowing from the Great Room

■ A corner fireplace highlighting the Great Room

■ A walk-in closet and a private double vanity bath in the Master Suite

■ An additional bedroom that easily accesses the full bath in the hall

■ This plan cannot be built in Clark County, WA

Main floor — 1,420 sq. ft.

■ Total living area 1,420 sq. ft. ■ Price Code A ■

MAIN AREA

Excellent Choice for First Time Buyer

No. 91055 ✂

This plan features:

— Three bedrooms

— Two full and one half baths

■ A friendly, covered Porch sheltering the front entrance

■ A formal Living Room with an expansive floor-to-ceiling triple window flowing into a formal Dining Room

■ A comfortable Family Room with a sliding glass door to the backyard, a Utility Closet with washer and dryer and access to the Kitchen

■ An efficient Kitchen with a peninsula counter/snackbar on the Family Room side and adjacent to the Dining Room for ease in serving

■ A cozy Master Bedroom with a recessed dormer window, an oversized, walk-in closet and a private Bath

■ Two additional bedrooms, on the second floor, sharing a full hall bath and a Playroom that could be a fourth bedroom

First floor — 805 sq. ft.
Second floor — 961 sq. ft.
Garage — 540 sq. ft.

■ Total living area 1,766 sq. ft. ■ Price Code B ■

FIRST FLOOR

SECOND FLOOR

Enhanced by a Columned Porch

■ *Total living area 1,754 sq. ft.* ■ *Price Code C* ■

No. 92531

■ This plan features:

— Three bedrooms

— Two full baths

■ A Great Room with a fireplace and decorative ceiling

■ A large efficient Kitchen with Breakfast Area

■ A Master Bedroom with a private Master Bath and walk-in closet

■ A formal Dining Room conveniently located near the Kitchen

■ Two additional bedrooms with walk-in closets and use of full hall bath

■ An optional crawl space or slab foundation available — please specify when ordering

Main floor — 1,754 sq. ft.
Garage — 552 sq. ft.

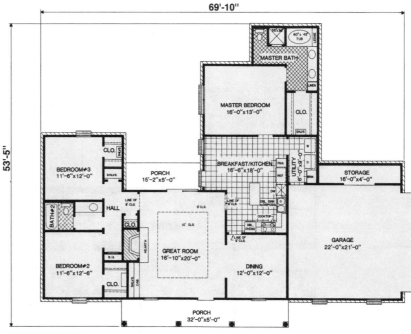

MAIN FLOOR

Energy Efficient Air-Lock Entry

■ *Total living area 1,771 sq. ft.* ■ *Price Code B* ■

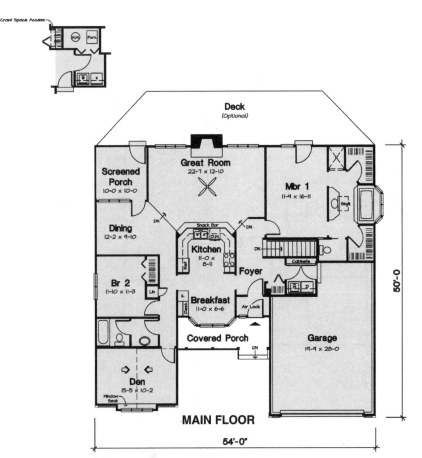

Deck
(Optional)

Crawl Space Access

MAIN FLOOR

54'-0"

50'-0"

Screened Porch
10-0 x 10-0

Great Room
22-7 x 12-10

Mbr 1
11-4 x 16-11

Skylt

Dining
12-2 x 9-10

Snack Bar

Kitchen
11-0 x 8-11

Foyer

Cabinets

Br 2
11-10 x 11-3

Breakfast
11-0 x 6-6

Air Lock

Covered Porch

Garage
19-9 x 20-0

Den
15-5 x 10-2

Window Seat

No. 24714

■ **This plan features:**

— Two bedrooms

— Two full baths

■ The attractive covered Porch highlights the curb appeal of this charming home

■ A cozy window seat and a vaulted ceiling enhance the private Den

■ The sunken Great Room is accented by a fireplace that is nestled between windows

■ A screened Porch, accessed from the Dining Room, extends the living space to the outdoors

■ The master bath features a garden tub, separate shower, his-n-her walk-in closets and a skylight

■ No materials list is available for this plan

Main floor — 1,771 sq. ft.
Basement — 1,194 sq. ft.
Garage — 517 sq. ft.

Lots of Space in this Small Package

No. 90378

This plan features:

– Two bedrooms with possible third bedroom/loft

– Two full baths

■ A Living Room with dynamic, soaring angles and a fireplace

■ A first floor Master Suite with full bath and walk in-closet

■ Walk-in closets in all bedrooms

Main floor — 878 sq. ft.
Upper floor — 405 sq. ft.

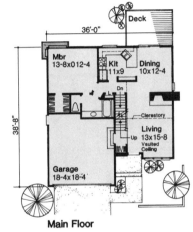

Total living area 1,283 sq. ft. ● Price Code A

Main Floor

Upper Floor

Enjoy a Summer Breeze on the Covered Porch

No. 91073

This plan features:

– Three bedrooms

– Two full and one half baths

■ A large Living Room enhanced by a fireplace and an open entry to the formal Dining Room

■ An efficient L-shaped Kitchen with cooktop island and open layout to the Family Room and Nook area creating a feeling of spaciousness

■ Two generously sized bedrooms that share a full bath

■ A Master Suite that includes a walk-in closet and spa tub with garden windows

■ A large Bonus Room for you to decide on

■ No materials list is available for this plan

■ This plan is available with a basement or crawl space foundation — please specify when ordering

Main floor — 1,240 sq. ft.
Upper floor — 969 sq. ft.
Bonus Room — 254 sq. ft.
Garage — 550 sq. ft.

Total living area 2,209 sq. ft. ● Price Code D

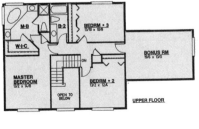

Adapt this Colonial to Your Lifestyle

Total living area 1,587 sq. ft. ■ Price Code B

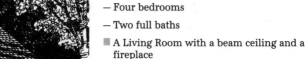

No. 90671

■ **This plan features:**

— Four bedrooms

— Two full baths

■ A Living Room with a beam ceiling and a fireplace

■ An eat-in Kitchen efficiently serving the formal Dining Room

■ A Master Bedroom with his-n-her closets

■ Two upstairs bedrooms sharing a split bath

First floor — 1,056 sq. ft.
Second floor — 531 sq. ft.

FIRST FLOOR

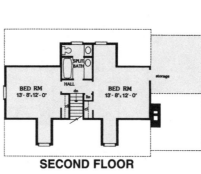

SECOND FLOOR

The Town House

No. 91325

Total living area 1,234 sq. ft. ■ Price Code G

■ **This plan features(per unit):**

— Two or three bedrooms

— One full and one three-quarter baths

■ Sheltered entrance leads to spacious Living/Dining area

■ Living area enhanced by a corner fireplace and sliding glass door to Patio with built-in barbecue

■ Efficient, U-shaped Kitchen easily serves Dining area

■ Den/Bedroom with a large closet and easy access to Patio and full bath

■ Spacious Master Bedroom offers three closets, a private Deck and full bath access

■ Secondary bedroom with a large closet and easy access to a full bath

■ No materials list is available for this plan

First floor — 722 sq. ft.
Second floor — 512 sq. ft.

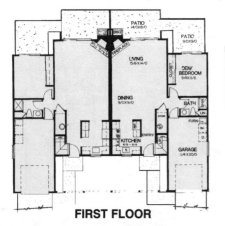

FIRST FLOOR

SECOND FLOOR

Distinguished Dwelling

■ *Total living area 2,733 sq. ft.* ■ *Price Code E* ■

No. 94112

■ **This plan features:**

— Four bedrooms

— Two full and one half baths

■ Grand two-story entry into Foyer with a lovely landing staircase

■ Living Room with a decorative window and a vaulted ceiling

■ Beautiful bay window highlights formal Dining Room

■ Convenient Kitchen with cooktop work island, pantry, octagon Dining area, and nearby Study, Laundry and Garage entry

■ Luxurious Master Bedroom offers a glass alcove, walk-in closet and pampering bath with a corner tub

■ No materials list is available for this plan

First floor — 1,514 sq. ft.
Second floor — 1,219 sq. ft.
Basement — 1,465 sq. ft.
Garage — 596 sq. ft.

Large Front Porch Adds a Country Touch

■ *Total living area 1,415 sq. ft.* ■ *Price Code A* ■

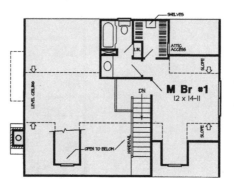

Second Floor

SHELVES

ATTIC ACCESS

M Br #1
12 x 14-11

DN

LEVEL CEILING

SLOPE

OPEN TO BELOW

HANDRAIL

SLOPE

No. 34601

■ **This plan features:**

– Three bedrooms

– Two full baths

■ A country-styled front Porch

■ Vaulted ceiling in the Living Room which includes a fireplace

■ An efficient Kitchen with double sinks and peninsula counter that may double as an eating bar

■ Two first floor bedrooms with ample closet space

■ A second floor Master Suite with sloped ceiling, walk-in closet and private master bath

First floor — 1,007 sq. ft.
Second floor — 408 sq. ft.
Basement — 1,007 sq. ft.

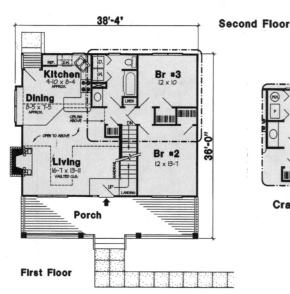

38'-4'

REF. D.W.

Kitchen
9-10 x 8-4
APPROX.

Dining
8-5 x 7-5
APPROX.

Br #3
12 x 10

LINEN

OPEN TO ABOVE

CEILING ABOVE

DN

Living
16-7 x 13-11
VAULTED CLG.

Br #2
12 x 13-7

HANDRAIL

UP
LANDING

36'-0"

Porch

First Floor

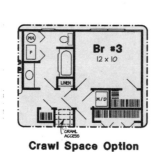

MUD
F

Br #3
12 x 10

LINEN

W/D

CRAWL ACCESS

Crawl Space Option

Gabled Roofline and Arched Windows

No. 91063

This plan features:

- Three bedrooms
- Two full baths
- Vaulted ceilings and an open interior creating a spacious feeling
- A private Master Bedroom with a generous closet and Master Bath
- Two additional bedrooms sharing the second full bath
- A Kitchen with ample storage, countertops, and a built-in pantry
- No materials list is available for this plan

Main area — 1,207 sq. ft.
Garage — 440 sq. ft.

■ *Total living area 1,207 sq. ft.* ■ *Price Code A* ■

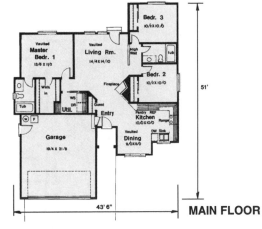

MAIN FLOOR

Spanish Style Affordable Home

No. 91340

This plan features:

- Two bedrooms
- Two full baths
- A beautiful arched entry leads guests to the porch and Great Room within
- A large Master Suite with vaulted ceilings and a handicap accessible private bath
- Vaulted ceilings in the Great Room
- An open Kitchen area with an eating bar
- A large wrap-around Porch punctuated by columns, spanning the length of the home
- Easy access from the Carport to the central hallway

Main area — 1,111 sq. ft.

■ *Total living area 1,111 sq. ft.* ■ *Price Code A* ■

MAIN FLOOR

Varied Roof Heights Create Interesting Lines

Total living area 1,613 sq. ft. ■ Price Code B

No. 90601

■ This plan features:

— Three bedrooms

— Two full and one half baths

■ A spacious Family Room with a heat-circulating fireplace, which is visible from the Foyer

■ A large Kitchen with a cooktop island, opening into the dinette bay

■ A Master Suite with his-n-her closets and a private Master Bath

■ Two additional bedrooms which share a full hall bath

■ Formal Dining and Living Rooms, flowing into each other for easy entertaining

Main area — 1,613 sq. ft.
Basement — 1,060 sq. ft.
Garage — 461 sq. ft.

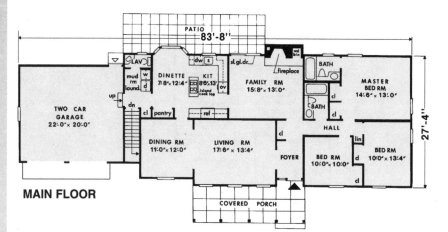

MAIN FLOOR

A Special Kind of Coziness

Total living area 1,089 sq. ft. ■ Price Code A

No. 98805

■ This plan features:

— Three bedrooms

— One full and one half baths

■ An open rail staircase compliments the central Foyer

■ The Living room with it's warm fireplace combines with the Dining area

■ The Kitchen is highlighted by a desk, a pantry, and a serving bar

■ Laundry conveniently located near the bedrooms

■ The Master suite includes a private half bath

■ Two secondary bedrooms have ample closet space

Main floor — 1,089 sq. ft.
Basement — 1,089 sq. ft.
Garage — 462 sq. ft.

MAIN FLOOR

B. NATHAN

■ *Total living area 1,864 sq. ft.* ■ *Price Code C* ■

No. 96468

■ This plan features:

— Three bedrooms

— Two full baths

■ Sunlit Foyer flows easily into the generous Great Room

■ Great Room crowned in a cathedral ceiling and accented by a fireplace

■ Accent columns define the open Kitchen and Breakfast Bay

■ Master Bedroom topped by a tray ceiling and highlighted by a well-appointed master bath

■ Two additional bedrooms, sharing a skylit bath in the hall, create the children's wing

Main floor—1,864 sq. ft.
Bonus room—319 sq. ft.
Garage—503 sq. ft.

BONUS RM.
12-8 x 20-10

attic storage   attic storage

down

skylights

BED RM.
10-8 x 11-0

BED RM.
10-8 x 11-0

skylight

bath

up

PORCH

UTIL.

storage

BRKFST.
11-4 x 9-0

GREAT RM.
16-4 x 18-8
(cathedral ceiling)

fireplace

MASTER
BED RM.
14-0 x 15-4

KIT.
11-4 x
12-6

GARAGE
21-8 x 20-10

lin.

walk-in
closet

storage

(optional door location)

master
bath

cl

FOYER
6-4 x
9-8

DINING
12-4 x 13-0

59-8

PORCH

FLOOR PLAN

65-0

© 1996 Donald A Gardner Architects, Inc.

Traditional Brick with Detailing

■ *Total living area 1,869 sq. ft.* ■ *Price Code D* ■

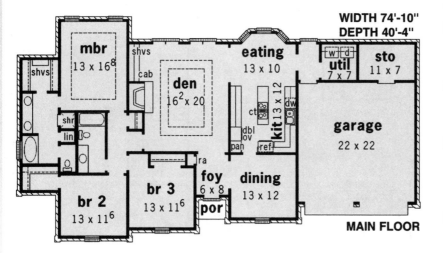

WIDTH 74'-10"
DEPTH 40'-4"

MAIN FLOOR

No. 92536 ☒

■ **This plan features:**

— Three bedrooms

— Two full baths

■ Covered entry leads into the Foyer, the formal Dining Room and the Den

■ Expansive Den with a decorative ceiling over a hearth fireplace and sliding glass doors to the rear yard

■ Country Kitchen with a built-in pantry, double ovens and a cooktop island easily serves the Breakfast area and Dining Room

■ Private Master Bedroom suite with a decorative ceiling, a walk-in closet, a double vanity and a whirlpool tub

■ Two additional bedrooms share a full bath

■ An optional slab or crawl space foundation — please specify when ordering

Main floor — 1,869 sq. ft.
Garage — 561 sq. ft.

Elegant Entertaining Indoors and Out

No. 90001

This plan features:

– Four bedrooms

– Two full and one half baths

■ Gracious double doors lead into the Reception Foyer with a unique bridge over a moat to the Living Room

■ Huge, stone fireplace with a barbeque and a wood storage on the Terrace side, a concealed bar and French doors enhance this Living Room

■ Gracious Dining Room equipped with an open grill

■ Efficient Kitchen with an eating bar as part of the Family Room, highlighted by a corner fireplace

■ Sunken Master Bedroom suite with a decorative window topped by a cathedral ceiling, three closets and a private bath with a Roman tub

■ Three large bedrooms with ample closet space share a full bath

Main floor — 2,177 sq. ft.

■ Total living area 2,177 sq. ft. ■ Price Code C ■

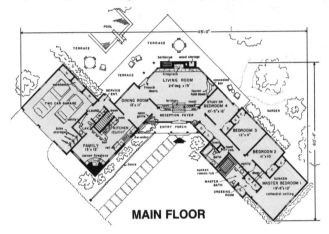

MAIN FLOOR

One-Level Family Living

No. 98808

This plan features:

– Three bedrooms

– Two full baths

■ Covered entry leading to a Foyer equipped with a convenient coat closet

■ Secluded Den or third bedroom to the left of the Foyer

■ Living Room open to the Dining Room for a perfect living space for entertaining

■ Cozy fireplace highlighting the Living Room while built-in china cabinet space is featured in the Dining Room

■ Tiled Kitchen/Nook area includes a built-in pantry, a work island and a French door to the patio

■ Master Bedroom includes a private bath creating a master suite

■ Secondary bedroom has easy access to the full bath in the hall

Main floor — 1,326 sq. ft.
Basement — 1,302 sq. ft.
Garage — 442 sq. ft.

■ Total living area 1,326 sq. ft. ■ Price Code A ■

MAIN FLOOR PLAN

An Estate of Epic Proportion

■ *Total living area 3,936 sq. ft.* ■ *Price Code F* ■

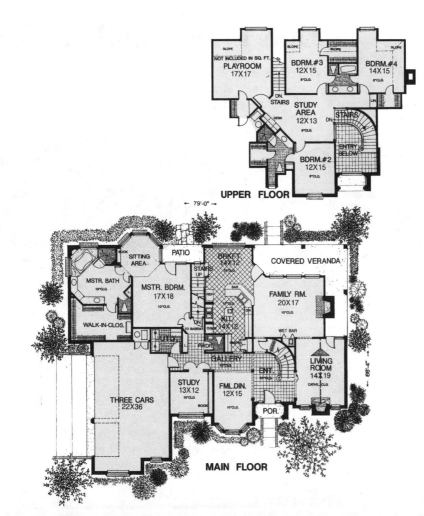

UPPER FLOOR

← 79'-0" →

MAIN FLOOR

No. 98539

■ **This plan features**

— Four bedrooms

— Three full and one half baths

■ Front door opening into a grand Entry way with a 20' ceiling and a spiral staircase

■ Living Room with cathedral ceiling and fireplace

■ Walk down the Gallery to the Study with a full wall, built-in bookcase

■ The enormous Master Bedroom has a walk-in closet, sumptuous bath and a bayed Sitting Area

■ Family Room has a wetbar and a fireplace

■ An optional basement or slab foundation — please specify when ordering

■ No materials list is available for this plan

First floor — 2,751 sq. ft.
Second floor — 1,185 sq. ft.
Bonus — 343 sq. ft.
Garage — 790 sq. ft.

■ *Total living area 1,552 sq. ft.* ■ *Price Code B* ■

No. 90844

This plan features:

- Three bedrooms
- Two full and one half baths

■ A wrap-around Deck providing outdoor living space, ideal for a sloping lot

■ Two-and-a-half story glass wall and two separate atrium doors providing natural light for the Living/Dining Room area

■ An efficient galley Kitchen with easy access to the Dining area

■ A Master Bedroom suite with a half bath and ample closet space

■ Another bedroom on the first floor adjoins a full hall bath

■ A second floor Bedroom/Studio, with a private Deck, adjacent to a full hall bath and a Loft area

First floor — 1,086 sq. ft.
Second floor — 466 sq. ft.
Basement — 1,080 sq. ft.

An EXCLUSIVE DESIGN
By Westhome Planners, Ltd.

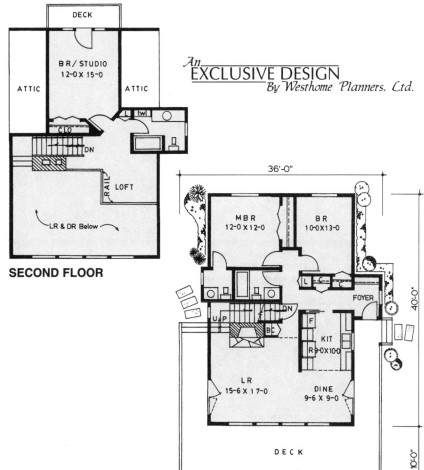

SECOND FLOOR

FIRST FLOOR

Country Brick

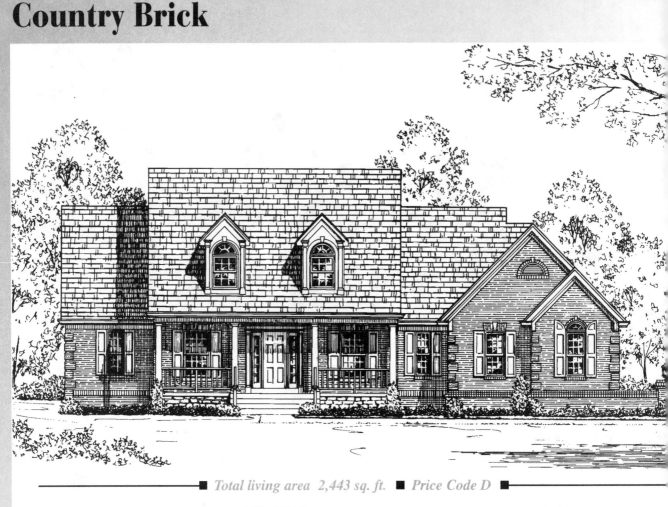

Total living area 2,443 sq. ft. ■ Price Code D

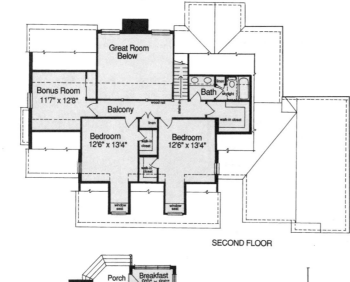

SECOND FLOOR

Great Room Below

Bonus Room
11'7" x 12'8"

Balcony

Bath

Bedroom
12'6" x 13'4"

Bedroom
12'6" x 13'4"

FIRST FLOOR

Porch

Breakfast
9'9" x 8'6"

Kitchen
9'2" x 11'8"

Master Bedroom
14' x 12'10"

Great Room
16'9" x 14'

Library
11' x 13'4"

Foyer

Dining Room
10'6" x 13'4"

Laun.

Two-car Garage
20'4" x 26'4"

Dressing

78'4"

47'8"

No. 92653

■ This plan features:

— Three or four bedrooms

— Two full and one half baths

■ Friendly front porch leads into a gracious open Foyer

■ Secluded Library offers a quiet space with built-in shelves

■ Great Room with a focal point fireplace topped by sloped ceiling

■ Kitchen with island snack bar, bright Breakfast area, pantry and nearby Laundry/Garage entry

■ Master Bedroom offers a deluxe bath and spacious walk-in closet

■ Two additional bedrooms with walk-in closets and window seats

■ No materials list is available for this plan

First floor — 1,710 sq. ft.
Second floor — 733 sq. ft.
Bonus — 181 sq. ft.
Basement — 1,697 sq. ft.
Garage — 499 sq. ft.

Traditional Two-Story with Special Details

■ *Total living area 2,157 sq. ft.* ■ *Price Code C* ■

No. 92631

■ **This plan features:**

— Four bedrooms

— Two full and one half baths

■ Front entrance into two-story Foyer with a plant shelf and lovely railing staircase

■ Expansive Great Room with corner fireplace and access to rear yard is topped by two-story ceiling

■ Efficient Kitchen with peninsula counter, walk-in Pantry, Breakfast Bay and access to Deck, Laundry, Garage and formal Dining Room

■ Secluded Master Bedroom offers a sloped ceiling and lavish bath with walk-in closet

■ No materials list is available for this plan

First floor — 1,511 sq. ft.
Second floor — 646 sq. ft.
Basement — 1,479 sq. ft.
Garage — 475 sq. ft.

Columned Keystone Arched Entry

■ *Total living area 2,256 sq. ft.* ■ *Price Code D* ■

No. 96503

■ **This plan features:**

— Three bedrooms

— Two full baths

■ Keystone arches and arched transoms above the windows

■ Formal Dining Room and Study flank the Foyer

■ Fireplace in Great Room

■ Efficient Kitchen with a peninsula counter and bayed Nook

■ A step ceiling in the Master Suite and interesting master bath with a triangular area for the oval tub

■ The secondary bedrooms share a full bath in the hall

Main floor — 2,256 sq. ft.
Garage — 514 sq. ft.

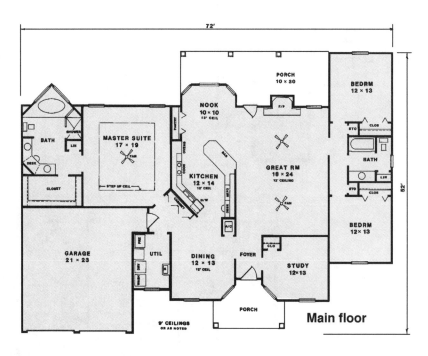

Main floor

L-Shaped Front Porch

■ *Total living area 1,280 sq. ft.* ■ *Price Code A* ■

No. 98747

■ This plan features:

— Three bedrooms

— Two full baths

■ Attractive wood siding and a large L-shaped covered porch

■ Front entry leading to generous living room with a vaulted ceiling

■ Large two-car garage with access through utility room

■ Roomy secondary bedrooms share the full bath in the hall

■ Kitchen highlighted by a built-in pantry and a garden window

■ Vaulted ceiling adds volume to the Dining Room

■ Master Suite in an isolated location enhanced by abundant closet space, separate vanity, and linen storage

Main floor — 1,280 sq. ft.

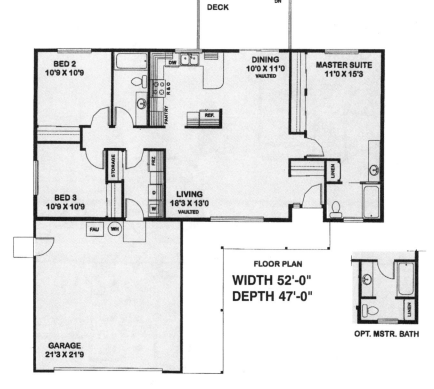

FLOOR PLAN
WIDTH 52'-0"
DEPTH 47'-0"

OPT. MSTR. BATH

Facade Communicates Success

■ *Total living area 3,166 sq. ft.* ■ *Price Code E* ■

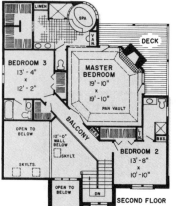

SECOND FLOOR

First floor — 1,807 sq. ft.
Second floor — 1,359 sq. ft.
Basement — 1,807 sq. ft.
Garage — 840 sq. ft.

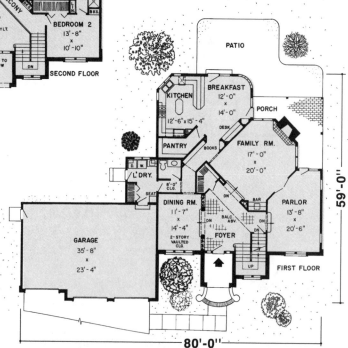

FIRST FLOOR

No. 20353 ⚒

■ This plan features:

— Three bedrooms

— Three full and one half baths

■ A sky-lit Foyer with a balcony above

■ A formal Dining Room made spacious by a vaulted ceiling

■ A large island Kitchen with peninsula counter that serves a glass-walled Breakfast Area equipped with an adjoining Pantry

■ A built-in bar in the huge Family Room with a cozy fireplace that is just steps away from the elegant Parlor

■ A magnificent Master Suite with pan-vault ceiling, fireplace, circular spa, two-way access to a private Deck and large walk-in closet

■ *Total living area 1,249 sq. ft.* ■ *Price Code A* ■

No. 91033

■ **This plan features:**

— Two bedrooms

— Two full baths

■ A two-story Living Room and Dining Room with a handsome stone fireplace

■ A well-appointed Kitchen with a peninsula counter

■ A Master Suite with a walk-in closet and private master bath

■ A large Utility Room with Laundry facilities

■ An optional basement or crawl space foundation — please specify when ordering

Main floor — 952 sq. ft.
Upper floor — 297 sq. ft.

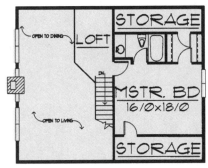

UPPER FLOOR PLAN

OPTIONAL
BASEMENT PLAN

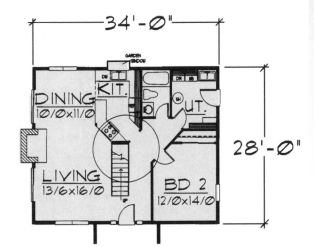

MAIN FLOOR PLAN

An Extraordinary Home

■ *Total living area 2,082 sq. ft.* ■ *Price Code C* ■

Bedroom
11'1" x 13'3"

Bedroom
11'5" x 12'0"

linen

Bath

bookshelves
computer desk

Balcony Foyer Below

wood rail

Bonus
Room
11'0" x 22'0"

wood rail

SECOND FLOOR

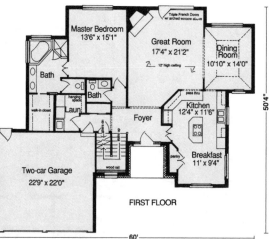

Master Bedroom
13'6" x 15'1"

Great Room
17'4" x 21'2"

Triple French Doors
w/ arched window above

Dining
Room
10'10" x 14'0"

12' high ceiling

Bath

hanging
space

Bath

pass thru

walk-in closet

Laun

Kitchen
12'4" x 11'6"

Foyer

50'4"

pantry

Two-car Garage
22'9" x 22'0"

Breakfast
11' x 9'4"

wood rail

FIRST FLOOR

60'

No. 92642

■ This plan features:

— Three bedrooms

— Two full and one half baths

■ A grand entry into the formal Dining Room with a volume ceiling

■ A roomy, well-equipped Kitchen that includes a pass-through

■ Large windows in the Breakfast area flooding the room with natural light

■ A private Master Bedroom with a luxurious, compartmented bath

■ Split stairs graced with wood railings

■ No materials list is available for this plan

First floor — 1,524 sq. ft.
Second floor — 558 sq. ft.
Basement — 1,460 sq. ft.

Carefree Convenience

■ *Total living area 1,600 sq. ft.* ■ *Price Code B* ■

No. 10674

This plan features:

- Three bedrooms

- Two full baths

■ A galley Kitchen, centrally-located between the Dining, Breakfast and Living Room areas

■ A huge Family Room which exits onto the patio

■ A Master Suite with double closets and vanity

Main floor — 1,600 sq. ft.
Garage — 465 sq. ft.

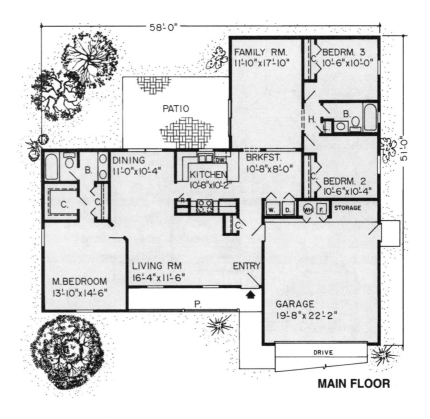

MAIN FLOOR

Tailored for a View to the Side

■ *Total living area 2,579 sq. ft.* ■ *Price Code D* ■

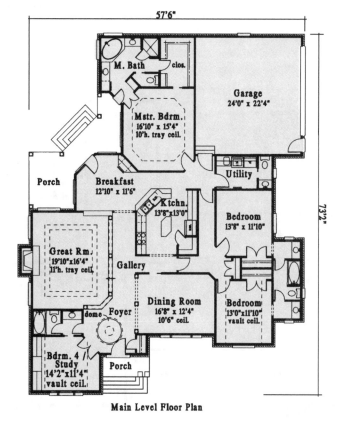

57'6"

73'2"

M. Bath

clos.

Garage
24'0" x 22'4"

Mstr. Bdrm.
16'10" x 15'4"
10'h. tray ceil.

Utility

Porch

Breakfast
12'10" x 11'6"

Kitchn.
13'8" x 13'0"

Bedroom
13'8" x 11'10"

Great Rm.
19'10"x16'4"
11'h. tray ceil.

Gallery

Dining Room
16'8" x 12'4"
10'6" ceil.

Bedroom
13'0"x11'10"
vault ceil.

dome

Foyer

Bdrm. 4 /
Study
14'2"x11'4"
vault ceil.

Porch

Main Level Floor Plan

Main floor — 2,579 sq. ft.
Garage — 536 sq. ft.

No. 93708

■ **This plan features:**

— Three/four bedrooms

— Three full and one half baths

■ Domed Foyer and French doors leading to the private study or guest bedroom with a vaulted ceiling

■ Arched entrance and columns introduce elegant Dining Room

■ A sunken Great Room with a high tray ceiling also punctuated by arches and columns and further enhanced by a fireplace

■ A Breakfast Room, with an optional planning desk, opens to the Kitchen via the eating bar

■ An island and walk-in Pantry adding to the Kitchen's efficiency

■ A tray ceiling and lavish bath pamper the owner in the Master Suite

■ No materials list is available for this plan

Southern Traditional Flavor

■ *Total living area 1,567 sq. ft.* ■ *Price Code B* ■

No. 99641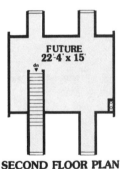

■ **This plan features:**

— Three bedrooms

— Two full baths

■ The Living Room is enhanced by nine foot ceilings and a bookcase flanked fireplace

■ Two mullioned French doors from the Dining Room to the rear terrace

■ Laundry area serving as a Mudroom between the Garage and Kitchen

■ A Master Suite with a large walk-in closet and a compartmented Bath has a separate shower stall, whirlpool tub, double vanity and linen closet

■ Bonus area can be finished into a study or recreation room

First floor — 1,567 sq. ft.
Future bonus area — 462 sq. ft.
Basement — 1,567 sq. ft.
Garage — 504 sq. ft.

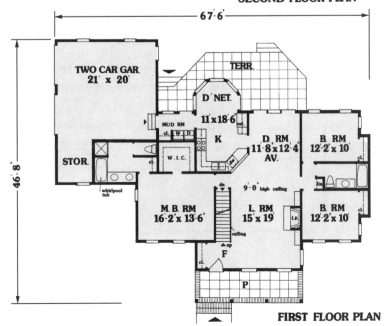

FUTURE
22'-4" x 15'

SECOND FLOOR PLAN

67'-6"

46'-8"

TWO CAR GAR.
21' x 20'

TERR.

D'NET.
11' x 18'-6"

MUD RM

STOR.

K

W.I.C.

D. RM
11'-8" x 12'-4"
AV.

B. RM
12'-2" x 10'

whirlpool tub

M. B. RM
16'-2" x 13'-6"

9'-0" high ceiling

L. RM
15' x 19

B. RM
12'-2" x 10'

railing

F

P

FIRST FLOOR PLAN

Cozy Three-Bedroom

■ *Total living area 1,770 sq. ft.* ■ *Price Code C* ■

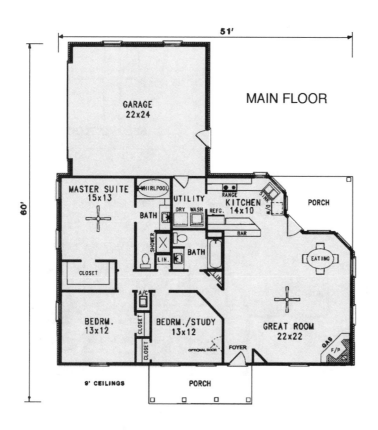

MAIN FLOOR

51'

60'

GARAGE
22x24

MASTER SUITE
15x13

WHIRLPOOL

UTILITY

RANGE

KITCHEN
14x10

STMS DN

PORCH

BATH

DRY WASH

REFG.

BAR

SHOWER

BATH

LIN.

EATING

CLOSET

A/C

CLOSET

BEDRM.
13x12

CLOSET

BEDRM./STUDY
13x12

OPTIONAL DOOR

FOYER

GREAT ROOM
22x22

GAS
F/P

9' CEILINGS

PORCH

PORCH

No. 96522

■ **This plan features:**

— Three bedrooms

— Two full baths

■ The triple arched front Porch adds to the curb appeal of the home

■ The expansive Great Room is accented by a cozy gas fireplace

■ The efficient Kitchen includes an eating bar that separates it from the Great Room

■ The Master Bedroom is highlighted by a walk-in closet and a whirlpool bath

■ Two secondary bedrooms share use of the full hall bath

■ The rear Porch extends dining to the outdoors

Main floor — 1,515 sq. ft.
Garage — 528 sq. ft.

Private Master Suite

■ *Total living area 2,069 sq. ft.* ■ *Price Code D* ■

No. 96505

■ This plan features:

– Three bedrooms

– Two full and one half baths

■ Secluded Master Bedroom tucked into the rear left corner of the home with a five-piece bath and two walk-in closets

■ Two additional bedrooms at the opposite side of the home sharing the full bath in the hall

■ Expansive Living Room highlighted by a corner fireplace and access to the rear Porch

■ Kitchen is sandwiched between the bright, bayed Nook and the formal Dining Room providing ease in serving

Main floor — 2,069 sq. ft.
Garage — 481 sq. ft.

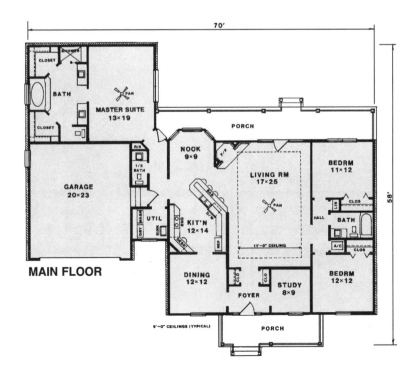

MAIN FLOOR

Dramatic Ranch

■ *Total living area 1,792 sq. ft.* ■ *Price Code B* ■

An EXCLUSIVE DESIGN
By Karl Kreeger

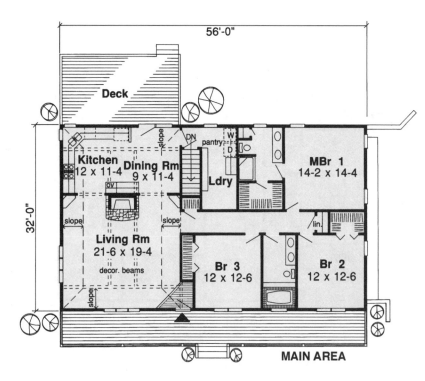

MAIN AREA

No. 20198

■ **This plan features:**

— Three bedrooms

— Two full baths

■ A large Living Room with a stone fireplace and a decorative beamed ceiling

■ A Kitchen/Dining Room arrangement which makes the rooms seem more spacious

■ A Laundry with a large Pantry located close to the bedrooms and the Kitchen

■ A Master Bedroom with a walk-in closet and a private master bath

■ Two additional bedrooms, one with a walk-in closet, that share the full hall bath

Main area — 1,792 sq. ft.
Basement — 818 sq. ft.
Garage — 857 sq. ft.

■ *Total living area 1,560 sq. ft.* ■ *Price Code B* ■

No. 34602

This plan features:

- Three bedrooms

- Two full and one half baths

■ A wrap-around Porch for views and visiting provides access into the Great Room and Dining area

■ A spacious Great Room with a two-story ceiling and dormer window above a massive fireplace

■ A combination Dining/Kitchen with an island work area and breakfast bar opening to a Great Room and adjacent to the Laundry/storage and half-bath area

■ A private two-story Master Bedroom with a dormer window, walk-in closet, double vanity bath and optional deck with hot tub

First floor — 1,061 sq. ft.
Second floor — 499 sq. ft.
Basement — 1,061 sq. ft.

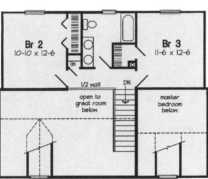

SECOND FLOOR

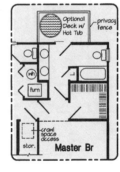

Alternate Foundation Plan

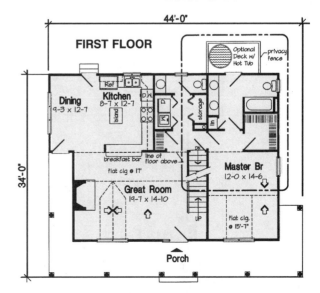

Country-Style Home for Quality Living

■ *Total living area 2,466 sq. ft.* ■ *Price Code D* ■

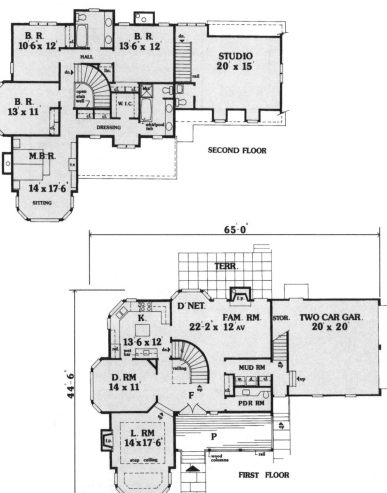

SECOND FLOOR

B. R. 10'-6" x 12'
HALL
B. R. 13'-6" x 12'
STUDIO 20' x 15'
open stair well
B. R. 13' x 11'
DRESSING
W. I. C.
whirlpool tub
M. B. R. 14' x 17'-6"
SITTING

FIRST FLOOR

65'-0"
44'-6"
TERR.
D' NET.
K.
FAM. RM. 22'-2" x 12' AV
STOR.
TWO CAR GAR. 20' x 20'
13'-6" x 12
wet bar
railing
MUD RM
D. RM 14' x 11'
F
PDR RM
L. RM 14 x 17'-6"
step ceiling
P
wood columns
rail

No. 99640 ✗

■ **This plan features:**

— Four bedrooms

— Two full and two half baths

■ A spacious central Foyer leads to all rooms

■ A sunken Living Room, enhanced by a focal point fireplace and a large windowed bay

■ An elegant formal Dining Room with interior corners angled to form an octagon

■ A fully equipped Kitchen with a center island

■ A luxurious Master Bedroom includes a dressing area, a walk-in closet and a deluxe bath

■ A Studio area above the garage that includes a half bath

First floor — 1,217 sq. ft.
Second floor — 1,249 sq. ft.
Basement — 1,217 sq. ft.
Garage — 431 sq. ft.

Friendly Front Porch

■ *Total living area 1,576 sq. ft.* ■ *Price Code C* ■

No. 94138

■ **This plan features:**

– Three bedrooms

– One full and one half baths

■ Country, homey feeling with wrap-around Porch

■ Adjoining Living Room and Dining Room

■ Efficient Kitchen easily serves Dining area with extended counter and a built-in pantry

■ Spacious Family Room with optional fireplace and access to Laundry/Garage entry

■ Large Master Bedroom with a walk-in closet and access to a full bath, offers a private bath option

■ No materials list is available for this plan

First floor — 900 sq. ft.
Second floor — 676 sq. ft.
Basement — 900 sq. ft.
Garage — 448 sq. ft.

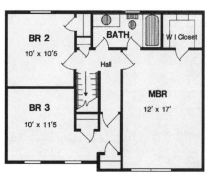

SECOND FLOOR

WIDTH 58'-0"
DEPTH 34'-0"

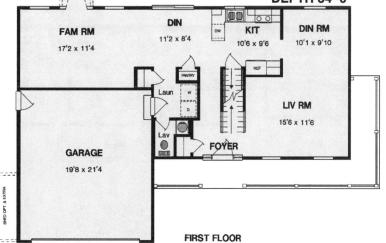

FIRST FLOOR

Attractive Ceiling Treatments and Open Layout

■ *Total living area 1,654 sq. ft.* ■ *Price Code B* ■

No. 96506 ✕

■ **This plan features:**

— Three bedrooms

— Two full and one half baths

■ Great Room and Master Suite with step-up ceiling treatments

■ A cozy fireplace providing warm focal point in the Great Room

■ Open layout between Kitchen, Dining and Great Room lending a more spacious feeling

■ Five-piece, private bath and walk-in closet pampering Master Suite

■ Two additional bedrooms located at opposite end of home from Master Suite

Main floor — 1,654 sq. ft.
Garage — 480 sq. ft.

MAIN FLOOR

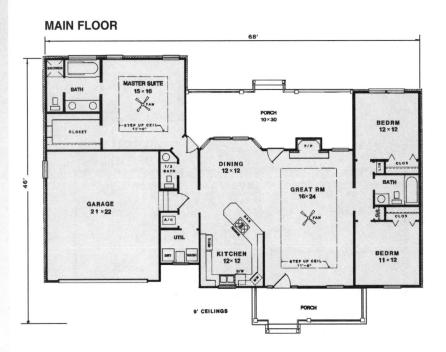

■ *Total living area 3,623 sq. ft.* ■ *Price Code F* ■

No. 94999

This plan features:

- Four bedrooms

- Two full, two three-quarter and one half baths

- The spider beamed Den with French doors includes arched transom windows

- The Dining Room opens to a dramatic high ceiling in the entry

- The Great Room features a fireplace wall with entertainment center, bookcases and wetbar

- Kitchen area includes a gazebo-shaped Dinette, large island/snack bar and walk-in pantry

- Each secondary bedroom includes a walk-in closet, a built-in desk and a private bath

- The first floor Master Suite includes a Sitting Room with a built-in bookcase and a fireplace

First floor — 2,603 sq. ft.
Second floor — 1,020 sq. ft.
Basement — 2,603 sq. ft.
Garage — 801 sq. ft.

SECOND FLOOR

FIRST FLOOR

© design basics, inc.

Expansive Covered Porch

Total living area 2,270 sq. ft. ■ Price Code D

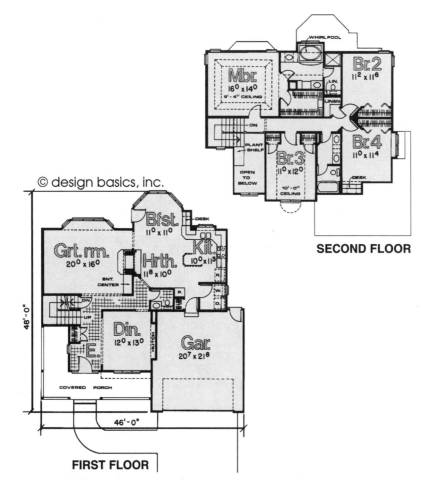

© design basics, inc.

SECOND FLOOR

FIRST FLOOR

No. 99457 ☒

■ This plan features:

— Four bedrooms

— Two full and one half baths

■ The spacious two-story entry surveys the formal Dining Room, which features a built-in hutch

■ A built-in entertainment center, a see-through fireplace and an elegant bay window highlight the Great Room

■ The Kitchen/Breakfast/Hearth Room with gazebo, wrapping counters and an open layout add an open airy feeling to the home

■ The luxurious Master Suite is topped by a decorative ceiling and has a lavish bath featuring a whirlpool tub and his-n-her vanities

First floor — 1,150 sq. ft.
Second floor — 1,120 sq. ft.
Basement — 1,150 sq. ft.
Garage — 457 sq. ft.

Impressive Elevation

■ Total living area 2,891 sq. ft. ■ Price Code E ■

No. 94231

■ This plan features:

— Three bedrooms

— Two full and one three-quarter baths

■ Glass arch entrance into Foyer and Grand Room

■ Decorative windows highlight Study and formal Dining Room

■ Spacious Kitchen with walk-in pantry and peninsula serving counter easily serves Nook, Veranda and Dining Room

■ Luxurious Master Suite with step ceiling, sitting area, his-n-her closets and pampering bath

■ Two additional bedrooms, one with a private Deck, have bay windows and walk-in closets

■ No materials list is available for this plan

First floor — 2,181 sq. ft.
Second floor — 710 sq. ft.
Garage — 658 sq. ft.

SECOND FLOOR

FIRST FLOOR

387

Country Influence

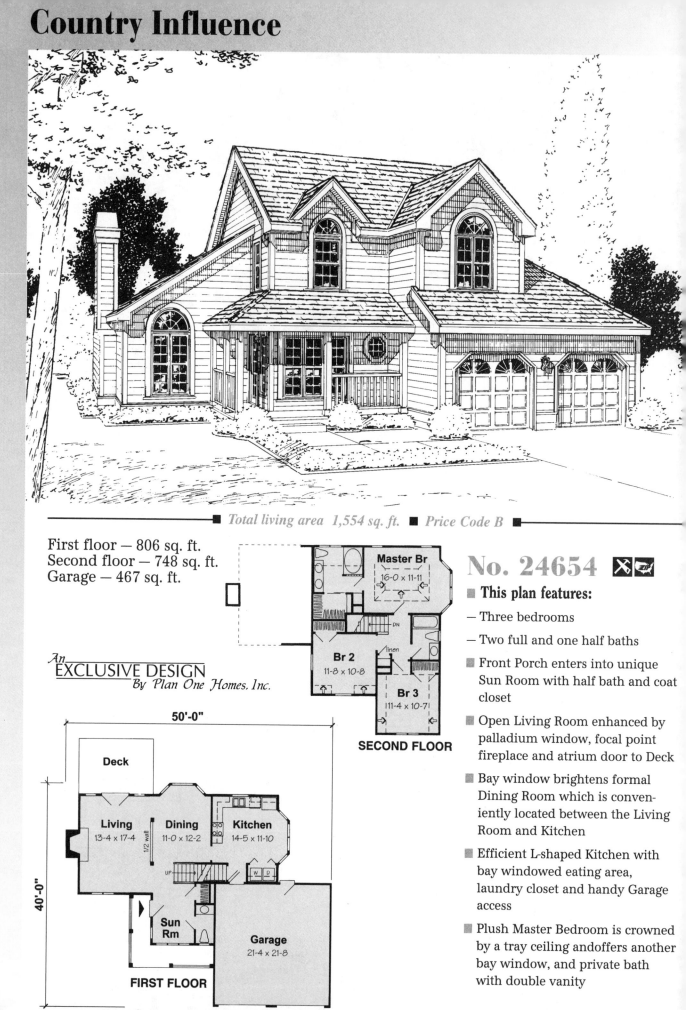

■ Total living area 1,554 sq. ft. ■ ■ Price Code B ■

First floor — 806 sq. ft.
Second floor — 748 sq. ft.
Garage — 467 sq. ft.

An
EXCLUSIVE DESIGN
By Plan One Homes, Inc.

Master Br
16-0 x 11-11

Br 2
11-8 x 10-8

linen

DN

Br 3
11-4 x 10-7

SECOND FLOOR

50'-0"

40'-0"

Deck

Living
13-4 x 17-4

1/2 wall

Dining
11-0 x 12-2

Kitchen
14-5 x 11-10

UP

W D

Sun Rm

Garage
21-4 x 21-8

FIRST FLOOR

No. 24654 ⚒ ✎

■ **This plan features:**

— Three bedrooms

— Two full and one half baths

■ Front Porch enters into unique Sun Room with half bath and coat closet

■ Open Living Room enhanced by palladium window, focal point fireplace and atrium door to Deck

■ Bay window brightens formal Dining Room which is conveniently located between the Living Room and Kitchen

■ Efficient L-shaped Kitchen with bay windowed eating area, laundry closet and handy Garage access

■ Plush Master Bedroom is crowned by a tray ceiling andoffers another bay window, and private bath with double vanity

Total living area 1,950 sq. ft. ■ **Price Code C**

No. 99757 ✕

■ This plan features:

— Three bedrooms

— Two full and one half baths

■ Front Porch invites visiting and leads into an open Entry with an angled staircase

■ Living Room with a wall of windows and an island fireplace

■ Kitchen with a work island, walk-in pantry, garden window over sink, skylit Nook and nearby Deck

■ Corner Master Suite enhanced by Deck access, vaulted ceiling, a large walk-in closet and spa bath

■ Guest/Utility Room offers a pullman bed and laundry

■ Two second floor bedrooms with large closets share a full bath

First floor — 1,472 sq. ft.
Second floor — 478 sq. ft.
Garage — 558 sq. ft.

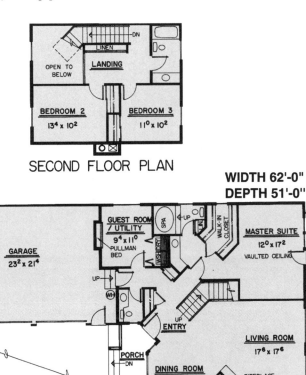

SECOND FLOOR PLAN

WIDTH 62'-0"
DEPTH 51'-0"

FIRST FLOOR PLAN

National Treasure

■ *Total living area 1,978 sq. ft.* ■ *Price Code C* ■

SECOND FLOOR

Master Br
12-7 x 16-1
cathedral

Br 2
10 x 12

railing

Sitting
9-6 x 8-6

Br 3
10 x 10-4

crawl access

Dining

furn. w/h

FIRST FLOOR

39'-6"

Living
21-2 x 12-4
decor clg.

Kitchen
14-11 x 12-4

W
D

Storage/Shop
16-2 x 12-7

Den/
Guest
10 x 10

Dining
10 x 12-3
decor clg.

Garage
23-2 x 19-3

67'-6"

No. 24400

■ **This plan features:**

— Three bedrooms

— Two full and one half baths

■ A wrap-around covered Porch

■ Decorative vaulted ceilings in the fireplaced Living Room

■ A large Kitchen with central island/breakfast bar

■ A sun-lit Sitting Area

First floor — 1,034 sq. ft.
Second floor — 944 sq. ft.
Basement — 944 sq. ft.
Garage & storage — 675 sq. ft.

An
EXCLUSIVE DESIGN
By Upright Design

©1994 Donald A. Gardner Architects, Inc.

B. NATHAN

■ *Total living area 1,639 sq. ft.* ■ *Price Code C* ■

No. 96456

■ This plan features:

— Three bedrooms

— Two full and one half baths

■ Creative use of natural lighting gives a feeling of spaciousness to this country home

■ Traffic flows easily from the bright Foyer into the Great Room which has a vaulted ceiling and skylights

■ The open floor plan is efficient for Kitchen/Breakfast area and the Dining Room

■ Master Bedroom features a walk-in closet and a private bath with whirlpool tub

■ Two second floor bedrooms with storage access share a full bath

First floor — 1,180 sq. ft.
Second floor — 459 sq. ft.
Bonus room — 385 sq. ft.
Garage & storage — 533 sq. ft.

SECOND FLOOR PLAN

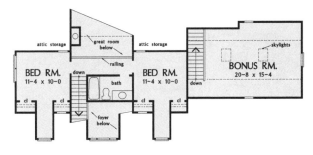

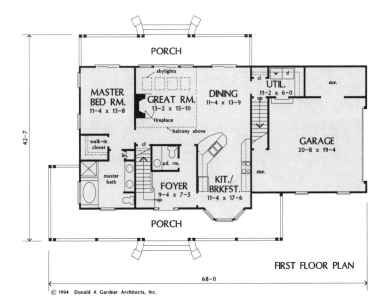

FIRST FLOOR PLAN

© 1994 Donald A Gardner Architects, Inc.

Every Luxurious Feature One Could Want

■ *Total living area 3,276 sq. ft.* ■ *Price Code F* ■

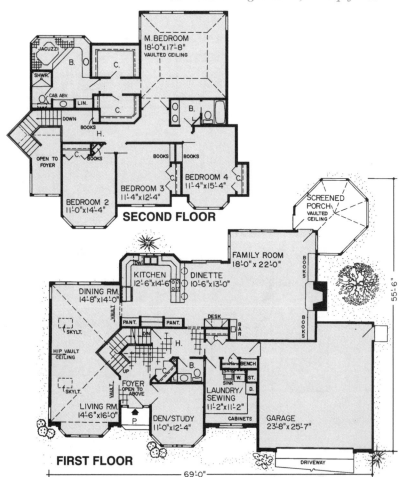

SECOND FLOOR

FIRST FLOOR

No. 10686

■ This plan features:

— Four bedrooms

— Two full and one half baths

■ An open staircase leading to the bedrooms and dividing the space between the vaulted Living and Dining Rooms

■ A wide family area including the Kitchen, Dinette and Family Room complete with built-in bar, bookcases and fireplace

■ A Master Bedroom with a vaulted ceiling, spacious closets and Jacuzzi

First floor — 1,786 sq. ft.
Second floor — 1,490 sq. ft.
Basement — 1,773 sq. ft.
Garage — 579 sq. ft.

Great Room With Columns

© 1995 Donald A Gardner Architects, Inc.

■ *Total living area 1,879 sq. ft.* ■ *Price Code C* ■

No. 99807

■ This plan features:

- Three bedrooms

- Two full baths

■ Great Room crowned with a cathedral ceiling and accented by columns and a fireplace

■ Tray ceilings and arched picture windows accent front bedroom and the Dining Room

■ Secluded Master Suite highlighted by a tray ceiling and contains a bath with skylight, a garden tub and spacious walk-in closet

■ Two additional bedrooms share a full bath

■ An optional crawl space or basement foundation — please specify when ordering

Main floor — 1,879 sq. ft.
Bonus — 360 sq. ft.
Garage — 485 sq. ft.

Floor Plan w/Basement Option

© 1995 Donald A Gardner Architects, Inc.

Floor Plan

© 1995 Donald A Gardner Architects, Inc.

Perfect for Entertaining

© 1997 Donald A. Gardner Architects, Inc.

■ Total living area 2,772 sq. ft. ■ Price Code E ■

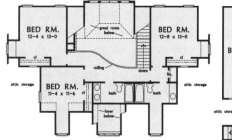

SECOND FLOOR PLAN

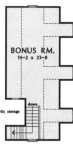

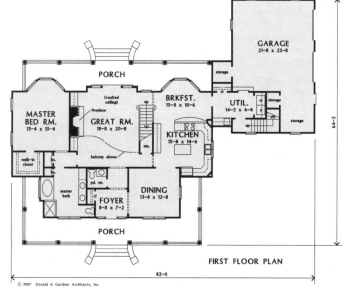

FIRST FLOOR PLAN

No. 96407

■ This plan features:

— Four bedrooms

— Three full and one half baths

■ With front dormers and wrap-around Porch, the home offers formal entertaining and casual living

■ Dramatic Great Room boasts cathedral ceiling and fireplace nestled between built-in shelves

■ French doors expand living space to full length rear Porch

■ Center island and peninsula counter create an efficient Kitchen/Breakfast Area

■ First floor Master Suite features a walk-in closet and spacious master bath

First floor — 1,831 sq. ft.
Second floor — 941 sq. ft.
Bonus room — 539 sq. ft.
Garage & storage — 684 sq. ft.

© 1997 Donald A Gardner Architects, Inc.

Convenient Country

■ *Total living area 1,767 sq. ft.* ■ *Price Code B* ■

No. 99045

■ **This plan features:**

– Three bedrooms

– Two full and one half baths

■ Full front Porch provides comfortable visiting and a sheltered entrance

■ Expansive Living Room with an inviting fireplace opens to bright Dining Room and Kitchen

■ U-shaped Kitchen with peninsula serving counter and nearby Pantry

■ Secluded Master Bedroom with two closets and a double vanity bath

■ Two second floor bedrooms share a full bath

■ No materials list is available for this plan

First floor — 1,108 sq. ft.
Second floor — 659 sq. ft.
Basement — 875 sq. ft.

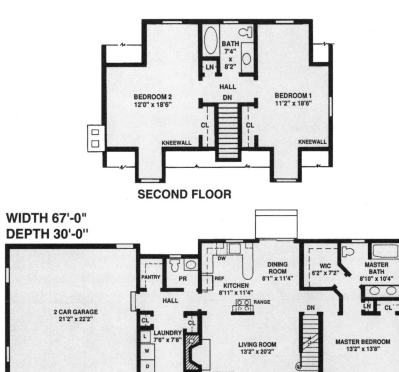

Skylight Brightens Master Bedroom

■ *Total living area 1,686 sq. ft.* ■ *Price Code B* ■

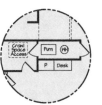

Slab/Crawl Space Option

An
EXCLUSIVE DESIGN
By Karl Kreeger

No. 34029

■ This plan features:

- Three bedrooms
- Two full baths

■ A covered Porch entry

■ A foyer separating the Dining Room from the Breakfast Area and Kitchen

■ A Living Room enhanced by a vaulted beam ceiling and a fireplace

■ A Master Bedroom with a decorative ceiling and a skylight in the private bath

■ An optional Deck accessible through sliding doors off the Master Bedroom

Main floor — 1,686 sq. ft.
Basement — 1,676 sq. ft.
Garage — 484 sq. ft.

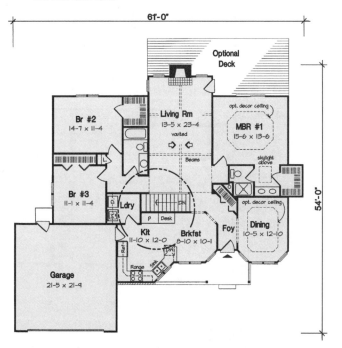

Unique and Desirable

© 1996 Donald A Gardner Architects, Inc.

■ *Total living area 1,977 sq. ft.* ■ • *Price Code C* ■

No. 99803

■ This plan features:

- Three bedrooms

- Two full baths

■ Private Master Bedroom has a walk-in closet and a skylit bath

■ Two additional bedrooms, one with a possible use as a study, share a full bath

■ From the Foyer columns lead into the Great Room with a cathedral ceiling and a fireplace

■ In the rear of the home is a skylit screen Porch and a Deck that features built-in seats and a spa

■ The Kitchen is conveniently located between the Dining Room and the skylit Breakfast Area

■ An optional basement or crawl space foundation — please specify when ordering

Main floor — 1,977 sq. ft.
Bonus room — 430 sq. ft.
Garage & storage — 610 sq. ft.

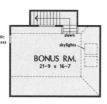

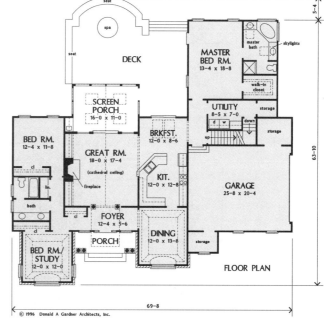

Small But Room To Grow

■ *Total living area 1,607 sq. ft.* ■ *Price Code B* ■

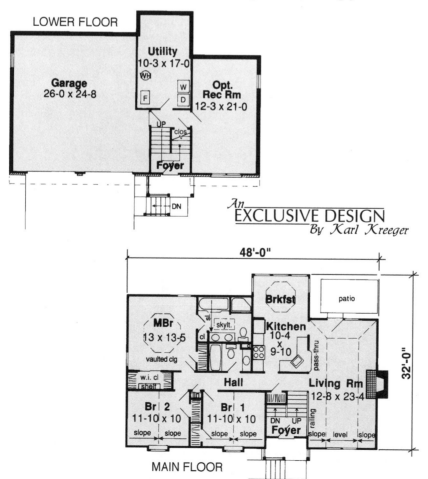

LOWER FLOOR

Utility
10-3 x 17-0

Garage
26-0 x 24-8

Opt.
Rec Rm
12-3 x 21-0

UP   clos

Foyer

DN

An EXCLUSIVE DESIGN *By Karl Kreeger*

48'-0"

MAIN FLOOR

32'-0"

Brkfst   patio

MBr
13 x 13-5
vaulted clg

skylt.

Kitchen
10-4 x 9-10

pass-thru

w.i. cl
shelf

Hall

Living Rm
12-8 x 23-4

Br 2
11-10 x 10
slope   slope

Br 1
11-10 x 10
slope   slope

DN UP

Foyer
slope level slope

No. 20205

■ **This plan features:**

— Three bedrooms

— Two full baths

■ A Master Suite with a vaulted
ceiling and private skylit bath

■ A fireplaced Living Room with a
sloped ceiling

■ Efficient Kitchen with a Breakfast
Nook

■ Options for growth on the lower
level

Main floor — 1,321 sq. ft.
Lower floor — 286 sq. ft.
Garage — 655 sq. ft.

■ *Total living area 2,978 sq. ft.* ■ *Price Code E* ■

No. 94242

■ **This plan features:**

- Three bedrooms

- Two full, one three quarter and one half baths

■ Wonderfully balanced exterior highlighted by triple arched glass in Entry Porch, leading into the Gallery Foyer

■ Triple arches lead into Formal Living and Dining Room, Verandah and beyond

■ Kitchen, Nook, and Leisure Room easily flow together

■ Owners' wing has a Master Suite with glass alcove to rear yard, a lavish bath and a Study offering many uses

■ No materials list is available for this plan

Main floor — 2,978 sq. ft.
Garage — 702 sq. ft.

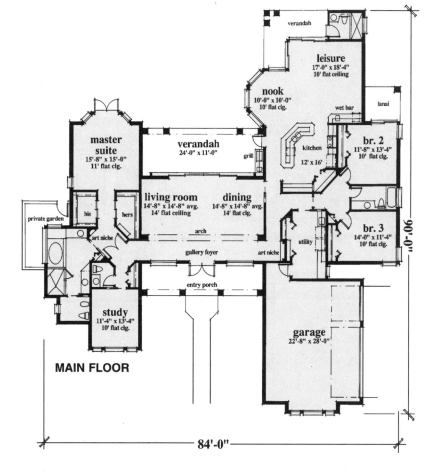

MAIN FLOOR

Exquisite Detail

■ *Total living area 3,262 sq. ft.* ■ *Price Code F* ■

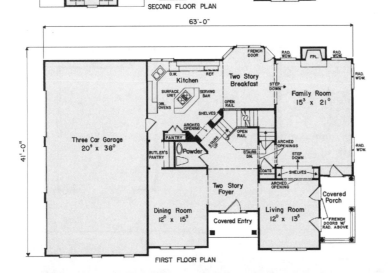

Master Suite 22⁴ x 14⁸

Sitting Room 12⁰ x 10¹⁰

Breakfast Below

Bedroom 4 13⁴ x 12⁰

Vaulted M. Bath

Bath

Laundry

Bath

Bedroom 2 12⁰ x 15³

Foyer Below

Bedroom 3 12⁰ x 13⁹

SECOND FLOOR PLAN

63'-0"

41'-0"

Three Car Garage 20⁹ x 38⁰

Kitchen

Two Story Breakfast

Family Room 15³ x 21⁰

Butler's Pantry

Powder

Dining Room 12⁰ x 15⁰

Two Story Foyer

Living Room 12⁰ x 13⁵

Covered Entry

Covered Porch

FIRST FLOOR PLAN

No. 98400

■ **This plan features:**

— Four bedrooms

— Three full and one half baths

■ Formal Living Room with access to Covered Porch

■ Radius windows and arches, huge fireplace enhance spacious Family Room

■ Kitchen has a pantry, cooktop/serving bar and a two-story Breakfast area

■ Expansive Master Bedroom offers a tray ceiling, a cozy Sitting Room a luxurious bath and huge walk-in closet

■ An optional basement or crawl space foundation — please specify when ordering

First floor — 1,418 sq. ft.
Second floor — 1,844 sq. ft.
Basement — 1,418 sq. ft.
Garage — 820 sq. ft.

■ *Total living area 1,625 sq. ft.* ■ *Price Code B* ■

No. 24701 ☒ ⬛

This plan features:

- Three bedrooms

- Two full baths

■ Central Foyer leads to Den/Guest room with arched window and Living Room accented by two-sided fireplace

■ U-shaped Kitchen with peninsula counter/breakfast bar serves Dining Room

■ Master Suite features walk-in closet and private bath

■ Two additional bedrooms with ample closet space share full bath

Main floor — 1,625 sq. ft.
Basement — 1,625 sq. ft.
Garage — 455 sq. ft.

Main Floor

Alternate Foundation Plan

Welcoming Exterior

© 1995 Donald A. Gardner Architects, Inc.

■ *Total living area 2,832 sq. ft.* ■ *Price Code E* ■

No. 96403 ✕ ℝ

■ This plan features:

— Four bedrooms

— Two full and one half baths

■ Columns between the Foyer and Living Room/Study hint at all the extras in this four bedroom country estate with a warm, welcoming exterior

■ Transom windows over French doors open up the Living Room/Study to the front Porch, while a generous Family Room accesses the covered back Porch

■ Deluxe Master Suite is topped by tray ceiling and includes a bath with a sunny garden tub bay and ample closet space

■ Bonus Room is accessed from the second floor - ready to expand family living space for future needs

First floor — 1,483 sq. ft.
Second floor — 1,349 sq. ft.
Garage — 738 sq. ft.

SECOND FLOOR PLAN

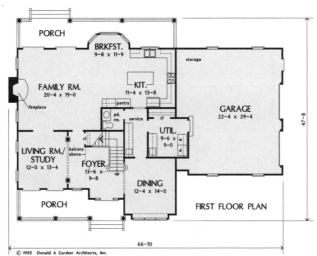

FIRST FLOOR PLAN

© 1995 Donald A Gardner Architects, Inc.

Brick Home of Distinction

■ *Total living area 3,023 sq. ft.* ■ *Price Code E* ■

No. 99109

This plan features:

- Four bedrooms

- Three full and one half baths

■ Past the covered front Porch you step into a two-story Entry way

■ Voluminous two-story Family Room has a fireplace centered along the back wall, and the Nook, while the Kitchen is in close proximity

■ Master Bedroom has a private bath and a big walk-in closet

■ Two additional bedrooms upstairs with ample closet space that share a full bath

■ This plan has a three-car Garage

■ No materials list is available for this plan

First floor — 1,873 sq. ft.
Second floor — 1,150 sq. ft.
Basement — 1,810 sq. ft.

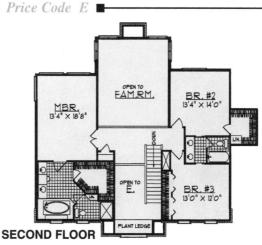

SECOND FLOOR

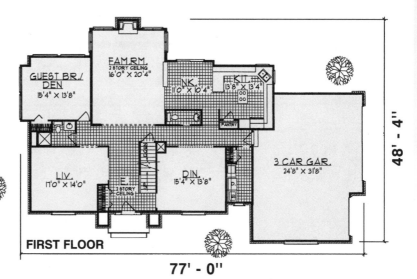

FIRST FLOOR

A Modern Slant On A Country Theme

■ *Total living area 1,648 sq. ft.* ■ *Price Code B* ■

No. 96513

■ **This plan features:**

— Three bedrooms

— Two full and one half baths

■ Country styled front porch highlighting exterior which is enhanced by dormer windows

■ Modern open floor plan for a more spacious feeling

■ Great Room accented by a quaint, corner fireplace and a ceiling fan

■ Dining Room flowing from the Great Room for easy entertaining

■ Kitchen graced by natural light from attractive bay window and a convenient snack bar for meals on the go

■ Master suite secluded in separate wing for total privacy

■ Two additional bedrooms sharing full bath in the hall

Main floor — 1,648 sq. ft.
Garage — 479 sq. ft.

MAIN FLOOR

■ *Total living area 1,203 sq. ft.* ■ *Price Code A* ■

No. 99365 ✗

■ **This plan features:**

- Three bedrooms

- Two full baths and opt. half bath

■ 10-foot high ceilings in the Living Room, Family Room and Dinette area

■ A heat-circulating fireplace in Living Room

■ A master bath with separate stall shower and whirlpool tub

■ A two-car Garage with access through the Mudroom

Main area — 1,203 sq. ft.
Basement — 676 sq. ft.
Garage — 509 sq. ft.

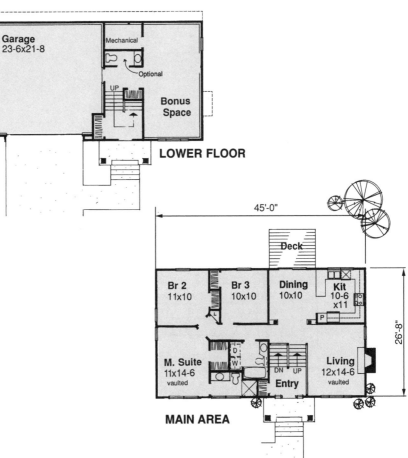

LOWER FLOOR

Garage
23-6x21-8

Mechanical

Optional

UP

Bonus
Space

MAIN AREA

45'-0"

26'-8"

Deck

Br 2
11x10

Br 3
10x10

Dining
10x10

Kit
10-6
x11

M. Suite
11x14-6
vaulted

DN   UP

Entry

Living
12x14-6
vaulted

Distinctive Detailing

© 1995 Donald A. Gardner Architects, Inc.

■ *Total living area 1,972 sq. ft.* ■ *Price Code C* ■

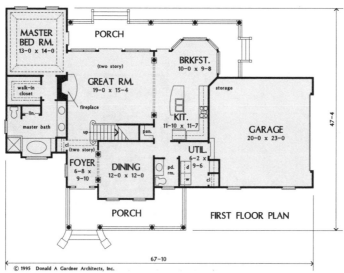

SECOND FLOOR PLAN

FIRST FLOOR PLAN

© 1995 Donald A Gardner Architects, Inc.

No. 99829 ⚒ ⓡ ®

■ This plan features:

— Three bedrooms

— Two full and one half baths

■ Interior columns distinguishing the inviting two-story Foyer from the Dining Room

■ Spacious Great Room set off by two-story windows and opening to the Kitchen and Breakfast Bay

■ Nine foot ceilings adding volume and drama to the first floor

■ Secluded Master Suite topped by a space amplifying tray ceiling and enhanced by a plush bath

■ Two generous additional bedrooms with ample closet and storage space

■ Skylit Bonus Room enjoying second floor access

First floor — 1,436 sq. ft.
Second floor — 536 sq. ft.
Bonus room — 296 sq. ft.
Garage & storage — 520 sq. ft.

Today's Family Living Made Easy

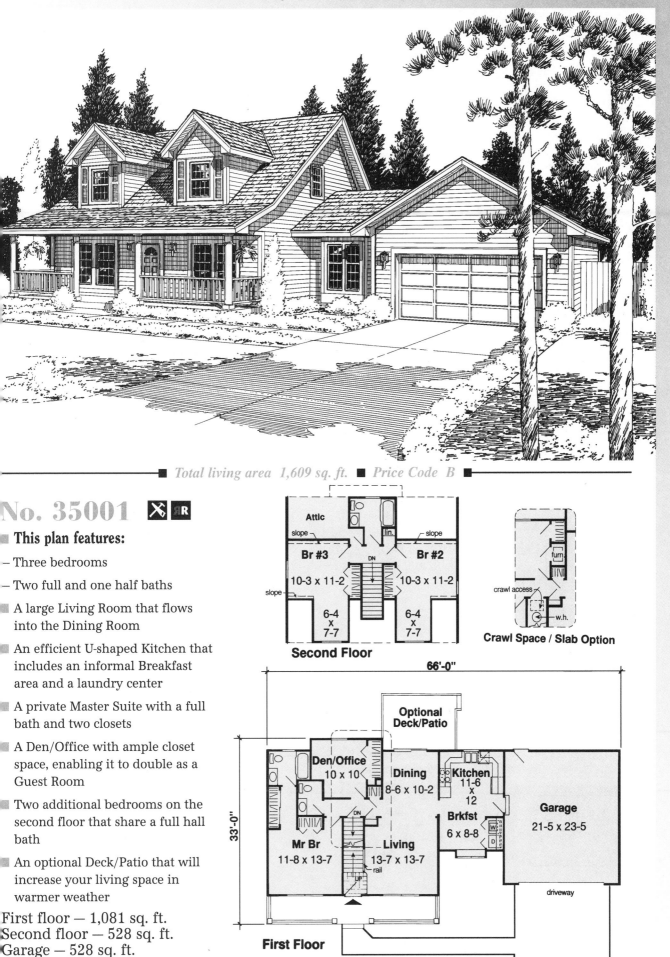

■ *Total living area 1,609 sq. ft.* ■ *Price Code B* ■

No. 35001

■ This plan features:

- Three bedrooms

- Two full and one half baths

■ A large Living Room that flows into the Dining Room

■ An efficient U-shaped Kitchen that includes an informal Breakfast area and a laundry center

■ A private Master Suite with a full bath and two closets

■ A Den/Office with ample closet space, enabling it to double as a Guest Room

■ Two additional bedrooms on the second floor that share a full hall bath

■ An optional Deck/Patio that will increase your living space in warmer weather

First floor — 1,081 sq. ft.
Second floor — 528 sq. ft.
Garage — 528 sq. ft.

Second Floor

Attic
slope   lin.   slope
Br #3   Br #2
10-3 x 11-2   DN   10-3 x 11-2
slope
6-4   6-4
x   x
7-7   7-7

Crawl Space / Slab Option

furn.
crawl access
w.h.

First Floor

66'-0"

Optional
Deck/Patio

Den/Office
10 x 10   Dining   Kitchen
8-6 x 10-2   11-6
x
12
33'-0"   Brkfst
DN   6 x 8-8
Mr Br   Garage
11-8 x 13-7   Living   21-5 x 23-5
13-7 x 13-7
UP   rail

driveway

Classic Country Farmhouse

© 1992 Donald A Gardner Architects, Inc.

■ *Total living area 1,663 sq. ft.* ■ *Price Code C* ■

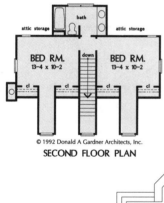

© 1992 Donald A Gardner Architects, Inc.
SECOND FLOOR PLAN

First floor — 1,145 sq. ft.
Second floor — 518 sq. ft.
Bonus room — 380 sq. ft.
Garage & storage — 509 sq. ft.

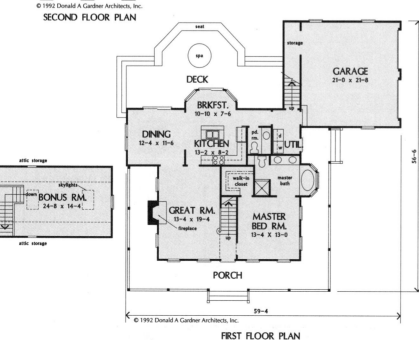

© 1992 Donald A Gardner Architects, Inc.

FIRST FLOOR PLAN

No. 99800 ✕

■ This plan features:

– Three bedrooms

– Two full and one half baths

■ Covered Porch gives classic country farmhouse look, and includes multiple dormers, a great layout for entertaining, and a Bonus Room

■ Clerestory dormer window bathes the two-story Foyer in natural light

■ Large Great Room with fireplace opens to the Dining/Breakfast/Kitchen space, which leads to a spacious Deck with optional spa and seating for easy indoor/outdoor entertaining

■ First floor Master Suite offers privacy and luxury with a separate shower, whirlpool tub and a double vanity

■ *Total living area 4,759 sq. ft.* ■ *Price Code F* ■

No. 94230

■ **This plan features:**

— Four bedrooms

— Two full, one three-quarter and one half baths

■ Triple arches at entry lead into Grand Foyer and Gallery with arched entries to all areas

■ Triple French doors catch the breeze and access to rear grounds in Living and Leisure rooms

■ Spacious Kitchen with large walk-in Pantry, cooktop/work island and angled serving counter/snack bar, glass Nook, Utility Room and Garage entry

■ Master Suite wing offers Veranda access, two closets and vanities, and a garden window tub

■ Three second floor bedrooms with walk-in closets, balcony and full bath access

■ No materials list is available for this plan

First floor — 3,546 sq. ft.
Second floor — 1,213 sq. ft.
Garage — 822 sq. ft.

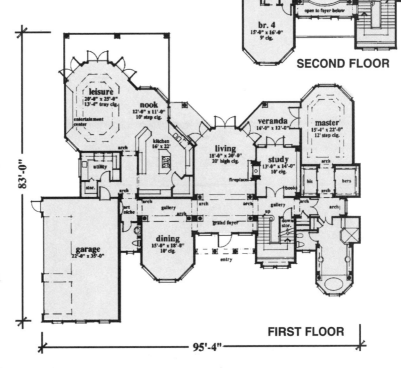

SECOND FLOOR

FIRST FLOOR

Designed for Entertaining

© The Sater Group, Inc.

■ *Total living area 2,875 sq. ft.* ■ *Price Code E* ■

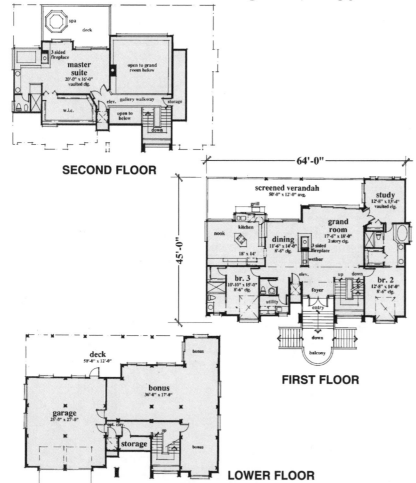

SECOND FLOOR

FIRST FLOOR

LOWER FLOOR

No. 94247

■ This plan features:

— Three bedrooms

— Three full and one half baths

■ Grand Room and Dining area separated by 3-sided fireplace and wetbar both access Screened Verandah

■ Spacious Kitchen with a cooktop island, eating Nook and access to Verandah and Dining Room

■ Secluded Master Suite enhanced by a private Spa Deck, huge walk-in closet and whirlpool tub

■ Study and two additional bedrooms have private access to full baths

■ No materials list is available for this plan

First floor — 2,066 sq. ft.
Second floor — 809 sq. ft.
Bonus — 1,260 sq. ft.
Garage — 798 sq. ft.

■ Total living area 2,563 sq. ft. ■ Price Code E ■

No. 99843

■ This plan features:

— Four bedrooms

— Two full and one half baths

■ Bay windows and a long, skylit, screened Porch make this four bedroom country home a haven for outdoor enthusiasts

■ Foyer is open to take advantage of the light from the central dormer with palladian window

■ Vaulted ceiling in the Great Room adds vertical drama to the room

■ Contemporary Kitchen is open to the Great Room creating a feeling of additional space

■ Master Bedroom is privately tucked away with a large luxurious bath complete with a bay window, corner shower and a garden tub

First floor — 1,907 sq. ft.
Second floor — 656 sq. ft.
Bonus room — 467 sq. ft.
Garage & storage — 580 sq. ft.

BONUS RM.
16-10 X 25-4

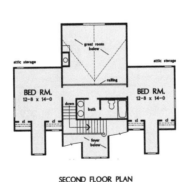

SECOND FLOOR PLAN

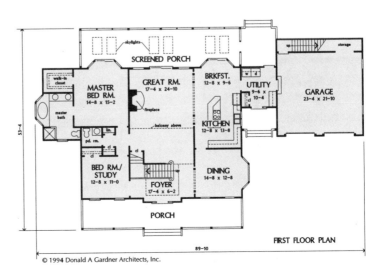

FIRST FLOOR PLAN

411

Second Floor Balcony Overlooks Great Room

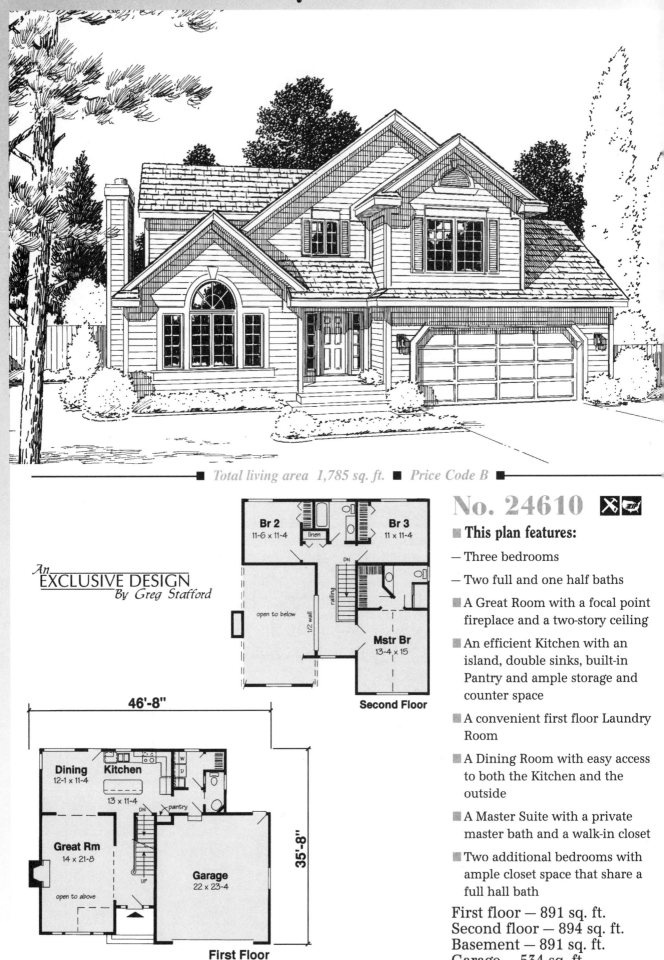

■ *Total living area 1,785 sq. ft.* ■ *Price Code B* ■

An EXCLUSIVE DESIGN *By Greg Stafford*

Br 2 11-6 x 11-4
linen
Br 3 11 x 11-4
open to below
1/2 wall
railing
DN
Mstr Br 13-4 x 15

Second Floor

46'-8"

35'-8"

Dining 12-1 x 11-4
Kitchen 13 x 11-4
W
D
DN
pantry
Great Rm 14 x 21-8
UP
Garage 22 x 23-4
open to above

First Floor

No. 24610

■ **This plan features:**

— Three bedrooms

— Two full and one half baths

■ A Great Room with a focal point fireplace and a two-story ceiling

■ An efficient Kitchen with an island, double sinks, built-in Pantry and ample storage and counter space

■ A convenient first floor Laundry Room

■ A Dining Room with easy access to both the Kitchen and the outside

■ A Master Suite with a private master bath and a walk-in closet

■ Two additional bedrooms with ample closet space that share a full hall bath

First floor — 891 sq. ft.
Second floor — 894 sq. ft.
Basement — 891 sq. ft.
Garage — 534 sq. ft.

Traditional Beauty

© 1993 Donald A Gardner Architects, Inc.

■ *Total living area 1,576 sq. ft.* ■ *Price Code C* ■

No. 99802

■ **This plan features:**

– Three bedrooms

– Two full baths

■ Traditional beauty with large arched windows, round columns, covered Porch, brick veneer, and an open floor plan

■ Clerestory dormers above covered Porch lighting the Foyer

■ Cathedral ceiling enhancing the Great Room along with a cozy fireplace

■ Island Kitchen with Breakfast area accessing the large Deck with an optional spa

■ Tray ceiling over the Master Bedroom, Dining Room and Bedroom/Study

■ Dual vanity, separate shower, and whirlpool tub in the master bath

Main floor — 1,576 sq. ft.
Garage — 465 sq. ft.

FLOOR PLAN

© 1993 Donald A Gardner Architects, Inc.

Backyard Views

■ *Total living area 1,746 sq. ft.* ■ *Price Code B* ■

WIDTH: 65' - 10"
DEPTH: 56' - 0"

MAIN FLOOR

No. 92655

■ **This plan features:**

— Three bedrooms

— Two full baths

■ Front Porch accesses open Foyer, and spacious Dining Room and Great Room with sloped ceilings

■ Corner fireplace, windows and atrium door to Patio enhance Great Room

■ Convenient Kitchen with a pantry, peninsula serving counter for bright Breakfast area and nearby Laundry/Garage entry

■ Luxurious bath, walk-in closet and back yard view offered in Master Bedroom

■ No materials list is available for this plan

Main floor — 1,746 sq. ft.
Garage — 480 sq. ft.
Basement — 1,697 sq. ft.

Simply Cozy

■ Total living area 1,325 sq. ft. ■ • Price Code A ■

No. 98912 ⚒

This plan features:

- Three bedrooms

- Two full baths

■ Quaint front porch sheltering Entry into the Living Area showcased by a massive fireplace and built-ins below a vaulted ceiling

■ Formal Dining Room accented by a bay of glass with Sun Deck access

■ Efficient, galley Kitchen with Breakfast area, laundry facilities and outdoor access

■ Secluded Master Bedroom offers a roomy walk-in closet and plush bath with two vanities and a garden window tub

■ Two additional bedrooms with ample closets, share a full skylit bath

Main floor — 1,325 sq. ft.

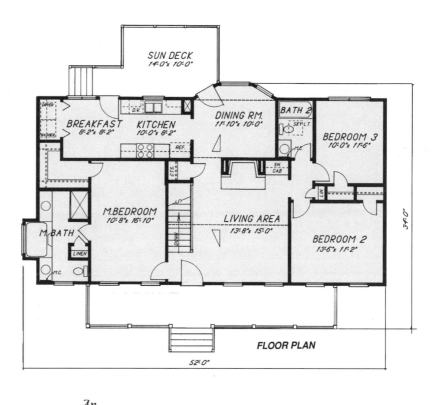

FLOOR PLAN

An
EXCLUSIVE DESIGN
By Jannis Vann & Associates, Inc.

Luxurious Yet Cozy

■ *Total living area 3,395 sq. ft.* ■ *Price Code F* ■

SECOND FLOOR

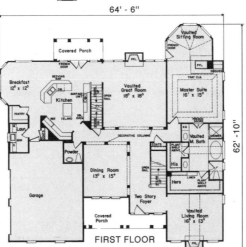

FIRST FLOOR

No. 98403

■ This plan features:

— Four bedrooms

— Three full and one half baths

■ Living Room is enhanced by a fieldstone fireplace and vaulted ceiling

■ Inviting fireplace between windows, and a vaulted ceiling enhance Great Room

■ Kitchen with a work island, serving bar, bright Breakfast area and walk-in pantry

■ Corner Master Suite includes a cozy fireplace, a vaulted Sitting Room and a lavish dressing area

■ Optional basement, crawl space o slab foundation — please specify when ordering

First floor — 2,467 sq. ft.
Second floor — 928 sq. ft.
Bonus — 296 sq. ft.
Basement — 2,467 sq. ft.
Garage — 566 sq. ft.

A-Frame for Year-Round Living

■ *Total living area 1,702 sq. ft.* ■ *Price Code B* ■

No. 90930 ✕

This plan features:

- Three bedrooms

- One full and one three-quarter baths

■ A vaulted ceiling in the Living Room with a massive fireplace

■ A wrap-around sun deck that gives you a lot of outdoor living space

■ A luxurious Master Suite complete with a walk-in closet, full bath and private deck

■ Two additional bedrooms that share a full hall bath

Main floor — 1,238 sq. ft.
Loft — 464 sq. ft.
Basement — 1,175 sq. ft.
Width — 34'-0"
Depth — 56'-0"

An EXCLUSIVE DESIGN
By Westhome Planners, Ltd.

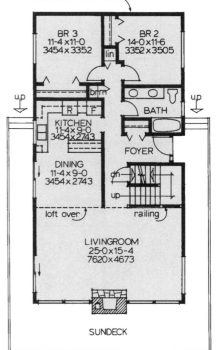

LOFT PLAN

DECK
MASTER SUITE
14-0 x 11-6
4267 x 3505
attic
attic
Bath
Dressing
Walk-in Closet
dn
LOFT
railing
Livingroom below

MAIN FLOOR

Full Basement under
BR 3
11-4 x 11-0
3454 x 3352
BR 2
14-0 x 11-6
3352 x 3505
lin
up
up
brm
BATH
KITCHEN
11-4 x 9-0
3454 x 2743
R F
FOYER
DINING
11-4 x 9-0
3454 x 2743
dn
up
loft over
railing
LIVINGROOM
25-0 x 15-4
7620 x 4673
SUNDECK

Easy Living

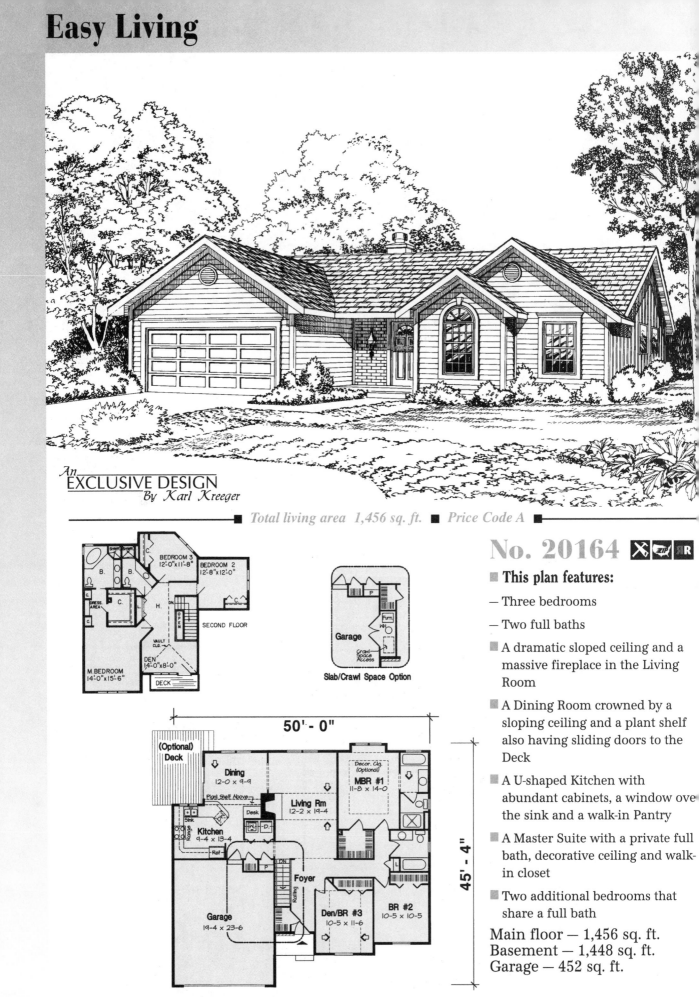

An EXCLUSIVE DESIGN
By Karl Kreeger

■ *Total living area 1,456 sq. ft.* ■ *Price Code A* ■

BEDROOM 3
12'-0"x11'-8"

BEDROOM 2
12'-8"x12'-0"

SECOND FLOOR

DRESS.
AREA

DEN
14'-0"x8'-0"

VAULT
CLG.

M. BEDROOM
14'-0"x15'-6"

DECK

Garage

Furn.

Crawl
Space
Access

Slab/Crawl Space Option

No. 20164

■ **This plan features:**

— Three bedrooms

— Two full baths

■ A dramatic sloped ceiling and a massive fireplace in the Living Room

■ A Dining Room crowned by a sloping ceiling and a plant shelf also having sliding doors to the Deck

■ A U-shaped Kitchen with abundant cabinets, a window over the sink and a walk-in Pantry

■ A Master Suite with a private full bath, decorative ceiling and walk-in closet

■ Two additional bedrooms that share a full bath

Main floor — 1,456 sq. ft.
Basement — 1,448 sq. ft.
Garage — 452 sq. ft.

50'- 0"

(Optional)
Deck

Dining
12-0 x 9-9

Decor. Clg.
(Optional)

MBR #1
11-8 x 14-0

Plant Shelf Above

Living Rm
12-2 x 19-4

Desk

Kitchen
9-4 x 13-4

Sink
Range

Ref

Foyer

45'- 4"

Garage
19-4 x 23-6

Den/BR #3
10-5 x 11-6

BR #2
10-5 x 10-5

First Floor Plan

© 1990 Donald A. Gardner Architects, Inc.

B. NATHAN

■ Total living area 2,692 sq. ft. ■ Price Code E ■

No. 99853

■ This plan features:

- Four bedrooms

- Three full and one half baths

■ Impressive double gable roof with front and rear palladian windows and wrap-around Porch

■ Vaulted ceilings in two-story Foyer and Great Room accommodates Loft/Study area

■ Spacious, first floor Master bedroom offers walk-in closet and luxurious bath

■ Living space extended outdoors by wrap-around Porch and large Deck

■ Upstairs, one of three bedrooms could be a second master suite

First floor — 1,734 sq. ft.
Second floor — 958 sq. ft.

SECOND FLOOR PLAN

FIRST FLOOR PLAN

© 1990 Donald A Gardner Architects, Inc.

Unique Turret Master Bedroom

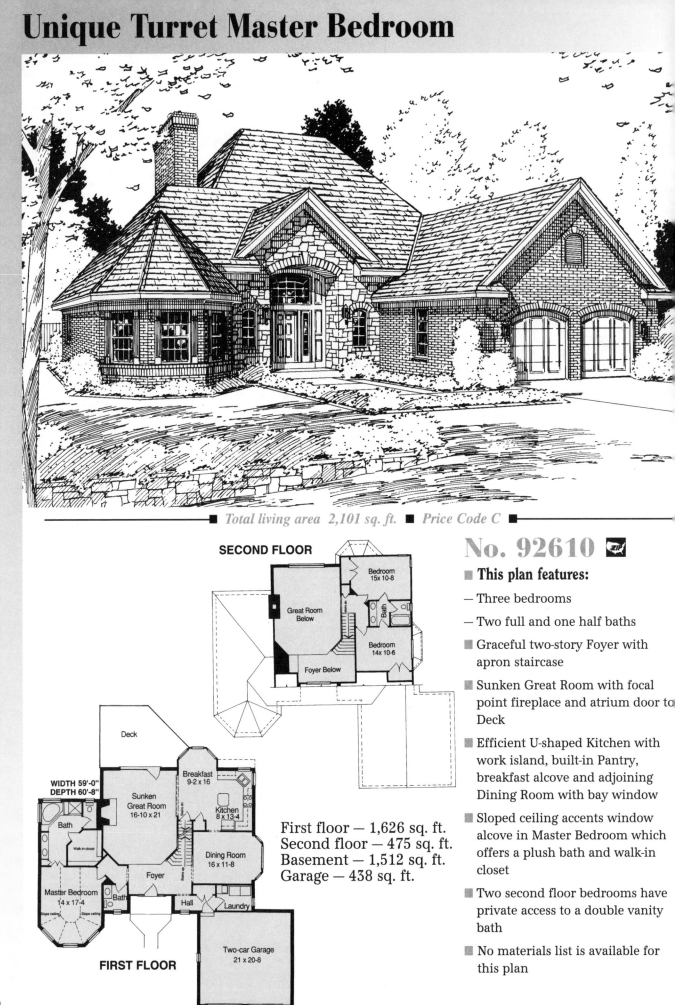

■ *Total living area 2,101 sq. ft.* ■ *Price Code C* ■

SECOND FLOOR

Great Room Below

Bedroom 15x 10-8

Bath

Bedroom 14x 10-6

Foyer Below

Deck

WIDTH 59'-0"
DEPTH 60'-8"

Sunken Great Room 16-10 x 21

Breakfast 9-2 x 16

Kitchen 8 x 13-4

Bath

Walk-in closet

Dining Room 16 x 11-8

Foyer

Master Bedroom 14 x 17-4

Slope ceiling   Slope ceiling

Bath

Hall

Laundry

Two-car Garage 21 x 20-8

FIRST FLOOR

First floor — 1,626 sq. ft.
Second floor — 475 sq. ft.
Basement — 1,512 sq. ft.
Garage — 438 sq. ft.

No. 92610

■ This plan features:

— Three bedrooms

— Two full and one half baths

■ Graceful two-story Foyer with apron staircase

■ Sunken Great Room with focal point fireplace and atrium door to Deck

■ Efficient U-shaped Kitchen with work island, built-in Pantry, breakfast alcove and adjoining Dining Room with bay window

■ Sloped ceiling accents window alcove in Master Bedroom which offers a plush bath and walk-in closet

■ Two second floor bedrooms have private access to a double vanity bath

■ No materials list is available for this plan

© 1995 Donald A Gardner Architects, Inc.

Total living area 1,417 sq. ft. ■ *Price Code B* ■

No. 99809 ✗ ⤴

■ **This plan features:**

— Three bedrooms

— Two full baths

■ Cathedral ceiling expanding the Great Room, Dining Room and Kitchen

■ A versatile bedroom or Study topped by a cathedral ceiling accented by double arched windows

■ Master Suite complete with a cathedral ceiling, including a bath with a garden tub, linen closet and a walk-in closet

Main floor — 1,417 sq. ft.
Garage — 441 sq. ft.

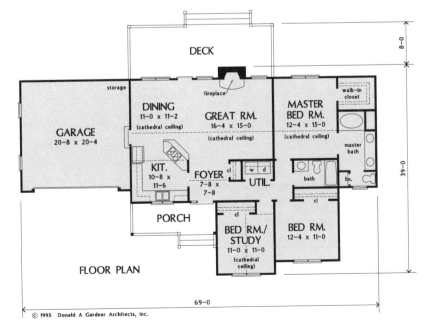

FLOOR PLAN

© 1995 Donald A Gardner Architects, Inc.

Delightful Home

■ *Total living area 1,853 sq. ft.* ■ *Price Code C* ■

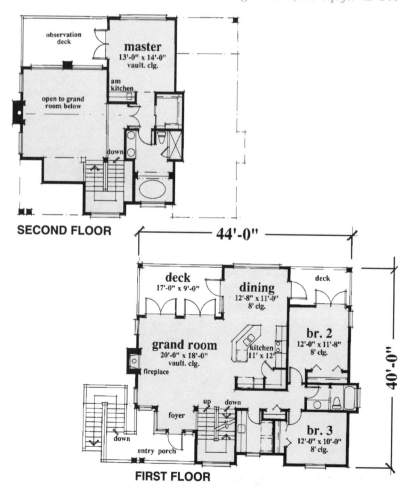

observation deck

master
13'-0" x 14'-0"
vault. clg.

am kitchen

open to grand room below

down

SECOND FLOOR

◄── 44'-0" ──►

deck
17'-0" x 9'-0"

dining
12'-8" x 11'-0"
8' clg.

deck

grand room
20'-0" x 18'-0"
vault. clg.

kitchen
11' x 12'

br. 2
12'-0" x 11'-8"
8' clg.

fireplace

40'-0"

up **down**

foyer

br. 3
12'-0" x 10'-0"
8' clg.

down

entry porch

FIRST FLOOR

No. 94248

■ This plan features:

— Three bedrooms

— Two full baths

■ Grand Room with a fireplace, vaulted ceiling and double French doors to the rear deck

■ Kitchen and Dining Room open to continue the overall feel of spaciousness

■ Kitchen has a large walk-in pantry, island with a sink and dishwasher creating a perfect triangular workspace

■ Dining Room with doors to both decks, has expanses of glass looking out to the rear yard

■ Master Bedroom features a double door entry, private bath and a morning kitchen

■ No materials list is available for this plan

First floor — 1,342 sq. ft.
Second floor — 511 sq. ft.
Garage — 1,740 sq. ft.

■ *Total living area 1,354 sq. ft.* ■ *Price Code A* ■

No. 91026

This plan features:

– Two bedrooms

– One full and one three-quarter baths

■ Sweeping panels of glass and a wood stove, creating atmosphere for the Great Room

■ An open plan that draws the Kitchen into the warmth of the Great Room's wood stove

■ A sleeping Loft that has a full bath all to itself

Main floor — 988 sq. ft.
Upper floor — 366 sq. ft.
Basement — 742 sq. ft.
Garage — 283 sq. ft.

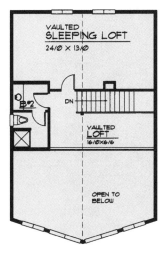

UPPER FLOOR PLAN

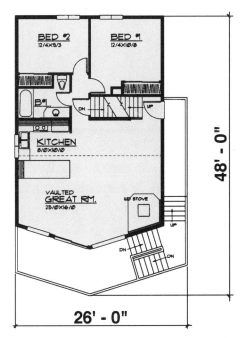

MAIN FLOOR PLAN

Spectacular Stucco and Stone

■ *Total living area 4,106 sq. ft.* ■ *Price Code F* ■

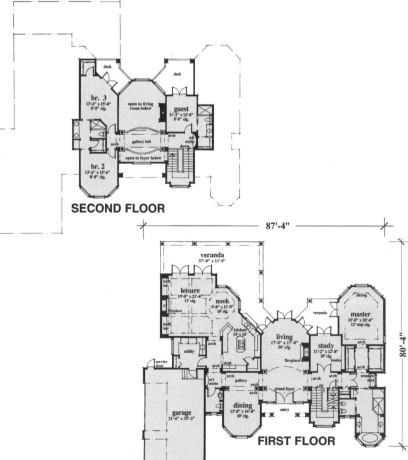

SECOND FLOOR

FIRST FLOOR

No. 94239

■ **This plan features:**

— Four bedrooms

— One full, two three-quarter and one half baths

■ Arches and columns accent Entry, Grand Foyer, Gallery, Living and Dining rooms

■ Open Living Room with fireplace and multiple glass doors

■ Formal Dining Room with bay windows conveniently located

■ Angled Kitchen with walk-in pantry and peninsula counter

■ Master wing offers a step ceiling, two walk-in closets and a lavish bath

■ No materials list is available for this plan

First floor — 3,027 sq. ft.
Second floor — 1,079 sq. ft.
Basement — 3,027 sq. ft.
Garage — 802 sq. ft.

Traditional Ranch

■ Total living area 1,568 sq. ft. ■ Price Code B ■

No. 20220

■ This plan features:

— Three bedrooms

— Two full baths

■ A large front palladian window provides great curb appeal, and allows a view of the front yard from the Living Room

■ A vaulted ceiling in the Living Room, adding to the architectural interest and the spacious feel of the room

■ Sliding glass doors in the Dining Room that lead to a wood Deck

■ A built-in Pantry, double sink and breakfast bar in the efficient Kitchen

■ A Master Suite that includes a walk-in closet and a private bath with a double vanity

Main floor — 1,568 sq. ft.
Basement — 1,568 sq. ft.
Garage — 509 sq. ft.

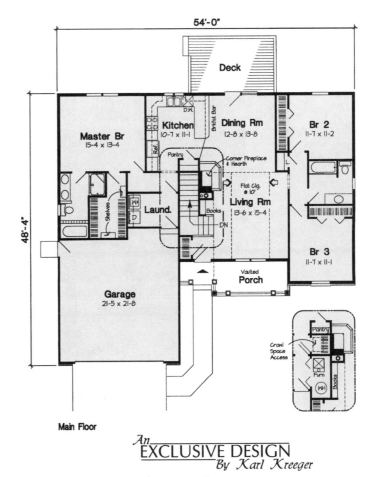

Main Floor

An
EXCLUSIVE DESIGN
By Karl Kreeger

Lots of Extras

■ *Total living area 3,511 sq. ft.* ■ *Price Code E* ■

SECOND FLOOR

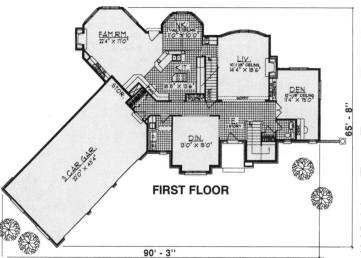

FIRST FLOOR

90' - 3"

65' - 8"

No. 99118

■ **This plan features:**

— Four bedrooms

— Three full and one half baths

■ Master Bedroom has French doors with niches on either side

■ Bedrooms 2 and 3 share a full bath, while bedroom 4 has a bath of its own and a cathedral ceiling

■ Bonus Room over the three-car garage

■ Kitchen has ample counter space, a pantry and a center island

■ The Den with built-in desk and cabinets is the perfect place to make a great home Office

■ No materials list is available for this plan

■ This plan is not to be built within a 75 mile radius of Cedar Rapids, IA

First floor — 1,931 sq. ft.
Second floor — 1,580 sq. ft.
Bonus — 439 sq. ft.
Basement — 1,931 sq. ft.

One-Level with a Twist

■ Total living area 1,575 sq. ft. ■ Price Code B ■

No. 20083

An
EXCLUSIVE DESIGN
By Karl Kreeger

■ This plan features:

– Three bedrooms

– Two full baths

■ Wide-open active areas that are centrally-located

■ A spacious Dining, Living, and Kitchen area

■ A Master Suite at the rear of the house with a full bath

■ Two additional bedrooms that share a full hall bath and the quiet atmosphere that results from an intelligent design

Main floor — 1,575 sq. ft.
Basement — 1,575 sq. ft.
Garage — 475 sq. ft.

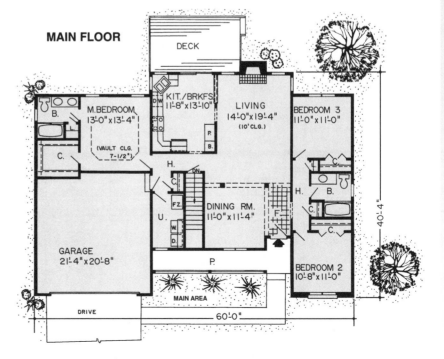

MAIN FLOOR

DECK

M.BEDROOM 13'-0"x13'-4"
(VAULT CLG. 7-1/2')

KIT./BRKFS 11'-8"x13'-10"

LIVING 14'-0"x19'-4" (10' CLG.)

BEDROOM 3 11'-0"x11'-0"

DINING RM. 11'-0"x11'-4"

GARAGE 21'-4"x20'-8"

BEDROOM 2 10'-8"x11'-0"

MAIN AREA

DRIVE

60'-0"

40'-4"

Casual Country Charmer

© 1997 Donald A. Gardner Architects, Inc.

B.NATHAN.

■ *Total living area 1,770 sq. ft.* ■ *Price Code C* ■

BONUS RM.
13-6 x 24-0

attic storage

down

PORCH

UTIL.
7-0 x 10-0

KIT.
13-0 x 12-0

DINING
11-4 x 12-0

(dormers above)

PORCH

walk-in closet

walk-in closet

master bath

lin.

pan.

storage

up

fireplace

(cathedral ceiling)

GREAT RM.
17-8 x 20-4

MASTER BED RM.
13-0 x 14-8

shelves

cl

lin.

bath

cl

FOYER
8-0 x 9-3

BED RM.
11-4 x 11-8

GARAGE
22-0 x 24-0

PORCH

BED RM.
11-0 x 11-0

57-4

FLOOR PLAN

54-0

© 1997 Donald A Gardner Architects, Inc.

No. 96493

■ **This plan features:**

— Three bedrooms

— Two full baths

■ Columns and arches frame the front Porch

■ The open floor plan combines the Great Room, Kitchen and Dining Room

■ The Kitchen offers a convenient breakfast bar for meals on the run

■ The Master Suite features a private bath oasis

■ Secondary bedrooms share a full bath with a dual vanity

Main floor — 1,770 sq. ft.
Bonus — 401 sq. ft.
Garage — 630 sq. ft.

Surrounded with Sunshine

■ *Total living area 1,731 sq. ft.* ■ *Price Code B* ■

No. 90986

■ This plan features:

– Three bedrooms

– Two full and one half baths

■ An Italianate style, featuring columns and tile originally designed to sit on the edge of a golf course

■ An open design with pananoramic vistas in every direction

■ A whirlpool tub in the elaborate and spacious Master Bedroom suite

■ A Great Room with a corner gas fireplace

■ A turreted Breakfast Nook and an efficient Kitchen with peninsula counter

■ Two family bedrooms that share a full hall bath

■ An optional basement or crawl space foundation — please specify when ordering

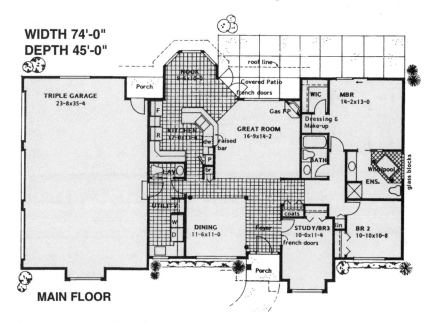

WIDTH 74'-0"
DEPTH 45'-0"

An
EXCLUSIVE DESIGN
By Westhome Planners, Ltd.

MAIN FLOOR

Main floor — 1,731 sq. ft.
Garage — 888 sq. ft.
Basement — 1,715 sq. ft.

Regal Residence

■ *Total living area 3,039 sq. ft.* ■ *Price Code F* ■

SECOND FLOOR

FIRST FLOOR

55' - 0"

57' - 4"

No. 98405

■ **This plan features:**

— Five bedrooms

— Four full baths

■ Keystone, arched windows accent entrance into two-story Foyer

■ Spacious two-story Family Room enhanced by a fireplace

■ Kitchen with a cooktop island/ serving bar and a walk-in pantry

■ First floor Guest Room/Study with roomy closet and adjoining full bath

■ Luxurious Master Suite offers a tray ceiling, Sitting Area, a huge walk-in closet and a vaulted bath

■ Optional basement or crawl space foundation — please specify when ordering

First floor — 1,488 sq. ft.
Second floor — 1,551 sq. ft.
Basement — 1,488 sq. ft.
Garage — 667 sq. ft.

Dressed to Impress

© 1997 Donald A Gardner Architects, Inc.

■ *Total living area 2,121 sq. ft.* ■ *Price Code D* ■

No. 99824 ✗

■ This plan features:

- Three bedrooms

- Two full and one half baths

■ A stone and stucco exterior plus a dramatic entry with square columns provide impressive curb appeal

■ The Great Room has a cathedral ceiling and adjoins the Breakfast Area

■ The Kitchen is enhanced by an angled counter with stove top, a Pantry and easy access to the formal Dining Room

■ A separate Utility Room with built-in cabinets and a counter top with laundry sink add efficiency

■ Double doors lead into the Master Suite with a box bay window, two walk-in closets and a lavish bath

■ Located upstairs are two more bedrooms a full bath, linen closet and skylit Bonus Room

First floor — 1,572 sq. ft.
Second floor — 549 sq. ft.
Bonus room — 384 sq. ft.
Garage & storage — 540 sq. ft.

SECOND FLOOR PLAN

FIRST FLOOR PLAN

© 1997 Donald A Gardner Architects, Inc.

431

Ranch Provides Great Kitchen Area

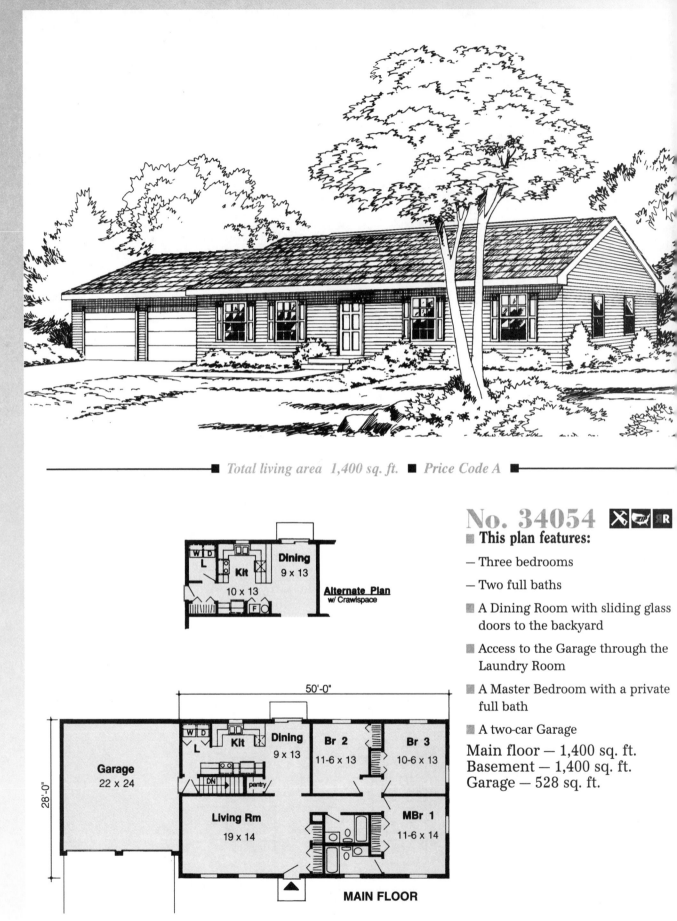

■ *Total living area 1,400 sq. ft.* ■ *Price Code A* ■

Alternate Plan
w/ Crawlspace

W D
L
Kit
10 x 13
Dining
9 x 13
F

No. 34054
■ This plan features:

— Three bedrooms

— Two full baths

■ A Dining Room with sliding glass doors to the backyard

■ Access to the Garage through the Laundry Room

■ A Master Bedroom with a private full bath

■ A two-car Garage

Main floor — 1,400 sq. ft.
Basement — 1,400 sq. ft.
Garage — 528 sq. ft.

50'-0"

28'-0"

Garage
22 x 24

W D
L
Kit
Dining
9 x 13
Br 2
11-6 x 13
Br 3
10-6 x 13

DN
pantry

Living Rm
19 x 14

MBr 1
11-6 x 14

MAIN FLOOR

Tradition Combined with Contemporary

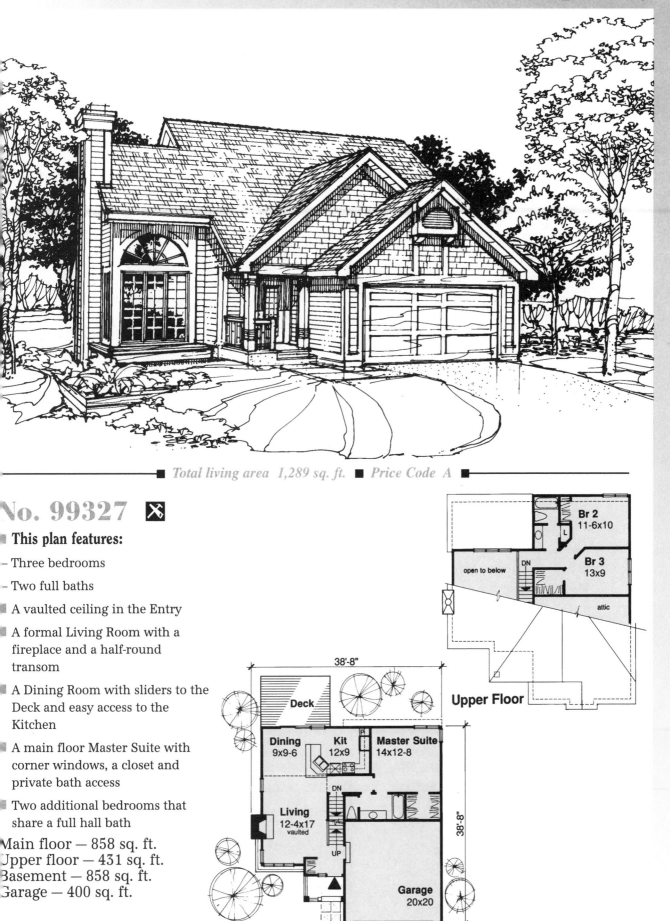

■ *Total living area 1,289 sq. ft.* ■ *Price Code A* ■

No. 99327 ✗

▪ This plan features:

– Three bedrooms

– Two full baths

▪ A vaulted ceiling in the Entry

▪ A formal Living Room with a fireplace and a half-round transom

▪ A Dining Room with sliders to the Deck and easy access to the Kitchen

▪ A main floor Master Suite with corner windows, a closet and private bath access

▪ Two additional bedrooms that share a full hall bath

Main floor — 858 sq. ft.
Upper floor — 431 sq. ft.
Basement — 858 sq. ft.
Garage — 400 sq. ft.

Upper Floor

Br 2
11-6x10

Br 3
13x9

open to below

DN

attic

Main Floor

38'-8"

Deck

Dining
9x9-6

Kit
12x9

Master Suite
14x12-8

DN

Living
12-4x17
vaulted

UP

38'-8"

Garage
20x20

Attractive Hip and Valley Style Roof

■ Total living area 2,411 sq. ft. ■ Price Code D ■

PATIO

LNDRY

KITCHEN
11'-10"x12'-8"

NOOK

OVEN REF. PAN

ALTERNATE KITCHEN

BEDROOM
11'-0"x12'-4"

MASTER
BEDROOM
VAULTED CEILING
16'-4"x15'-0"

OPEN TO
BELOW

DN

BATH

MASTER
BATH

WALK
IN
CLOSET
SHELVES

LINEN

LIN

BEDROOM
11'-0"x13'-0"

BEDROOM
11'-0"x11'-0"

WALK IN
CLOSET

SECOND FLOOR

PATIO

NOOK
11'-0"x13'-0"

DW

LNDRY

KITCHEN
11'-10"x12'-8"

OVEN REF. PAN

OPTIONAL
WORKBENCH

BUTLER
PANTRY

DESK

DN

POWDER
ROOM

UP

FAMILY ROOM
12'-0" CEILING
19'-0"x15'-2"

FIREPLACE

OPTIONAL
DOOR

GARAGE

DINING
ROOM
11'-8"x13'-0"

FOYER

LIVING
ROOM
12'-0" CEILING
11'-10"x13'-8"

43'-0"

PORCH

FIRST FLOOR

52'-0"

OPTIONAL
RETREAT
11'-0"x12'-4"

MASTER
BEDROOM

CABINETS

DN

OPTIONAL RETREAT

No. 24262

■ This plan features:

— Four bedrooms

— Two full and one half baths

■ A see-through fireplace between the Living Room and the Family Room

■ A gourmet Kitchen with an island built-in Pantry and double sink

■ A Master Bedroom with a vaulted ceiling

■ A master bath with large double vanity, linen closet, corner tub, separate shower, compartmented toilet and huge walk-in closet

■ Three additional bedrooms, one with walk-in closet, share full hall bath

First floor — 1,241 sq. ft.
Second floor — 1,170 sq. ft.
Garage — 500 sq. ft.

An
EXCLUSIVE DESIGN
By Energetic Enterprises

Cathedral Ceiling Enlarges Great Room

© 1996 Donald A Gardner Architects, Inc.

■ *Total living area 1,699 sq. ft.* ■ *Price Code B* ■

No. 99811

■ This plan features:

- Three bedrooms

- Two full baths

■ Two dormers add volume to the Foyer

■ Great Room, topped by a cathedral ceiling, is open to the Kitchen and Breakfast area

■ Accent columns define the Foyer, Great Room, Kitchen, and Breakfast area

■ Private Master Suite crowned in a tray ceiling and highlighted by a skylit bath

■ Front bedroom topped by a tray ceiling

Main floor — 1,699 sq. ft.
Garage — 498 sq. ft.
Bonus — 336 sq. ft.

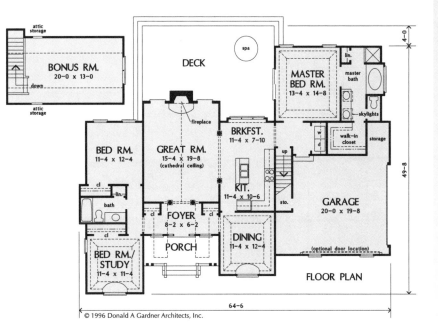

© 1996 Donald A Gardner Architects, Inc.

Growing Families Take Note

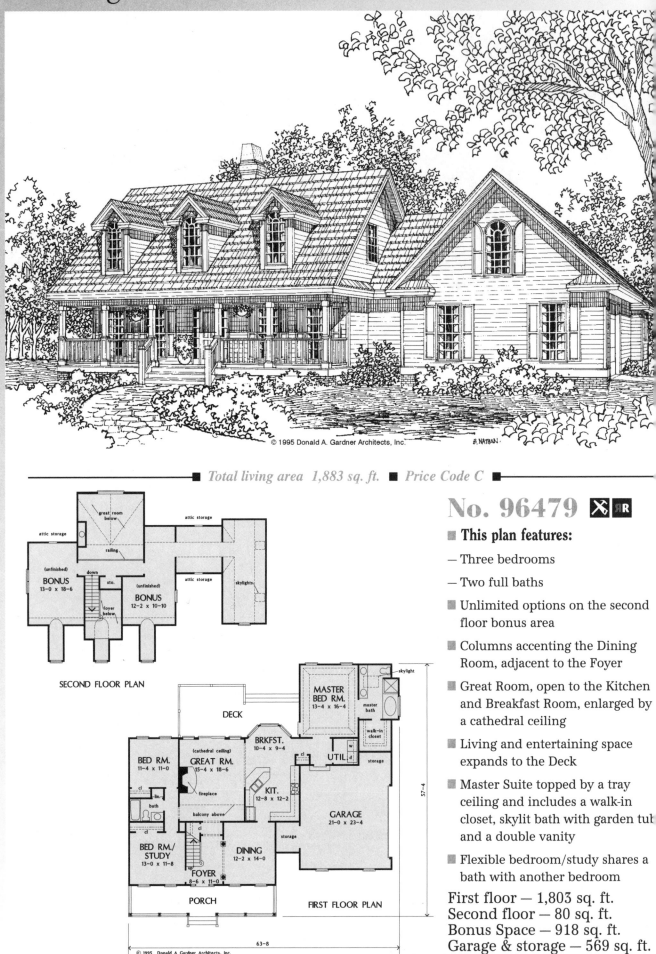

© 1995 Donald A. Gardner Architects, Inc.

B. NATHAN

■ *Total living area 1,883 sq. ft.* ■ *Price Code C* ■

No. 96479

■ This plan features:

— Three bedrooms

— Two full baths

■ Unlimited options on the second floor bonus area

■ Columns accenting the Dining Room, adjacent to the Foyer

■ Great Room, open to the Kitchen and Breakfast Room, enlarged by a cathedral ceiling

■ Living and entertaining space expands to the Deck

■ Master Suite topped by a tray ceiling and includes a walk-in closet, skylit bath with garden tub and a double vanity

■ Flexible bedroom/study shares a bath with another bedroom

First floor — 1,803 sq. ft.
Second floor — 80 sq. ft.
Bonus Space — 918 sq. ft.
Garage & storage — 569 sq. ft.

SECOND FLOOR PLAN

great room below

attic storage

attic storage

railing

attic storage

(unfinished)
BONUS
13-0 x 18-6

down

sto.

foyer below

(unfinished)
BONUS
12-2 x 10-10

attic storage

skylights

FIRST FLOOR PLAN

skylight

MASTER BED RM.
13-4 x 16-4

master bath

DECK

walk-in closet

BRKFST.
10-4 x 9-4

UTIL

storage

BED RM.
11-4 x 11-0

(cathedral ceiling)
GREAT RM.
15-4 x 18-6

KIT.
12-8 x 12-2

fireplace

balcony above

GARAGE
21-0 x 23-4

bath

57-4

BED RM./
STUDY
13-0 x 11-8

DINING
12-2 x 14-0

FOYER
8-6 x 11-0

up

storage

PORCH

63-8

© 1995 Donald A Gardner Architects, Inc.

Three Porches Offer Outdoor Charm

■ *Total living area 1,274 sq. ft.* ■ *Price Code A* ■

No. 90048 ✕

■ This plan features:

– Three bedrooms

– Two full baths

■ An oversized log burning fireplace
in the spacious Living/Dining
area which is two stories high
with sliding glass doors

■ Three porches offering the
maximum in outdoor living space

■ A private bedroom located on the
second floor

■ An efficient Kitchen including an
eating bar and access to the
covered Dining Porch

First floor — 974 sq. ft.
Second floor — 300 sq. ft.

second floor plan

first floor plan

Dramatic Dormers

© 1996 Donald A. Gardner Architects, Inc.

B. NATHAN.

■ *Total living area 1,685 sq. ft.* ■ *Price Code D* ■

No. 99810

■ **This plan features:**

— Three bedrooms

— Two full baths

■ A Foyer open to the dramatic
dormer, defined by columns

■ The Dining Room is augmented
by a tray ceiling

■ The Great Room expands into the
open Kitchen and Breakfast Room

■ A privately located Master Suite is
topped by a tray ceiling

■ Two additional Bedrooms are
located at the opposite side of the
home from the Master Suite

Main floor — 1,685 sq. ft.
Bonus area — 331 sq. ft.
Garage & storage — 536 sq. ft.

BONUS RM.
12-0 x 21-8

attic storage

skylights

down

PORCH

BED RM.
11-4 x 11-0

GREAT RM.
15-4 x 18-6
(cathedral ceiling)

fireplace

BRKFST.
11-4 x 8-8

KIT.
11-4 x 12-10

MASTER
BED RM.
13-4 x 16-4

skylight

master
bath

walk-in
closet

storage

GARAGE
21-0 x 21-8

BED RM./
STUDY
11-0 x 11-8

FOYER
6-0 x
8-4

DINING
11-0 x 11-8

storage

PORCH

FLOOR PLAN

57-4

62-4

© 1996 Donald A Gardner Architects, Inc.

European Sophistication

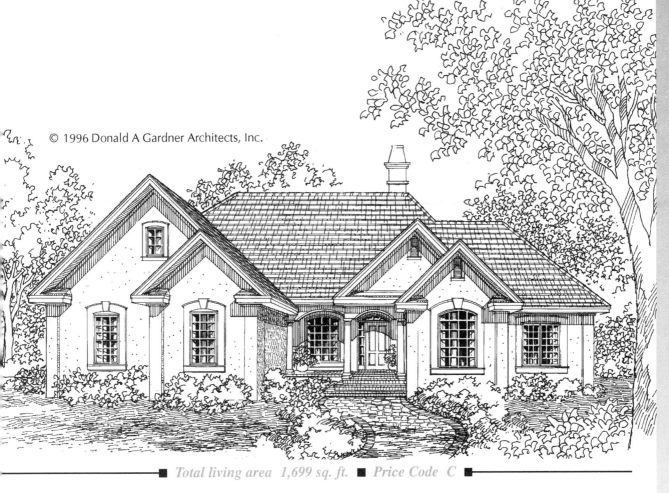

© 1996 Donald A Gardner Architects, Inc.

■ *Total living area 1,699 sq. ft.* ■ *Price Code C* ■

No. 99831 ✕

■ This plan features:

— Three bedrooms

— Two full baths

■ Keystone arches, gables, and stucco give the exterior European sophistication

■ Large Great Room with fireplace, and U-shaped Kitchen with a large Utility Room nearby

■ Octagonal tray ceiling dresses up the Dining Room

■ Special ceiling treatments include a cathedral ceiling in the Great Room and tray ceilings in the Master and front bedrooms

■ Indulgent master bath with a separate toilet area, a garden tub, shower and twin vanities

Main floor — 1,699 sq. ft.
Bonus — 386 sq. ft.
Garage — 637 sq. ft.

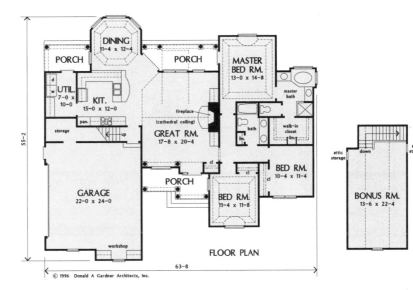

Home With Many Views

■ *Total living area 1,710 sq. ft.* ■ *Price Code B* ■

An
EXCLUSIVE DESIGN
By Marshall Associates

No. 24319

■ **This plan features:**

— Three bedrooms

— Two full baths

■ Large Decks and windows taking full advantage of the view

■ A fireplace that divides the Living Room from the Dining Room

■ A Kitchen flowing into the Dining Room

■ A Master Bedroom with full master bath

■ A Recreation Room sporting a whirlpool tub and a bar

Main floor — 728 sq. ft.
Upper floor — 573 sq. ft.
Lower floor — 409 sq. ft.
Garage — 244 sq. ft.

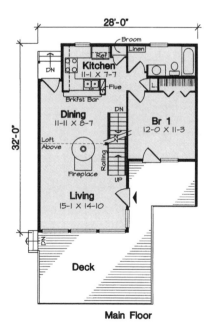

Main Floor

28'-0"
32'-0"

Kitchen
11-1 X 7-7

Broom
Ref
Linen

Dining
11-11 X 8-7

Br 1
12-0 X 11-3

Brkfst Bar
Flue
DN
Loft Above
Railing
Fireplace
UP

Living
15-1 X 14-10

Deck

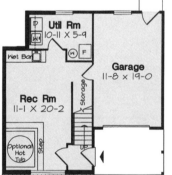

Util Rm
10-11 X 5-9

Wet Bar

Garage
11-8 X 19-0

Rec Rm
11-1 X 20-2

Optional Hot Tub

storage
Step
UP

Lower Floor

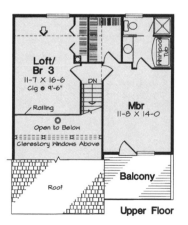

Loft/
Br 3
11-7 X 16-6
Clg @ 9'-6"

Railing

DN

Mbr
11-8 X 14-0

Whirlpool Tub

Open to Below

Clerestory Windows Above

Roof

Balcony

Upper Floor

Master Retreat Welcomes You Home

■ *Total living area 1,486 sq. ft.* ■ *Price Code A* ■

No. 34154

■ This plan features:

— Three bedrooms

— Two full baths

■ Foyer opens into an huge Living Room with a fireplace below a sloped ceiling and Deck access

■ Efficient Kitchen with a Pantry, serving counter, Dining area, laundry closet and Garage entry

■ Corner Master Bedroom offers a walk-in closet and pampering bath with a raised tub

■ Two more bedrooms, one with a Den option, share a full bath

Main area — 1,486 sq. ft.
Garage — 462 sq. ft.

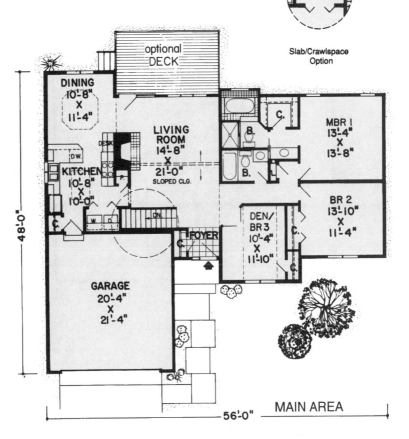

Easy Maintenance

■ *Total living area 786 sq. ft.* ■ *Price Code A* ■

No. 94307

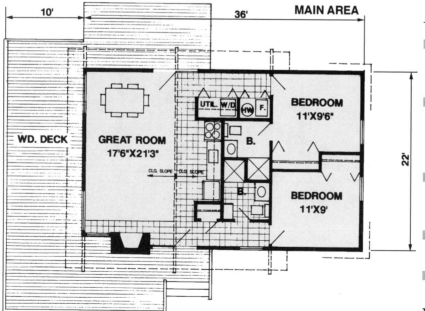

■ **This plan features:**

— Two bedroom

— Two three quarter baths

■ Abundant glass and a wrap-around Deck to enjoy the outdoors

■ A tiled entrance into a large Great Room with a fieldstone fireplace and dining area below a sloped ceiling

■ A compact tiled Kitchen open to a Great Room and adjacent to the Utility area

■ Two bedrooms, one with a private bath, offer ample closet space

■ No materials list is available for this plan

Main area — 786 sq. ft.

An
EXCLUSIVE DESIGN
By Marshall Associates

French Country Styling

■ *Total living area 3,352 sq. ft.* ■ *Price Code F* ■

No. 98513

■ **This plan features:**

– Three bedrooms

– Three full and one half baths

■ Brick and stone blend masterfully for an impressive French country exterior

■ Separate Master Suite with expansive bath and closet

■ Study containing a built-in desk and bookcase

■ Angled island Kitchen highlighted by walk-in Pantry and open to the Breakfast Bay

■ Fantastic Family Room including a brick fireplace and a built-in entertainment center

■ Three additional bedrooms with private access to a full bath

■ No materials list is available for this plan

Main floor — 3,352 sq. ft.
Garage — 672 sq. ft.

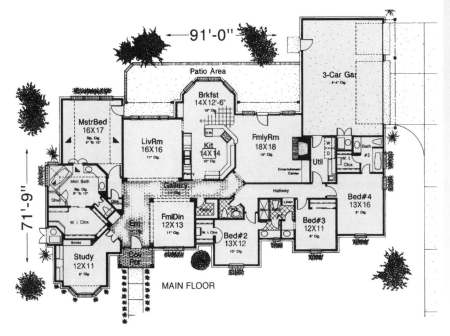

MAIN FLOOR

Lattice Trim Adds Nostalgic Charm

■ *Total living area 1,359 sq. ft.* ■ *Price Code A* ■

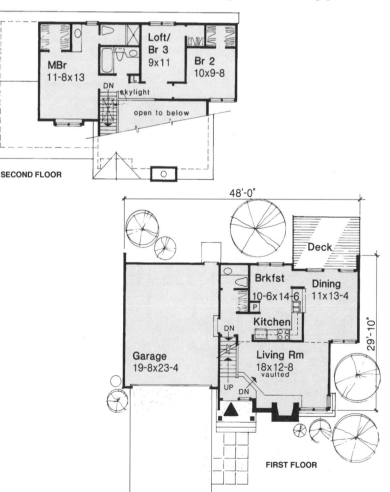

SECOND FLOOR

MBr
11-8x13

Loft/
Br 3
9x11

Br 2
10x9-8

DN skylight

open to below

FIRST FLOOR

48'-0"

29'-10"

Deck

Brkfst
10-6x14-6

Dining
11x13-4

Kitchen

Living Rm
18x12-8
vaulted

Garage
19-8x23-4

DN

P

UP   DN

No. 99315 ✖

■ **This plan features:**

— Three bedrooms

— Two full and one half baths

■ Wood and fieldstone exterior

■ A vaulted Living Room with balcony view and floor-to-ceiling corner window treatment

■ A Master Suite with private bath and dressing area

■ A two-car Garage with access to Kitchen

First floor — 668 sq. ft.
Second floor — 691 sq. ft.
Garage — 459 sq. ft.

Gazebo Porch Creates Old-Fashioned Feel

■ *Total living area 1,452 sq. ft.* ■ *Price Code A* ■

No. 24718

■ **This plan features:**

— Three bedrooms

— Two full baths

■ An old-fashioned welcome is created by the covered Porch

■ The Breakfast Area overlooks the Porch and is separated from the Kitchen by an extended counter

■ The Dining Room and the Great Room are highlighted by a two sided fireplace

■ The roomy Master Suite is enhanced by a whirlpool bath with double vanity and a walk-in closet

■ Each of the two secondary bedrooms feature a walk-in closet

■ No materials list is available for this plan

Main floor — 1,452 sq. ft.
Garage — 584 sq. ft.

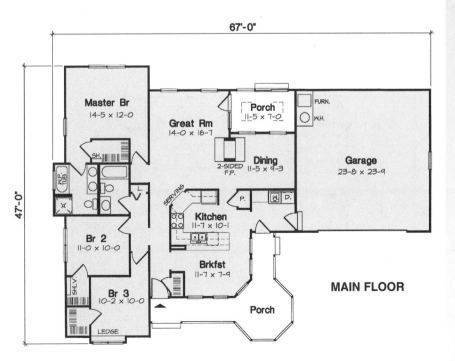

MAIN FLOOR

Family Favorite

■ *Total living area 1,359 sq. ft.* ■ *Price Code A* ■

No. 20156

■ This plan features:

— Three bedrooms

— Two full baths

■ An open arrangement with the Dining Room that combines with ten foot ceilings to make the Living Room seem more spacious

■ Glass on three sides of the Dining Room, which overlooks the Deck

■ An efficient, compact Kitchen with a built-in Pantry and peninsula counter

■ A Master Suite with a romantic window seat, a compartmentalized private bath and a walk-in closet

■ Two additional bedrooms that share a full hall bath

Main floor — 1,359 sq. ft.
Basement — 1,359 sq. ft.
Garage — 501 sq. ft.

Crawl Space/Slab Option

58'-0"

34'-4"

Deck

Dining
11-0 x 11-2
Decor. Ceiling

Br #2
10-10 x 11-10

Den/Br #3
10-0 x 11-10

Optional
Door
Location

Sink

Kit
10-0 x 11-2
Ref.   Pan.

Ldry

Ceiling

Solid Wall
w/ Opt. Door
Location

Plant
Ledge

DN

Decor. Ceiling

lin.

Living Rm
14-10 x 17-0

10' clg

Garage
20-4 x 21-8

MBr #1
11-7 x 13-0

Seat

MAIN FLOOR

An
EXCLUSIVE DESIGN
By Karl Kreeger

Easy Living Plan

■ *Total living area 1,600 sq. ft.* ■ *Price Code B* ■

No. 98406 ⚒

■ This plan features:

- Three bedrooms

- Two full and one half baths

■ Kitchen, Breakfast Bay, and Family Room blend into a spacious open living area

■ Convenient Laundry Center is tucked into the rear of the Kitchen

■ Luxurious Master Suite is topped by a tray ceiling while a vaulted ceiling is in the bath

■ Two roomy secondary bedrooms share the full bath in the hall

■ An optional basement, crawl space or slab foundation — please specify when ordering

First floor — 828 sq. ft.
Second floor — 772 sq. ft.
Basement — 828 sq. ft.
Garage — 473 sq. ft.

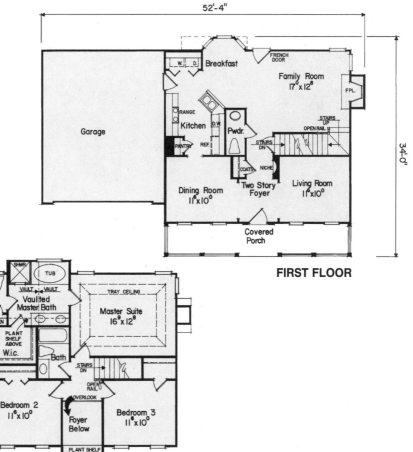

Magnificent Presence

■ *Total living area 4,500 sq. ft.* ■ *Price Code F* ■

© Carmichael & Dame

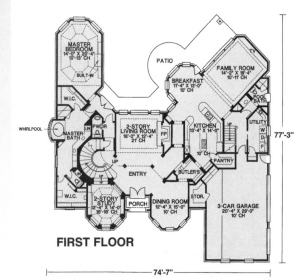

SECOND FLOOR

FIRST FLOOR

No. 99410

■ **This plan features:**

— Four bedrooms

— Three full, one three quarter, and one half baths

■ Curved staircase leads to elevated two-story Study and the Master Suite

■ Dining Room is connected to the Kitchen by a butler's pantry

■ Two-story Living Room has a fireplace and distinctive windows

■ Breakfast Bay adjoins family room with built-in entertainment center

■ Three bedrooms, a Game Room, and two full baths on the upper level

■ Three-car garage has an adjoining Storage Room

■ No materials list is available for this plan

First floor — 2,897 sq. ft.
Second floor — 1,603 sq. ft.
Basement — 2,897 sq. ft.
Garage — 793 sq. ft.

Private Master Suite

© 1997 Donald A. Gardner Architects, Inc.

B. NATHAN

■ *Total living area* 1,515 sq. ft. ■ *Price Code* C ■

No. 99835

■ This plan features:

- Three bedrooms

- Two full baths

■ Working at the Kitchen island focuses your view to the Great Room with its vaulted ceiling and a fireplace

■ Clerestory dormers emanate light into the Great Room

■ Both the Dining Room and Master Suite are enhanced by tray ceilings

■ Skylights flood natural light into the Bonus space

■ The private Master Suite has its own bath and an expansive walk-in closet

Main floor — 1,515 sq. ft.
Bonus — 288 sq. ft.
Garage — 476 sq. ft.

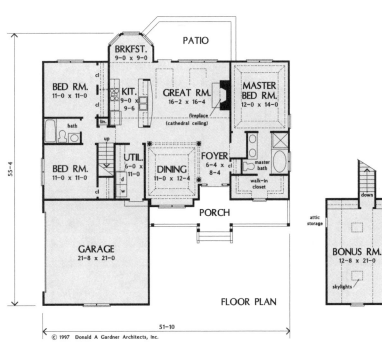

FLOOR PLAN

© 1997 Donald A Gardner Architects, Inc.

Elegant Living

Total living area 2,592 sq. ft. ■ Price Code D ■

SECOND FLOOR

First floor — 1,408 sq. ft.
Second floor — 1,184 sq. ft.
Basement — 1,408 sq. ft.

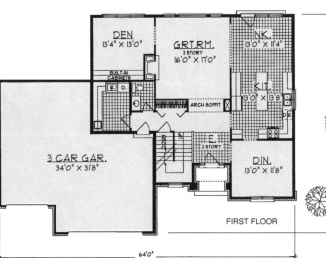

FIRST FLOOR

No. 99142

■ This plan features:

— Three bedrooms

— Two full and one half baths

■ The spacious Great Room has a two-story ceiling and a fireplace

■ The Den features built-in cabinetry

■ The formal Dining Room located at the front of the house provides a quiet place for entertaining

■ The main floor Laundry is located just off the three-car Garage

■ A Nook is adjacent to the Kitchen which has access to the backyard

■ The Master Suite with generous windows to the rear, also has a private bath and an extra-large walk-in closet

■ No materials list is available for this plan

Multiple Porches Provide Added Interest

■ *Total living area 3,149 sq. ft.* ■ *Price Code E* ■

No. 94622

■ **This plan features:**

- Four bedrooms

- Three full and one half baths

■ Great Room with large fireplace and French doors to Porch and Deck

■ Country-size Kitchen with cooktop work island, walk-in pantry and Breakfast Area with Porch access

■ Pampering Master Bedroom offers a decorative ceiling, sitting area, Porch and Deck access, a huge walk-in closet and lavish bath

■ Three second floor bedrooms with walk-in closets have private access to a full bath

■ An optional crawl space or slab foundation — please specify when ordering

■ No materials list is available for this plan

First floor — 2,033 sq. ft.
Second floor — 1,116 sq. ft.

WIDTH 66'-0"
DEPTH 56'-0"

brz'way to detached garage

Deck

Covered Porch

Deck

Porch

Ma. Ba.

Sitting Rm.
10'-2" x 5'-9"

Util.

Brkfst.
13'-8" x 9'

Great Room
23'-6" x 17'-8"

Hall

Ma. Bdrm.
13'-8" x 18'-10"

Kit.
13'-8" x 13'-6"

1/2 Ba.

Porch
14' x 6'

Dining
12'-8" x 15'-6"

Foyer

Living
13'-6" x 12'-8"

Porch
14' x 6'

Porch
38' x 7'

FIRST FLOOR

Bdrm. 2
13'-6" x 12'

attic storage

Dr.

Ba. 2

Balcony

Ba. 3

Dr.

Bdrm. 3
13'-6" x 15'

attic storage

Bdrm. 4
12'-8" x 13'-6"

open to below

SECOND FLOOR

Comfort and Style

■ *Total living area 1,423 sq. ft.* ■ *Price Code A* ■

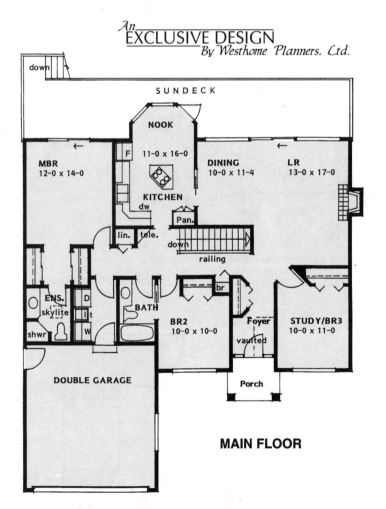

An EXCLUSIVE DESIGN
By Westhome Planners, Ltd.

MAIN FLOOR

No. 90990 ✖

■ **This plan features:**

— Two bedrooms with possible third bedroom/den

— One full and one three quarter baths

■ An unfinished daylight basement providing possible space for family recreation

■ A Master Suite complete with private bath and skylight

■ A large Kitchen including an eating nook

■ A sundeck that is easily accessible from the Master Suite, Nook and the Living/Dining area

Main floor — 1,423 sq. ft.
Basement — 1,423 sq. ft.
Garage — 399 sq. ft.
Width — 46'-0"
Depth — 52'-0"

Impressive Brick

An EXCLUSIVE DESIGN
By Britt J. Willis

■ Total living area 2,716 sq. ft. ■ Price Code E ■

No. 24550

■ This plan features:

- Four bedrooms

- Two full and one half baths

■ Two-story, raised Foyer with a splendid curved staircase

■ A dramatic cathedral ceiling and a two-way fireplace in the Living Room

■ A formal Dining Room accented by a lovely bay window

■ A Family Room with the unique fireplace and built-in entertainment center

■ An efficient, island Kitchen with an atrium sink, walk-in pantry, expanding to bright Breakfast area

■ A Master Suite with a vaulted ceiling, walk-in closet, and a plush bath

First floor — 1,433 sq. ft.
Second floor — 1,283 sq. ft.
Basement — 1,433 sq. ft.
Garage — 923 sq. ft.

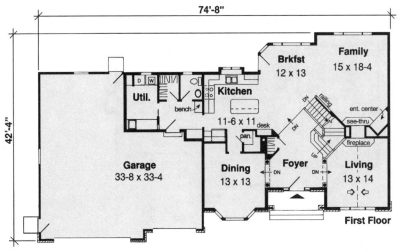

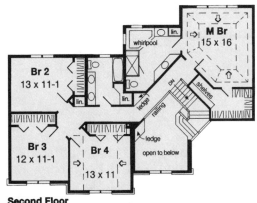

Charming Country Style

■ *Total living area 1,596 sq. ft.* ■ *Price Code B* ■

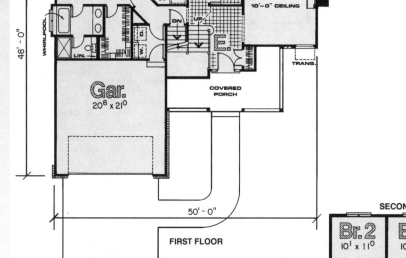

© design basics, inc.

Mbr.
15⁰ x 12⁰
9'-0" CEILING

Kit.
10⁰ x 12⁰

Bfst.
10⁰ x 11²
SNACK BAR

Grt. rm.
13⁸ x 19⁴
10'-0" CEILING

TRANSOMS

WHIRLPOOL

48' - 0"

LIN.

P.   R.

DN   UP

W. D.

Gar.
20⁸ x 21⁰

COVERED PORCH

TRANS.

50' - 0"

FIRST FLOOR

First floor — 1,191 sq. ft.
Second floor — 405 sq. ft.
Basement — 1,191 sq. ft.
Garage — 454 sq. ft.

No. 99404

■ **This plan features:**

— Three bedrooms

— Two full and one half baths

■ Spacious Great Room enhanced by a fireplace and transom windows

■ Breakfast Room with a bay window and direct access to the Kitchen

■ Snack bar extending work space in the Kitchen

■ Master Suite enhanced by a crowning in a boxed nine foot ceiling, a compartmental whirlpool bath and a large walk-in closet

■ Second floor balcony overlooking the U-shaped stairs and Entry

■ Two second floor bedrooms share a full hall bath

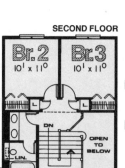

SECOND FLOOR

Br. 2
10¹ x 11⁰

Br. 3
10¹ x 11⁰

DN

LIN.

OPEN TO BELOW

■ *Total living area* 1,762 sq. ft. ■ *Price Code* B ■

No. 99498

■ This plan features:

– Three bedrooms

– Two full and one half baths

■ The subtle detailing of the entry includes dentil molding offsetting a triple window and square side columns

■ The private Master Suite has a walk-in closet, whirlpool tub and a dual sink vanity

■ Patio doors in the Breakfast Area lead to the rear Deck

■ Tall windows in the corners of the Great Room allow in an abundance of light

■ There is a snack bar in the Kitchen for meals on the go

■ A large closet on the second floor for storing toys or games

First floor — 1,363 sq. ft.
Second floor — 399 sq. ft.
Garage — 524 sq. ft.

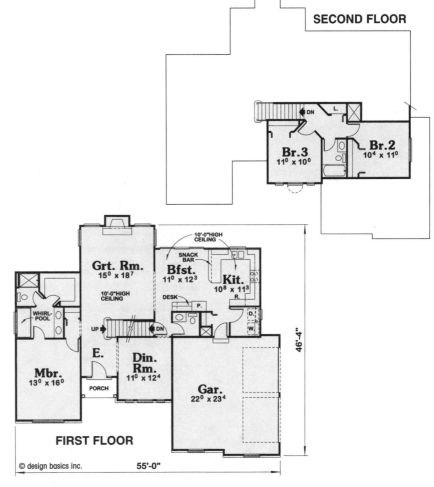

SECOND FLOOR

Br.3 11⁰ x 10⁰

Br.2 10⁴ x 11⁰

FIRST FLOOR

10'-0"HIGH CEILING

SNACK BAR

Grt. Rm. 15⁰ x 18⁷

Bfst. 11⁰ x 12³

Kit. 10⁸ x 11³

10'-0"HIGH CEILING

DESK

P.

WHIRL-POOL

UP

DN

Mbr. 13⁰ x 16⁰

E.

Din. Rm. 11⁰ x 12⁴

Gar. 22⁰ x 23⁴

46'-4"

PORCH

© design basics inc.

55'-0"

455

Covered Porch with Columns

■ *Total living area 1,856 sq. ft.* ■ *Price Code C* ■

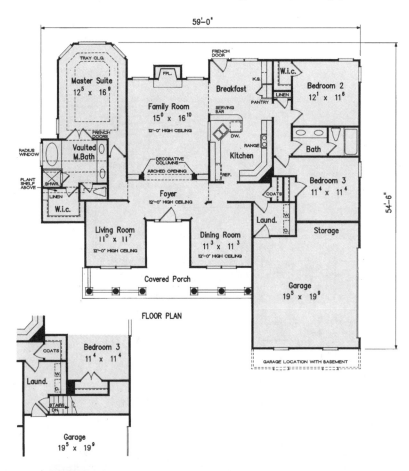

FLOOR PLAN

OPT. BASEMENT STAIR LOCATION

No. 98408

■ **This plan features:**

— Three bedrooms

— Two full baths

■ The foyer with 12' ceiling leads past decorative columns into the Family Room with a center fireplace

■ The Living and Dining rooms are linked by Foyer and have windows overlooking the front Porch

■ The Kitchen has a serving bar and is adjacent to the Breakfast Nook which has a French door that opens to the backyard

■ The private Master Suite has a tray ceiling and a vaulted bath with a double vanity

■ An optional basement, slab or crawl space foundation — please specify when ordering

Main floor — 1,856 sq. ft.
Basement — 1,856 sq. ft.
Garage — 429 sq. ft.

A Touch of Country

An EXCLUSIVE DESIGN
By Upright Design

■ *Total living area 2,647 sq. ft.* ■ *Price Code E* ■

No. 24403

■ This plan features:

- Three or four bedrooms

- Two full and one three quarter baths

■ A large Foyer with an attractive staircase

■ Study/Guest Room with convenient access to a full, hall bath

■ Elegant Dining Room topped by a decorative ceiling treatment

■ Expansive Family Room equipped with a massive fireplace with built-in bookshelves

■ Breakfast Room with a convenient built-in planning desk

■ Peninsula counter/eating bar, a built-in pantry, double sink and ample counter space in the Kitchen

■ A cathedral ceiling crowning the Master Suite

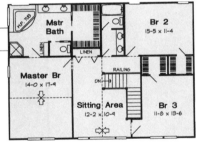

Second Floor

First floor — 1,378 sq. ft.
Second floor — 1,269 sq. ft.
Basement — 1,378 sq. ft.
Garage — 717 sq. ft.

Shop
14-5 x 15-5

Crawl Space/Slab Option

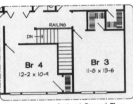

Br 4
12-2 x 10-4

Br 3
11-8 x 13-6

Optional Second Floor

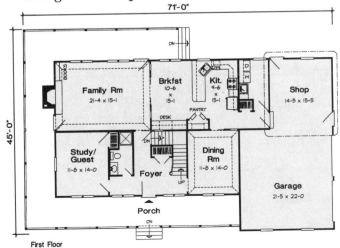

First Floor

Classic Country Farmhouse

© 1995 Donald A Gardner Architects, Inc.

■ Total living area 1,832 sq. ft. ■ Price Code C ■

No. 99808

This plan features:

— Three bedrooms

— Two full baths

■ Dormers, arched windows and multiple columns give this home country charm

■ Foyer, expanded by vaulted ceiling, accesses Dining Room, Bedroom/Study and Great Room

■ Expansive Great Room, with hearth fireplace topped by cathedral ceiling, opens to rear Porch and efficient Kitchen

■ Tray ceiling adds volume to private Master Bedroom with plush bath and walk-in closet

■ Extra room for growth offered by Bonus Room with skylight

Main floor — 1,832 sq. ft.
Bonus room — 425 sq. ft.
Garage & storage — 562 sq. ft.

© 1995 Donald A Gardner Architects, Inc.

Open Plan is Full of Air & Light

■ *Total living area 1,505 sq. ft.* ■ *Price Code B* ■

No. 98463

■ This plan features:

– Three bedrooms

– Two full and one half baths

■ Foyer open to the Family Room and highlighted by a fireplace

■ Dining Room with a sliding glass door to rear yard adjoins Family Room

■ Kitchen and Nook in an efficient open layout

■ Second floor Master Suite topped by tray ceiling over the bedroom and a vaulted ceiling over the lavish bath

■ Two additional bedrooms sharing a full bath in the hall

■ An optional basement or crawl space foundation — please specify when ordering

■ No materials list is available for this plan

First floor — 767 sq. ft.
Second floor — 738 sq. ft.
Bonus room — 240 sq. ft.
Basement — 767 sq. ft.
Garage — 480 sq. ft.

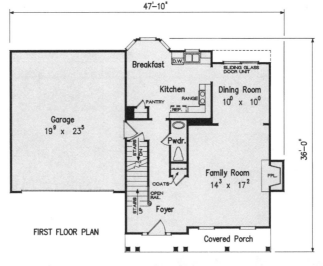

Sunny Dormer Brightens Foyer

© 1996 Donald A Gardner Architects, Inc.

■ *Total living area 1,386 sq. ft.* ■ *Price Code B* ■

No. 99812

DECK

DINING
9–10 x 11–0
(cathedral ceiling)

GREAT RM.
15–10 x 16–10
(cathedral ceiling)

fireplace

MASTER
BED RM.
12–4 x 13–6
(cathedral ceiling)

walk-in
closet

master
bath

KIT.
9–10 x
11–8

FOYER
9–6 x 5–6

bath

storage

up

d
w

PORCH

cl

cl
cl

BED RM.
11–0 x 11–0

BED RM.
11–0 x 11–0
(cathedral ceiling)

GARAGE
22–0 x 20–8

FLOOR PLAN

54–10

10–0

48–0

© 1996 Donald A Gardner Architects, Inc.

down

skylights

attic storage

BONUS RM.
12–0 x 20–8
(cathedral ceiling)

■ **This plan features:**

—Three bedrooms

—Two full baths

■ Today's comforts with cost
effective construction

■ Open Great room, Dining Room,
and Kitchen topped by a cathedral
ceiling emphasizing spaciousness

■ Adjoining Deck providing extra
living or entertaining room

■ Front bedroom crowned in
cathedral ceiling and pampered
by a private bath with garden tub
dual vanity and a walk-in closet

■ Skylighted Bonus Room above the
garage offering flexibility and
opportunity for growth

Main floor — 1,386 sq. ft.
Garage — 517 sq. ft.
Bonus room — 314 sq. ft.

■ Total living area 1,303 sq. ft. ■ Price Code A ■

No. 99339 ⚒

■ This plan features:

- Three bedrooms

- Two full baths

■ A vaulted ceiling in the Living Room with a half-round transom window and a fireplace

■ A Dining area flowing into either the Kitchen or the Living Room with sliders to the Deck

■ A main floor Master Suite with corner windows, walk-in closet and private access to a full bath

■ Two additional bedrooms on the second floor, one with a walk-in closet, having use of a full bath

Main floor — 857 sq. ft.
Upper floor — 446 sq. ft.
Garage — 400 sq. ft.

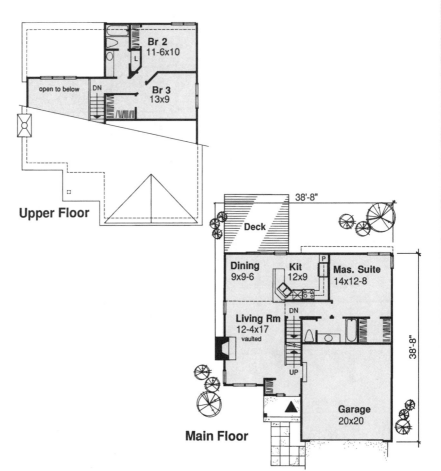

Upper Floor

Br 2
11-6x10

open to below   DN

Br 3
13x9

Main Floor

38'-8"

Deck

Dining
9x9-6

Kit
12x9

P

Mas. Suite
14x12-8

Living Rm
12-4x17
vaulted

DN

UP

38'-8"

Garage
20x20

Lovely Second Home

■ *Total living area 1,096 sq. ft.* ■ *Price Code A* ■

No. 91002

■ **This plan features:**

— Three bedrooms

— One full and one half baths

■ Fireplace warms both entryway and Living Room

■ Dining and Living Rooms opening onto the Deck, which surrounds the house on three sides

Main floor — 808 sq. ft.
Upper floor — 288 sq. ft.

BDRM-2
VAULTED
9/2x9/6

B-2

DN

VAULTED
LOFT
10/10x11/6

PLANT
SHELF

OPEN TO BELOW

UPPER FLOOR PLAN

BEDRM-1
10/10x11/10

B-1

UP

KIT.
9/6x11/0

VAULTED
LIVING
13/2x16/0

VAULTED
DINING
9/0x11/10

32'-0"

24'-0"

MAIN FLOOR PLAN

Old-Fashioned With Contemporary Interior

■ *Total living area 2,052 sq. ft.* ■ *Price Code C* ■

No. 98407

This plan features:

Four bedrooms

Three full baths

A two-story Foyer is flanked by the Living Room and the Dining Room

The Family Room features a fireplace and a French door

The bayed Breakfast Nook and Pantry are adjacent to the Kitchen

The Master Suite with a trayed ceiling has an attached bath with a vaulted ceiling

Upstairs are two additional bedrooms, a full bath, a laundry closet, and a Bonus Room

An optional basement, slab or crawl space foundation — please specify when ordering

First floor — 1,135 sq. ft.

Second floor — 917 sq. ft.

Bonus — 216 sq. ft.

Basement — 1,135 sq. ft.

Garage — 452 sq. ft.

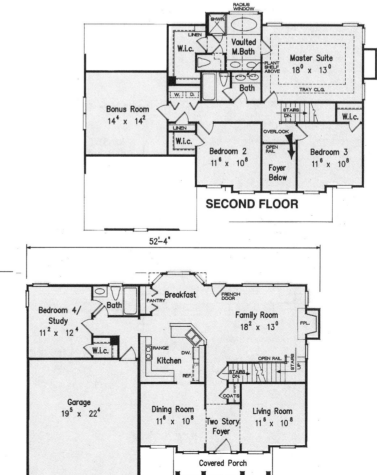

Easy, Economical Building

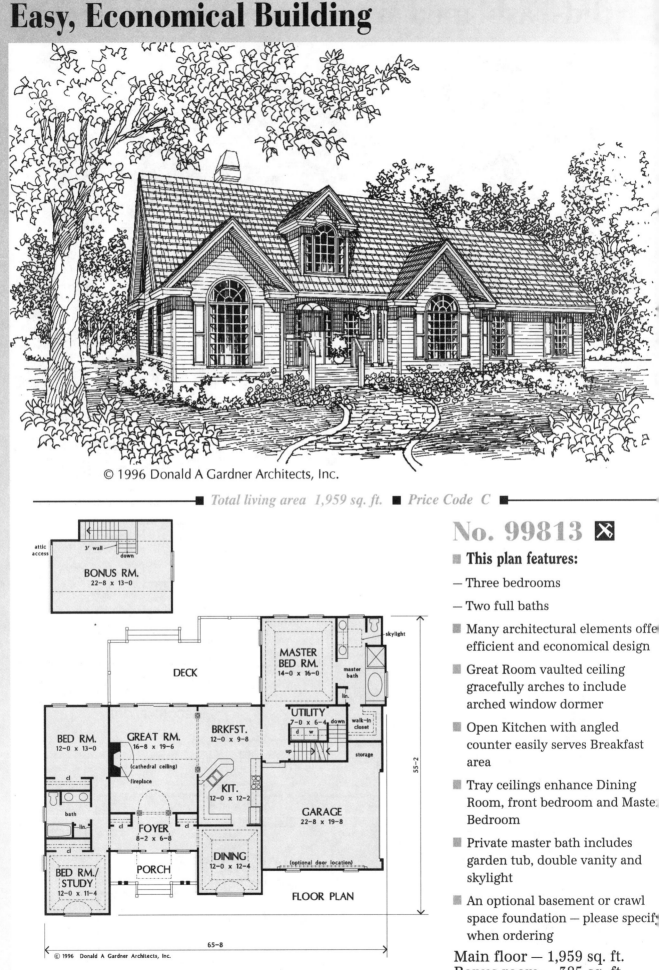

© 1996 Donald A Gardner Architects, Inc.

■ *Total living area 1,959 sq. ft.* ■ *Price Code C* ■

BONUS RM.
22-8 x 13-0

attic access

3' wall

down

DECK

MASTER BED RM.
14-0 x 16-0

skylight

master bath

lin.

UTILITY
7-0 x 6-4

down

walk-in closet

storage

BED RM.
12-0 x 13-0

GREAT RM.
16-8 x 19-6

(cathedral ceiling)

fireplace

BRKFST.
12-0 x 9-8

KIT.
12-0 x 12-2

up

GARAGE
22-8 x 19-8

cl

bath

lin.

cl

FOYER
8-2 x 6-8

cl

cl

BED RM./ STUDY
12-0 x 11-4

PORCH

DINING
12-0 x 12-4

(optional door location)

FLOOR PLAN

55-2

65-8

© 1996 Donald A Gardner Architects, Inc.

No. 99813 ✖

■ **This plan features:**

— Three bedrooms

— Two full baths

■ Many architectural elements off[e] efficient and economical design

■ Great Room vaulted ceiling gracefully arches to include arched window dormer

■ Open Kitchen with angled counter easily serves Breakfast area

■ Tray ceilings enhance Dining Room, front bedroom and Maste[r] Bedroom

■ Private master bath includes garden tub, double vanity and skylight

■ An optional basement or crawl space foundation — please specif[y] when ordering

Main floor — 1,959 sq. ft.
Bonus room — 385 sq. ft.
Garage & storage — 484 sq. ft.

A Comfortable Informal Design

■ *Total living area 1,300 sq. ft.* ■ *Price Code B* ■

No. 94801

This plan features:

- Three bedrooms

- Two full baths

■ Warm, country front Porch with wood details

■ Spacious Activity Room enhanced by a pre-fab fireplace

■ Open and efficient Kitchen/Dining area highlighted by bay window, adjacent to Laundry and Garage entry

■ Corner Master Bedroom offers a pampering bath with a garden tub and double vanity topped by a vaulted ceiling

■ Two additional bedrooms with ample closets, share a full bath

■ An optional crawl space or slab foundation available — please specify when ordering

Main floor — 1,300 sq. ft.
Garage — 576 sq. ft.

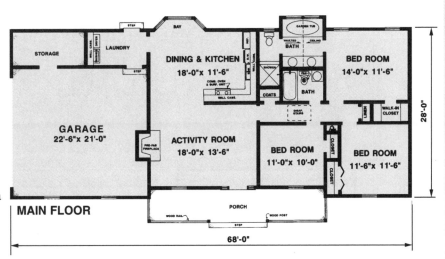

Grand Country Porch

■ *Total living area 2,665 sq. ft.* ■ *Price Code E* ■

No. 94615

■ **This plan features:**

— Four bedrooms

— Three full baths

■ Large front Porch provides shade and Southern hospitality

■ Spacious Living Room with access to Covered Porch and Patio, and a cozy fireplace between built-in shelves

■ Country Kitchen with a cooktop island, bright Breakfast bay, Utility Room and Garage entry

■ Corner Master Bedroom with a walk-in closet and private bath

■ First floor bedroom with private access to a full bath

■ Two second floor bedrooms with dormers, walk-in closets and separate vanities, share a full bath

■ An optional crawl space or slab foundation — please specify when ordering

■ No materials list available

First floor — 1,916 sq. ft.
Second floor — 749 sq. ft.
Garage — 479 sq. ft.

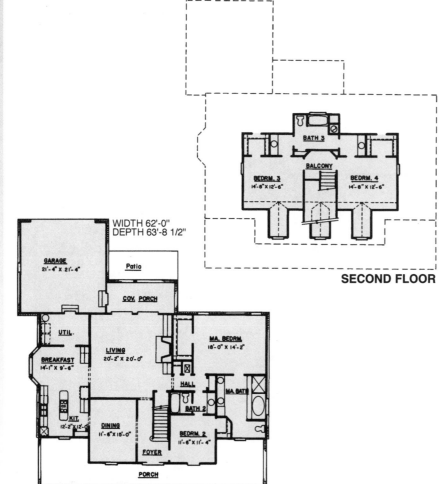

WIDTH 62'-0"
DEPTH 63'-8 1/2"

SECOND FLOOR

FIRST FLOOR

Balcony Overlooks Living Room Below

■ *Total living area 1,351 sq. ft.* ■ *Price Code A* ■

No. 90356 ✗

■ **This plan features:**

- Three bedrooms

- Two full and one half baths

■ A vaulted ceiling Living Room with a balcony above, and a fireplace

■ An efficient, well-equipped Kitchen with stovetop island and easy flow of traffic into the Dining Room

■ A Deck accessible from the Living Room

■ A luxurious Master Suite with a bay window seat, walk-in closet, dressing area and a private shower

■ Two additional bedrooms that share a full hall bath

First floor — 674 sq. ft.
Second floor — 677 sq. ft.

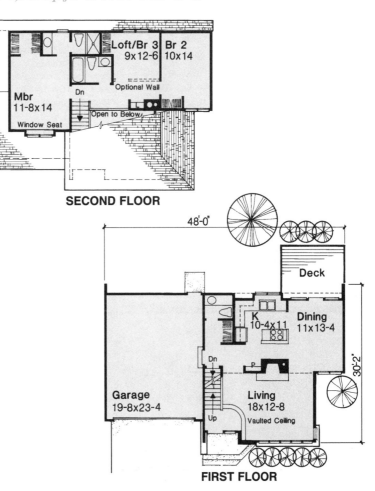

SECOND FLOOR

Loft/Br 3
9x12-6

Br 2
10x14

Optional Wall

Mbr
11-8x14

Dn

Window Seat

Open to Below

FIRST FLOOR

48'-0"

30'-2"

Deck

K
10-4x11

Dining
11x13-4

Dn

Garage
19-8x23-4

Living
18x12-8

Up

Vaulted Ceiling

Everything You Need...
...to Make Your Dream Come True

You pay only a fraction of the original cost for home designs by respected professionals.

You've Picked Your Dream Home!

You can imagine your new home situated on your lot in the morning sunlight. You can visualize living there, enjoying your family, entertaining friends and celebrating holidays. All that remains are the details. That's where we can help. Whether you plan to build it yourself, act as your own general contractor or hire a professional builder, your Garlinghouse Co. home plans will provide the perfect design and specifications to help make your dream home a reality.

We can offer you an array of additional products and services to help you with your planning needs. We can supply materials lists, construction cost estimates based on your local material and labor costs and modifications to your selected plan if you would like.

For over 90 years, homeowners and builders have relied on us for accurate, complete, professional blueprints. Our plans help you get results fast... and save money, too! These pages will give you all the information you need to order. So get started now... We know you'll love your new Garlinghouse home!

Sincerely,

President

Chief Executive Officer

EXTERIOR ELEVATIONS

Elevations are scaled drawings of the front, rear, left, and right sides of a home. All of the necessary information pertaining to the exterior finish materials, roof pitches, and exterior height dimensions of your home are defined.

CABINET PLANS

These plans, or in some cases elevations, will detail the layout of the kitchen and bathroom cabinets at a larger scale. This gives you an accurate layout for your cabinets or an ideal starting point for a modified custom cabinet design. Available for most plans. You may also show the floor plan without a cabinet layout. This will allow you to start from scratch and design your own dream kitchen.

TYPICAL WALL SECTION

This section is provided to help your builder understand the structural components and materials used to construct the exterior walls of your home. This section will address insulation, roof components, and interior and exterior wall finishes. Your plans will be designed with either 2x4 2x6 exterior walls, but most professional contractors can easily adapt the plans to the wall thickness you require.

FIREPLACE DETAILS

If the home you have chosen includes a fireplace, the fireplace detail will show typical methods to construct the firebox, hearth and flue chase for masonry units, or a wood frame chase for a zero-clearance unit. Available for most plans.

FOUNDATION PLAN

These plans will accurately dimension the footprint of your home including load bearing points and beam placement if applicable. The foundation style will vary from plan to plan. Your local climatic conditions will dictate whether a basement, slab or crawlspace is best suited for your area. In most cases, if your plan comes with one foundation style, a professional contractor can easily adapt the foundation plan to an alternate style.

ROOF PLAN

The information necessary to construct the roof will be included with your home plans. Some plans will reference roof trusses, while many others contain schematic framing plans. These framing plans will indicate the lumber sizes necessary for the rafters and ridgeboards based on the designated roof loads.

TYPICAL CROSS SECTION

A cut-away cross-section through the entire home shows your building contractor the exact correlation of construction components at all levels of the house. It will help to clarify the load bearing points from the roof all the way down to the basement. Available for most plans.

DETAILED FLOOR PLANS

The floor plans of your home accurately dimension the positioning of all walls, doors, windows, stairs and permanent fixtures. They will show you the relationship and dimensions of rooms, closets and traffic patterns. The schematic of the electrical layout may be included in the plan. This layout is clearly represented and does not hinder the clarity of other pertinent information shown. All these details will help your builder properly construct your new home.

STAIR DETAILS

If stairs are an element of the design you have chosen, the plans will show the necessary information to build these, either through a stair cross section, or on the floor plans. Either way, the information provides your builders the essential reference points that they need to build the stairs.

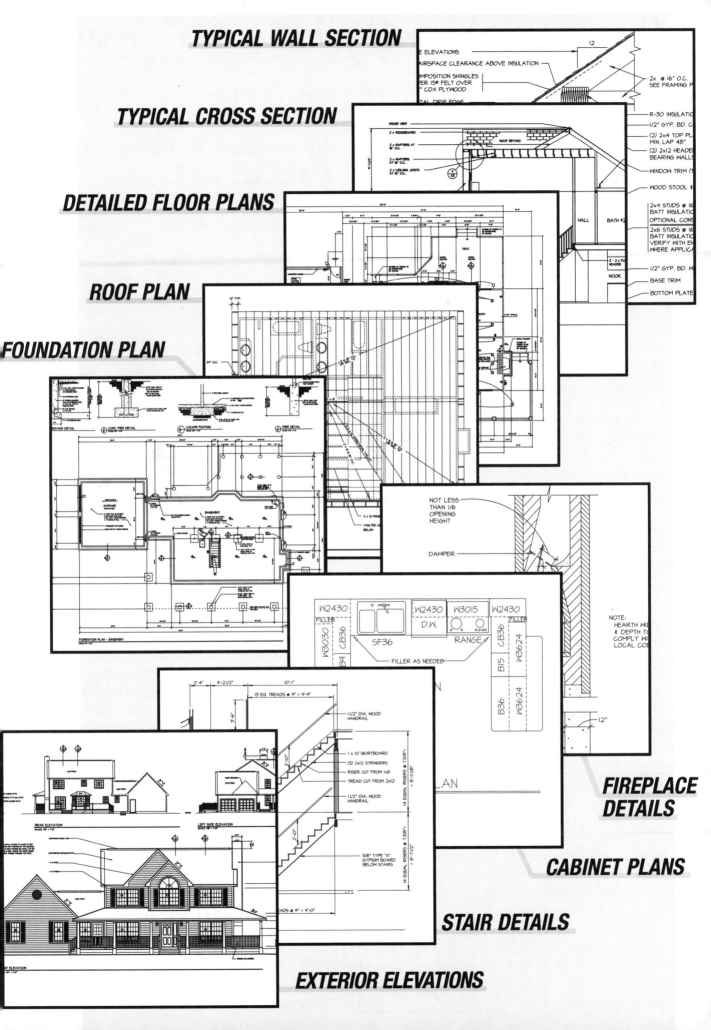

TYPICAL WALL SECTION

TYPICAL CROSS SECTION

DETAILED FLOOR PLANS

ROOF PLAN

FOUNDATION PLAN

FIREPLACE DETAILS

CABINET PLANS

STAIR DETAILS

EXTERIOR ELEVATIONS

Garlinghouse Options & Extras ...Make Your Dream A Home

Reversed Plans Can Make Your Dream Home Just Right!

"That's our dream home...if only the garage were on the other side!"

You could have exactly the home you want by flipping it end-for-end. Check it out by holding your dream home page of this book up to a mirror. Then simply order your plans "reversed." We'll send you one full set of mirror-image plans (with the writing backwards) as a master guide for you and your builder.

The remaining sets of your order will come as shown in this book so the dimensions and specifications are easily read on the job site...but most plans in our collection come stamped "REVERSED" so there is no construction confusion.

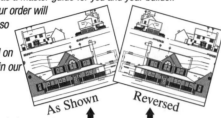

As Shown   Reversed

We can only send reversed plans with multiple-set orders. There is a $50 charge for this service.

Some plans in our collection are available in Right Reading Reverse. Right Reading Reverse plans will show your home in reverse, with the writing on the plan being readable. This easy-to-read format will save you valuable time and money. Please contact our Customer Service Department at (860) 343-5977 to check for Right Reading Reverse availability. (There is a $150 charge for plan series 964, 980, 981 & 998. $125 for all other plans.)

Specifications & Contract Form

We send this form to you free of charge with your home plan order. The form is designed to be filled in by you or your contractor with the exact materials to use in the construction of your new home. Once signed by you and your contractor it will provide you with peace of mind throughout the construction process.

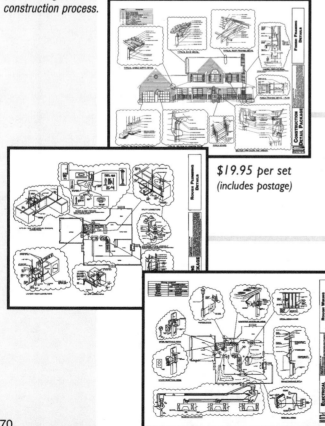

$19.95 per set
(includes postage)

Remember To Order Your Materials List

It'll help you save money. Available at a modest additional charge, the Materials List gives the quantity, dimensions, and specifications for the major materials needed to build your home. You will get faster, more accurate bids from your contractors and building suppliers — and avoid paying for unused materials and waste. Materials Lists are available for all home plans except as otherwise indicated, but can only be ordered with a set of home plans. Due to differences in regional requirements and homeowner or builder preferences... electrical, plumbing and heating/air conditioning equipment specifications are not designed specifically for each plan. However, non-plan specific detailed typical prints of residential electrical, plumbing and construction guidelines can be provided. Please see below for additional information.

Detail Plans Provide Valuable Information About Construction Techniques

Because local codes and requirements vary greatly, we recommend that you obtain drawings and bids from licensed contractors to do your mechanical plans. However, if you want to know more about techniques — and deal more confidently with subcontractors — we offer these remarkably useful detail sheets. These detail sheets will aid in your understanding of these technical subjects. **The detail sheets are not specific to any one home plan and should be used only as a general reference guide.**

RESIDENTIAL CONSTRUCTION DETAILS

Ten sheets that cover the essentials of stick-built residential home construction. Details foundation options — poured concrete basement, concrete block, or monolithic concrete slab. Shows all aspects of floor, wall and roof framing. Provides details for roof dormers, overhangs, chimneys and skylights. Conforms to requirements of Uniform Building code or BOCA code. Includes a quick index and a glossary of terms.

RESIDENTIAL PLUMBING DETAILS

Eight sheets packed with information detailing pipe installation methods, fittings, and sizes. Details plumbing hook-ups for toilets, sinks, washers, sump pumps, and septic system construction. Conforms to requirements of National Plumbing code. Color coded with a glossary of terms and quick index.

RESIDENTIAL ELECTRICAL DETAILS

Eight sheets that cover all aspects of residential wiring, from simple switch wiring to service entrance connections. Details distribution panel layout with outlet and switch schematics, circuit breaker and wiring installation methods, and ground fault interrupter specifications. Conforms to requirements of National Electrical Code. Color coded with a glossary of terms.

470

Modifying Your Favorite Design, Made EASY!

OPTION #1

Modifying Your Garlinghouse Home Plan

Simple modifications to your dream home, including minor non-structural changes and material substitutions, can be made between you and your builder by marking the changes directly on your blueprints. However, if you are considering making significant changes to your chosen design, we recommend that you use the services of The Garlinghouse Design Staff. We will help take your ideas and turn them into a reality, just the way you want. Here's our procedure!

When you place your Vellum order, you may also request a free Garlinghouse Modification Kit. In this kit, you will receive a red marking pencil, furniture cut-out sheet, ruler, a self addressed mailing label and a form for specifying any additional notes or drawings that will help us understand your design ideas. Mark your desired changes directly on the Vellum drawings. NOTE: Please use only a **red pencil** to mark your desired changes on the Vellum. Then, return the redlined Vellum set in the original box to us. **IMPORTANT**: Please **roll** the Vellums for shipping, **do not fold** the Vellums for shipping.

We also offer modification estimates. We will provide you with an estimate to draft your changes based on your specific modifications before you purchase the vellums, for a $50 fee. After you receive your estimate, if you decide to have us do the changes, the $50 estimate fee will be deducted from the cost of your modifications. If, however, you choose to use a different service, the $50 estimate fee is non-refundable. (Note: Personal checks cannot be accepted for the estimate.)

Within 5 days of receipt of your plans, you will be contacted by the Design Staff with an estimate for the design services to draw those changes. A 50% deposit is required before we begin making the actual modifications to your plans.

Once the design changes have been completed to your vellum plan, a representative will call to inform you that your modified Vellum plan is complete and will be shipped as soon as the final payment has been made. For additional information call us at 1-860-343-5977. Please refer to the Modification Pricing Guide for estimated modification costs.

OPTION #2

Reproducible Vellums for Local Modification Ease

If you decide not to use Garlinghouse for your modifications, we recommend that you follow our same procedure of purchasing our Vellums. You then have the option of using the services of the original designer of the plan, a local professional designer, or architect to make the modifications to your plan.

With a Vellum copy of our plans, a design professional can alter the drawings just the way you want, then you can print as many copies of the modified plans as you need to build your house. And, since you have already started with our complete detailed plans, the cost of those expensive professional services will be significantly less than starting from scratch. Refer to the price schedule for Vellum costs.

IMPORTANT RETURN POLICY: Upon receipt of your Vellums, if for some reason you decide you do not want a modified plan, then simply return the Kit and the unopened Vellums. Reproducible Vellum copies of our home plans are copyright protected and only sold under the terms of a license agreement that you will receive with your order. Should you not agree to the terms, then the Vellums may be returned, **unopened,** for a full refund less the shipping and handling charges, plus a 20% restocking fee. For any additional information, please call us at 1-860-343-5977.

MODIFICATION PRICING GUIDE

CATEGORIES	ESTIMATED COST
KITCHEN LAYOUT — PLAN AND ELEVATION	$175.00
BATHROOM LAYOUT — PLAN AND ELEVATION	$175.00
FIREPLACE PLAN AND DETAILS	$200.00
INTERIOR ELEVATION	$125.00
EXTERIOR ELEVATION — MATERIAL CHANGE	$140.00
EXTERIOR ELEVATION — ADD BRICK OR STONE	$400.00
EXTERIOR ELEVATION — STYLE CHANGE	$450.00
NON BEARING WALLS (INTERIOR)	$200.00
BEARING AND/OR EXTERIOR WALLS	$325.00
WALL FRAMING CHANGE — 2X4 TO 2X6 OR 2X6 TO 2X4	$240.00
ADD/REDUCE LIVING SPACE — SQUARE FOOTAGE	QUOTE REQUIRED
NEW MATERIALS LIST	QUOTE REQUIRED
CHANGE TRUSSES TO RAFTERS OR CHANGE ROOF PITCH	$300.00
FRAMING PLAN CHANGES	$325.00
GARAGE CHANGES	$325.00
ADD A FOUNDATION OPTION	$300.00
FOUNDATION CHANGES	$250.00
RIGHT READING PLAN REVERSE	$575.00
ARCHITECTS SEAL (Available for most states.)	$300.00
ENERGY CERTIFICATE	$150.00
LIGHT AND VENTILATION SCHEDULE	$150.00

Questions?

Call our customer service department at 1-860-343-5977

"How to obtain a construction cost calculation based on labor rates and building material costs in <u>your</u> Zip Code area!"

ZIP-QUOTE!
HOME COST CALCULATOR

ZIP QUOTE
HOME COST CALCULATOR

WHY?

Do you wish you could quickly find out the building cost for your new home without waiting for a contractor to compile hundreds of bids? Would you like to have a benchmark to compare your contractor(s) bids against? *Well, Now You Can!!,* with **Zip-Quote** Home Cost Calculator. Zip-Quote is only available for zip code areas within the United States.

HOW?

Our new **Zip-Quote** Home Cost Calculator will enable you to obtain the calculated building cost to construct your new home, based on labor rates and building material costs within your zip code area, without the normal delays or hassles usually associated with the bidding process. Zip-Quote can be purchased in two separate formats, an itemized or a bottom line format.

"How does **Zip-Quote** actually work?" When you call to order, you must choose from the options available, for your specific home, in order for us to process your order. Once we receive your **Zip-Quote** order, we process your specific home plan building materials list through our Home Cost Calculator which contains up-to-date rates for all residential labor trades and building material costs in your zip code area. "The result?" A calculated cost to build your dream home in your zip code area. This calculation will help you (as a consumer or a builder) evaluate your building budget. This is a valuable tool for anyone considering building a new home.

All database information for our calculations is furnished by Marshall & Swift, L.P. For over 60 years, Marshall & Swift L.P. has been a leading provider of cost data to professionals in all aspects of the construction and remodeling industries.

OPTION 1

The **Itemized Zip-Quote** is a detailed building material list. Each building material list line item will separately state the labor cost, material cost and equipment cost (if applicable) for the use of that building material in the construction process. Each category within the building material list will be subtotaled and the entire Itemized cost calculation totaled at the end. This building materials list will be summarized by the individual building categories and will have additional columns where you can enter data from your contractor's estimates for a cost comparison between the different suppliers and contractors who will actually quote you their products and services.

OPTION 2

The **Bottom Line Zip-Quote** is a one line summarized total cost for the home plan of your choice. This cost calculation is also based on the labor cost, material cost and equipment cost (if applicable) within your local zip code area.

COST

The price of your **Itemized Zip-Quote** is based upon the pricing schedule of the plan you have selected, in addition to the price of the materials list. Please refer to the pricing schedule on our order form. The price of your initial **Bottom Line Zip Quote** is $29.95. Each additional **Bottom Line Zip-Quote** ordered in conjunction with the initial order is only $14.95. **Bottom Line Zip-Quote** may be purchased separately and does NOT have to be purchased in conjunction with a home plan order.

FYI

An **Itemized Zip-Quote** Home Cost Calculation can ONLY be purchased in conjunction with a Home Plan order. The **Itemized Zip-Quote** can not be purchased separately. The **Bottom Line Zip-Quote** can be purchased separately and doesn't have to be purchased in conjunction with a home plan order. Please consult with a sales representative for current availability. If you find within 60 days of your order date that you will be unable to build this home, then you may exchange the plans and the materials list towards the price of a new set of plans (see order info pages for plan exchange policy). The **Itemized Zip-Quote** and the **Bottom Line Zip-Quote** are NOT returnable. The price of the initial **Bottom Line Zip-Quote** order can be credited towards the purchase of an **Itemized Zip-Quote** order only. Additional **Bottom Line Zip-Quote** orders, within the same order can not be credited. Please call our Customer Service Department for more information.

Itemized Zip-Quote is available for plans where you see this symbol.
Bottom Line Zip-Quote is available for all plans under 4,000 square feet.

SOME MORE INFORMATION

Itemized and Bottom Line Zip-Quotes give you approximated costs for constructing the particular house in your area. These costs are not exact and are only intended to be used as a preliminary estimate to help determine the affordability of a new home and/or as a guide to evaluate the general competitiveness of actual price quotes obtained through local suppliers and contractors. However, Zip-Quote cost figures should never be relied upon as the only source of information in either case. Land, sewer systems, site work, landscaping and other expenses are not included in our building cost figures. Garlinghouse and Marshall & Swift L.P. can not guarantee any level of data accuracy or correctness in a Zip-Quote and disclaim all liability for loss with respect to the same, in excess of the original purchase price of the Zip-Quote product. All Zip-Quote calculations are based upon the actual blueprints and do not reflect any differences or options that may be shown on the published house renderings, floor plans, or photographs.

Ignoring Copyright Laws Can Be
A $1,000,000 Mistake

Recent changes in the US copyright laws allow for statutory penalties of up to **$100,000** per incident for copyright infringement involving any of the copyrighted plans found in this publication. The law can be confusing. So, for your own protection, take the time to understand what you can and cannot do when it comes to home plans.

··· WHAT YOU CANNOT DO ···

You Cannot Duplicate Home Plans

Purchasing a set of blueprints and making additional sets by reproducing the original is **illegal**. If you need multiple sets of a particular home plan, then you must purchase them.

You Cannot Copy Any Part of a Home Plan to Create Another

Creating your own plan by copying even part of a home design found in this publication is called "creating a derivative work" and is **illegal** unless you have permission to do so.

You Cannot Build a Home Without a License

You must have specific permission or license to build a home from a copyrighted design, even if the finished home has been changed from the original plan. It is **illegal** to build one of the homes found in this publication without a license.

What Garlinghouse Offers

Home Plan Blueprint Package

By purchasing a multiple set package of blueprints or a vellum from Garlinghouse, you not only receive the physical blueprint documents necessary for construction, but you are also granted a license to build one, and only one, home. You can also make simple modifications, including minor non-structural changes and material substitutions, to our design, as long as these changes are made directly on the blueprints purchased from Garlinghouse and no additional copies are made.

Home Plan Vellums

By purchasing vellums for one of our home plans, you receive the same construction drawings found in the blueprints, but printed on vellum paper. Vellums can be erased and are perfect for making design changes. They are also semi-transparent making them easy to duplicate. But most importantly, the purchase of home plan vellums comes with a broader license that allows you to make changes to the design (ie, create a hand drawn or CAD derivative work), to make an unlimited number of copies of the plan, and to build one home from the plan.

License To Build Additional Homes

With the purchase of a blueprint package or vellums you automatically receive a license to build one home and only one home, respectively. If you want to build more homes than you are licensed to build through your purchase of a plan, then additional licenses may be purchased at reasonable costs from Garlinghouse. Inquire for more information.

IMPORTANT INFORMATION TO READ BEFORE YOU PLACE YOUR ORDER

How Many Sets Of Plans Will You Need?

The Standard 8-Set Construction Package

Our experience shows that you'll speed every step of construction and avoid costly building errors by ordering enough sets to go around. Each tradesperson wants a set — the general contractor and all subcontractors; foundation, electrical, plumbing, heating/air conditioning and framers. Don't forget your lending institution, building department and, of course, a set for yourself. * Recommended For Construction *

The Minimum 4-Set Construction Package

If you're comfortable with arduous follow-up, this package can save you a few dollars by giving you the option of passing down plan sets as work progresses. You might have enough copies to go around if work goes exactly as scheduled and no plans are lost or damaged by subcontractors. But for only $50 more, the 8-set package eliminates these worries. * Recommended For Bidding *

The Single Study Set

We offer this set so you can study the blueprints to plan your dream home in detail. They are stamped "study set only-not for construction", and you cannot build a home from them. In pursuant to copyright laws, it is illegal to reproduce any blueprint.

An Important Note About Building Code Requirements:

All plans are drawn to conform to one or more of the industry's major national building standards. However, due to the variety of local building regulations, your plan may need to be modified to comply with local requirements — snow loads, energy loads, seismic zones, etc. Do check them fully and consult your local building officials.

A few states require that all building plans used be drawn by an architect registered in that state. While having your plans reviewed and stamped by such an architect may be prudent, laws requiring non-conforming plans like ours to be completely redrawn forces you to unnecessarily pay very large fees. If your state has such a law, we strongly recommend you contact your state representative to protest.

The rendering, floor plans, and technical information contained within this publication are not guaranteed to be totally accurate. Consequently, no information from this publication should be used either as a guide to constructing a home or for estimating the cost of building a home. Complete blueprints must be purchased for such purposes.

Order Form

Plan prices guaranteed until 2/15/01— After this date call for updated pricing

Order Code No. **CHP11**

Foundation _____

____ set(s) of blueprints for plan #_____ $_____

____ Vellum & Modification kit for plan #_____ $_____

____ Additional set(s) @ $30 each for plan #_____ $_____

____ Mirror Image Reverse @ $50 each $_____

____ Right Reading Reverse $_____

____ Materials list for plan #_____ $_____

____ Detail Plans @ $19.95 each _____

____ ❑ Construction ❑ Plumbing ❑ Electrical $_____

____ Bottom line ZIP Quote @ $29.95 for plan #_____ $_____

Additional Bottom Line Zip Quote

@ $14.95 for plan(s) #_____ $_____

Zip Code where you are building_____

Itemized ZIP Quote for plan(s) #_____ $_____

Shipping (see charts on opposite page) $_____

Subtotal $_____

Sales Tax (CT residents add 6% sales tax, KS residents add 6.15% sales tax) (Not required for all states) $_____

TOTAL AMOUNT ENCLOSED $_____

Email address _____

Send your check, money order or credit card information to:
(No C.O.D.'s Please)

Please submit all United States & Other Nations orders to:

Garlinghouse Company
P.O. Box 1717
Middletown, CT. 06457

ADDRESS INFORMATION:

NAME: _____

STREET: _____

CITY: _____ STATE: _____ ZIP: _____

DAYTIME PHONE: _____

TERMS OF SALE FOR HOME PLANS: All home plans sold through this publication are copyright protected. Reproduction of these home plans, either in whole or in part, including any direct copying and/or preparation of derivative works thereof, for any reason without the prior written permission of Garlinghouse, Inc., is strictly prohibited. The purchase of a set of home plans in no way transfers any copyright or other ownership interest in it to the buyer except for a limited license to use that set of home plans for the construction of one, and only one, dwelling unit. The purchase of additional sets of that home plan at a reduced price from the original set or as a part of a multiple set package does not entitle the buyer with a license to construct more than one dwelling unit.

Payment must be made in U.S. funds. Foreign Mail Orders: Certified bank checks in U.S. funds only

Credit Card Information

Charge To: ❑ Visa ❑ Mastercard

Card # | | | | | | | | | | | | | | | |

Signature _____ Exp. ____/____

ORDER TOLL FREE — 1-800-235-5700
Monday-Friday 8:00 a.m. to 8:00 p.m. Eastern Time
or FAX your Credit Card order to 1-860-343-5984
All foreign residents call 1-800-343-5977

BEST PLAN VALUE IN THE INDUSTRY!

Please have ready: 1. Your credit card number   2. The plan number   3. The order code number ⟹ CHP11

Garlinghouse 2000 Blueprint Price Code Schedule

Additional sets with original order $30

PRICE CODE	A	B	C	D	E	F	G	H
8 SETS OF SAME PLAN	$405	$445	$490	$530	$570	$615	$655	$695
4 SETS OF SAME PLAN	$355	$395	$440	$480	$520	$565	$605	$645
1 SINGLE SET OF PLANS	$305	$345	$390	$430	$470	$515	$555	$595
VELLUMS	$515	$560	$610	$655	$700	$750	$795	$840
MATERIALS LIST	$60	$60	$65	$65	$70	$70	$75	$75
ITEMIZED ZIP QUOTE	$75	$80	$85	$85	$90	$90	$95	$95

Shipping — (Plans 1-54999)

	1-3 Sets	4-6 Sets	7+ & Vellums
Standard Delivery (UPS 2-Day)	$25.00	$30.00	$35.00
Overnight Delivery	$35.00	$40.00	$45.00

International Shipping & Handling

	1-3 Sets	4-6 Sets	7+ & Vellums
Regular Delivery Canada (7-10 Days)	$25.00	$30.00	$35.00
Express Delivery Canada (5-6 Days)	$40.00	$45.00	$50.00
Overseas Delivery Airmail (2-3 Weeks)	$50.00	$60.00	$65.00

Shipping — (Plans 60000-99999)

	1-3 Sets	4-6 Sets	7+ & Vellums
Ground Delivery (7-10 Days)	$15.00	$20.00	$25.00
Express Delivery (3-5 Days)	$20.00	$25.00	$30.00

Our Reorder and Exchange Policies:

If you find after your initial purchase that you require additional sets of plans you may purchase them from us at special reorder prices (please call for pricing details) provided that you reorder within 6 months of your original order date. There is a $28 reorder processing fee that is charged on all reorders. For more information on reordering plans please contact our Customer Service Department.

Your plans are custom printed especially for you once you place your order. For that reason we cannot accept any returns.

If for some reason you find that the plan you have purchased from us does not meet your needs, then you may exchange that plan for any other plan in our collection. We allow you sixty days from your original invoice date to make an exchange. At the time of the exchange you will be charged a processing fee of 20% of the total amount of your original order plus the difference in price between the plans (if applicable) plus the cost to ship the new plans to you. Call our Customer Service Department for more information. Please Note: Reproducible vellums can only be exchanged if they are unopened.

Important Shipping Information

Please refer to the shipping charts on the order form for service availability for your specific plan number. Our delivery service must have a street address or Rural Route Box number — never a post office box. (PLEASE NOTE: Supplying a P.O. Box number _only_ will delay the shipping of your order.) Use a work address if no one is home during the day.

Orders being shipped to APO or FPO must go via First Class Mail.

For our International Customers, only Certified bank checks and money orders are accepted and must be payable in U.S. currency. For speed, we ship international orders Air Parcel Post. Please refer to the chart for the correct shipping cost.

Thank you

BL — Bottom-line Zip Quote Available · **X** — Materials List Available · **ZIP** — Zip Quote Available · **RR** — Right Reading Reverse · **Duplex** — Duplex Pla...

Plan#	Page#	Price Code	Sq. Ft.	Features
1078	40	A	1024	BL X RR
10274	217	B	1783	BL X RR
10507	294	C	2194	BL X ZIP
10570	316	D	2450	BL X
10619	310	D	2352	BL X
10656	244	C	1899	BL X
10674	166	B	1600	BL X ZIP
10839	2	B	1738	BL X ZIP RR
20062	136	A	1500	BL X ZIP RR
20083	159	B	1575	BL X
20087	157	B	1568	BL X
20100	205	B	1737	BL X ZIP RR
20108	281	C	2120	BL X
20156	83	A	1359	BL X ZIP
20161	73	A	1307	BL X ZIP RR
20164	116	A	1456	BL X ZIP RR
20198	30	B	1792	BL X
20220	156	B	1568	BL X ZIP
22004	276	C	2070	BL X
24256	280	C	2108	BL X
24259	268	C	2010	BL X
24302	38	A	988	BL X ZIP
24304	38	A	993	BL X
24317	171	B	1620	BL X ZIP
24661	348	E	2860	BL X
24700	20	A	1312	BL X ZIP
24701	172	B	1625	BL X ZIP
24708	161	B	1576	BL X ZIP
24709	79	A	1330	BL
24714	213	B	1771	BL
24717	181	B	1642	BL
24718	113	A	1452	BL
24719	202	B	1702	BL
24721	146	A	1539	BL
24723	44	A	1112	BL
24738	152	B	1554	BL
24743	265	C	1990	BL
32122	4	A	1112	BL X
34003	48	A	1146	BL X ZIP RR
34011	193	B	1672	BL X ZIP RR
34029	196	B	1686	BL X ZIP RR
34031	228	C	1831	BL X
34043	162	B	1583	BL X ZIP RR
34054	101	A	1400	BL X ZIP RR
34150	133	A	1492	BL X
34154	129	A	1486	BL X ZIP RR
35003	94	A	1373	BL X RR
35005	129	A	1484	BL X
84014	245	C	1901	BL
84020	33	A	768	BL
84056	182	B	1644	BL
84330	45	A	1114	BL
90001	290	C	2177	BL X
90007	228	C	1830	BL X
90288	97	A	1387	BL X
90324	39	A	1016	BL X
90354	85	A	1360	BL X
90357	90	A	1368	BL X
90398	175	B	1630	BL X
90409	192	B	1670	BL X
90412	115	A	1454	BL X
90423	214	B	1773	BL X
90433	37	A	928	BL X
90441	226	C	1811	BL X
90454	298	D	2218	BL X
90461	317	D	2485	BL X
90466	232	C	1845	BL X
90467	306	D	2290	BL X
90476	223	C	1804	BL X
90478	309	D	2344	BL X
90479	122	A	1472	BL X
90484	287	C	2167	BL X
90485	304	D	2271	BL X
90502	181	B	1642	BL X
90601	170	B	1613	BL X
90620	127	A	1476	BL X
90630	53	A	1207	BL X
90680	100	A	1393	BL X
90682	57	A	1243	BL X
90684	163	B	1590	BL X
90689	128	A	1476	BL X
90697	165	B	1597	BL X
90865	76	A	1313	BL X
90934	35	A	884	BL X
90954	171	B	1617	BL X
90986	204	B	1731	BL X
90990	106	A	1423	BL X
91021	69	A	1295	BL X
91105	248	C	1908	BL
91122	229	C	1838	BL
91129	263	C	1983	BL
91333	36	G	914	BL Duplex
91342	81	A	1345	BL X
91346	291	C	2185	BL X RR
91349	197	B	1694	BL X
91418	190	B	1665	BL X
91501	358	E	3160	BL X RR
91545	104	A	1420	BL X
91731	236	C	1857	BL X
91746	203	B	1717	BL X
91749	354	E	3051	BL X
91750	359	E	3188	BL X RR
91753	132	A	1490	BL
91807	102	A	1410	BL X
92056	107	A	1425	BL X
92220	27	C	1830	BL X ZIP
92221	357	G	3121	BL Duplex
92238	189	B	1664	BL X ZIP
92243	347	E	2858	BL
92247	283	C	2149	BL
92254	318	D	2495	BL
92265	368	F	3818	BL
92268	202	B	1706	BL
92271	326	E	2615	BL
92273	363	F	3254	BL ZIP
92283	185	B	1653	BL
92284	303	D	2261	BL
92285	328	E	2620	BL
92400	41	A	1050	BL
92404	305	D	2275	BL
92501	338	F	2727	BL
92502	56	B	1237	BL
92514	271	D	2045	BL X
92515	258	D	1959	BL X
92517	223	D	1805	BL X
92520	54	B	1208	BL X
92523	68	B	1293	BL X
92527	196	C	1680	BL X
92528	89	B	1363	BL X
92531	208	C	1754	BL X
92538	341	F	2733	BL X
92542	237	D	1866	BL X
92544	264	D	1987	BL X
92546	311	E	2387	BL X
92550	342	F	2735	BL X
92552	240	D	1873	BL X
92557	99	B	1390	BL X
92559	64	B	1265	BL X
92560	189	C	1660	BL X
92561	235	D	1856	BL X
92562	234	C	1856	BL X
92625	207	B	1746	BL X ZIP
92628	266	C	1998	BL
92630	16	B	1782	BL ZIP
92655	207	B	1746	BL X ZIP
92657	17	F	4328	BL ZIP
92658	209	B	1756	BL
92660	260	C	1964	BL
92677	239	B	1869	BL
92685	113	A	1442	BL
92688	270	D	2041	BL
92694	145	B	1537	BL
92704	42	A	1078	BL
92705	233	C	1849	BL
92900	286	C	2166	BL
92901	337	E	2691	BL
93004	63	A	1260	BL
93017	47	A	1142	BL
93018	47	A	1142	BL
93019	46	A	1136	BL
93021	65	A	1282	BL
93026	101	A	1402	BL
93027	136	A	1500	BL
93031	257	C	1955	BL
93048	74	A	1310	BL
93049	307	D	2292	BL
93061	206	B	1742	BL
93068	346	E	2777	BL
93073	53	A	1202	BL
93075	49	A	1170	BL
93078	186	B	1654	BL
93080	243	C	1890	BL
93085	256	C	1955	BL
93086	332	E	2648	BL
93095	314	D	2409	BL
93097	345	E	2757	BL
93098	257	C	1932	BL
93107	238	C	1868	BL RR
93133	211	B	1761	BL X ZIP RR
93134	96	A	1387	BL
93143	222	C	1802	BL
93161	147	B	1540	BL X ZIP
93165	122	A	1472	BL
93171	180	B	1642	BL
93190	295	C	2196	BL
93191	210	B	1756	BL
93193	222	C	1802	BL
93222	67	A	1292	BL X ZIP RR
93261	215	B	1778	BL X ZIP
93279	98	A	1388	BL X ZIP
93311	226	C	1810	BL
93414	100	A	1393	BL
93416	124	A	1475	BL
93426	187	B	1655	BL
93427	234	B	1849	BL
93440	311	D	2361	BL
93447	123	A	1474	BL
93449	63	A	1253	BL
93453	80	A	1333	BL
93454	97	A	1388	BL
93455	151	B	1550	BL
93608	275	C	2060	BL
93708	324	D	2579	BL
93718	321	D	2525	BL
93722	291	C	2184	BL
94116	151	C	1546	BL X
94200	217	B	1784	BL
94206	297	D	2214	BL
94209	6	C	2072	BL
94220	10	F	3477	BL X
94224	369	F	4028	BL
94242	350	E	2978	BL X
94243	352	E	2998	BL
94260	29	C	2068	BL
94263	66	A	1288	BL
94307	34	A	786	BL
94640	323	D	2558	BL
94641	313	D	2400	BL
94703	59	G	1245	BL X Duplex
94724	163	B	1589	BL X
94729	103	A	1417	BL X
94738	215	B	1779	BL X
94800	52	C	1199	BL X
94801	71	C	1300	BL X
94810	336	E	2690	BL X
94811	286	D	2165	BL X
94827	164	C	1595	BL X
94913	55	A	1212	BL X RR
94914	114	A	1453	BL X RR
94921	184	B	1651	BL X
94923	191	B	1666	BL X
94966	249	C	1911	BL X
94967	310	D	2355	BL X
94971	290	C	2172	BL X
94972	162	B	1580	BL X
94973	320	D	2512	BL X
94979	314	D	2404	BL X RR
94982	86	A	1360	BL X RR
94985	64	A	1279	BL X RR
94986	169	B	1604	BL X
96402	269	E	2027	BL X RR
96405	246	D	1903	BL X RR
96413	28	E	2349	BL X ZIP RR
96417	32	D	1561	BL X ZIP RR
96418	15	C	1452	BL X ZIP RR
96419	148	D	1541	BL X RR
96420	139	D	1512	BL X RR
96421	272	E	2045	BL X RR
96435	322	F	2526	BL X RR
96447	296	E	2207	BL X RR
96449	297	E	2211	BL X RR
96450	279	E	2090	BL X RR
96452	125	C	1475	BL X RR
96453	225	D	1807	BL X RR
96454	144	A	1537	BL X RR
96458	22	D	1512	BL X RR
96463	178	D	1633	BL X RR
96465	273	E	2050	BL X RR
96467	289	E	2170	BL X RR
96468	236	D	1864	BL X RR
96478	296	E	2203	BL X RR
96482	195	D	1677	BL X RR
96483	274	E	2057	BL X RR
96484	60	C	1246	BL X RR
96488	198	D	1695	BL X RR
96489	170	D	1609	BL X RR
96493	212	D	1770	BL X RR
96496	305	E	2282	BL X RR
96503	302	D	2256	BL X RR
96504	285	C	2162	BL X RR
96505	275	D	2069	BL X RR
96506	186	B	1654	BL X RR
96508	128	A	1481	BL X RR
96509	112	A	1438	BL X RR
96510	92	A	1372	BL X RR
96511	62	A	1247	BL X RR
96513	183	B	1648	BL X RR
96516	117	A	1458	BL X RR
96517	120	A	1463	BL X RR
96518	187	B	1657	BL X RR
96519	58	A	1243	BL
96521	355	E	3084	BL X
96522	141	B	1515	BL X
96523	185	B	1652	BL X

Legend:
- **BL** Bottom-line Zip Quote Available
- ✕ Materials List Available
- 🏳 Zip Quote Available
- **ЯR** Right Reading Reverse
- 🏠 Duplex Plan

Plan#	Page#	Price Code	Sq. Ft.	Icons
96527	261	C	1972	BL ✕
96529	278	C	2089	BL ✕
96530	306	D	2289	BL ✕
96537	194	B	1676	BL
96539	279	C	2098	BL
96600	335	E	2678	BL
96601	244	C	1890	BL
96602	343	E	2745	BL
96902	254	C	1950	BL
96913	334	E	2677	BL
97105	280	C	2112	BL
97108	219	B	1794	BL
97124	103	A	1416	BL
97135	299	D	2229	BL
97137	120	A	1461	BL
97148	91	A	1370	BL
97151	267	C	2007	BL
97152	154	B	1557	BL
97224	88	B	1363	BL
97233	206	B	1743	BL
97242	277	C	2080	BL
97246	308	D	2311	BL
97253	241	C	1875	BL
97254	197	B	1692	BL
97256	52	A	1198	BL
97259	55	A	1222	BL
97262	121	A	1467	BL
97274	111	A	1432	BL ✕
97277	251	C	1927	BL
97278	292	D	2188	BL ✕
97294	284	C	2158	BL
97299	318	D	2491	BL
97404	308	D	2311	BL ✕
97410	360	C	3225	BL ✕
97415	216	B	1782	BL ✕
97442	183	B	1650	BL ✕
97445	174	B	1628	BL ✕
97503	307	D	2310	BL
97505	327	D	2618	BL
97507	332	E	2659	BL
97511	353	E	3032	BL
97513	361	F	3230	BL
97514	366	F	3430	BL
97600	87	A	1361	BL
97601	118	A	1459	BL
97623	262	C	1978	BL
97702	168	B	1601	BL
97703	259	D	1963	BL
97714	367	D	3570	BL
97724	131	A	1488	BL
97730	77	A	1315	BL
97731	76	A	1315	BL
97800	312	D	2393	BL
98000	132	C	1488	BL ✕ ЯR
98003	295	E	2198	BL ✕ ЯR
98004	141	D	1517	BL ✕ ЯR
98005	149	D	1542	BL ✕ ЯR
98006	245	D	1899	BL ✕ ЯR
98007	304	E	2273	BL ✕ ЯR
98008	249	D	1911	BL ✕ ЯR
98009	255	D	1954	BL ✕ ЯR
98010	371	H	4523	✕ ЯR
98011	268	E	2024	BL ✕ ЯR
98018	269	E	2027	BL ✕ ЯR
98019	271	E	2042	BL ✕ ЯR
98020	220	D	1795	BL ✕ ЯR
98026	126	C	1476	BL ✕ ЯR
98027	150	D	1544	BL ✕ ЯR
98029	95	C	1377	BL ✕ ЯR
98034	250	D	1918	BL ✕ ЯR
98054	218	D	1792	BL ✕

Plan#	Page#	Price Code	Sq. Ft.	Icons
98056	229	D	1844	BL
98058	184	D	1652	BL
98059	109	C	1428	BL
98060	317	E	2487	BL
98061	251	D	1925	BL
98062	188	D	1658	BL ✕
98068	309	E	2342	BL ✕
98075	50	C	1182	BL ✕
98076	303	E	2262	BL ✕
98081	123	C	1473	BL ✕
98082	276	E	2078	BL ✕
98083	138	D	1511	BL ✕
98086	201	D	1700	BL ✕
98087	204	D	1733	BL ✕
98095	302	E	2250	BL ✕
98096	119	C	1460	BL ✕
98097	253	C	1933	BL ✕
98100	219	D	1792	BL ✕
98101	231	D	1845	BL ✕
98103	283	E	2152	BL ✕
98238	252	C	1928	BL
98327	300	D	2235	BL
98337	177	B	1633	BL ✕
98354	111	A	1431	BL ✕
98408	235	C	1856	BL ✕
98411	93	A	1373	BL ✕
98412	152	B	1553	BL ✕
98414	160	B	1575	BL ✕
98415	110	A	1429	BL ✕
98423	193	B	1671	BL ✕
98424	301	D	2236	BL ✕
98425	230	C	1845	BL ✕
98426	329	E	2622	BL ✕
98427	273	C	2051	BL ✕
98430	243	C	1884	BL ✕
98432	192	B	1670	BL ✕
98434	82	A	1346	BL ✕
98435	253	C	1945	BL ✕
98441	137	B	1502	BL
98443	84	A	1359	BL
98456	203	B	1715	BL ✕
98460	150	B	1544	BL
98461	51	A	1185	BL
98464	216	B	1779	BL
98466	293	C	2193	BL
98468	44	A	1104	BL
98472	133	A	1492	BL
98479	158	B	1575	BL
98498	46	A	1135	BL
98500	288	C	2169	BL
98501	294	C	2194	BL
98503	242	C	1876	BL
98511	316	D	2445	BL 🏳
98512	287	C	2167	BL
98513	364	F	3352	BL 🏳
98521	300	D	2233	BL
98522	142	B	1528	BL
98528	344	E	2748	BL 🏳
98538	370	F	4082	
98544	301	D	2238	BL
98547	330	E	2626	BL
98549	110	A	1431	BL
98550	319	D	2506	BL
98559	278	C	2081	BL 🏳
98569	349	E	2911	BL
98580	179	B	1640	BL
98584	333	E	2674	BL
98589	246	C	1902	BL
98597	356	E	3089	BL
98598	362	F	3239	BL
98732	319	D	2508	BL

Plan#	Page#	Price Code	Sq. Ft.	Icons
98743	258	C	1958	BL
98744	315	D	2424	BL ✕
98747	65	A	1280	BL ✕
98748	281	C	2126	BL ✕
98802	270	D	2035	BL
98804	91	A	1372	BL
98805	43	A	1089	BL
98807	130	A	1487	BL
98808	78	A	1326	BL
98814	199	B	1699	BL
98912	82	A	1345	BL ✕ 🏳
98915	54	A	1208	BL ✕
98920	182	B	1646	BL
98936	214	B	1772	BL
99081	164	B	1590	BL
99106	134	A	1495	BL
99113	247	C	1906	BL
99115	254	C	1947	BL ЯR
99152	153	B	1557	BL
99154	248	C	1907	BL
99160	340	E	2731	BL
99162	339	E	2730	BL
99163	167	B	1600	BL
99167	142	B	1537	BL
99208	227	C	1830	BL ✕
99216	142	B	1521	BL ✕
99303	105	A	1421	BL ✕
99321	90	A	1368	BL ✕
99324	72	A	1307	BL ✕
99487	224	C	1806	BL ✕
99503	172	B	1620	BL
99504	45	A	1127	BL
99639	89	A	1367	BL ✕
99641	155	B	1567	BL ✕
99657	180	B	1641	BL ✕
99662	121	A	1466	BL ✕
99668	188	B	1658	BL ✕
99669	102	A	1412	BL ✕
99721	365	F	3417	BL
99727	242	C	1876	BL ✕
99774	292	C	2192	BL ✕
99784	351	E	2987	BL ✕
99802	161	D	1576	BL ✕ 🏳 ЯR
99803	8	D	1977	BL ✕ 🏳 ЯR
99804	12	D	1815	BL ✕ 🏳 ЯR
99805	218	D	1787	BL ✕ 🏳 ЯR
99806	61	C	1246	BL ✕ ЯR
99807	14	D	1879	BL ✕ 🏳 ЯR
99808	18	D	1832	BL ✕ 🏳 ЯR
99809	21	C	1417	BL ✕ 🏳 ЯR
99810	24	D	1685	BL ✕ 🏳 ЯR
99811	23	D	1699	BL ✕ ЯR
99812	96	C	1386	BL ✕ ЯR
99813	259	D	1959	BL ✕ 🏳 ЯR
99814	221	D	1800	BL ✕ 🏳 ЯR
99815	250	D	1912	BL ✕ 🏳 ЯR
99820	325	F	2602	BL ✕ ЯR
99826	31	C	1346	BL ✕ 🏳 ЯR
99828	70	C	1298	BL ✕ ЯR
99830	31	C	1372	BL ✕ ЯR
99831	200	D	1699	BL ✕ ЯR
99833	112	C	1440	BL ✕ ЯR
99834	160	D	1575	BL ✕ ЯR
99835	140	D	1515	BL ✕ ЯR
99838	293	E	2192	BL ✕ 🏳 ЯR
99840	176	D	1632	BL ✕ ЯR
99844	205	D	1737	BL ✕ ЯR
99845	25	D	1954	BL ✕ ЯR
99846	282	E	2136	BL ✕ ЯR
99849	77	C	1322	BL ✕ ЯR
99850	32	D	1590	BL ✕ ЯR

Plan#	Page#	Price Code	Sq. Ft.	Icons
99854	173	D	1625	BL ✕ ЯR
99856	75	C	1310	BL ✕ ЯR
99857	237	C	1865	BL ✕ ЯR
99858	62	C	1253	BL ✕ 🏳 ЯR
99860	135	C	1498	BL ✕ 🏳 ЯR
99864	108	C	1426	BL ✕ ЯR
99868	83	C	1350	BL ✕ ЯR
99870	88	C	1362	BL ✕ ЯR
99871	19	D	1655	BL ✕ 🏳 ЯR
99878	26	D	1864	BL ✕ 🏳 ЯR

CREATIVE HOMEOWNER®

How-To Books for...

REMODELING BASEMENTS, ATTICS & GARAGES

Cramped for space? This book shows you how to find space you may not know you had and convert it into useful living areas. 40 colorful photographs and 530 full-color drawings.

BOOK #: 277680   192pp.   8½"x10⅞"

BASIC WIRING
(Third Edition, Conforms to latest National Electrical Code)

Included are 350 large, clear, full-color illustrations and no-nonsense step-by-step instructions. Shows how to replace receptacles and switches; repair a lamp; install ceiling and attic fans; and more.

BOOK #: 277048   160pp.   8½"x10⅞"

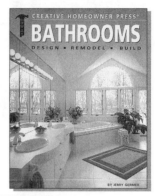

BATHROOMS: Design, Remodel, Build

Shows how to plan, construct, and finish a bathroom. Remodel floors; rebuild walls and ceilings; and install windows, skylights, and plumbing fixtures. Specific tools and materials are given for each project. Includes 90 color photos and 470 color illustrations.

BOOK #: 277053   192pp.   8½"x10⅞"

The Smart Approach to BATH DESIGN

Everything you need to know about designing a bathroom like a professional is explained in *this book*. Creative solutions and practical advice about space, the latest in fixtures and fittings, and safety features accompany over 150 photographs.

BOOK #: 287225   176pp.   9"x10"

BUILD A KIDS' PLAY YARD

Here are detailed plans and step-by-step instructions for building the play structures that kids love most: swing set, monkey bars, balance beam, playhouse, teeter-totter, sandboxes, kid-sized picnic table, and a play tower that supports a slide. 200 color photographs and illustrations.

BOOK #: 277662   144 pp.   8½"x10⅞"

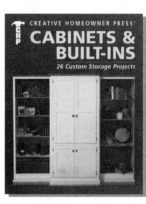

CABINETS & BUILT-INS

26 custom cabinetry projects are included for every room in the house, from kitchen cabinets to a bedroom wall unit, a bunk bed, computer workstation, and more. Also included are chapters on tools, techniques, finishing, and materials.

BOOK #: 277079   160 pp.   8½"x10⅞"

DECKS: Plan, Design, Build

With this book, even the novice builder can build a deck that perfectly fits his yard. The step-by-step instructions lead the reader from laying out footings to adding railings. Includes three deck projects, 500 color drawings, and photographs.

BOOK #: 277180   176pp.   8½"x10⅞"

FURNITURE REPAIR & REFINISHING

From structural repairs to restoring older finishes or entirely refinishing furniture: a hands-on step-by-step approach to furniture repair and restoration. More than 430 color photographs and 60 full-color drawings.

BOOK #: 277335   240pp.   8½"x10⅞"

HOUSE FRAMING

Written for those with beginning to intermediate building skills, this book is designed to walk you through the framing basics, from assembling simple partitions to cutting compound angles on dormer rafters. More than 400 full-color drawings.

BOOK #: 277655   240pp.   8½"x10⅞"

the Home Planner, Builder & Owner

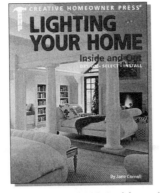

KITCHENS: Design, Remodel, Build

This is the reference book for modern kitchen design, with more than 100 full-color photos to help homeowners plan the layout. Step-by-step instructions illustrate basic plumbing and wiring techniques; how to finish walls and ceilings; and more.

BOOK #: 277065   192pp.   8½"x10⅞"

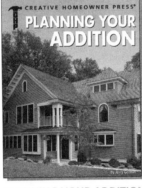

LIGHTING YOUR HOME: Inside and Out

Lighting should be selected with care. This book thoroughly explains lighting design for every room as well as outdoors. It is also a step-by-step manual that shows how to install the fixtures. More than 125 photos and 400 drawings.

BOOK #: 277583   176pp.   8½"x10⅞"

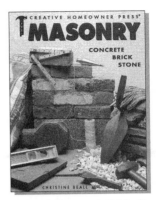

MASONRY: Concrete, Brick, Stone

Concrete, brick, and stone choices are detailed with step-by-step instructions and over 35 color photographs and 460 illustrations. Projects include a brick or stone garden wall, steps and patios, a concrete-block retaining wall, a concrete sidewalk.

BOOK #: 277106   176pp.   8½"x10⅞"

The Smart Approach to KITCHEN DESIGN

Transform a dated kitchen into the spectacular heart of your home. Learn how to create a better layout and more efficient storage. Find out about the latest equipment and materials. Savvy tips explain how to create style like a pro. More than 150 color photos.

BOOK #: 279935   176 pp.   9"x10"

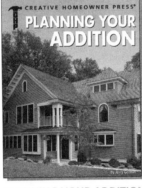

PLANNING YOUR ADDITION

Planning an addition to your home involves a daunting number of choices, from choosing a contractor to selecting bathroom tile. Using 280 color drawings and photographs, architect/author Jerry Germer helps you make the right decision.

BOOK #: 277004   192pp.   8½"x10⅞"

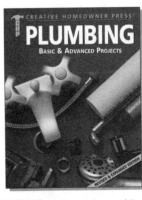

PLUMBING: Basic & Advanced Projects

Take the guesswork out of plumbing repair and installation for old and new systems. Projects include replacing faucets, unclogging drains, installing a tub, replacing a water heater, and much more. 500 illustrations and diagrams.

BOOK #: 277620   176pp.   8½"x10⅞"

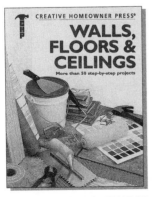

WALLS, FLOORS & CEILINGS

Here's the definitive guide to interiors. It shows you how to replace old surfaces with new professional-looking ones. Projects include installing molding, skylights, insulation, flooring, carpeting, and more. Over 500 color photos and drawings.

BOOK #: 277697   176pp.   8½"x10⅞"

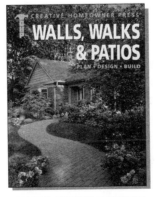

WALLS, WALKS & PATIOS

Learn how to build a patio from concrete, stone, or brick and complement it with one of a dozen walks. Learn about simple mortarless walls, landscape timber walls, and hefty brick and stone walls. 50 photographs and 320 illustrations, all in color.

BOOK #: 277994   192pp.   8½"x10⅞"

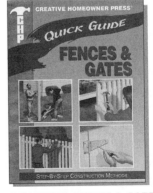

QUICK GUIDE: FENCES & GATES

Learn how to build and install all kinds of fences and gates for your yard, from hand-built wood privacy and picket fences to newer prefabricated vinyl and chain-link types. Over 200 two-color drawings illustrate step-by-step procedures.

BOOK #: 287732   80pp.   8½"x10⅞"

Place your Order ....

WORKING WITH TILE

Design and complete interior and exterior tile projects on walls, floors, countertops, shower enclosures, patios, pools, and more. 425 color illustrations and over 80 photographs.

BOOK #: 277540   176pp.   8½"x10⅞"

COLOR IN THE AMERICAN HOME

Find out how to make the most of color in your home with ideas for analyzing, selecting, and coordinating color schemes. Over 150 photographs of traditional and contemporary interiors.

BOOK #: 287264   176pp.   9"x10"

The Smart Approach to HOME DECORATING

Learn how to work with space, color, pattern, and texture with the flair of a professional designer. More than 300 color photos.

BOOK #: 279667   256pp.   9"x10"

CREATIVE HOMEOWNER®

BOOK ORDER FORM   *Please Print*
SHIP TO:

Name: _____

Address: _____

City: _____ State: _____ Zip: _____ Phone Number: _____

(Should there be a problem with your order)

Quantity	Title	Price	CH #	Cost
____	380 Country & Farmhouse Home Plans	$9.95	277035	____
____	400 Affordable Home Plans	9.95	277012	____
____	408 Vacation & Second Home Plans	8.95	277036	____
____	450 One-Story Home Plans	9.95	277014	____
____	450 Two-Story Home Plans	9.95	277042	____
____	375 Southern Home Plans	9.95	277037	____
____	Adding Value to Your Home	16.95	277006	____
____	Basic Wiring	14.95	277048	____
____	Bathrooms: Design, Remodel, Build	16.95	277053	____
____	Better Lawns, Step by Step	14.95	274359	____
____	Bird Feeders	10.95	277102	____
____	Build a Kids' Play Yard	14.95	277662	____
____	Cabinets & Built-Ins	14.95	277079	____
____	Color in the American Home	19.95	287264	____
____	Complete Guide to Wallpapering	14.95	278910	____
____	Complete Guide to Water Gardens	19.95	274452	____
____	Complete Home Landscaping	24.95	274615	____
____	Creating Good Gardens	16.95	274244	____
____	Custom Closets	12.95	277132	____
____	Decks: Plan, Design, Build	14.95	277180	____
____	Decorating with Paint & Paper	19.95	279723	____
____	Decorative Paint Finishes	10.95	287371	____
____	Drywall: Pro Tips for Hanging & Finishing	14.95	278315	____
____	Easy-Care Guide to Houseplants	19.95	275243	____
____	Fences, Gates & Trellises	14.95	277981	____
____	Furniture Repair & Refinishing	19.95	277335	____
____	Gazebos & Other Outdoor Structures	14.95	277138	____
____	Home Landscaping: Mid-Atlantic Reg.	19.95	274537	____
____	Home Landscaping: Midwest Reg./S Can.	19.95	274385	____
____	Home Landscaping: Northeast Reg./SE Can.	19.95	274618	____
____	Home Landscaping: Southeast Reg.	19.95	274762	____
____	House Framing	19.95	277655	____
____	Kitchens: Design, Remodel, Build (New Ed.)	16.95	277065	____
____	Lighting Your Home Inside & Out	16.95	277583	____
____	Masonry: Concrete, Brick, Stone	16.95	277106	____
____	Mastering Fine Decorative Paint Techniques	27.95	279550	____
____	Planning Your Addition	16.95	277004	____
____	Plumbing: Basic and Advanced Projects	14.95	277620	____
____	Remodeling Basements, Attics & Garages	16.95	277680	____
____	Smart Approach to Bath Design	19.95	287225	____
____	Smart Approach to Home Decorating	24.95	279667	____
____	Smart Approach to Kitchen Design	19.95	279935	____
____	Smart Approach to Window Decor	19.95	279431	____
____	Trees, Shrubs & Hedges for Home Landscaping	19.95	274238	____

Quantity	Title	Price	CH #	Cost
____	Walls, Floors & Ceilings	$16.95	277697	____
____	Walls, Walks & Patios	14.95	277994	____
____	Working with Tile	16.95	277540	____

Quick Guide Series

Quantity	Title	Price	CH #	Cost
____	Quick Guide - Attics	$7.95	287711	____
____	Quick Guide - Basements	7.95	287242	____
____	Quick Guide - Ceramic Tile	7.95	287730	____
____	Quick Guide - Decks	7.95	277344	____
____	Quick Guide - Fences & Gates	7.95	287732	____
____	Quick Guide - Floors	7.95	287734	____
____	Quick Guide - Garages & Carports	7.95	287785	____
____	Quick Guide - Gazebos	7.95	287757	____
____	Quick Guide - Insulation & Ventilation	7.95	287367	____
____	Quick Guide - Interior & Exterior Painting	7.95	287784	____
____	Quick Guide - Masonry Walls	7.95	287741	____
____	Quick Guide - Patios & Walks	7.95	287778	____
____	Quick Guide - Plumbing	7.95	287863	____
____	Quick Guide - Ponds & Fountains	7.95	287804	____
____	Quick Guide - Pool & Spa Maintenance	7.95	287901	____
____	Quick Guide - Roofing	7.95	287807	____
____	Quick Guide - Shelving & Storage	7.95	287763	____
____	Quick Guide - Siding	7.95	287892	____
____	Quick Guide - Stairs & Railings	7.95	287755	____
____	Quick Guide - Storage Sheds	7.95	287815	____
____	Quick Guide - Trim (Crown Molding, Base & more)	7.95	287745	____
____	Quick Guide - Walls & Ceilings	7.95	287792	____
____	Quick Guide - Windows & Doors	7.95	287812	____
____	Quick Guide - Wiring, Third Edition	7.95	287884	____

Number of Books Ordered _____ Total for Books _____

NJ Residents add 6% tax _____

Prices subject to change without notice.   Subtotal _____

Postage/Handling Charges _____
$3.75 for first book / $1.25 for each additional book

Total _____

Make checks (in U.S. currency only) payable to:

CREATIVE HOMEOWNER®
P.O. BOX 38, 24 Park Way
Upper Saddle River, New Jersey 07458-9960

Please visit us at our Web site: **www.creativehomeowner.com**